100

FIGHTING FOR ATLANTA

CIVIL WAR AMERICA

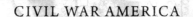

Peter S. Carmichael, Caroline E. Janney,
and Aaron Sheehan-Dean, editors

This landmark series interprets broadly the history and culture
of the Civil War era through the long nineteenth century and
beyond. Drawing on diverse approaches and methods, the
series publishes historical works that explore all aspects of
the war, biographies of leading commanders, and tactical and
campaign studies, along with select editions of primary sources.
Together, these books shed new light on an era that remains
central to our understanding of American and world history.

FIGHTING FOR
ATLANTA

Tactics, Terrain, and Trenches in the Civil War

Earl J. Hess

THE UNIVERSITY OF NORTH CAROLINA PRESS

Chapel Hill

Designed by Jamison Cockerham
Set in Arno, Cutright, Sorts Mill Goudy, and Scala Sans
by Tseng Information Systems, Inc.

Cover photographs: Sherman's men in a Confederate fort
east of Atlanta (front); Federal Fort No. 9, Atlanta (back).
Photographs by George N. Bernard. Courtesy of the
Library of Congress Prints and Photographs Division.

Manufactured in the United States of America

The University of North Carolina Press has been a member
of the Green Press Initiative since 2003.

LIBRARY OF CONGRESS CATALOGING-IN-PUBLICATION DATA
Names: Hess, Earl J., author.
Title: Fighting for Atlanta : tactics, terrain, and trenches in the Civil War / Earl J. Hess.
Description: Chapel Hill : The University of North Carolina Press, [2018] |
Includes bibliographical references and index.
Identifiers: LCCN 2018010413 | ISBN 9781469643427 (cloth : alk. paper) |
ISBN 9781469643434 (ebook)
Subjects: LCSH: Atlanta Campaign, 1864. | Fortification—Georgia—Atlanta. | Atlanta
(Ga.)—Defenses. | United States—History—Civil War, 1861–1865—Campaigns.
Classification: LCC E476.7 .H4654 2018 | DDC 973.7/371—dc23
LC record available at https://lccn.loc.gov/2018010413

For Pratibha and Julie, with love

contents

figures, maps, and tables

MAPS

East Point Line *211*

Manigault's Brigade's skirmish lines, August 1864 *228*

Jonesboro *252*

Federal defenses of Atlanta *274*

TABLES

preface

In early May 1864, Federal generals moved two large concentrations of troops against the Confederacy in a massive resumption of their war effort against the South. While Lt. Gen. Ulysses S. Grant personally directed 100,000 men of the Army of the Potomac in Virginia, Maj. Gen. William T. Sherman commanded an army group of equal size in northwest Georgia. Grant, the new general-in-chief of Union armies, instructed Sherman to make the Confederate Army of Tennessee his chief target as he advanced 100 miles from Chattanooga toward Atlanta. Sherman had the task of maintaining contact with the Confederate commander, Gen. Joseph E. Johnston, and not letting up pressure.

In both the Virginia and Georgia campaigns that unfolded as spring gave way to summer, the extensive and intensive use of field fortifications became a major feature of operations. Spurred by continuous contact between the opposing armies, temporary earthworks sprang up as soldiers on all levels sought means to protect themselves from rifle fire and artillery rounds now that they remained within range of enemy guns for extended periods of time. Fieldworks became an all-important element of operations in 1864, helping to determine which army succeeded in its tactical and strategic goals.

In two previous books, I have detailed the role played by earthworks in the Overland and Petersburg campaigns that Grant conducted against Gen. Robert E. Lee's Army of Northern Virginia.[1] This volume carries that story into the western theater of war by examining the role of field fortifications in Sherman's Atlanta campaign. It is based on extensive research in a variety of sources, including official reports and dispatches, personal letters, diaries, and memoirs of soldiers and officers, archaeological reports, historical photographs, and exhaustive field research on battlefields between Chattanooga and Atlanta. My field work began in 1986, when I initially became aware of the rich storehouse of earthwork remnants at Kennesaw Mountain National Battlefield Park. I have been gathering material for this book ever since.

My approach to the study of earthworks developed into a wider effort than merely understanding how the field fortifications were constructed and what shape and design they assumed. It became apparent from an early stage that the relationship between the earthworks and the landscape was all-important. Moreover, the relationship between the earthworks and the tactical history of the campaign that they were a part of was equally important. In my trilogy on the history of field fortifications in the eastern theater, I discussed this triad relationship, especially in the second volume on the Overland campaign and the third volume on the Petersburg campaign. In this book on Atlanta, the triad relationship is made even more explicit. Most studies of weapons in the Civil War tend to focus on hardware rather than on how those guns were actually used in combat; that trend misses an important point. It would be equally dangerous to consider the topic of field fortification without seeing it in its larger operational context. One gets only a sliver of the true story in that way.

Therefore, this study attempts to gain as wide a spectrum of views on the use of field fortifications in the Atlanta campaign as possible. That spectrum includes the tactical approach to operations as it related to the use of fieldworks; an understanding of how terrain and vegetation affected those operations and were linked to field defenses; and a good deal of attention paid to the earthworks themselves. The engineering resources (officers, troops, pioneers, and tools) that were the foundation of siting and constructing earthworks are studied. The story includes the role of infantry and artillery officers and enlisted men in helping to build the works; the details of construction, design, and layout according to the lay of the land; and a sense of how much digging took place.

Moreover, the human dimension of fortification use is important. What was it like to dig under imminent threat of enemy attack? Long-term occupation of trenches under a broiling sun or a drenching rain created unusual living conditions for men stuck in ditches, and veterans of the campaign were not shy about discussing those matters in detail. Trenches became a bizarrely confined theater of life and death for both Union and Confederate enlisted men and their officers, and this to me represents one of the more fascinating aspects of their history in the Civil War.

Both sides utilized earthworks in the Atlanta campaign but they used them for different purposes. While the Confederates learned how to construct impressive fortification systems as the campaign progressed, they almost always used them for *defensive* purposes. The Federals not only built strong defensive works, but more importantly sought ways to use them for *offensive* purposes, too. Sherman's aim was to penetrate Georgia, break up the Army of Tennessee, capture Atlanta, and keep the Confederates from sending reinforcements to Lee's army in Virginia. He had to remain on the move. Therefore, using earthworks to hold his advanced positions and organizing men to conduct flanking moves became his modus operandi. But he had to develop tactics and use terrain to facilitate that mode of operation.

The sources for understanding the combination of tactics, terrain, and trenches in the Atlanta campaign are plentiful. The campaign lasted four months, as many as 160,000 men participated in it, and the reports, letters, diaries, memoirs, and other personal accounts are voluminous. The campaign left behind some of the best earthwork remnants of the entire war, especially at Kennesaw Mountain.

Despite this, no one has yet written a study of the link between tactics, terrain, and fortifications during the Atlanta campaign. Sherman's drive to the city has called forth numerous books and articles, but they tend to follow the lead of Thomas Lawrence Connelly's discussion of the campaign in his landmark study, *Autumn of Glory: The Army of Tennessee, 1862–1865*, published in 1971. Connelly focused on the high command of that army. He discussed personal relations among its leaders and how those relations influenced the course of the army's campaigns, as well as the grand tactics and strategy associated with the army's operations. Connelly's view is strictly on the higher levels of military operations.

Most subsequent studies of the Atlanta campaign tend to do more or less the same things that Connelly did in his book. We have many interesting discussions of whether Johnston or his successor, Gen. John Bell Hood, did well in managing the Confederate army. There are good discussions of whether Hood's replacement of Johnston significantly hurt soldier morale.[2]

While topics associated with strategy and tactics obviously were important in the history of the fight for Atlanta, they do not constitute a full list of significant factors in understanding the campaign. Everything from supply and logistics, medical care of the troops, field communications, soldier attitudes toward a wide variety of issues, and the competency of lower-level commanders played equally important roles in events that transpired in the hill and piedmont country of northwest Georgia that summer of 1864.

Even the best overall study of the campaign, Albert Castel's *Decision in the West*, gives only passing mention of field fortifications. The handful of historians who had written books on individual battles of the campaign before the 2013 appearance of my study of the actions around Kennesaw Mountain also paid scant attention to the role of fieldworks in their engagements. In my series of battle books on Kennesaw Mountain, Ezra Church, and Peach Tree Creek, I give full attention to the earthworks associated with each phase of the campaign that is covered. In addition, I discuss the effect of terrain and tactics in each of my Atlanta campaign battle books.[3]

But there is a need to understand the matrix of tactics, terrain, and trenches for the campaign as a whole. Given the length of the operation, the fact that the Confederates dug eighteen separate fieldwork systems, the fact that hundreds of miles of parapet were thrown up by both armies, and that Sherman was compelled to adjust his tactics and his use of terrain to deal with those earthwork systems, there is ample justification for devoting one book to the study of these three vital factors in one of the most important campaigns of the war. The struggle for Atlanta involved a classic example of persistent penetration of enemy territory over a long period of time and across varied and rugged terrain. Hopefully this book will be but the beginning of a new trend to explore many previously ignored topics associated with a well-rounded picture of military operations in the Civil War.

I wish to thank the staff of all the archival institutions listed in the bibliography for their cooperation in making their sources available. My thanks also go to Steve Acker for sharing information with me about his circle of reenactors' efforts to reconstruct and fire from a Civil War earthwork in Wisconsin.

Most of all, thanks to my wife, Pratibha, for being here and enriching my life beyond expression.

1

Tactics, Terrain, and Trenches

The armies that assembled for the Atlanta campaign were among the largest concentrations of fighting men in the western theater during the Civil War. Maj. Gen. William T. Sherman, commander of the Military Division of the Mississippi, drew troops from three geographic departments to mass 110,000 men and 254 guns for the campaign, scattering them in winter camps across Middle Tennessee, northern Alabama, eastern Tennessee, and around Chattanooga. Maj. Gen. George H. Thomas led 73,000 men and 130 guns in the Army of the Cumberland, while Maj. Gen. James B. McPherson's Army of the Tennessee consisted of 24,500 men and ninety-six guns. Maj. Gen. John M. Schofield's Army of the Ohio fielded 13,559 troops and twenty-eight guns. Opposing this array stood Gen. Joseph E. Johnston's Army of Tennessee with 63,000 men.[1]

TACTICS

In order to understand the tactical history of the Atlanta campaign, it is necessary to differentiate between two levels of this complicated subject. This chapter will not deal with one of those levels, which has often been termed lower tactics, minor tactics, or small unit tactics. I prefer to call this level primary tactics because that is exactly what it was: the most fundamental aspect of Civil War tactics. The primary level consisted of the various formations used to organize men in a shoulder-to-shoulder linear fashion so officers could control their movement. Primary tactics also consisted of the various maneuvers officers used to shift those linear formations from one place to another or to change from one formation to a different one.[2]

Both armies used the same primary tactics during the Atlanta campaign. Union and Confederate soldiers were well versed in forming lines and columns, the two basic formations employed by Civil War armies. They also had trained incessantly in the process of moving forward while guiding on a unit within their own battle line so as to maintain well-dressed formations; in moving by the flank; in marching obliquely; and in changing front forward on a subunit. Neither Sherman's nor Johnston's troops changed these basic formations and maneuvers to suit the needs of the campaign.[3]

This chapter will discuss the so-called higher level of tactics, which used to be termed grand tactics but now is more generally referred to as the operational level. This term refers to a wide range of factors that illuminate how a commander handled his army on campaign, and can range from logistics and communications to tactics. For our purposes in this study, the operational discussion will mostly involve how commanders handled their troops while advancing toward or defending Atlanta. The context of that discussion will center on terrain and the use of field fortifications.[4]

The basic operational mode followed by Sherman was fairly simple. He relied almost entirely on his line of communications to supply the large army group under his command. That line consisted of a single track of railroad stretching back to Chattanooga, Nashville, and Louisville for a total of 350 miles. Sherman had to maintain contact with this line and protect it with defenses and garrisons of troops; he could afford to break away from the railroad only for short periods while feeding his men with wagon trains linking the units with the nearest railhead. Johnston also relied on the railroad to supply his men but had in many ways an easier time of it in that Atlanta was his nearest base and he retired toward that city.[5]

In addition to maintaining close contact with the railroad, the other element in Sherman's operational art lay in his approach to dealing with the many well-fortified Confederate lines of defense he encountered in northwestern Georgia. From Dalton to Palmetto Station, the Army of Tennessee built eighteen major lines of fieldworks during and immediately after the campaign. Sherman soon adopted a more subtle and effective way of dealing with enemy fieldworks than did Ulysses S. Grant, his commander and friend. Grant tended to launch massive frontal assaults against Robert E. Lee's earthworks during the Overland campaign and during some phases of the Petersburg campaign, and they usually resulted in heavy casualties that severely degraded the combat readiness

Tactics, Terrain, and Trenches

Table 1.1. Confederate fortified lines in the Atlanta campaign

Sequence	Location and name	Duration
First	Dalton (Rocky Face Ridge) Line	May 8–12, 1864
Second	Resaca Line	May 13–15, 1864
Third	Adairsville Line	May 17, 1864
Fourth	Cassville Line	May 19, 1864
Fifth	New Hope Church, Pickett's Mill, and Dallas Line	May 25–June 3, 1864
Sixth	Mountain Line	June 5–14, 1864
Seventh	Gilgal Church Line	June 15–16, 1864
Eighth	Mud Creek Line	June 17–18, 1864
Ninth	Kennesaw Mountain Line	June 19–July 2, 1864
Tenth	Smyrna Line	July 3–4, 1864
Eleventh	Chattahoochee River Line (Shoup Line)	July 5–9, 1864
Twelfth	Peach Tree Creek Line and Confederate Outer Line	July 18–21, 1864
Thirteenth	Atlanta City Line	July 21–September 2, 1864
Fourteenth	Hood's Addition to City Line	July 21–September 2, 1864
Fifteenth	East Point Line	July 29–September 2, 1864
Sixteenth	Jonesboro Line	August 31–September 1, 1864
Seventeenth	Lovejoy's Station Line	September 2–4, 1864
Eighteenth	Palmetto Station Line	September 20–29, 1864

of the Army of the Potomac. Those frontal assaults rarely achieved much and even at their most successful merely wore down Lee's troop strength.[6]

Sherman, who kept abreast of Grant's progress, consciously chose not to adopt his mentor's operational mode. He also rejected another model in the way Maj. Gen. Henry W. Halleck had conducted his advance toward Corinth, Mississippi, in May 1862. Seared by the surprise Confederate attack at Shiloh the month before, Halleck adopted an operational mode of extreme caution. He fortified nearly every daily position his huge army group adopted and thus advanced the short distance from Pittsburg Landing to Corinth at a snail's pace. In the end Halleck minimized his losses and captured Corinth without a major battle, but he was heavily criticized for letting the opposing Confederate Army of the Mississippi (later renamed the Army of Tennessee) escape with little punishment.[7]

Sherman's operational art was a good blend of caution and maneuver mixed with an occasional willingness to try a limited attack on fortified positions. It blended the best of Halleck's and Grant's approaches. As it developed, Sherman relied on closing in on Johnston's fortifications, establishing his own troops in fortified lines to confront those enemy works, and trying to find a way to shift the Confederates out of their trenches with minimal losses. That meant making large-scale flanking movements, and Sherman honed that tedious and risky process to a fine art as the campaign lengthened.

In other words, the Federals used field fortifications more effectively than their opponents did because they learned how to use them for offensive purposes, not just defensive aims. Union trenches fixed the enemy in their fortified positions and enabled the Federals, who outnumbered their opponents, to send troops off to either enemy flank. Sherman also understood the topography of northwestern Georgia and keenly used it to his advantage whenever that was possible. Terrain features could either help or hinder flank movements. Terrain helped Sherman advance more quickly than usual north of the Etowah River, while it slowed his advance to a crawl south of the Etowah.

Johnston's operational art was overly simplistic. For the most part, he acted on the defensive, encouraging his troops to dig in ever more strongly upon defensible ground in the hopes of wearing down Sherman's manpower and will to continue the campaign. Only occasionally was Johnston willing to mix limited tactical offensives with his defensive policy, and those few occasions offered little trouble to the Federals. It also has to be pointed out that Johnston did not always do a good job of watching his flanks and was too ready to abandon his fortified positions at the first hint that the enemy was about to turn them. In short, Johnston was good at judging defensive ground and authorizing a stand on it, but he was not tenacious at keeping that position when threatened by anything except a direct frontal assault—and Sherman did not oblige him in offering such assaults very often.

Johnston failed to take advantage of all the terrain features that could have aided his policy. Sherman's path was crossed by several major rivers, including the Oostanaula, the Etowah, and the Chattahoochee. Johnston too often failed to protect all the crossings within reach of the enemy and usually did not offer much resistance when Federal troops began to use them. He seems to have been blind to the tactical possibilities of forcing the Yankees to expend time and manpower in forcing crossings of large streams, allowing them remarkable opportunities to cross those rivers and establish bridgeheads on the enemy side of them with impunity.

When John Bell Hood replaced Johnston on July 18, he adopted a drastically different operational policy of offensive action. The Army of Tennessee conducted the first full-scale attacks it had essayed since the battle of Chickamauga when it struck Thomas north of Atlanta at Peach Tree Creek two days later, McPherson east of Atlanta on July 22, and Maj. Gen. Oliver O. Howard (McPherson's replacement) west of the city on July 28. None of those assaults achieved the desired result and cost the Confederates at least 11,000 casualties. Hood then adopted Johnston's defensive policy but tried another major assault (that failed) on the first day of fighting at Jonesboro on August 31. Hood was unable to take advantage of terrain opportunities because by the time he took command, the army was south of the Chattahoochee River and the landscape offered little if any advantage to his operations.

TERRAIN

The armies contending for control of Atlanta operated in an interesting mix of terrain as they moved south from Dalton, crossing major geographical boundaries in northwestern Georgia. Initially, the combatants operated in the edge of the Appalachian Highlands, which stretched down to the Oostanaula River at Resaca. This region was characterized by long, high ridges that stretched for dozens of miles on a northeast-to-southwest axis, with wide valleys between the ridges. These terrain features were typical of the valley regions of southern Appalachia. The ridges contained numerous gaps of varied depths. These gaps could be transformed into strong defensive positions quite easily, as demonstrated by the Confederate defense of Mill Creek Gap and Dug Gap on top of Rocky Face Ridge near Dalton. Federal operations against fortified gaps such as these proved to be futile and costly.

But the Federals had a distinct advantage in this Appalachian terrain, for there always were more gaps farther along the ridgeline they could use to turn the fortified positions. That is exactly what Sherman did in the first phase of the Atlanta campaign, using the unguarded Snake Creek Gap to force Johnston out of his defenses at Dalton. The same was true of earlier Federal operations in Appalachia, including those against Cumberland Gap, the advance on Chattanooga, and the Union occupation of Knoxville.

South of Resaca, however, the armies left Appalachian terrain and began to enter the outer edges of the Piedmont, an intermediate zone between the mountains and the coastal plain. The terrain was much more mixed south of the Oostanaula, without the long ridges that shaped the topography near Dalton. Yet one could easily find some remnants of such high ridges, as at Cassville, upon which to plant a defensive line to tactical advantage.

South of Cassville and south of the Etowah River, the armies entered an area dotted with a few high, commanding hills or clusters of hills, with large areas of rolling terrain in between. The rolling terrain often was covered with thick vegetation and only a few clearings; small farms appeared here and there. The road system, consisting of dirt pathways for wheeled vehicles, constituted the principal markers in this relatively undeveloped landscape. Here the Federals found their worst physical obstacle to rapid movement, especially when the spring rains descended in torrents for days on end, making it almost impossible to move troops along the dirt roads. This area between the Etowah River and the town of Marietta also was the most advantageous for the Confederates. Terrain, vegetation, and the weather conspired to give Johnston an opportunity to slow Sherman to an agonizing crawl. There were no high ridges to shield his flanking movements, no valleys to offer good routes for travel. This phase of the Atlanta campaign, from the Etowah to the Chattahoochee, was the most frustrating for Sherman and his men also because of Johnston's skill at conducting a delaying action at minimal cost to the Confederate army.

South of the Chattahoochee the terrain is typical, rolling Piedmont country, with comparatively few high hills or ridges, and leveling out even more south of Atlanta. By the time Sherman's army group captured the city in September, the Federals had fought and dug their way out of the mountains and into the open country, which offered them opportunities to penetrate the Confederacy toward Savannah, Macon, or even the Gulf Coast. In a sense, the end of the Atlanta campaign finished a long, grueling Union effort begun by Maj. Gen. William S. Rosecrans when he moved the Army of the Cumberland across the mountains in August 1863 in an effort to flank Braxton Bragg's Army of Tennessee out of Chattanooga. Crossing the Appalachian Highlands in successive campaigns had proven to be the most difficult part of the Federal war in the West in terms of logistics and troop mobility. That great, natural barrier was now past, and the war in the West had taken a new turn.[8]

FEDERAL MAPS

While Sherman had had some personal experience with the terrain of northwest Georgia as a young army officer in the 1840s, most of his subordinates had little idea what to expect as the campaign started. Most of their understanding of the topography to be encountered came from maps. Until 1863, the U.S. Army maintained the Corps of Topographical Engineers, which was separate from the Corps of Engineers. The former organization had an important task to perform in mapping the western frontier and the coastal regions of the United

States. But many officers and administrators had urged that the two corps be merged for efficiency, and by the time of the Atlanta campaign all engineer officers were expected to turn their hand to map-making as needed. Within Sherman's army group, chief engineer Orlando M. Poe relied mostly on volunteer engineers, officers detailed from the infantry regiments, to scout terrain and sketch maps. His subordinates issued 4,000 copies of maps to various commanders during the campaign. Thomas's Army of the Cumberland boasted a large and efficient staff of topographical officers, with one serving each corps and division commander, and most of the brigade leaders as well. The Army of the Tennessee and the Army of the Ohio had far fewer topographers.[9]

Poe relied heavily on the mapping capabilities of the Department of the Cumberland. William E. Merrill, Thomas's chief engineer before the campaign, organized a thriving map-making industry for Sherman's army group. He started with a base map of northern Georgia, enlarged it to a scale of one inch per mile, and gathered information from spies, refugees, and anyone else caught by the provost marshal. He then divided the map into sixteen sections and assigned draftsmen to work on each one. Four adjacent sections were joined and placed on one stone to be lithographed, for Merrill found that the lithography process was the fastest and best way to reproduce large numbers of maps. He made 200 copies of each quadrant and joined the four quadrants together to make 200 large maps of north Georgia. Each corps, division, and brigade leader in Sherman's army group thus had a copy before the campaign started. Map copies issued to cavalry commanders were printed on muslin rather than paper, to be more flexible, durable, and washable. Sherman's command "was the best supplied with maps of any that fought in the civil war," Merrill concluded.[10]

CONFEDERATE MAPS

Wilbur F. Foster was primarily responsible for the maps Confederate commanders possessed of the terrain between Chattanooga and Atlanta. A civil engineer before the war who had been involved in the construction of Fort Henry and Fort Donelson, he received orders from Bragg in November 1863 to create a survey and map-making party to chart the country ten miles to either side of the Western and Atlantic Railroad in anticipation of future operations along the line. Foster used the results of surveys conducted by the state government before the war as a start, but relied mostly on field reconnaissance to create a series of reliable maps for the Army of Tennessee. He began work on November 3, assigning sectors to different officers, who used pocket compasses to get their bearings and then counted their horses' paces to estimate distance.

After coordinating the results with each other, every sector map was sent in to the engineer office in Atlanta (or Macon, after it was moved there in May 1864). At the office, these sketches were reproduced and added to the general map. A total of fifteen men were involved in this project, and it was not finished until after the Atlanta campaign started. A. J. Riddle of Macon made photographic copies of the finished maps to be distributed to officers in the field.[11]

TRENCHES

The third element in the combination of tactics, terrain, and trenches had been developing since the onset of the Civil War and had roots stretching deeply into prewar America. The technical expertise to build and utilize field fortifications had been in place for decades. The Corps of Engineers was the strongest arm of the U.S. Army and was placed in charge of the Military Academy at West Point. It was responsible for managing the largest government building project of early America, the Third System of masonry seacoast fortifications. West Point taught cadets the rudiments of how to plan and build earthen fortifications as well as masonry forts, and Dennis Hart Mahan, the most prominent professor at the academy, had written the American textbook on fortifications. Published in 1836 and entitled *A Treatise on Field Fortification*, it became the most important discussion of fieldwork construction in the country.

Theory and doctrine concerning the use of temporary fieldworks were simple and straightforward. Of course, a well-made earthwork thoughtfully sited on the best ground could be used defensively, but Mahan also pointed out that it could be used offensively to shield troops before they launched an attack. Neither Mahan nor anyone else offered anything like a full-scale doctrine on the use of field fortifications. All they could do was provide the technical details about constructing them and offer a bit of advice about how to use them.

Actual experience on the battlefield counted for everything when it came to making decisions about when and where to dig in, or whether to remain on the defensive or conduct an attack against an enemy. The Civil War generation's readiest example from the past was the Mexican War of 1846–1848, but the American army that won every battle of that war of territorial conquest had made only scant use of fieldworks. It had more experience at taking Mexican fortifications than in constructing and defending entrenchments of its own.

Nevertheless, when the Civil War broke out, the country entered a new phase of its fortification history. This was by far the largest, most engrossing conflict to hit the United States, and from the beginning armies in blue and gray used temporary fieldworks more often than ever before in American history. The construction of semipermanent earthen fortifications to protect cities and other fixed assets exploded because America was, in a sense, a fortification-poor society and these assets needed protection. But the Union and Confederate soldiers soon came to understand the value of a quickly thrown-together breastwork or parapet of earth, something to protect their bodies even for a few hours, which could easily be abandoned after they were no longer needed during active operations by armies in the field.

In many early battles of the Civil War, including Big Bethel, Fredericksburg, Chancellorsville, and Gettysburg in the East, and Stones River, Chickamauga, and Chattanooga in the West, soldiers threw up temporary works during an engagement or immediately before or after the fight. It is probably true that more temporary fortifications were deployed during the first half of the Civil War than during all American wars before 1861 combined, and yet soldiers of both armies were not prepared for the intense use to be seen in the Overland and Petersburg campaigns in Virginia or the Atlanta campaign in Georgia during 1864.

The key to the intense reliance on hasty fortifications in 1864 was the Federal policy of continuous contact, maintaining the pressure of a campaign against the major Confederate field armies without letup for months at a time. This kind of pressure put a massive premium on protection because it placed opposing armies within gunshot range of each other for hours, days, weeks, and even months at a time.[12]

The handling of fieldwork construction was a communal affair, not restricted to any one person or category of soldier. It is true that trained military engineers were mostly responsible for deciding where to place the field defenses and to a degree supervised their construction, but these engineers were in short supply during the Atlanta campaign. Many infantry officers had to be detailed from the ranks to serve as engineers. These officers sited the positions of earthworks and often supervised their construction, but most of the digging actually was performed by infantrymen rather than trained engineers. Few engineer units operated with the Union and Confederate armies in northwestern Georgia, and they typically performed the more intricate and sophisticated aspects of earthwork construction: fashioning embrasures for artillery pieces or setting up complicated layers of wooden obstructions in front of the trenches to trip up attackers. The heavy, drudging labor was overwhelmingly performed by foot soldiers.

In addition to engineer officers, engineer units, and infantrymen, pioneer troops also performed a good deal of work on the field fortifications. Pioneers were infantrymen detailed from the ranks to use shovels, picks, and axes to perform a variety of duties associated with operations in the field. These included repairing existing civilian roads or cutting new military roads, burying the dead after a battle, or clearing trees and brush for a campsite. They also worked normally on the more complicated aspects of field fortifications, leaving the heavy work for large infantry details.

Given all of these groups of men who contributed to the construction of field fortifications, it is not surprising that the earthworks springing up in the Atlanta campaign were a mix of the highly improvised and the traditional, textbook version. One can see trenches constructed along Mahan's basic outlines mixed in with peculiar elements fashioned by individuals to suit a particular need or adapted to a quirk in the landscape. In studying the Atlanta campaign, one must keep in mind this curious mix of the standard and the improvised in understanding the design and construction of fieldworks. One must also consider the types and availability of entrenching tools in the two competing armies.

FEDERAL ENGINEER OFFICERS

The armies that were poised to begin the Atlanta campaign possessed few engineer officers, but that was not unusual for the western forces. Sherman had a superb engineer serving on the staff of his military division, Capt. Orlando Metcalfe Poe. Ohio born, a graduate of the West Point class of 1856, and a topographical engineer before the war, Poe had served in western Virginia under George B. McClellan in 1861 before accepting command of the 2nd Michigan, which he led in the Peninsula campaign. Poe commanded a brigade during the Second Bull Run campaign, in Maryland, and at Fredericksburg, but the Senate failed to confirm his commission as brigadier general, and he spent the rest of the war in engineer work. Poe was chiefly responsible for planning the strong defenses of Knoxville, Tennessee, when Confederate forces under Lt. Gen. James Longstreet tried to wrest that mountain stronghold from the Federals late in 1863. In fact, Sherman's inspection of those earthworks led him to appoint Poe to his staff.[13]

Capt. William E. Merrill served as Thomas's chief of engineers in the Army of the Cumberland until early May, when he organized and took command of the 1st U.S. Veteran Volunteer Engineers. Merrill was succeeded by Lt. Henry C. Wharton, a twenty-two-year-old graduate of the West Point class of 1862.[14]

McPherson had only one regular engineer officer, Capt. Chauncey B. Reese, at the start of the Atlanta campaign. Reese served as his chief engineer, taking up his duties on April 29, 1864. He had graduated in the West Point class

Tactics, Terrain, and Trenches

Capt. Orlando M. Poe. As chief engineer of the Military Division of the Mississippi, Poe brought his expertise and experience to bear on managing Sherman's engineer resources during the long campaign for Atlanta. *Brady National Photographic Art Gallery, Library of Congress, LC-DIG-cwpb-05945.*

Capt. Chauncey B. Reese. Having graduated from the U.S. Military Academy five years before, Reese served as chief engineer of the Army of the Tennessee during the Atlanta campaign. *Library of Congress, LC-DIG-cwpb-07072.*

of 1859 and had gained experience on the Peninsula and in operations along the South Carolina coast. Reese managed to obtain engineer officers to serve corps and division commanders in the Army of the Tennessee, although many of the officers were detailed from infantry and artillery units rather than trained at West Point. They were men who had demonstrated an aptitude for engineer work, and were often referred to as volunteer engineers. They spent most of

Tactics, Terrain, and Trenches

their time superintending construction by the pioneer details. Capt. James R. Percy of the 53rd Ohio, for example, had been a civil engineer before the war and was detailed to engineer work on the Fourth Division staff in the Fifteenth Corps. Percy was killed on August 18, 1864, at age thirty-two. Four more engineer officers were detailed to Sherman in early July, all of them recent graduates of West Point, but the Union armies continued to rely heavily on volunteer engineers by necessity.[15]

Maj. Gen. Francis P. Blair issued a general order in early August mandating that all division commanders in the Seventeenth Corps maintain an engineer officer on their staff. He charged this officer with the responsibility of reporting to corps headquarters any change in the division's position and illustrating his reports with maps. The engineer officer also constructed military roads parallel to the division line and maintained the strength of the division pioneer corps. The officer was specially charged with superintending the fieldworks that secured the division's position, "as the direction of a very small portion of the line may decidedly affect the issue of an attack on it."[16]

Sherman never had enough engineer officers during the campaign, forcing those available to do a variety of tasks including scouting terrain, making maps of the road system, laying out fortifications, and supervising pontoons. Sherman had two pontoon trains, one for McPherson's army and the other for Thomas's, with two more in reserve at Nashville. The engineers were forced to improvise in order to provide medical care for men detailed to their units. When his pontoniers became ill, Capt. William Kossak prevailed on the surgeon of the 12th Missouri to care for them because he had no other recourse within the administrative structure of the Army of the Tennessee.[17]

FEDERAL ENGINEER UNITS

The Federal army also had few engineer troops available for service during the Atlanta campaign. As Poe put it, he possessed an engineer organization that was "altogether inadequate." There were only two engineer regiments within the limits of Sherman's Military Division of the Mississippi early in 1864, the 1st Michigan Engineers and Mechanics and the 1st Missouri Engineers (formerly designated the Engineer Regiment of the West). Both units reported to Thomas and both remained on railroad duty behind the lines to repair Sherman's fragile supply system. Schofield had a small engineer battalion, originally created by Poe when the Federals entered East Tennessee, but it operated more like a pioneer unit than an engineer organization. The Army of the Tennessee had no engineer units at all, but as Poe reported, it possessed "an excellent pio-

Table 1.2. Federal engineer officers in the Atlanta campaign

Name and commission	Assignment	Position and time occupied
Capt. Orlando Metcalfe Poe, Corps of Engineers	Military Division of the Mississippi	Chief engineer
Capt. William E. Merrill, Corps of Engineers	Department and Army of the Cumberland	Chief engineer until early May 1864
Lt. Henry C. Wharton, Corps of Engineers	Department and Army of the Cumberland	Chief engineer from early May 1864
Lt. William Ludlow, Corps of Engineers	Twentieth Corps, Army of the Cumberland	Chief engineer from July 19 to late August 1864
Capt. Chauncey B. Reese, Corps of Engineers	Department and Army of the Tennessee	Chief engineer
Lt. Oswald H. Ernst, Corps of Engineers	Department and Army of the Tennessee	Assistant to chief engineer, July 16 to August 5, 1864
Capt. Leopold Helmle, Corps of Engineers	Department and Army of the Tennessee	Assistant to chief engineer
Capt. Herman Klostermann, 3rd Missouri	Fifteenth Corps, Army of the Tennessee	Chief engineer
Capt. James R. Percy, 53rd Ohio	Fourth Division, Fifteenth Corps, Army of the Tennessee	Killed August 18, 1864
Capt. William Kossak, staff appointment as aide-de-camp	Left Wing, Sixteenth Corps, Army of the Tennessee	Chief engineer, June 16 to 29, 1864
Lt. Col. Dedrick F. Tiedemann, 110th USCT	Left Wing, Sixteenth Corps, Army of the Tennessee	Chief engineer, June 29 to September 2, 1864
Col. Oscar Malmborg, 55th Illinois	Seventeenth Corps, Army of the Tennessee	Chief engineer, June 6 to July 18, 1864
Capt. John W. Barlow, Corps of Engineers	Seventeenth Corps, Army of the Tennessee	Chief engineer, July 18 to August 28, 1864
Capt. William Kossak, staff appointment as aide-de-camp	Seventeenth Corps, Army of the Tennessee	Chief engineer, August 28 to September 2, 1864
Capt. William J. Twining, Corps of Engineers	Department and Army of the Ohio	Chief engineer
Lt. A. M. Damrell, Corps of Engineers	Department and Army of the Ohio	Specific assignment unknown
Capt. William Kossak, staff appointment as aide-de-camp	Pontoon Train	Department of the Tennessee, June 30 to September 10, 1864

neer organization." At Poe's suggestion, Sherman ordered the 1st Missouri Engineers to report to the Army of the Tennessee, but the regiment did not arrive until the very end of the campaign.[18]

It is a mark of the importance attached to logistical matters that all engineer troops available were devoted to keeping the railroad running rather than placed on the front line where they could construct fieldworks. The Army of the Cumberland had the largest resource of engineer troops of any Union or Confederate army in the West. Capt. James St. Clair Morton created the Pioneer Brigade, consisting of three battalions, before the Stones River campaign. The Pioneers and the 1st Michigan Engineers and Mechanics were under fire during that terrible engagement on December 31, 1862. Neither unit engaged in the battle of Chickamauga on September 19–20, 1863, because they worked behind the lines on railroads. The Federals created a volunteer engineer brigade in the fall of 1863 to work on the defenses of Chattanooga, consisting of five regiments detailed from their parent brigades. This unit continued to operate throughout the summer of 1864 and worked on Sherman's logistical network in the area near Chattanooga. A handful of African American units also worked on the railroad system, including the 12th and 13th U.S. Colored Troops. By the end of April 1864, Thomas could boast of having 3,377 engineer soldiers in his Department of the Cumberland, but not one of them accompanied his large army when it set out for Atlanta. All of them remained clustered around Chattanooga and Nashville to maintain the vital rail line supplying Sherman's army group, all of which lay within the jurisdiction of Thomas's departmental command.[19]

Thomas prevailed on Secretary of War Edwin M. Stanton to authorize the creation of a new engineer unit, the 1st Veteran Volunteer Engineer Regiment. It was recruited from men of the Pioneer Brigade whose terms of enlistment in their original regiments were due to expire that summer. Thomas sent his chief engineer back to Chattanooga to oversee the recruitment process and take command of the regiment when it was ready.[20]

In addition, as noted earlier, the 1st Missouri Engineers managed to join the Army of the Tennessee just before the Atlanta campaign ended. The regiment had started as the Engineer Regiment of the West in 1861 and had mostly served within the boundaries of the Department of the Tennessee, although normally not on active campaigns. It had merged with the 25th Missouri early in 1864, was renamed the 1st Missouri Engineers, and was transferred to the Department of the Cumberland. When the regiment received orders to join the Army of the Tennessee, it arrived on August 30 near Jonesboro and thus was present for the climactic battle of the campaign. The regiment acted as infantry in the trenches and tore up railroads from September 2 to 4. It seems to have done little in the way of constructing the earthworks used in the fighting at Jonesboro or Lovejoy's Station.[21]

Schofield's small Engineer Battalion in the Army of the Ohio had seen continuous service since the previous year in Kentucky and East Tennessee. It consisted of men detailed from their parent regiments and was organized into two companies. At full strength, the battalion consisted of 300 men, but at the time of the Atlanta campaign it apparently was far smaller. Moreover, the men apparently received no specialized engineer training. At least one member of the battalion later tried to bill the government for extra pay, at the rate of forty cents per day, based on the practice of allowing such pay for soldiers who performed heavy labor for at least ten days, but Congress disallowed such rates through a resolution passed on March 3, 1865.[22]

FEDERAL PIONEERS

With essentially no engineer troops available to do the specialized work of creating field fortifications such as fashioning artillery embrasures, magazines, and mines, Sherman was forced to rely on infantry units, pioneers, and details of black laborers. The western armies had a long history of improvising engineer resources, relying heavily on the native talent of the rank and file to come forward and do work that normally was performed by regularly organized engineer units. Sherman also allowed each division to have a pioneer corps consisting of African Americans, promising to pay them ten dollars per month. He recommended to Adj. Gen. Lorenzo Thomas that this system should be followed in the entire Union army.[23]

But there is no evidence that Sherman was able to implement his system uniformly throughout the three armies that conducted the Atlanta campaign. Those armies made do with a haphazard organization of pioneers at all levels of command, from corps and division down to the company, usually taking white soldiers from the ranks. All told, perhaps 4,000 to 5,000 men, white and black, served as pioneers in the Union forces during the Atlanta campaign. They performed the normal duties of pioneers, which was to improve roads for the passage of troops and wheeled vehicles, bury the dead after an engagement, and do any other labor involved in camp duty. In addition, the pioneers substituted for engineer troops in digging earthworks, although they never performed the bulk of the labor in that important task. The fieldworks constructed by the Federals during the Atlanta campaign were far too extensive for the pioneers alone to dig, and the rank and file of the infantry units were responsible for most of the dirt-moving in that campaign.[24]

Tactics, Terrain, and Trenches

George Thomas used the well-known Pioneer Brigade, which Maj. Gen. William S. Rosecrans had created solely for railroad work in Tennessee. But he also had inherited the pioneer organization of the old Eleventh and Twelfth Corps of the Army of the Potomac (with 100-man companies attached to each brigade) when those two units were merged to form the Twentieth Corps. He wanted the remainder of his army to create new pioneer organizations. Maj. Gen. Oliver O. Howard formed units of twenty pioneers for each regiment in the Fourth Corps; they could be grouped into larger organizations if necessary. The commanders of the Fourteenth Corps, however, never created a permanent organization of pioneers, detailing men on an ad hoc basis as needed.[25]

Lt. Chesley A. Mosman of the 59th Illinois was assigned to command a regimental pioneer unit in the Fourth Corps early in May 1864. His men worked mostly at night during the campaign and often on fortifications. John K. Ely of the 88th Illinois, another Fourth Corps soldier, was detailed to pioneer duty in late May and recorded almost nightly labor on field fortifications. His unit lost three men due to enemy fire while making works one night in June. Mosman tired of his work in July because of the need to perform at night and sleep during the day; he welcomed an opportunity to return to company command.[26]

The Army of the Tennessee fielded the best organization of pioneers in Sherman's army group. Grant had created that force in late 1862. He established regulations for the pioneer organization a few months later, requiring 146 men for every division. Three hundred black laborers were later added to every division pioneer corps. The actual size of each corps varied. When Brig. Gen. John M. Corse took command of the Second Division, Sixteenth Corps, on July 26, it had a pioneer contingent of 123 whites and 190 blacks serving a division of 3,754 men. Andrew Hickenlooper, McPherson's chief engineer, indicated that the selection of pioneers was in part based on the men's skill with axes and other tools.[27]

In Schofield's Army of the Ohio, Brig. Gen. Jacob D. Cox created a pioneer corps for his division that was separate from the Engineer Battalion. He did this just before the onset of the Atlanta campaign, forming 100-man detachments for each brigade in the division.[28]

The work of a typical pioneer detachment, which some Federals called a "shovel brigade," did not always meet with approval. Lt. Lyman A. White of Bridges's Illinois Battery complained that a gun emplacement constructed by pioneers was readily torn apart by enemy counterbattery fire, even at a range of 1,800 yards. White's gunners rebuilt the work and fashioned their own embrasures as a result. Peter J. Osterhaus, a division commander in the Fifteenth Corps, wrote in his diary that "pioneer Captains made blunder of course" when they constructed gun emplacements on his sector, but his artillerymen "could mend" the mistakes. Every battery commander seems to have taken it for granted that pioneer-built works had to be improved by their own men.[29]

The pioneers, black as well as white, often fled at the sound of Confederate gunfire. Marshall Hurd, an enlisted man of the 2nd Iowa, insisted that the pioneers under his control carry their weapons and return fire, even when exposed in front of the Union line. Hurd worked his way up through the pioneer ranks of Grenville M. Dodge's Left Wing, Sixteenth Corps so that the men called him major, even though he never held a commission. He was an intelligent, practical engineer. In William B. Hazen's Fifteenth Corps division, one-fourth of the black pioneers were listed as absent without leave or having "deserted" during the last month of the Atlanta campaign.[30]

The availability of entrenching tools varied from army to army within Sherman's command, and this affected the ability of the pioneer units to do their job. Pioneer companies were allowed 150 shovels, 150 axes, 50 picks, and a variety of carpenter tools. They probably never actually possessed such an abundance of materials. In late September 1864, Hazen's division fielded 187 spades and shovels and 100 axes to be used by both the line infantry and the pioneers. In Oliver O. Howard's Fourth Corps, each pioneer company had ten axes, five picks, and five shovels, too few to arm every man in the company. Schofield counted only twenty axes in each division of the Twenty-Third Corps, so his pioneers must have suffered a good deal for lack of usable implements.[31]

SHERMAN'S RAILROAD DEFENSES

Sherman fully understood that logistics were the foundation of his success at Atlanta, and he devoted considerable time and energy to maintaining the flow of railcars toward his advancing army. The last year of the war witnessed a dramatic improvement in the type of defenses the Federals erected at key rail points, particularly important bridges. The Tullahoma and Chickamauga campaigns, which saw the Army of the Cumberland penetrating mountainous terrain to capture Chattanooga, had been supported with small earthworks and simple wooden stockades at these important rail points. Such defenses soon proved inadequate, as the Confederates often used field guns to batter them down. William E. Merrill took the lead in developing a stronger blockhouse that could withstand artillery fire, basing the design on a structure the Confederates had left half-finished at Strawberry Plains, east of Knoxville, Tennessee. Merrill also tested the effect of artillery fire on wood to conclude that the log walls had to be at least forty inches thick. The resulting structure was a massive blockhouse, with a tower and a roof, capable of withstanding field guns. It was difficult and time-consuming to build, demanding the attention of trained engineer troops, but the Merrill blockhouse represented the state of the art in railroad defenses of the Civil War.[32]

The blockhouses were still being constructed in late July 1864, as Merrill neared the completion of his system. When finished, the railroads that fed Sherman's army group were lined with formidable defenses. Quartermasters used a total of 351 miles of track between Nashville and Chattanooga, which included not only the direct line between those two cities but also the route by way of Decatur and Stevenson. Engineers constructed a total of ninety-five blockhouses along that mileage to protect the tracks. Merrill also built blockhouses along the rail line that linked Chattanooga with Atlanta, 137 miles, and eventually constructed twenty-two blockhouses along the route.[33]

CONFEDERATE ENGINEER OFFICERS

Gen. Joseph E. Johnston and his successor, John Bell Hood, had similar problems with finding engineer officers as Sherman, but they managed to more or less adequately staff the Army of Tennessee to meet the demands of the campaign. Johnston started with Lt. Col. Stephen Wilson Presstman as his chief engineer. Born in Delaware, and a railroad engineer before the war, Presstman had served as a captain in the 17th Virginia until receiving a wound at Blackburn's Ford on July 18, 1861. After Presstman recovered, Gen. P. G. T. Beauregard ordered him to the western theater, where he remained for the rest of the war. Presstman gained valuable experience as a staff engineer in the Army of the Mississippi, soon to be renamed the Army of Tennessee, and served as Gen. Braxton Bragg's chief engineer for a time. Presstman yearned for an order to return to Virginia, where his brother-in-law, Isaac R. Trimble, commanded a division. But that would never happen; engineer officers were too scarce in the West.[34]

Presstman served Johnston as chief engineer of the Army of Tennessee, even though he also commanded the 3rd Confederate Engineers. That regiment had only recently been created for assignment to the Army of Tennessee. When Hood replaced Johnston on July 18, he reshuffled his staff and brought in Maj. Gen. Martin L. Smith as chief engineer. Born in Danbury, New York, Smith had graduated from West Point in 1832 and served as a topographical engineer in the prewar army. He married a woman from Athens, Georgia, and thus sided with the Confederacy. Initially given a commission in the small Confederate Corps of Engineers, Smith angled himself into field command, first as

Table 1.3. Confederate engineer officers in the Atlanta campaign

Name	Assignment	Position and time occupied
Lt. Col. Stephen W. Presstman	Department and Army of Tennessee	Chief engineer until August 1, 1864
Maj. Gen. Martin L. Smith	Department and Army of Tennessee	Chief engineer, August 1, 1864, to end of campaign
Capt. George H. Hazlehurst	Hardee's Corps, Army of Tennessee	Chief engineer
Capt. Thaddeus Coleman	Hood's Corps, Army of Tennessee	Chief engineer
Capt. Walter J. Morris	Army of Mississippi–Stewart's Corps	Chief engineer before August 25, 1864
Maj. Wilbur F. Foster	Army of Mississippi–Stewart's Corps	Chief engineer as of August 25, 1864
Capt. John A. Porter	Army of Mississippi–Stewart's Corps	Specific assignment unknown
Lt. John W. Glenn	Stewart's Division, Hood's Corps, Army of Tennessee	Specific assignment unknown
Lt. A. B. DeSaulles	Army of Mississippi–Stewart's Corps	Specific assignment unknown
Lt. James K. P. McFall	Army of Mississippi–Stewart's Corps	Specific assignment unknown
Lt. Col. B. W. Frobel	Army of Tennessee	Sent August 4, 1864, specific assignment unknown
Maj. J. W. Green	Army of Tennessee	As of June 30, 1864, specific assignment unknown
Capt. John Batist Vinet	Army of Tennessee	Specific assignment unknown
Lt. George R. McRee	Army of Tennessee	Sent May 6, 1864, specific assignment unknown
Lt. M. M. Farrow	Army of Tennessee	Sent July 13, 1864, specific assignment unknown
Lt. D. W. Currie	Army of Tennessee	Sent May 23, 1864, specific assignment unknown
Lt. G. H. Browne	Army of Tennessee	Sent May 23, 1864, specific assignment unknown
Lt. Thomas E. Marble	Army of Tennessee	As of May 24, 1864, specific assignment unknown
Capt. L. P. Grant	Atlanta City Line	Chief engineer
Lt. W. A. Hansell	Atlanta City Line	Sent May 6, 1864, assistant to chief engineer

colonel of the 21st Louisiana and then as a brigade and division commander. He led one of the four Confederate divisions that defended Vicksburg during the siege of that river town. Smith served as Gen. Robert E. Lee's chief engineer during the Overland campaign and in the early phases of the Petersburg campaign, chalking up an impressive record with the Army of Northern Virginia.[35]

Lee told Smith to expect orders to move to Georgia on July 20, 1864, and he departed the next day. Smith visited Jefferson Davis, as well as his wife and child, along the way. He reported to Hood on August 1 and began inspecting the massive defenses around Atlanta. By that stage of the campaign, Smith's best talents were wasted. He had a keen sense of topography and fully understood how to maneuver large bodies of troops, and thus was a superb field engineer for a commander engaged in fluid movements. Now that the Army of Tennessee was stuck in its earthworks around Atlanta, earthworks which already had been designed and constructed, there was far less for Smith to do than he had hoped.[36]

The subordinate engineer officers in the Army of Tennessee performed yeoman's work in conceiving and building fortifications during the Atlanta campaign. They had help from Johnston's chief of artillery, Brig. Gen. Francis A. Shoup, who often was put to engineer work during the campaign before Hood named him chief of staff in late July.[37]

Among the subordinate engineer officers, Capt. George H. Hazlehurst had had extensive railroad experience in Georgia before the war. Hazlehurst, a slave owner who lived near Chattanooga, had worked on engineering projects for the Confederacy but refused to accept a commission in the Corps of Engineers until April 1864. He then served on the staff of Lt. Gen. William J. Hardee. Capt. Thaddeus Coleman had served in the artillery and as an engineer in North Carolina early in the war and had come west with Lt. Gen. Daniel Harvey Hill in 1863. He served as chief engineer of Hood's Corps throughout the Atlanta campaign. Capt. Walter J. Morris of the Confederate Engineer Corps had operated a business in East Tennessee before the war, and had served as an engineer at Fort Donelson when that post fell in February 1862. He had particular skills as a topographical engineer and a draftsman, and he served as chief engineer in Lt. Gen. Leonidas Polk's Army of Mississippi soon after that field force joined Johnston's army in mid-May 1864.[38]

The Confederate Engineer Bureau in Richmond worked hard to funnel engineer officers to the Army of Tennessee during the Atlanta campaign. From early May until early August, it sent at least nine officers to Georgia, one of whom was assigned to assist Capt. Lemuel P. Grant in working on the city defenses of Atlanta. While most of those men held commissions in the Corps of

Maj. Gen. Martin L. Smith. A superb field engineer, this New York native served as chief engineer of the Army of Northern Virginia before Hood called him west to serve in the same capacity in the Army of Tennessee in August 1864. *Library of Congress, LC-DIG-cwpb-05324.*

Engineers, some were ordnance and artillery officers, and one was a brigade-level staff member in the Army of Northern Virginia. The bureau also refused requests to have engineer officers transferred from the Army of Tennessee to other theaters, even when the officers requested it.[39]

Confederate engineer officers performed the same types of duties as their counterparts in blue: laying out positions for infantry units, designing field-works, and delivering messages. Maj. Gen. Jeremy F. Gilmer, the head of the bureau, even tried to influence strategy by urging Martin L. Smith to tell Hood that Atlanta should be held at least until the Democratic Party completed its nominating convention in Chicago on September 29. He hoped that a length-ening stalemate in Georgia might increase war weariness in the North and lead to a Democratic victory in the general elections that fall.[40]

CONFEDERATE ENGINEER TROOPS

The Confederate government did not begin to organize engineer regiments until the middle of 1863, with Jeremy Gilmer authorizing Presstman to do so within the ranks of the Army of Tennessee on June 19. Presstman was to orga-nize one company from each division in the army; by late August, he had com-pleted the formation of four companies with more to come. By mid-December, after its disastrous defeat at Chattanooga, the Army of Tennessee had nearly 450 engineer troops present for duty. Gilmer designated these companies as the 3rd Confederate Engineer Regiment, with Presstman as commander. Presst-man therefore filled two important roles for Johnston as his chief engineer and commander of the available engineer troops, an unusual circumstance in the Civil War. The regiment consisted of only seven companies, and three of them (Companies A, D, and E) were on detached duty in western Virginia and east-ern Tennessee to work on railroads. Capt. A. W. Clarkson's previously orga-nized company of Sappers and Miners was added to the regiment as the eighth company and served during the Atlanta campaign. Presstman's five companies averaged about 400 men during the period from May to September 1864.[41]

Polk's Army of Mississippi brought no engineer troops with it when the men transferred from the Department of Mississippi, East Louisiana, and Ala-bama in May 1864. The Engineer Bureau bemoaned the fact that attempts to organize engineer companies in that department had failed because of lack of support by Polk and his subordinate officers.[42]

After taking command of the Army of Tennessee, Hood sought to re-inforce his engineer units as much as possible. He requested at least 200 re-placements from the conscript depot at Macon in late July. There also were several vacancies in the grade of first lieutenant in the 3rd Confederate Engineers. Hood called on an old friend from Texas, who urged a relative named R. H. Griffin to request a transfer to Hood's army. Griffin, who held a commission in the 1st Confederate Engineers in Lee's army, did so out of a sense of duty to Hood, even though he would have preferred a transfer to the Trans-Mississippi. The transfer, however, was not approved because Lee needed engineer troops as badly as Hood.[43]

The 3rd Confederate Engineers saw some combat during the Atlanta campaign. At Jonesboro, on August 31, the companies cooperated with the 3rd Mississippi Cavalry to screen the extreme left flank of the Confederate line as it swept forward in an ill-advised attack on the Army of the Tennessee. While the assault was bluntly repulsed, the troops on the left managed to drive some Federals from an open field and across Flint River. Two days later, a corporal of the 3rd Confederate Engineers was captured by the Federals while the Army of Tennessee briefly held works at Lovejoy's Station. All told, Confederate reports indicate that a total of two engineers were killed and twenty-one wounded during the Atlanta campaign.[44]

CONFEDERATE PIONEERS

The Army of Tennessee had a substantial pioneer organization, but information on it is spotty. John C. Brown's Brigade formed a pioneer corps in early January 1864, while Stewart's Division of Hood's Corps created a pioneer organization led by Capt. J. R. Oliver of the 44th Tennessee. One of its members, Hiram Smith Williams of the 40th Alabama, joined the pioneers only after "some hesitation." A carpenter and carriage maker before the war, Williams soon wearied of the exhausting work involved in cutting brush and trees before earthworks to make a clear field of fire, complaining that Oliver "tried to see how much he could get for us to do, and he seems to have an idea that no one of us can ever get worn out." Carter L. Stevenson's Division and Maj. Gen. Samuel G. French's Division also created pioneer corps.[45]

CONFEDERATE TOOLS

Of course, the pioneers and the infantrymen who dug earthworks during the Atlanta campaign needed entrenching tools and axes, and the Engineer Bureau in Richmond was under pressure to provide them. Several shipments were sent by rail. In early May, when the campaign had just started, a bureau employee took thirty-three boxes filled with 396 axes to Atlanta. Another shipment of 500 shovels and 1,000 spades went to Lt. John W. Glenn in late May, with an additional 500 spades and 500 shovels, which were "indispensably necessary to the operations" of Johnston's army, sent in early June. The supply of entrenching tools dried up by the midpoint of the campaign; when Glenn requested more in early July, the bureau informed him that it had none to send.[46]

Archaeologists conducting a dig in the Rebel works at Gilgal Church in the 1980s uncovered a sample of the type of entrenching tool used by the Confederates. They found a shovel blade at the bottom of the trench, covered by a layer of dirt that had washed back into the work. It had a rounded point and was 11 inches long and 9.4 inches wide. "Two triangular pieces of iron, one about half the size as the other, were riveted to the shovel" to attach the blade to the handle. This rare find helps us to understand a basic, often ignored aspect of field fortifications—the size and shape of the common shovel.[47]

2

Dalton and Resaca

When Maj. Gen. Ulysses S. Grant still commanded the Military Division of the Mississippi, he envisioned a two-pronged advance toward Atlanta to take place in the spring of 1864. One column was to move south from Chattanooga and another north from Mobile as soon as that Gulf port city should fall into Union hands. Such a move would slice through the heart of the southeastern part of the Confederacy, further dividing the rebellious states as Grant's capture of Vicksburg the previous year had already done in a spectacular way.[1]

But Sherman planned to conduct a midwinter raid to disrupt Confederate rail transportation before it was time for the major spring campaign to begin. He intended to move from Vicksburg to Meridian, Mississippi, tearing up track and destroying that rail center as a hub of logistics for the Confederates in the state. Grant therefore ordered a supporting move out of Chattanooga to divert Rebel attention from Sherman's raid. He directed George H. Thomas to threaten the town of Dalton, where Joseph E. Johnston was rebuilding the Army of Tennessee after its dismal defeat at Chattanooga the previous November. Such a move would have to be conducted within the context of a projected thrust against Atlanta, and Grant hoped Thomas could seize Dalton "and hold it as one step towards a Spring Campaign." Grant also suggested to Thomas that the Army of the Cumberland avoid the fortified high ground near Dalton and bypass Johnston's main force by finding a suitable gap farther south to threaten the Confederate rail link with Atlanta. If successful, Thomas was to garrison Dalton and rebuild the railroad from Chattanooga to that point; if not, he was to remain near the town and threaten it until he was ready to launch a major drive in the spring.[2]

The first Federal strike against Dalton, in late February 1864, was a foretaste of Sherman's Atlanta campaign. Sherman's raid toward Meridian compelled Confederate president Jefferson Davis to order troops from Johnston's Army of Tennessee to Mississippi. Hardee's Corps received orders to ship out as soon as possible by rail to reinforce Polk's Department of Mississippi, East Louisiana, and Alabama on February 17. Maj. Gen. Benjamin Franklin Cheatham's Division left three days later, and Maj. Gen. Patrick R. Cleburne's Division left on February 22. Totaling 16,000 troops, these were two of Johnston's best divisions. But then on the morning of February 22, Thomas sent 25,000 of his own men toward Dalton under Maj. Gen. John M. Palmer, commander of the Fourteenth Corps, because he was too ill to accompany the expedition.[3]

As soon as he discovered the Federal move, Johnston prepared to defend Mill Creek Gap, which was a wide and deep passage through Rocky Face Ridge that accommodated both the wagon road and the railroad running from Chattanooga to Atlanta. Maj. Gen. Alexander P. Stewart placed three brigades and two batteries of his division in the gap, with the last brigade held to the rear as a reserve. More Confederate troops under Maj. Gen. John C. Breckinridge held the height south of the gap. As Breckinridge's men moved up the high, steep slope, John S. Jackman of the 9th Kentucky was reminded "of pictures seen of Hannibal crossing the Alps."[4]

The Federals began skirmishing with Johnston's outposts on February 23 and closed in on his position two days later, appearing in force before Mill Creek Gap as well as in Crow Valley east of Rocky Face Ridge. In short, Palmer was advancing both from the northwest and the north, on both sides of the high ridge. It did not take Federal commanders long to conclude that Johnston's position was "a very strong one," offering immense natural advantages for the defender and few opportunities for the attacker.[5]

The opposing sides engaged only in skirmishing during this first Union advance on Dalton. Thomas, who now felt well enough to take charge of the expedition, sought to gather information about the topography while skirmishing took place before Mill Creek Gap and in Crow Valley. He also sent a Federal force looking for gaps farther south and briefly occupied Dug Gap four miles south of Stewart's position. It was a shallow, high passage across Rocky Face Ridge, defended at the last minute by a brigade of Cleburne's Division, which

Dalton and Resaca   27

had rushed back to Dalton at the first word of Thomas's advance. This brigade, commanded by Brig. Gen. Hiram Granbury, routed the Federals out of the gap in a brief skirmish on February 26. Thomas broke contact soon after this fight and returned to Chattanooga, having discovered a deeper, wider pass at Snake Creek Gap about twelve miles south of Mill Creek Gap that could serve Union purposes very well on the next visit to Dalton.[6]

The Federal demonstration against the Army of Tennessee had diverted some troops intended for Mississippi, but Sherman had already reached Meridian without a major battle by February 17. He remained there five days before returning to Vicksburg. As a result, the troops Johnston sent had no opportunity to participate in the defense of Mississippi.[7]

Thomas's men had begun building field defenses as soon as they reached Mill Creek Gap on February 25, throwing together breastworks with logs and stones. These were crude structures, to be sure, but the men, hardened by defeat at Chickamauga and accustomed to elaborate, semipermanent works at Chattanooga, were taking no chances in this next open-field encounter. This tendency was evident in Fourth and Fourteenth Corps units. Ironically, the Confederates seem not to have constructed defenses at all during the first Dalton fight. Three years later, one of Stewart's staff officers recalled that there was a small fort at Mill Creek Gap and that one brigade of Stewart's Division constructed traverses to protect itself from enfilading artillery fire, but there is no supporting evidence to clear up this officer's somewhat unreliable memory. He admitted that he confused the February confrontation with digging that took place in April and with the second Dalton fight of early May. It is quite possible that the Confederates did not feel the need for earthworks to defend the high, dominating ground guarding the approaches to Dalton.[8]

But Johnston soon changed his mind about the need for earthworks. A Federal scout brought word to Thomas in early April that the Confederates were fortifying key points along the route from Chattanooga to Atlanta, including Dalton, Resaca, Mill Creek Gap (which also was known as Buzzard Roost), and the crossing of the Chattahoochee and Etowah Rivers. In addition to earthworks, the Confederates were constructing a dam on Mill Creek to flood the area inside Mill Creek Gap. The pace of Rebel fortifying picked up in late April as Johnston began to build works along the top of Rocky Face Ridge and across Crow Valley, having learned a lesson from the Federal approach in February. While Confederate soldiers did most of the work, Johnston also employed black laborers, presumably slaves, to work on the defenses.[9]

Sherman, the new commander of the Military Division of the Mississippi, realized that Rocky Face Ridge was a "very strong" position and that Johnston "had fortified it to the maximum." He was therefore ready to accept Thomas's proposal that the Federals flank Mill Creek Gap by using Snake Creek Gap to gain access to the railroad at Resaca. Sherman chose McPherson's Army of the Tennessee as the turning element, with Thomas and Schofield assigned to hold Johnston at Dalton. The scattered parts of Sherman's army group moved from their winter camps to converge on Dalton during the first week of May to start the Atlanta campaign.[10]

Rocky Face Ridge dominated the landscape around Dalton. Starting at a point seven miles northwest of the town, it stretched twenty-five miles toward the southwest. The ridge rises about 700 feet above the surrounding landscape. North of Mill Creek Gap, Rocky Face is taller and bulkier than the section to the south, and it has two enlarged areas, or humps. The Confederates constructed a signal station on the second hump and placed the angle in their line here as well. Eastward from the second hump, Stevenson's Division held the line across Crow Valley to Hamilton Ridge, a similar feature that ran parallel to Rocky Face Ridge. Capt. Willis Herbert Claiborne of Stevenson's Division was impressed by the view from Rocky Face. It was "magnificent—for ten miles around, the country lay like a map before us," he wrote.[11]

Johnston positioned his army to guard against a Federal approach from the north and northwest, anticipating a repeat of the February engagement. By May he had Cheatham's Division back, plus Brig. Gen. James Cantey's Brigade, which had been transferred from the Department of the Gulf. Cantey was assigned to hold Resaca and cover the roads to that railroad town from the west. But Johnston did not specify Snake Creek Gap as a point of importance to Cantey, who failed to position troops there.[12]

As the Federals approached, the Confederates set to work to improve their fortifications. Atop Rocky Face Ridge, south of Mill Creek Gap, members of the 37th Alabama "prized up huge stones and poised them, so that one man could easily set them off" in case the Federals tried to climb up the western slope. Near the angle of the Confederate line, Maj. Flavel C. Barber of the 3rd Tennessee found the top of Rocky Face Ridge to be ten to twenty feet wide, with a rock palisade sticking up along the western edge of the top and a small stone breastwork erected by compatriots. This rock palisade continued southward, in places high enough to serve as a breastwork itself. The western slope of Rocky Face tended to be covered with trees and was very steep.[13]

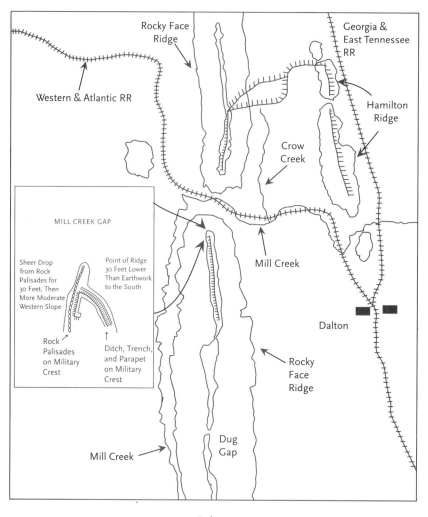

Dalton

As McPherson made his way south to find Snake Creek Gap, Thomas and Schofield approached Johnston's position from the northwest and north. When the Army of the Cumberland neared the area around Mill Creek Gap, its members automatically constructed field defenses, piling up logs and fence rails and using bayonets and tin plates to pile dirt on top. Harvey Reid marveled as his regiment, the 22nd Wisconsin, "pitched in" to gather "rails, dead trees, logs and so forth" and within an hour made a breastwork of them "that would have been hard to take."[14]

Thomas conducted several advances against the Dalton line to keep John-

Dalton and Resaca

Rock palisades on Rocky Face Ridge, near Dalton. This natural rock formation lines the western edge of the top of Rocky Face Ridge and provided a ready-made breastwork for defending Confederate troops. This image was taken from a short distance down the western slope of the ridge to indicate the perspective of approaching Federal soldiers. *Photograph by Earl J. Hess.*

ston occupied. On May 8, Brig. Gen. Charles Harker's brigade of the Fourth Corps ascended Rocky Face, which, according to his men, was twice as difficult to climb as Missionary Ridge. The brigade drove in the Confederate skirmishers and moved southward toward Mill Creek Gap as elements of the Fourth, Fourteenth, and Twentieth Corps moved up to cover the gap area from the west. Harker sent word to headquarters that the top of the ridge was, as Sherman put it, "a perfect couteau, knife edge, a sharp ridge." The Federals also learned firsthand the truth of earlier reports that the gap was impassable except along the railroad embankment and perhaps along the northern and southern edges. This obstruction was accomplished by building two dams, which flooded most of the gap, and all of the passages were covered by Confederate fire. The rocky palisade kept Harker's and other Union troops off the top of Rocky Face Ridge. The palisade even withstood an occasional direct hit by Union artillery. The surviving remnants of Confederate fortifications on top of the ridge, just south of Mill Creek Gap, indicate that a continuous line of trench was impossible due to the narrowness of the ridge top and all the rocks that crop out of the ground. But wherever feasible, the Rebels constructed works and utilized the continuous line of rock palisade to secure control of the high ground.[15]

Mill Creek Gap was the centerpiece of Johnston's defensive posture at Dalton. Stewart turned it into what division leader Daniel Butterfield called "a very ugly place to send troops." Mill Creek crossed the railroad twice inside the gap, making it easy to dam the stream at the crossings. Stewart relied on his engineer officer, Lt. John W. Glenn, to strengthen the dams with lumber and create a floodgate to control the flow of water. The work was performed by Stewart's pioneers under Capt. J. R. Oliver, with help from Stevenson's Division's pioneers. Work on the dams had started as early as March 13 and was finished by April 21, but Stewart improved them during the early days of May. The pioneers also tried to conceal the dams from prying Union eyes by piling brush in front of them. On May 7, after Johnston's cavalry corps under Maj. Gen. Joseph Wheeler retired through the gap, the pioneers also cut the bridges to prevent easy passage along the railroad embankment. The pioneers then cut trees across the roads leading to the gap as far as they could without running into Federal skirmishers.[16]

The Yankees made tentative efforts to deal with the obstructions so carefully placed in Mill Creek Gap. On May 9, men from a Fourteenth Corps brigade tried to reach the western dam and dismantle it. Reports indicated that the Confederates had stuffed "stones, logs, earth" into the railroad culvert so well that it was impossible to do anything about it. But that same dam broke apart the next day when a downpour caused Mill Creek to run wild. Stewart's pioneers cleared the debris that washed from the culvert over the road while under fire by Union skirmishers.[17]

Glenn also built earthworks and obstructions in and near the gap, spurred on by a dispatch from Hood urging Stewart to place abatis to disrupt an enemy advance. Stewart fortified his skirmish line to the point where he believed the works were "artillery proof" and argued that his skirmishers alone could have held the gap if needed. Sherman certainly thought his opponent had done an extraordinary job of fortifying the main passage of Rocky Face Ridge, calling Mill Creek Gap a "terrible door of death."[18]

North of the gap, at the angle in Johnston's line, the Confederates realized that their position was not as secure as at Mill Creek. When the Federals moved against this part of the line on May 8, Hood ordered Stevenson to shift another brigade to the top of Rocky Face Ridge so Edmund Pettus could contract his brigade line more compactly at the angle. This strengthened the critical junction of Johnston's westward-facing line with the troops who opposed

Schofield's advance from the north. Sherman warned Schofield not to waste manpower in futile assaults. "I do not want you to encounter field-works," he wrote. Schofield approached the Crow Valley line with caution and demonstrated on May 9 when he realized the strength of Stevenson's works. His skirmishers also reported "strong barricades of timber and stones" on top of Hamilton Ridge, facing east. Schofield was concerned about the security of his left flank, which also was the left flank of Sherman's army group. Division commander Jacob D. Cox protected that sector by ordering his men to construct breastworks. They gathered logs and treetops already lying on the ground and piled them up. Cox explained that some type of protection was necessary because the land in this area was "covered by dense forest" and the enemy could advance quite close before he would know about it.[19]

DUG GAP

The Federals made a vigorous attempt to force their way through Dug Gap at the same time that McPherson sought to use Snake Creek Gap to turn Johnston's position. It was a shallow gap, extending no more than about a quarter of the way into Rocky Face Ridge, and accessible by a steep climb up the western slope. Johnston held the gap with the 1st and 2nd Arkansas Mounted Rifles (dismounted) and Col. J. Warren Grigsby's cavalry brigade, 1,050 men all told, but he sent Hardee and Cleburne there on May 8 to investigate the situation.[20]

Brig. Gen. John W. Geary's division of the Twentieth Corps advanced to the gap with 4,500 men on May 8. When the Federals began the long climb at midafternoon, they encountered abatis placed along the mountainside and received heavy fire about 300 to 400 yards short of the rock palisade at the summit. Two regiments of Col. Adolphus Bushbeck's brigade, the 134th and 154th New York, made it to the palisade. Narrow crevices allowed some passage through the rocky barrier, and a few members of the 154th New York managed to get through but not in sufficient numbers to secure the crest. The two regiments fell back some distance to find suitable ground upon which to re-form. They advanced again with other units but failed to break through.[21]

The small Confederate force at Dug Gap held Geary's division all afternoon until Cleburne rushed elements of his division to replace them that evening. Capt. Samuel T. Foster of Granbury's Brigade found places on top of Rocky Face Ridge where he could see down both the western and eastern slopes at the same time, and at most the crest was no more than thirty feet wide. Cleburne's men worked all night to construct rock breastworks, which still exist today. A section of the works near Dug Gap was renovated in modern times,

Confederate rock breastworks at Dug Gap, Rocky Face Ridge, near Dalton.
Constructed by Cleburne's men, these breastworks have been renovated since the
war to a height that probably is close to their original appearance on the night
of May 8, 1864. They are located on the north side of Dug Gap; the Confederates
were positioned to the right of the work, and the Federals had to approach up
the steep side of Rocky Face Ridge from the left. *Photograph by Earl J. Hess.*

but the rest of the line has been allowed to remain in its eroded state after more
than 150 years. The Confederate defense of Dug Gap against Geary's attack involved nothing in the way of field defenses except the rock palisade, which was
a considerable obstacle to Union movement. Col. W. C. P. Breckinridge of the
9th Kentucky Cavalry, in Grigsby's Brigade, later argued that nothing more was
needed for his resolute men. Geary never tried another advance, but he ordered
his men to erect breastworks of their own near the bottom of the ridge on the
night of May 9 because local civilians had warned him of a possible counterattack on his position.[22]

SNAKE CREEK GAP

Soon after Geary's repulse at Dug Gap, the forward elements of McPherson's
Army of the Tennessee reached Snake Creek Gap on the evening of May 8. It
was a large passageway through Rocky Face Ridge, slashing through the feature

Dalton and Resaca

at a sharp angle. The gap was wide, deep, and four miles long. Grigsby moved his Kentucky cavalrymen from Dug Gap to the southern end of Snake Creek Gap on the night of May 8 and contested McPherson's cautious advance the next morning. Sixteenth Corps troops pushed the mounted Rebels east along the road that passed through the gap and linked Lafayette with Resaca. They secured the junction of this road with the wagon road from Dalton east of the gap. Cantey moved his brigade out to hold Bald Hill, a ridge that lay east of the junction, but the Federals pushed him back and sent men across Camp Creek, the last natural feature before Resaca. These men advanced to a point within 200 yards of the railroad before they were recalled. McPherson feared he might be walking into a trap; he ordered his men to pull away without snipping Johnston's vital rail link with Atlanta.[23]

Sherman was deeply disappointed in his friend and protégé for making this decision but rearranged his plans to accommodate the change in circumstances. He left behind the Fourth Corps and most of his cavalry while ordering the rest of Thomas's army and Schofield's command to move to Snake Creek Gap and move on Resaca from the west. McPherson justified his caution by arguing that the Confederates appeared to be "pretty well fortified" at Resaca and were holding the town with artillery.[24]

While waiting for reinforcements, Sherman ordered McPherson to construct fieldworks to secure possession of Snake Creek Gap. Chauncey Reese and Andrew Hickenlooper selected a line to cover the wide southern mouth of the gap on the evening of May 9. A heavy rainstorm delayed work until dawn the next morning, when troops were placed along the selected line. Reese ordered Herman Klostermann and Dedrick F. Tiedemann, chief engineers of the Fifteenth and Sixteenth Corps, to supervise the construction. The infantrymen worked hard on May 10–11, piling up logs and throwing dirt on them. A scarcity of entrenching tools delayed progress, as work details also cut military roads parallel to and behind the breastworks for easier movement of troops.[25]

When Butterfield's division of the Twentieth Corps arrived, it was assigned the task of improving the existing road and making a new route through Snake Creek Gap. It was not an easy job. The Federals wanted two lanes fixed for wagons, all holes filled in with stone, bridges across the creek, and a path for infantrymen east of the twin lanes. While Butterfield's pioneers worked on the roads, his infantrymen extended McPherson's breastworks, the men in some cases lifting whole trees and carrying them to the construction site. "A fellow can work twice as much on such occasions than when at a loging [sic] bee of his neighbors," commented William Wallace of the 3rd Wisconsin. After a couple of days, the Union line at Snake Creek Gap was "unassailable," in Sherman's words. Meanwhile, the holding force left behind at Mill Creek Gap maintained its position with the aid of a fortified skirmish line consisting of logs and other material "which can be easily got together."[26]

Fears of a Confederate strike at Snake Creek Gap proved to be groundless. As soon as Johnston realized he had been outmaneuvered, partly through the negligence of someone who had failed to identify Snake Creek Gap as an important point, he made preparations to evacuate Dalton and secure Resaca. The bulk of Polk's Army of Mississippi was beginning to arrive, and Johnston ordered it to stay at Resaca and cover the western approaches to the town. The Confederates abandoned Dalton on the night of May 12, and Fourth Corps troops entered it the next morning. Day Elmore of the 36th Illinois thought that nature alone was sufficient defense for the town, but he noted that the Confederates had added artificial defenses to make Johnston's position all but impregnable to a frontal attack. The obstructions and embrasured artillery positions in Mill Creek Gap especially impressed passing Union soldiers. For those who took the time and energy to ascend Rocky Face Ridge, the unique rock palisades combined with man-made fieldworks offered a treat. Some Federals recorded seeing sharpened stakes in addition to abatis in the valley between Rocky Face Ridge and Hamilton Ridge. For the time being, Sherman wanted Fourth Corps commander Howard to prepare a defensive position along the south side of Dalton in case Johnston returned. If there were no detached Confederate forts in that location, he told Howard to select good ground and begin to dig his own works.[27]

RESACA

But Johnston had no intention of going back to Dalton. Resaca was now the focus of his attention. He had, as early as May 10, sent Stephen W. Presstman "to mark out defensive works" to protect the town and construct them without delay. Before May 1864, Resaca had only one earthwork, a redoubt near the railroad bridge spanning the Oostanaula River, built by the Georgia militia in 1862. Two years later, Polk's command was primarily responsible for the early phase of fieldwork construction at Resaca in the Atlanta campaign. Polk rotated details from each unit of his Army of Mississippi to work on the defenses, increasing the number of commissioned officers to supervise the enlisted men to three from each regiment.[28]

The Confederates dug in with a will on May 13. Maj. Gen. William W. Loring deployed his division in two lines and ordered both of them to construct

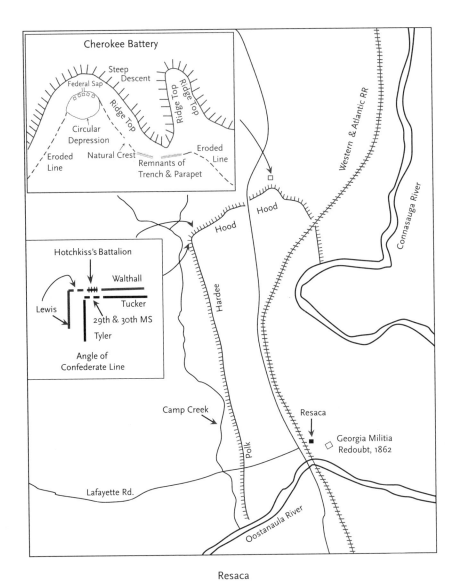

Cherokee Battery

Steep Descent

Federal Sap

Ridge Top

Ridge Top

Ridge Top

Circular Depression

Eroded Line

Natural Crest

Remnants of Trench & Parapet

Eroded Line

Eroded Line

Hotchkiss's Battalion

Walthall

Tucker

Lewis

29th & 30th MS

Tyler

Angle of Confederate Line

Hood

Hood

Western & Atlantic RR

Connasauga River

Hardee

Camp Creek

Resaca

Georgia Militia Redoubt, 1862

Polk

Lafayette Rd.

Oostanaula River

Resaca

works. The line of the 27th Alabama extended into low ground, where mud and water came up to the men's ankles, but they piled up logs and rails to make a breastwork across the muck. On the evening of May 13, the Alabamans received a supply of spades and picks and threw mud up onto the logs, finishing their work at midnight. Farther to the Confederate right, other units found higher ground and "hard and gravely soil." Unit commanders organized their men into shifts to keep their limited supply of tools engaged continuously. The 9th Tennessee made a trench three feet deep with a parapet in front by dawn the next day. "We have splendid entrenchments," crowed a staff officer in Cleburne's Division. "The best I ever saw."[29]

McPherson's men caught a glimpse of this developing Confederate line as they moved closer to Resaca on the evening of May 13. McPherson made sure that his division commanders placed their pioneers forward with tools in their hands to clear roads and make works as needed during his cautious advance. The valley of Camp Creek separated Polk and Hardee from the Army of the Tennessee on the west side of Johnston's defensive posture covering the town and its important railroad bridge. Sherman planned to attack the Confederates on May 14 to hold Johnston in place while elements of McPherson's army attempted to cross the Oostanaula at Lay's Ferry, some distance downstream.[30]

The key to Johnston's defensive posture at Resaca was the angle in his line that connected the western with the northern face. It lay about two miles north of the river on the highest ground outside the town, representing the junction of Hardee's Corps with Hood's Corps. Brig. Gen. Joseph H. Lewis's Kentucky Brigade was assigned the task of holding the angle. Regimental commanders issued a ration of whiskey on the morning of May 14 and set their men to work. They laid down a line of rails and logs and dug a trench behind it, piling the dirt onto the wooden foundation. Lewis placed two regiments facing north and three regiments facing west to hold the angle. Hardee told Johnston that this angle was "the weakest point" of the Confederate line, and he insisted on having a reserve brigade there in case it folded. As a result, Brig. Gen. Robert C. Tyler's Brigade took post in a rear, reserve line facing west inside the angle.[31]

Hood positioned Brig. Gen. Edward C. Walthall's Brigade to connect with Hardee at the angle. Walthall moved into position early on the morning of May 14, deploying all his available tools to dig in and to cut trees and brush in front of the north-facing position. Brig. Gen. William F. Tucker's Brigade took post to Walthall's rear as a reserve. Maj. T. R. Hotchkiss's Battalion of artillery was placed between Lewis's right and Walthall's left, with the 29th and 30th Mississippi under Col. William F. Brantley in works to the rear of Hotchkiss's guns. These artillery pieces occupied "a bare knob, the highest to be seen on the ridge along which the army line extended." While much of the valley before this line was open, a wooded ridge about half a mile away was waiting to be occupied by the enemy.[32]

The Federals went into action late on the morning of May 14 with an advance by Schofield along with elements of Palmer's Fourteenth Corps. These troops extended McPherson's line northward along the valley of Camp Creek. Heavy skirmishing ensued, followed by three Federal advances. The first made it to a point 300 yards from Walthall's position. The second attack lodged at the base of the ridge in front of Hotchkiss's guns only to be driven back by a heavy Confederate skirmish line, while the third assault made little headway across the wide, open valley. The Federals pressed the right of Hardee's Corps as well as Walthall's Brigade in this action.[33]

The Confederates had relatively little difficulty repelling the heavy reconnaissance in force that Sherman mounted, but they suffered a good deal from concentrated Union artillery fire on their exposed position at the angle. Some regiments had not yet finished their works before the Federals advanced, and others, which thought they had dug good defenses, discovered that they were not deep enough to protect the men. Lewis's Kentucky Brigade lost more than forty troops from the artillery fire alone on May 14. The 1st and 3rd Florida of Brig. Gen. Jesse J. Finley's Brigade occupied a spot ten paces behind the main line, well south of the angle, yet they suffered as much from the artillery fire as if they had been in front. "We got the worst shelling here that we ever had," reported Capt. John L. Inglis of the 3rd Florida, who lost ten of his men to the fire.[34]

As the day wore on, the Federals deployed more and more guns along the wooded ridge to pound the angle. The Kentuckians took the brunt of this fire behind works that seemed smaller with each passing round. John S. Jackman watched as two artillery shells killed four of his comrades and wounded several others. "I saw the men tossed about like chaff," he recalled. Projectiles often passed along the length of Walthall's trench, just inches above the heads of the men. Exploding shells set the exposed logs and rails within the earthworks on fire. One officer estimated that rounds from twenty-four Federal guns saturated the angle, many of them hitting the breastworks and taking big chunks out of the parapets.[35]

Another result of the action that day was the placement of many Federals in forward positions inside a skirt of trees near Walthall's right. Thick vegetation and uneven ground offered perfect cover for skirmishers. There also were some crude Confederate earthworks in this cover, dug by units that had previously held the area before Walthall took position, which the Federals used as shelter. The Yankees had nearly the equivalent of a battle line ensconced in this area, pelting the Confederates with rifle fire. Bullets often "grazed the breastwork and struck close to the inner bank of the trench," forcing Walthall's men to crouch low for safety. The skirmish firing also limited the ability of Confederate gunners to use their artillery.[36]

On the far Confederate right, the Federals had their left flank in the air, and Johnston ordered Hood to strike it. At 5:00 P.M., he sent Stevenson's and

Stewart's Divisions forward, guiding to the left to catch the flank at a disadvantage. But only Stevenson found the Union position, and he was repulsed by heavy fire from the 5th Indiana Battery. Besides the unsuccessful flank movement, Hood's men busied themselves with digging in to extend Walthall's line eastward, utilizing rails, logs, and "such things as could be picked up in the woods."[37]

On the far Confederate left, McPherson was busy trying to close in on the enemy line. The Army of the Tennessee sent two brigades across Camp Creek, and they took an advanced Rebel line. It had been held by two regiments behind a slight earthwork on the east bluff of the valley. Brigade leader Giles A. Smith ordered his pioneers to improve it, and the 127th Illinois detailed some men from each company to collect logs to help them. The Confederates tried to recapture the position but failed. Farther away, at Lay's Ferry, Thomas W. Sweeny sent 400 men across the Oostanaula to establish a bridgehead on the south side. When Confederate skirmishers confronted them, he withdrew the force to the north side about dusk, believing he had accomplished his mission to feint a crossing of the stream.[38]

The Confederates learned from the artillery pounding of May 14 that their earthworks were inadequate. Company C, 9th Tennessee, had endured repeated hits on its parapet, located in a reserve line to the rear of the main position. While it lost no men, the Union guns had knocked down a good deal of dirt into the trench. Cheatham rode by that night and told the troops, "Boys, you'll have to stay here another day. You'd better get down in the ground as deep as you can." The men discussed the idea and agreed to work as hard as possible until midnight but then take much-needed sleep. The trench was already three feet deep; the Tennesseeans made it deeper and placed head logs on the parapet. When they finished at midnight, they passed their tools to the next company and went to sleep. Before dawn, the rest of the 9th Tennessee had dug even deeper than the men of Company C.[39]

Everywhere else along the Confederate line, tired soldiers continued to strengthen their light defenses. Not only the main line, but also the Rebel picket line received attention. Most units worked all night.[40]

The Federals also dug in, but their effort seems to have been less uniform and far less desperate than that of the Confederates. Sherman reported to Henry Halleck that "an immense amount of rifle trenches" confronted him at Resaca. His subordinates seemed to understand the need to approximate what the Rebels had done. Division leader Daniel Butterfield ordered his officers to construct defenses strong enough to allow him to use as few troops as possible to protect the main line. McPherson's men were "pretty well fortified already," in Sherman's words, and Fifteenth Corps troops planted a battery on the east side of Camp Creek big enough to house two twelve-pounder and two twenty-pounder Parrotts and close enough to bombard the two bridges across the Oostanaula.[41]

Sherman's plan for May 15 continued to focus Federal attention on operations north of the river, rather than exploiting a bridgehead at Lay's Ferry. He wanted the Fourth and Twentieth Corps to attack the Confederate right and center, with Schofield attempting to extend the Union line in that area. Sherman told McPherson to concentrate his force in case the enemy mounted attacks on the Union right.[42]

When Federal artillery began to bombard the Confederate line on the morning of May 15, many gray-clad troops were glad they had stayed up all night digging. In William B. Bate's Division, near the angle, many traverses had been constructed, and they proved their worth as effective protection against enfilade fire. Those regiments nearest the angle constructed the most traverses, but in some cases it was still not enough. Members of the 9th Kentucky realized that they had failed to cover one stretch of their line adequately, and Union shells continued to sail "right into our trenches." The men evacuated that portion and lay on the open ground just to the rear for a while. Then they crawled to the right into a more protected segment, "leaving that portion of the works which their fire enfiladed unoccupied." Farther south of the angle, a round squarely hit a head log and knocked it "down on the men" of Company C, 9th Tennessee. "We were all pretty badly scared," admitted Capt. James I. Hall, "but no one was seriously hurt." Other rounds continued to hit the parapet, gouging chunks out of it, and one artillery projectile broke through the weakened parapet to kill two men and wound another in a different company of the 9th Tennessee.[43]

On Walthall's sector, just east of the angle, the Confederates apparently did not construct any traverses. The men suffered terribly from enfilade fire. Walthall estimated that thirty Union guns pounded his brigade all day on May 15. Fortunately, his left flank ended on a part of the ridge that was higher than the rest "and in consequence furnished a partial protection" for most of his line. Col. Robert P. McKelvaine, who commanded the consolidated 24th and 27th Mississippi, reported that the Union artillery fire was very effective, "in some places almost annihilating our frail defenses." He lost nine men killed and twenty-five wounded that day. One of McKelvaine's officers, Lt. W. P. Wiygle of the 24th Mississippi, "abandoned his command and fled from the field" when a shell killed six of his company and wounded five more. With good reason, Mc-Kelvaine referred to "the blood-dyed hills of Resaca" in his official report. He could obtain no tools to repair his works.[44]

The heaviest Federal attacks at Resaca took place on May 15. While Fourth Corps assaults on Hood's Corps resulted in little good, Twentieth Corps troops lodged within a few yards of an advanced Confederate emplacement filled with the guns of Capt. Max Van Den Corput's Cherokee Battery of Georgia. The Federals started at 1:30 P.M., bringing Brig. Gen. William T. Ward's brigade of Butterfield's division opposite the battery.[45]

Van Den Corput's guns were exposed and vulnerable because Hood had told Stevenson to place a battery thirty yards in front of the main Confederate line to obtain a better angle of fire on Union guns to the west, which were annoying Maj. Gen. Thomas C. Hindman's Division. Stevenson received "repeated and peremptory orders" to open fire before the emplacement was finished, drawing Federal attention to the guns. The battery took post in a small bowl, or "natural basin," about six feet deep and fifty yards wide, with five gun emplacements dug into the north side of the bowl so as to use the lip for protection. The Confederates cut five embrasures into the lip; the two on the left fired left oblique, the next two straight forward toward the north, and the right one aimed toward the right oblique. The main Confederate infantry trench was located to the rear of the guns, with a gentle ascending slope connecting the two positions. That gentle slope continued descending north of the gun emplacement for about twenty yards before a very steep slope began. The terrain allowed the attacking Federals to lodge very close to Van Den Corput's position.[46]

In fact, the men of Ward's brigade advanced to the very muzzles of the Rebel guns. Here they caught their breath and were encouraged to see the Confederate infantry supports abandon the artillery. The center companies of the 70th Indiana and 102nd Illinois, units of Ward's first and second lines that had merged before hitting the target, crossed the small lip of the bowl that barely protected the guns and entered the work. The 32nd Tennessee of Brig. Gen. John C. Brown's Brigade was surprised by the sudden appearance of these Federals, shielded as they were by the terrain and vegetation. The 32nd fell back to the main Confederate line, where aided by the 36th Tennessee, they held firm and fired down the slope. This forced the Yankees to retire out of the artillery fieldwork and take shelter just outside. More Federal troops gathered near the battery, including Col. David Ireland's brigade of Geary's division, to Ward's left. They discovered that the Confederate pieces were "sunk so as to bring the muzzles . . . near the ground." The Federals were close enough to literally touch the muzzles but could go no farther because of heavy fire from the Confederate main line only thirty yards away.[47]

Nowhere else along the contending lines at Resaca were the opponents so close to each other, and yet neither side could drive the other away. Neither side could take possession of Van Den Corput's four guns either. For the rest of that day, the opponents continued to skirmish until Stevenson was forced to replace Brown's Brigade with that of Brig. Gen. Daniel H. Reynolds, because the former ran out of ammunition.[48]

The only other action on May 15 took place on the far Confederate right, where Hood instructed Stewart to advance and "gradually wheel toward the left" to once again strike the Union flank. Stewart arrayed his division in two lines and moved as ordered, hitting Brig. Gen. Alpheus S. Williams's division of the Twentieth Corps behind log breastworks. Some of the Confederates got as close as thirty yards before retiring, but none of Stewart's brigades were able to turn the flank or force Williams out of his light works. Stevenson's Division, to Stewart's left, failed to advance toward Geary and Williams from the front as intended, so Stewart called off further action that evening. Williams suffered barely a third as many casualties as Stewart in this encounter.[49]

After Stewart's failed advance came to an end, Stevenson attempted to re-take the Cherokee Battery soon after dusk on May 15. He meant to use most of his division, with the 54th Virginia on his far right leading the way. But that regiment soon lost touch with the left flank of Stewart's Division, which was supposed to move forward in support. The Virginians fell back, losing more than 100 men in fifteen minutes.[50]

Darkness put an end to the major action at Resaca, but the Federals took advantage of it to secure the guns of Van Den Corput's Battery. Geary put Col. George Cobham Jr. of Ireland's brigade in charge of the work. Cobham examined the ground and planned to open fire on the Rebels, sending details out to draw the pieces off in the confusion. But Lt. Col. Philo B. Buckingham of the 20th Connecticut suggested the Federals dig a passage through the parapet and pull the guns out without making such a fuss. A detail of 250 men from the 20th moved into position at about 9:00 P.M. and began to dig shallow saps, starting three rods downhill. They dug toward the muzzle of each gun, making a trench wide enough to roll the carriage through. The Confederates fired on the party occasionally, especially so at about midnight, but the Federals simply lay down until the worst was over and then continued digging. When the details working on two saps were frightened away by Rebel fire, Capt. Austin T. Shirer of the 5th

Capture of Van Den Corput's Cherokee Battery at Resaca. This image depicts a clever plan concocted by Lt. Col. Philo B. Buckingham of the 20th Connecticut to dig saps through the Confederate parapet and pull these four guns out of their emplacements without being unduly exposed to fire from Confederates located only thirty yards away during the night of May 15, 1864. Harper's Weekly, *June 18, 1864, 389.*

Ohio replaced them with five companies of his own regiment. Shirer called on the 33rd New Jersey for help when he found that the digging was more difficult than expected and received fifty additional men.[51]

Many troops supported the operation, digging infantry works to the right and left of the Cherokee Battery and firing on the Confederates from the trenches. A detail of fifty men from the 27th Pennsylvania dropped their guns and knapsacks and carried fence rails up the slope to a point only a few yards from the enemy and began to construct works. After fifteen minutes, they received a startling amount of fire from the front and some from the flank as well. The Pennsylvanians fell back when the Union skirmish line, just in their front, retired. Unfortunately, they caused confusion by falling back into the 154th New York and 73rd Pennsylvania, compelling portions of those regiments to retire as well. The mass went all the way back to the foot of the slope.[52]

But all this confusion did not deter the Federals from finishing their saps. They managed to pull all four guns out of the battery emplacement. The Federals also found a flag in the work, "the usual blue bunting red flag, with the blue St. Andrew's Cross, with stars," as Lt. Col. R. L. Kilpatrick of the 5th Ohio described it. Buckingham bragged to his wife that he had given "the rebs a specimen of a yankee trick for I literally stole the guns from under their very eyes." Van Den Corput's guns were "4 bright, almost new, Brass 12 Pdr Napoleons," with double canister still in the tubes. The gunners had prepared to fire them but evacuated the position before they had a chance to do so. The struggle for the guns demonstrated the tenacity of the Federals and the danger of putting artillery in front of friendly infantry support.[53]

The Federals did not duplicate Hood's mistake in placing artillery. Capt. Otho Herron Morgan made certain the guns of his 7th Indiana Battery, assigned to Brig. Gen. Absalom Baird's division of the Fourteenth Corps, were well protected. His gunners received a good deal of annoying musketry all day on May 15. They sank their gun emplacements several feet below the surface, cutting ramps toward the rear so they could reload and then run the pieces forward. The body of a Union soldier lay near the battery's position on slightly higher ground, exposed to Confederate view, and the gray-clad skirmishers shot it so often that it "made the body look like a pepper-box," in Morgan's words.[54]

Two days of spirited fighting at Resaca resulted in a draw. Sherman continued to envision the possibility of flanking Johnston by crossing the river downstream from town. Sweeny had moved his division to Calhoun's Ferry, farther downstream from Lay's Ferry, upon reports that the Confederates were attempting to cross at that location. He then moved a sizeable force over the Oostanaula where Chauncey B. Reese constructed a fortified bridgehead big enough for a Union brigade at Calhoun's Ferry. The Confederates skirmished toward this bridgehead before it was completed, but they were forced to retire on May 15.[55]

Johnston decided to evacuate his position at Resaca that evening. Elements of Bate's Division began leaving their works at 9:00 P.M., as members of the 9th Kentucky were instructed to make certain the bright moonlight did not reflect the polished barrels of their muskets and alert nearby Union skirmishers. Stevenson wrote off the four guns of Van Den Corput's battery as a loss, for he calculated it would cost too many lives to attempt to recapture them. Hood agreed and so reported to Johnston the loss of the battery. The Army of Tennessee crossed the Oostanaula by dawn.[56]

Both sides suffered seriously at Resaca. The Federals lost 4,000 men, while the Confederates suffered 3,000 casualties. Walthall lost 164 men out of 1,158 engaged; many of them had been shot in the head and upper part of the body

Confederate earthworks at Resaca. George N. Barnard exposed a classic image of abandoned Confederate fieldworks in the Atlanta campaign several months after the battle here. By this time, local citizens had begun efforts to reclaim the land and degrade the earthworks. The fence rails seen leaning on the parapet have been pulled out of the works and left to dry before reuse. Notice the traverses stretching back at an angle from the parapet to provide flank protection for troops. *Barnard,* Photographic Views, *no. 22. Courtesy of the Metropolitan Museum of Art.*

by Union skirmishers as they tried to fire across the parapet. Apparently, they had not yet learned how to fix head logs as cover. Loring's Division engaged in no attack or defense at Resaca, yet suffered 184 casualties due to Union artillery fire and sharpshooting.[57]

The Federals had plenty of opportunity to observe the Confederate field-works at Resaca on May 16. David Nichol of Geary's division found the defenses "very strong. I don't see where they will stand & fight as I don't think they can find a better position." Daniel Wait Howe of the 79th Indiana also thought the Confederate works were impressive, but he noticed how much the ground had been scarred by Union artillery. Howe counted a dozen projectile holes within an area ten feet square on one part of the battlefield. Many Federals saw the Cherokee Battery emplacement and described its unique features.[58]

Sherman reported to Halleck that Resaca was "a strongly fortified position,

Dalton and Resaca

besides being a strong natural position." Like David Nichol, he was surprised that the Confederates gave it up so readily. But Johnston wrote after the war that his opponent had "a very exaggerated idea of our field-works" at Resaca and Dalton. Due to an inadequate supply of tools, Johnston felt his defenses were less substantial than the Federal works that opposed his army. While there is inadequate information on the details of Union earthworks at Resaca, the evidence is clear that the Confederate defenses were far less strong than Union observers reported. Johnston was closer to the truth in characterizing his works as slight, and he could have gone further in reporting his position as tenuous. The Confederates did well enough along the straight lines that faced west and north, but the angle of the two lines was exposed to devastating cross fire. The Kentuckians of Lewis's Brigade and the Mississippians of Walthall's Brigade failed to dig sophisticated works to protect themselves and paid the price for it. Many of them did not construct traverses until the night of May 14, halfway through the battle, and even then some Confederates failed to provide any kind of shelter against cross fire. Also, the depth of the initial trench, at only three feet, was far too shallow for the exposed position. Most of the Confederate commanders learned through hard experience, and thus ordered their men to dig deeper on the night of May 14. But there appears to have been no experience before the Atlanta campaign that could impress lessons such as these on the rank and file, and no engineer officers handy to tell the men what to do.[59]

The terrain offered Johnston only a slight advantage at Resaca. It was no higher than the ground upon which Sherman planted his line. John Geary described the landscape as "an irregular conglomerate of hills, with spurs running in every direction." The division commander thought this type of ground offered the defender "unusual facilities for cross-firing and enfilading the ground to be passed over." That was true, but the irregular terrain also had many abrupt drops in front of the Confederate line that allowed the Federals to take shelter within a few yards of the works. What happened at the Cherokee Battery was a clear example of how the landscape sometimes favored the attacker rather than the defender. In general, there was no clear terrain advantage for either side at Resaca, and the Confederate works were not sophisticated enough to give Johnston an added, decisive advantage. It was questionable how long the Confederates could have held out at Resaca if Johnston had not evacuated the position on the night of May 15.[60]

3

Cassville

After leaving Resaca, Johnston searched for good defensive ground south of the Oostanaula River. A string of railroad towns stretched south and then east, with Calhoun four miles south of the Oostanaula, Adairsville eight miles south of Calhoun, Kingston nine miles south of Adairsville, and Cassville six miles east of Kingston. The Western and Atlantic Railroad ran through the wide, flat valley of Oothcaloga Creek that stretched between Calhoun and Adairsville. It was a "beautiful" country, thought John S. Jackman of the 9th Kentucky, with "large fields of corn." Wheat also grew in abundance, and the valley displayed many well-to-do farmhouses and even a few plantations. Hiram Smith Williams of Stewart's pioneer corps thought the region was the repository of "wealth, refinement and taste in greater degree" than the more jumbled, Appalachian terrain to the north.[1]

The Confederates reached Calhoun on May 16. Upon scouting the terrain, Johnston decided to keep moving a few hours later and attempt a stand at Adairsville. Later that day, Hardee's Corps established a line two miles north of Adairsville, the third defensive position of the Army of Tennessee in the campaign. Cheatham's Division straddled the railroad along a ridge, with Cleburne's Division to his left and rear on the other side of Oothcaloga Creek. Bate's and W. H. T. Walker's Divisions filled out the rest of the position. Elements of Cheatham's command established a sharpshooter's post inside a unique structure called the Octagon House, which had been built by R. C.

Saxon in an eight-sided design. The walls had been constructed of concrete consisting of cement studded with stones, and thus it was often referred to as the gravel house.[2]

Johnston held a council on the night of May 16 in which his officers concluded that the position appeared untenable because both flanks were insecure. While Hardee advised that the army stay and fight anyway, Hood wanted to retire across the Etowah River. Johnston opted for a middle course, falling back to Cassville, and the army began to evacuate the position at Adairsville in the early morning hours of May 17. Heavy fog aided the withdrawal. Johnston tried to lure Sherman into a vulnerable position by dividing his army, sending Hardee first to Kingston, while Polk and Hood moved directly from Adairsville to Cassville. He hoped the Federals would follow both columns, offering him the opportunity to strike one of them while the other was too far away for support.[3]

Before he approached Cassville, Sherman felt obliged to deal with another railroad town called Rome, which was located twelve miles west of Kingston and connected to the Western and Atlantic Railroad by a spur. The Oostanaula flowed into the Etowah near Rome. In late February 1864, Sherman had received intelligence from a Federal scout that the Rebels had constructed a large fort mounting thirty-two-pounder guns to protect the junction of the two rivers. A line of trench was staked out along the Oostanaula to cover the approaches to Rome from the north. Sherman wanted to secure the town to protect his right flank from a Confederate approach from Alabama and sent Brig. Gen. Jefferson C. Davis's division of the Fourteenth Corps to do so. Rome was held by a tiny garrison, which offered only light opposition as Davis closed in and skirmished before occupying the town on May 18.[4]

As Davis took possession of Rome, the Army of Tennessee continued to move toward Cassville. The Confederates refrained from digging in because Johnston was maneuvering to place his units where they could attack the head of Sherman's northern column, the one that was marching directly from Adairsville to Cassville. Early on the morning of May 19, certain he could offer battle on his own terms, Johnston wrote an order announcing that the Army of Tennessee would turn and strike. It was read to the troops later that morning, eliciting cheers in nearly every unit of the army. The Confederates were more than ready to take the offensive.[5]

But the anticipated action never took place. When Hood moved out to strike Joseph Hooker and Schofield along the Adairsville Road, two divisions of Federal cavalry suddenly appeared on his flank and rear. Those horsemen had been sent to cut the railroad near Cass Station; they had no idea they were

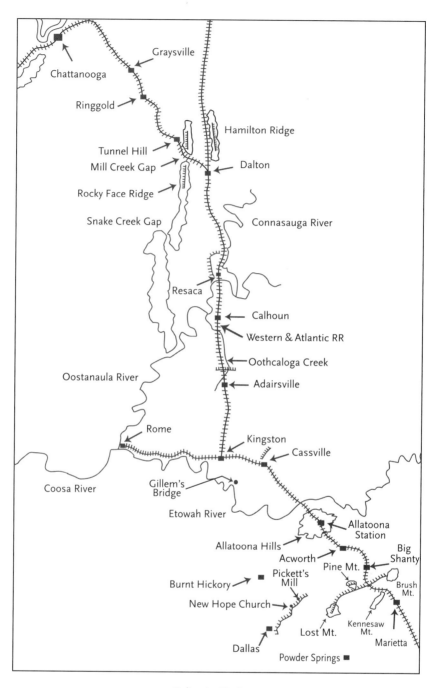

Dalton to Marietta

disrupting Confederate plans to engulf two corps of Sherman's army. When informed, Johnston ordered all his units to call off the plan and retire to Cassville for a defensive stand on high ground east of town.[6]

Disappointed by the turn of events, a large group of Confederates rode along the high ridge east of Cassville to stake out a defensive line. The group included engineer officers as well as Johnston and his chief of staff, Brig. Gen. William W. Mackall. Polk and several engineer officers participated in the survey as well. The ridge rose 140 feet above the town and had an elevation of 900 feet. From the top, reported Johnston, his men could completely command the open valley between the ridge and Cassville. It was an "excellent" position, in Johnston's view, in some ways better than any he had yet seen in the campaign. In fact, in his memoirs he called it "the best that I saw occupied during the war."[7]

The right flank of Johnston's position on the ridge lay about one mile east of Cassville, and the far left extended about three and a half miles toward the southwest. Hood positioned his corps on the right, with the city cemetery at about the center of his line, and his left, ending at a shallow gap where modern Mac Johnson Road crosses the ridge. Polk positioned the Army of Mississippi in Johnston's center, while Hardee placed his men on the rest of the ridge and along the low land southwest of it to straddle the wagon road and railroad linking Chattanooga with Atlanta.[8]

Confederate troops all along the intended line began to dig in with a will on the afternoon of May 19. If tools were not available, they used bayonets to loosen the earth. Pioneers cut brush for some distance in front of the works where needed. Everyone who commented on the position thought it one of the strongest they had ever seen. Confidence seemed to pervade the Rebel ranks, even on the left where the Confederates had less advantageous ground. Hardee's men constructed a redoubt on a knoll which was surrounded by open fields. Johnston felt very confident. If Hardee could hold, then the rest of the army, which "had very decided advantage of ground," would be impregnable.[9]

But before the day ended, developments took place that compelled Johnston to evacuate the ridge without a battle. Those developments involved a weak spot in the line where Hood's Corps joined Polk's Army of Mississippi. Maj. Gen. Samuel G. French was given the responsibility of managing this part of the line. He found that a gap, or "a dry water gully," had caused an irregularity in the line of the ridge. The gap was about fifty feet deep, cutting about one-third of the way down into the ridge. In general, the ridgeline ran roughly south to north, but the peaks lay a bit farther west along the section south of the gap compared to those located north of the cleavage. No troops had yet been

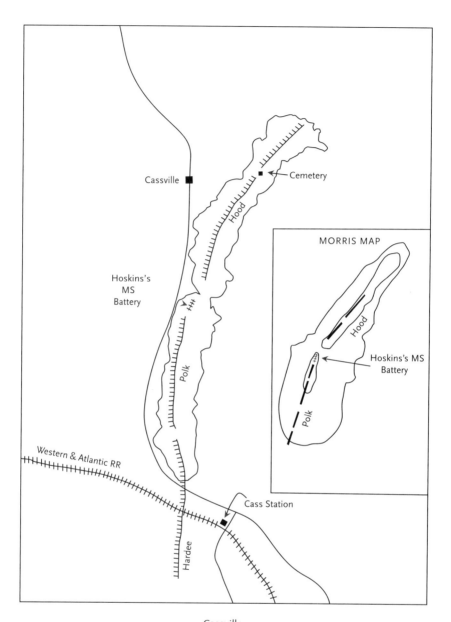

Cassville

placed to cover the area of the gap, so French put Capt. James Hoskins's Mississippi Battery and half of Brig. Gen. Matthew D. Ector's Brigade in the interval between Hood's left and the right flank of James Cantey's Brigade, which was the right flank of Polk's command. Because of the configuration of the terrain, Hoskins was fifty yards forward of Ector's men and somewhat exposed. The ridgetop was bare for about 1,000 feet south of the gap. French believed that Hood's line bent back at an angle of about twenty-five degrees compared to Polk's line.[10]

The army's chief of artillery, Brig. Gen. Francis A. Shoup, alerted Johnston to this problem spot late in the afternoon. He brought the army leader to Polk's right, where he pointed out a space of up to 200 yards where the line could be enfiladed by Federal guns located to the north. But Johnston noted the distance to the Union artillery, more than a mile, and thought the danger was "trifling." He suggested the infantry build traverses for flank protection and take shelter in the ravines to the rear if needed. The guns that concerned Shoup were tenpounder Parrotts of Capt. Luther Smith's Battery I, 1st Michigan Light Artillery, which were placed on two knolls along the sector held by Butterfield's division of the Twentieth Corps.[11]

Word of this controversial spot in the line reached Polk and he sent an engineer officer to investigate. Capt. Walter J. Morris had arrived at Cassville from Alabama at 3:30 P.M. on May 19 and was immediately hustled into Polk's headquarters for the assignment. Polk showed him a sketch map of the line and charged Morris to examine the position and report on whether traverses would be adequate to shelter the men. The general also wanted Morris to report on whether the ground in front of the line would permit a Confederate advance and to note the location of all Federal guns, in case Polk decided to attack and capture the batteries that threatened his right flank. Morris spent a half hour arranging for a copy of the map to be made and making notes, before setting out on a horse he borrowed from Polk and with one of the general's escorts as a guide. He had orders to return soon after dusk.[12]

This was a new kind of work for Morris. A native of eastern Tennessee, he had served as an engineer since the fall of 1862 on the staff of Brig. Gen. Lloyd Tilghman and later on Polk's staff in Mississippi. He was noted as a very good draftsman but had little, if any, experience evaluating infantry positions and the terrain of potential battlefields.[13]

Morris conducted a thorough examination, despite the constricted time period in which he was allowed to work, and concluded that the situation was very dangerous. He reported that Yankee guns could cover the gap area with fire and reach up to 600 feet behind the ridge, "therefore giving no cover for the men." During his examination, Morris noted that Ector's troops took shelter at the eastern foot of the ridge, leaving only a few pickets on top of the ground to give warning in case the enemy approached. Hoskins lost two or three horses at each gun during the time Morris was in the area. Morris concluded that Polk's right could not be held and that digging traverses would be futile, for they "would have covered nearly the entire surface" of the ridgetop. Moreover, he did not think there was time enough to dig such works. Morris also recommended against any attempt to attack the Federal guns, as the infantry would be shredded by enfilade artillery fire. Although he did not have an opportunity to so thoroughly examine Hood's sector, Morris believed that Federal guns were far enough north to enfilade Hood's right flank as well.[14]

Morris later prepared a map of the Confederate position on the ridge. Comparing it with modern topographical maps, it is clear that Morris drew a greater angle in the ridgeline, bent at the gap, than was warranted. There is no reason to believe he did this deliberately to bolster his contention that the ridge was untenable. Because of the fact that the ridgeline south of the gap lay a bit farther west than the portion located north of the gap, any Confederate line would have been at least partially exposed to enfilade fire, but probably not as much as Morris believed based on his somewhat faulty survey of the terrain.[15]

The Federals were not aware that they were causing concern on the enemy ridgetop, for they did not have a particularly clear view of Johnston's position. Sherman noted that trees between the Union line and the town of Cassville shielded much of the Rebel position from his line of sight. The Federals could see the top of the ridge above the trees but it lay about a mile away. Sherman spied "fresh-made parapets" and could see gray-clad troops moving about on the ridge, and he concluded that Johnston meant to make a determined stand. Butterfield pushed skirmishers into town in the late afternoon, and they found the streets barricaded by lines of fence rails, broken-down wagons, and even furniture taken from houses. Confederate cavalry evacuated the town and many citizens fled while others staunchly refused to leave their homes.[16]

As the skirmishers occupied Cassville, the Federals took position on top of an irregular series of hills west and north of town. Some of this high ground was up to thirty feet higher than the ridge on which the Confederates were located. Schofield's corps, on Sherman's left, curved far enough eastward so as to nearly overlap Hood's right flank.[17]

A number of Federal guns opened to support the advance of Butterfield's skirmishers at about 5:30 P.M., and they continued firing well into the night. It was this fire that Morris observed during his late evening scout. Several Union batteries have been identified as contributing to the enfilade fire delivered on Polk's right flank. In addition to Smith's Michigan gunners, they included Capt. Marco Gary's Battery C, 1st Ohio Light Artillery (on Geary's left wing); Capt. Alfred Morrison's 5th Indiana Battery and Capt. Samuel M. McDowell's Battery B, Pennsylvania Light Artillery (both on David S. Stanley's division front in the Fourth Corps); and Bridges's Illinois Battery (commanded by Lt. Lyman A. White, on Wood's division front of the Fourth Corps). As many as forty Union guns bombarded the Confederate position that evening, although not all of them targeted Polk's right flank.[18]

The guns punished the Confederates for two hours, until about 7:30 P.M. Shoup saw it as confirmation of his fears, and many infantry units along the line fell back to obtain some degree of shelter on the east slope of the ridge. Hood rode along his corps line during the bombardment and came to the conclusion that he could not hold his position. Brigade leader Arthur M. Manigault saw the Federals knock a Confederate battery to pieces on Hood's sector. But French's Division, located at the worst spot of the line, lost only ten men wounded during the two hours' bombardment, far less than one would have anticipated given the faulty terrain.[19]

At the insistence of Hood and Polk, the Confederate high command engaged in a council of war that night. It took place in a rough cabin Polk used as his headquarters. Hood took the lead in arguing that his corps could not hold its position the next day due to the enfilading artillery fire. Polk also reported that his position was dangerously exposed to the same fire. While both officers, especially Polk, were willing to take the offensive and attack the Federals from the ridge, they also agreed that retreating would be better than acting strictly on the defensive. Morris was present and supported Polk's position. French also was present for part of the meeting; he admitted that his men at the gap suffered from the enemy fire but refrained from urging a retreat. After one or two hours of discussion, Johnston reluctantly decided to retire across the Etowah River. Hardee arrived after that point and was surprised at the tenor of discussion and Johnston's decision. He expressed confidence in holding the left, even though he had less advantageous ground to defend. But Johnston felt it unwise to adopt a course of action that was not supported by two of his three second-tier subordinates.[20]

French was also surprised by the decision to evacuate the ridge. He had slipped out of the conference during a lull in the discussion, before Johnston decided to retire, and planned to have his men dig in more thoroughly during the night. It seemed to him, thus far in the discussion, that Johnston would decide to stay. He set his men to work, but then an officer rode by and suggested he stop, for word was circulating that the army would pull out. A bit later, the official order arrived. French was ready to use better fieldworks to hold the crooked angle across the gap as long as required, but that now was a moot point.[21]

Many of Hood's men also had begun to strengthen their works after dusk, when the Federal artillery fire ended, and were disgusted when the order to evacuate arrived at about midnight. Hastily preparing, they started at 2:00 A.M., leaving a skirmish line in place to shield the movement. Hardee's troops also had worked hard to make their earthworks stronger and felt a deep sense of disappointment at the order to give them up. On Polk's sector, many unit commanders detailed men to remain in the trenches to give the appearance of continued occupation. Polk also sent Morris with a detail of 300 men from Loring's Division to build fires, cut trees, and drive stakes on top of the ridge until dawn. After Polk pulled out, Morris could hear the Federals cutting trees along their own line, and he heard enemy movements in the town below. The detailed men and the skirmishers were gone by sunrise, and the Army of Tennessee crossed the Etowah on May 20.[22]

When the Yankees realized what had happened and advanced to secure the ridge, they had a chance to observe the nature of the position and the earthworks that adorned its top. Poe made a sketch map of the line and found the works "strong to resist a direct front attack, but could have been easily turned." Thomas viewed them as "a series of very formidable breast-works and batteries." The few civilians who remained in Cassville were upset that Hood's men had cut up graves and overturned headstones in the town cemetery while building the Confederate line near and through it.[23]

After seeing the works, Sherman could not understand why his opponents gave up such a strong position. He finally learned the reason in the fall of 1865 when he happened to meet Johnston on a Mississippi River steamboat. Sherman repeated the story during a speech in Cleveland in 1868, which was printed in the newspapers. Hood read it and arranged to meet Sherman in New Orleans two years later to give his own version of the story. The "affair" at Cassville became one of the salient points in a long-brewing controversy between Johnston and Hood, a controversy that tended to color the recollections of both officers for the rest of their lives.[24]

Historians have tended to believe Hood and Polk when evaluating the Confederate position at Cassville. They have concluded that the line was rendered untenable by enfilading artillery fire. In his memoirs, Hood argued that "traverses could not, in this instance, have provided a sufficient protection to the troops." Historians also agree with Hood that, even if the Confederates had remained in position, they would have had to evacuate anyway due to the opportunities Sherman would have had to outflank the line. Federal cavalry had secured Gillem's Bridge across the Etowah southwest of Cassville on the night of May 19, and it is likely Sherman would have placed troops south of the river the next day.[25]

But Johnston and French argued that the Confederates could have stayed on the ridge despite the enfilading fire. Johnston thought the position was less exposed to Federal guns than the angle of his army's line had been at Resaca. In his official report, filed in October 1864, he referred to the decision to retreat from Cassville as a "step which I have regretted ever since." French pointed out that later in the campaign, he was "obliged to hold enfiladed lines nearly an entire day" and did so successfully by employing proper fieldworks. French went further in calling Hood and Polk "almost disobedient in their acts at Cassville," and he noted that Polk never visited the endangered angle in the line even though his headquarters were but a fifteen-minute ride away.[26]

The views of Johnston and French are more convincing than of those who supported Hood and Polk. The latter two officers were too ready to cut and run from a strong position. Hood's attitude was shaped by personally experiencing the effect of the enfilade fire while riding through it in the open, and Polk's attitude was shaped by Morris's detailed report. Hood had little appreciation of the value of earthworks, as would be keenly demonstrated by his actions and words later in the campaign when he commanded the Army of Tennessee. For his part, Morris had more experience at drawing maps than in combat engineering. Throughout the Atlanta campaign, the Confederates demonstrated a growing appreciation for fieldworks; they nurtured an improving facility for constructing effective trenches and traverses in battlefield situations that were as bad as, and even worse than, the one they faced at Cassville. Resaca has already been noted as a point of comparison, and an even better example is to be found at Cheatham's Hill on the Kennesaw Line in late June, where an angle in the Confederate position was reinforced with dozens of traverses and held under great duress for many days.

Patrick R. Cleburne, one of Hardee's division commanders, demonstrated another way to deal with enfilading artillery fire when he placed Brig. Gen. Lucius E. Polk's Brigade on a slight ridgetop while taking post on the far Confederate right on May 26. Polk arrayed his regiments en echelon, in staggered positions to the right and rear, "to avoid an artillery enfilade from a neighboring position held by the enemy." Lucius Polk probably had no more room to place these units on his ridgetop than his uncle Leonidas Polk had at Cassville. Even if, as Morris put it, Leonidas Polk's men would have had to cover the ridgetop with traverses to achieve adequate protection, they could have and should have done so. The men seemed willing to dig all night to protect themselves. What happened at Cassville was a breakdown of confidence among two of Johnston's major subordinates, not a well-considered evaluation of the tactical situation, as it involved fieldworks. Johnston bears some of the blame for giving up a good defensive position at Cassville; he would have had the support of Hardee and most of the rank and file if he had rejected Hood and Polk's recommendation.[27]

The mood of the troops was dealt a blow by the order to evacuate the ridge. They could not understand the reason for it, and the hasty, confused manner of crossing the Etowah River further eroded morale. Many of the men now feared that Johnston would not make a determined stand north of the Chattahoochee River, close to Atlanta. Johnston elected not to establish a new position north of the Etowah, even though a modern historian has argued that the terrain favored such a stand at Cartersville, nine miles south of Cassville. The railroad ran through a fairly narrow valley as it approached Cartersville. Yet, Johnston seems to have been willing to give up long stretches of territory as he drew the Federals farther away from their base of supplies and into hostile country.[28]

Sherman paused for a bit now that he had cleared enemy troops from the area north of the Etowah River. Reese scouted out the line for a fortified bridge-head on the south side of the river at Gillem's Bridge on May 20. It was con-structed by Klostermann and the pioneers of the Fifteenth Corps on May 21 and 22. The bridgehead was designed to hold two batteries and included 840 yards of infantry trench. Sherman ordered McPherson to detail a garrison of 2,000 men to hold Rome and cover the town with "earth-works or stone build-ings." Resaca also was to be held by a strong garrison to protect its large depot of supplies.[29]

As Sherman took stock of the campaign thus far, the Allatoona Mountains loomed impressively just south of the Etowah River. He knew that the railroad ran through these hills and the Confederates could establish a strong position that would be very difficult to reduce. He intended to bypass the mountains and hoped to move swiftly to Atlanta, given how much ground Johnston had already yielded in only three weeks of campaigning. "I will cross the Etowah & Chattahoochee, & swing round Atlanta," he boasted to his wife. "If I can break up that nest it will be a splendid achievement." He was expecting "a terrific Battle at some point near the Chattahoochee" but appeared to assume the way would be relatively clear for some distance south of the Etowah.[30]

4

New Hope Church, Pickett's Mill, and Dallas

Sherman pushed his command across the Etowah River on May 23, utilizing four crossing points some distance west of the Allatoona Mountains. In an effort to avoid the rugged terrain, he cut loose from the railroad temporarily, hoping to regain contact with his supply line at Marietta. In the meanwhile, the Federals had to move thirty miles through a region cluttered with thick vegetation and which they only dimly understood by reading the maps available to them. Dallas was the first important crossroads, located fourteen miles south of the Etowah and sixteen miles west of Marietta. McPherson, on the right, headed for Dallas, while Thomas moved to his left and Schofield covered the left flank.[1]

As the Federals marched south, the landscape leveled off into an undulating terrain punctuated by hills and ridges. Sherman called it "very obscure, mostly in a state of nature, densely wooded, and with few roads." The woods sported heavy undergrowth, and the irregular hills, ridges, and valleys tended to confuse the unwary visitor. Thomas Speed of the 12th Kentucky in Schofield's corps reported "winding along narrow dark roads, with a thick jungle of undergrowth on each side." Speed thought the area south of the Etowah River was "a fine fertile country for surprises bushwhacking &c." It was one of the worst terrains in which to maneuver large masses of men. Sherman hoped that Johnston would not detect his movement in time to oppose it.[2]

But Johnston anticipated the move and sent Hardee and Polk toward Dallas on May 23 when his cavalry delivered confirmation that Sherman was trying to flank his position. Hood moved west late on May 24 as the Confeder-

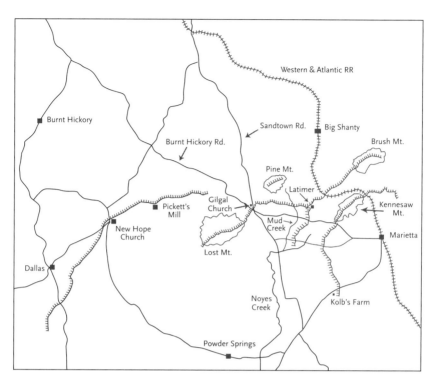

New Hope Church, Pickett's Mill, and Dallas

ates abandoned their stronghold at Allatoona. By the morning of May 25, Johnston's army established a strong position that stretched from Dallas eastward to New Hope Church, taking advantage of all contiguous high ground available. Hood was responsible for the New Hope Church area, and he placed Stewart's Division in his corps center, at the church, with Carter L. Stevenson to the right and Thomas C. Hindman to the left.[3]

Stewart positioned three of his brigades in line with one in reserve and sent out skirmishers as his men began to improvise breastworks. Alpheus Baker's Brigade and Henry De Lamar Clayton's Brigade "piled up a few logs," but Marcellus A. Stovall's Brigade prepared no defenses of any kind before the Federals appeared. As Johnston was careful to note, the log breastworks were very insubstantial. They were made of fence rails and "poles" as well as fallen timber, hastily gathered from nearby. Often referred to as "slight" or "rude" by the men who made them, the works hardly provided a couple of feet of cover. It "was barely enough to serve for a kneeling rest of their pieces," noted one of Stewart's staff officers. Stovall's men had less underbrush in their front and were on the top of a gently rising slope.[4]

New Hope Church, Pickett's Mill, and Dallas

Hindman's Division, to Stewart's left, managed to construct breastworks before the enemy appeared. Half the troops in Manigault's Brigade remained in line while the rest gathered logs, limbs, and stones. "I never saw men work so hard or so expeditiously," Manigault admitted. "All seemed to be endowed with superhuman strength, and the pile seemed to grow out of the ground." The men could not dig trenches because there was no time to find tools. Nor did they have time to cut brush in front of the line. As a result, they could not see more than 100 yards forward. Their only protection consisted of a linear pile of old wood and rock, but they considered it better than nothing.[5]

Thomas's Army of the Cumberland was heading directly toward New Hope Church, with Hooker's Twentieth Corps in the lead and Howard's Fourth Corps in close support. Geary's division led Hooker's column. Geary took a few prisoners while skirmishing with the enemy, and from them the high command learned of Hood's presence at the crossroads. Sherman authorized an attack, hoping to catch the Rebels before they were firmly established, and Hooker moved Williams's division in the lead. Williams struck Stewart with a column of brigades a little after 5:00 P.M. The fire delivered by the gray-clad defenders proved too much, and Williams's men stopped to take shelter behind rocks and trees. Intense firefights developed at short ranges along the line as the rest of Hooker's command and Howard's people closed up, but they could offer no hope of restarting the forward movement. The landscape was too cluttered and the defense was too strong. All of Stewart's Division amounted to about 4,000 men, while the Federals brought 16,000 troops to oppose him. Yet, as one historian has noted, all of Stewart's men could fire at the enemy, but only about one-third of the Federals could get into position to do the same. At least some of Williams's men "threw up a barricade of logs" to shelter themselves. The fighting ended by 7:30 P.M. when it began to rain. The Federals lost 665 men compared to casualties of about 300 to 400 on the Confederate side.[6]

That night, the Federals sought every means to dig in. Most units were about 100 yards from the Confederate position but shielded somewhat by the cover of trees and brush. Like their gray counterparts, the Unionists gathered logs, but they also used bayonets and tin plates to begin clawing into the earth. During the night, picks, shovels, and spades arrived to enable them to dig in faster and better. Pioneers began to cut down trees in front and the infantrymen used the logs to strengthen their parapets. Trees located well behind the line also were cut and brought forward to the works. Head logs began to appear, raised by supports to create a four-inch slit above the top of the parapet, through which to fire muskets. On many parts of the line, the Confederates sent a shower of bullets in the direction of any unusual noise, so the Federals worked as quietly, and in as stooped a position, as possible. By the morning of May 26, the works were good enough to provide basic protection from rifle fire. Work on them continued as more tools appeared.[7]

Stewart's men also dug in on the night of May 25, as videttes were placed only fifty paces out from the main line to give warning in case the enemy tried to advance. These men took shelter in the tree cover, shielded by the darkness. Few tools were available among the Confederates: only "a few dull axes," two picks, and four shovels in the 37th Alabama of Baker's Brigade. Capt. Charles L. Lumsden's Alabama Battery took position 100 yards to the right of New Hope Church, with the graveyard between, and the gunners constructed "a pretty fair earthwork" by dawn. The guns were 200 yards away from a Federal battery, and a good deal of skirmish fire began as soon as the sun rose on May 26.[8]

McPherson approached Dallas on the afternoon of May 26 and positioned available units east of the village. Hardee was already in place opposite his position, both lines arrayed along an irregular range of hills separated by a timbered valley. A one-mile gap existed between McPherson at Dallas and Thomas at New Hope Church, and a similar gap existed between Hardee and Polk-Hood. Both sides covered the interval with lines of pickets.[9]

PICKETT'S MILL

Stymied in his hope for a quick march to Marietta, Sherman now sought to flank Johnston's right, hoping to maneuver before the Confederates could extend and fortify. Howard was given the task of doing so with his Fourth Corps troops. Thomas J. Wood's division led the way on May 27, supported by Richard W. Johnson's division of the Fourteenth Corps. The Federals encountered rough, timbered terrain. They crawled along at a snail's pace until late afternoon, when Howard judged that he had gone far enough and ordered Wood to turn south and approach the Confederate position. Unknown to the Federals, Johnston had shifted Cleburne's Division from Hardee to extend Hood's line on May 26. Cleburne deployed two brigades, which dug in the rest of that day and on the morning of May 27, and held two others in reserve.[10]

Howard caught a glimpse of Cleburne's two brigades digging in, but he hoped his men could break the line before the Confederates completed their entrenchments. At about 5:00 P.M., Wood sent his troops forward one brigade at a time. William B. Hazen's command led the way. Hazen directed the movement of his 1,500 men up a timbered ravine, using a compass because of the confusing nature of the terrain. Pushing back Confederate cavalry who had deployed as skirmishers, Hazen's men caught sight of the ridgetop that was their

New Hope Church, Pickett's Mill, and Dallas

target when they reached the head of the ravine about 100 yards away from the top of the rise. But much to their dismay, Granbury's Brigade of Texas troops was just then taking position on the ridge.[11]

The Texans had no time to construct breastworks and had to fight the battle of Pickett's Mill without protection. They lay flat on the ground to minimize casualties. "Ah! Damn you, we have caught you without your logs now," some Federals yelled as they advanced toward the ridge crest.[12]

The battle mostly took place in the narrow space between the upper end of the ravine and the top of the ridge. Hazen's men surged to within twenty paces of Granbury's line. Brig. Gen. Daniel C. Govan's Arkansas Brigade, to Granbury's left, was protected by works; two of his regiments opened an oblique fire on Hazen. Also, two guns of Capt. Thomas J. Key's Arkansas Battery obtained an enfilade fire on Hazen's right flank. Cleburne had personally seen to it that Key was able to fire laterally. When the gunners had constructed their emplacement earlier that day, Cleburne inspected the work and saw that they had allowed only for a frontal fire. He told them to tear down the embrasures and reconstruct them to give the tubes more sweep, and now the benefits were obvious.[13]

Hazen's men advanced to within very close range of Granbury's guns, but could go no farther. The line of dead and wounded clearly demarked the high tide of his attack. Ambrose Bierce, Hazen's topographer, recalled that one-third of the fallen lay within fifteen paces of the Confederates, but none lay within ten paces. Hazen's brigade fell back at about 5:45 P.M., having lost 467 men. Hazen recalled that his troops retired "from sheer necessity." About 200 yards to the rear they met the next brigade coming up to test the Confederate line. Col. William H. Gibson pushed his brigade forward up the same ravine, duplicating Hazen's line of advance, at about 6:00 P.M. His troops also came within ten yards of Granbury's line before falling back sometime after 6:30. Gibson lost 681 troops in this futile assault.[14]

By this time, Howard received a dispatch from Sherman that had been written an hour earlier. In it, the commanding general told Howard to call off the offensive. Sherman had come to the conclusion that Howard had moved too slowly to take advantage of the Confederate position and did not want unnecessary losses. "It is useless to look for the flank of the enemy," Sherman told him, "as he makes temporary breast-works as fast as we travel. We must break his line without scattering our troops too much, and then break through." That message had arrived too late to save nearly 1,200 Union soldiers in what Howard later termed "a race of breastworks and intrenchments." Howard laid himself open to criticism by not moving farther to the east and for allowing

Wood to attack piecemeal. Granbury's men demonstrated that breastworks were not indispensable to a stubborn defense if other terrain features and the enemy's mode of attack favored the defender. The Confederates possessed many tactical advantages at Pickett's Mill, despite their lack of entrenchments at the point of battle.[15]

Howard advanced another brigade, commanded by Frederick Knefler, to establish a line close to the Confederate position at 6:30 P.M. Knefler's men constructed breastworks of rails and rocks inside the tree cover near the head of the ravine and opened a skirmish fire at the Confederates. Then at 10:00 P.M., Knefler's men pulled back to a new line Howard had established half a mile to the rear, which is today known as Howard's Knoll. William P. Carlin's brigade and John H. King's brigade of Johnson's division constructed works along this new line. Hazen's and Gibson's men also contributed to the defenses of Howard's position, making a trench three feet wide and four feet deep.[16]

During the heaviest action, when Hazen and then Gibson were fighting, other Federal units swung out to their left and drove back the Confederate cavalry that extended Granbury's line. But Cleburne was able to shift more infantry forces to shore up the flank, eventually sending two more brigades to that area.[17]

Elsewhere along the Federal line, other commanders adjusted the positions of their units to accommodate Howard's flanking movement. Stanley's division relieved Wood when the latter started on the maneuver, and his men found "a partial line of breastworks." Stanley's pioneers went to the front to strengthen the works, carrying logs forward. The skirmishers were already well protected in "snug, crescent-shaped" pits, most of which had head logs. On the main line, the pioneers and infantrymen used "heavy logs" to revet the parapet and increased its size until it was up to four feet thick. They deepened the trench so that men could stand up in it without exposing their heads. "Heavy head-logs" completed the adornment. That night, Stanley's men placed an abatis before the line. It consisted of "small trees cut for the purpose and staked to the ground, their limbs sharpened and interwoven so as to make a pretty serious obstruction," according to members of the 96th Illinois in Walter C. Whitaker's brigade.[18]

The 96th Illinois held a section of the Union line that constituted a sharp angle atop a rise of ground, and it became the target of intense artillery fire on the evening of May 27. For more than an hour, the projectiles cut tree limbs and leaves and threw dirt up around the angle. When the bombardment ceased at dark, the Federals obtained more tools and improved their works at the angle, widening the trench and making the parapet up to ten feet thick. They

New Hope Church, Pickett's Mill, and Dallas

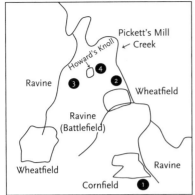

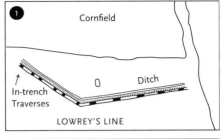

LOWREY'S LINE

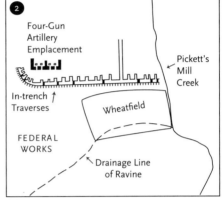

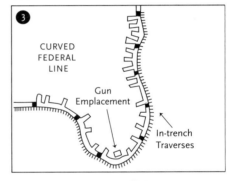

Pickett's Mill

also constructed traverses of logs and dirt "at frequent intervals." Skirmishing continued all night. One-third of the regiment's manpower stood ready in the trench as some of the others worked on the defenses and the rest tried to catch some sleep to the rear. Everyone had a fitful, restless night because the skirmishing often rose to such a pitch as to cause the regimental commander to assume an attack was underway. He regularly called everyone into the trenches with guns at the ready.[19]

Skirmishing also was heavy on the Twentieth Corps front that day and night. Geary's skirmishers drove the opposing Rebel skirmishers back into their main position. They could see "entrant angles" in the Confederate line of earthworks, stretching back to form traverses, from their new position. On Stevenson's part of the line, members of Alfred Cumming's Georgia Brigade endured heavy shelling by Federal guns only 200 yards away. The enemy battery "soon knocked down our weak works, then it poured in its iron hail of grape & canister & shell & solid shot which was fatal to a great many of our troups," wrote a man in the 39th Georgia.[20]

At Pickett's Mill, the epicenter of battle that day, Cleburne wanted Granbury to advance under cover of darkness and push the Federals farther away from his position. Granbury's men spent an hour preparing for this dangerous mission, placing a heavy skirmish line only ten feet before the main line. At 10:00 P.M., a bugle sounded the advance, and Granbury's men started with bayonets fixed, raising "a regular Texas Yell, or an Indian Yell or perhaps both together," wrote Capt. Samuel T. Foster of the 24th Texas Cavalry (dismounted). Knefler was just then pulling back anyway, so Granbury's men had little difficulty clearing some breathing space for the Confederates atop the ridge.[21]

While Cleburne lost 460 men out of 4,683 engaged, the Federals suffered 1,600 losses from among the 14,000 who were present on the battlefield. The Confederates picked up 1,200 abandoned guns. The dead littered the small space in front of Granbury's line on the morning of May 28, many of them hit multiple times by the hail of gunfire. Samuel Foster was sickened by the sight and rushed away before he fainted. Even Johnston, Hardee, and Cleburne were awed by the sight of massed bodies when they viewed the field that morning.[22]

DALLAS

The flow of action at Dallas proceeded in a very different direction than it did at Pickett's Mill. McPherson never tried to find and turn Johnston's left flank. His orders from Sherman had been, from the start, to close up to his left toward

New Hope Church, Pickett's Mill, and Dallas

Thomas at New Hope Church. Sherman wanted to slide back toward the railroad and regain contact with his line of communications. Because Johnston blocked his march to Marietta, Sherman had to be content with merely flanking the enemy out of the Allatoona Mountains. He directed McPherson to move left and connect firmly with Thomas, and then everyone would make their way east. But it would take time and effort. "I cannot well work toward the left," McPherson warned Sherman, "for as soon as we uncover this flank (the right), the enemy will be on it." Only with the construction of fortified flank positions could McPherson safely fulfill Sherman's directive.[23]

McPherson's caution was justified because Johnston was attentive to an opportunity to strike at Sherman. Sixteenth Corps headquarters directed division leaders to make sure their lines were as strong as possible, and a heavy skirmish force was placed in front. They also were to order all their men to stand to in the trenches at 3:00 A.M. on May 28 and place cooking fires well to the rear. With precautions like these, the Confederates were presented with few opportunities to attack the Federals frontally, but Johnston was eager to try a flank. When Confederate cavalry reported that Sherman's left was in the air, Hood proposed he take his corps out of line and attack. Johnston approved, but an all-night march through rugged terrain exhausted and slowed the Confederates. By dawn of May 28, the Federals secured the left flank and Hood called off the planned strike.[24]

During the day on May 28, Johnston received word (which proved to be false) that McPherson was pulling away toward the north. He ordered a reconnaissance in force to determine what was going on. William B. Bate's Division, on the army's far left, conducted the maneuver with support from William H. Jackson's Division of cavalry to the left. A plan was worked out to minimize exposure. Frank C. Armstrong's Brigade of cavalry would advance first on foot. If it encountered little opposition, a signal consisting of four rapid artillery rounds would propel Bate's Division into action. If the Federals were still there in force, there would be no signal and no infantry advance.[25]

Armstrong started his dismounted troopers at 3:45 P.M. and captured the Yankee pickets. It soon became obvious that McPherson had not moved away, and when Bate received word from Armstrong he ordered that the signal guns not be fired. But not all of his brigade commanders understood the situation. Col. Robert Bullock, who commanded Finley's Florida Brigade, and Joseph H. Lewis, who led the Kentucky Brigade, received no message that the attack had been canceled. They believed that the firing of Armstrong's command had drowned out the sound of the signal cannon, so both men ordered their commands forward.[26]

Bullock's troops managed to capture a section of the Union skirmish line, with the 1st and 4th Florida fighting the Federals hand to hand. The skirmish works were stronger than usual, and the Confederates assumed they had taken a section of the main Union line. Not until they advanced another 100 yards beyond the captured works did they see the main Federal position another fifty yards ahead on top of a "very precipitous hill." The Confederates discovered a small gap in the Union line on the Fifteenth Corps sector and captured three guns of the 1st Iowa Battery. But a counterattack by the 6th Iowa reclaimed the cannon and sealed the hole in the line. For the rest, Fifteenth Corps troops opened fire and stopped the Confederate advance. Many Federals reported that it was the first time the Fifteenth Corps had repelled an enemy attack from behind earthworks. Sherman reported the result of the May 28 attack to Halleck by noting that McPherson's men were protected "by log breast-works, like our old Corinth lines" in the spring of 1862.[27]

The Confederates lost between 1,000 and 1,500 men in this botched reconnaissance, with the Federals losing only about 400. Bate tried to explain the fiasco to army headquarters, arguing, in the words of staff officer Thomas B. Mackall, that the "ardor of men could not be restrained, went too far before could be recalled." One small result of Bate's attack was that it caused a delay in Union plans to shift to the left. McPherson was supposed to begin the movement after dark on May 28, but he postponed those plans for fear of further enemy attacks. The 76th Ohio in the Fifteenth Corps stood to at midnight for a half hour and then again at 5:00 A.M. due to nervousness regarding what the Rebels might do. The Federals also conducted no major movements the next day although the skirmishing was heavy on McPherson's front.[28]

Preparations to shift the Army of the Tennessee had been mostly completed by the time Armstrong and Bate launched their ill-coordinated attack. Andrew Hickenlooper, McPherson's trusted artillery and engineer officer from the days he commanded the Seventeenth Corps, had spent all day laying out a refused line that stretched as much as two miles toward the Union rear. He plotted out sectors for each division and began to cut military roads through the tangled landscape so all units could find their way to the new position and know where to align during the night. This position was designed to secure McPherson's right flank after the pullout from Dallas. Hickenlooper was nearly finished when the Confederates attacked in the late afternoon of May 28. Dodge spelled out the process of withdrawing in special field orders to his Sixteenth Corps subordinates. While the skirmish line remained in place, with a staff officer to guide it to the rear when the time was right, the first of two main lines in the corps would pull away first, followed by the second line. Staff officers attached to each division would guide the commands along their assigned routes and to their places in the new position. Details would remain in the old works to chop trees and divert Rebel attention, coming away with the skirmishers.[29]

McPherson hoped to put this carefully laid plan into operation on the evening of May 29, and Chauncey Reese instructed staff officers from each corps on what they were supposed to do. The Federals had just begun to pull out, when firing flared up along the Fifteenth and Sixteenth Corps fronts; McPherson immediately canceled the move. Skirmish firing continued off and on until dawn, but everyone seemed confused as to exactly why it took place. The Federals assumed they were under attack again, but the Confederates were certain they were the targets of a Yankee advance. "This was truly a night of alarms," commented Capt. Charles Dana Miller of the 76th Ohio. "Whether there was any real occasion for the great turmoil it was hard to find out." On the other side of no-man's-land, John S. Jackman of the 9th Kentucky remembered the "perfect sheet of flame coming over the enemy's works," and his comrades thought it was a good time "to get rid" of the extra sixty rounds of cartridges they had earlier been issued. Skirmishers on both sides were caught in the middle of this deluge of fire that seemed never to cease. Rumors circulated that some of the Florida troops mistook lightning bug flashes for Union muzzle blasts and opened fire, causing the noisy demonstration that night.[30]

Whatever the cause of the night firing, Sherman decided to give McPherson's exhausted men some rest. He set the night of May 31 as the new target hour for starting the pullout. Reese added another element to the plan by assigning corps engineers to supervise the digging of a new line of works 500 to 600 yards to the rear of the present line, to be held by a rear guard as the main force pulled away in the darkness. This was done all day on May 31. That evening, the Federals began to execute their plan without interruption. They retired to Hickenlooper's refused line by dawn. When the Confederates failed to sally forth and challenge them, the Federals began to move out of Hickenlooper's position toward Hooker's troops at New Hope Church. It proved to be an easy pullout, but several more days of careful sliding were necessary before Sherman reestablished a firm connection with his railroad supply line.[31]

SIEGE CONDITIONS ALONG THE NEW HOPE CHURCH, PICKETT'S MILL, AND DALLAS LINES

South of the Etowah River, the Federals began to cope with the most difficult conditions they had yet encountered in the Atlanta campaign. There was no well-defined ridge here, as there had been at Dalton and Cassville, only rolling, rugged terrain engulfed by sometimes choking woods. The opposing lines stretched for about ten miles and were anywhere from fifty yards to half a mile apart. "I rarely saw a dozen of the enemy at any one time," Sherman remembered of his almost daily rides along the line, "and there were always skirmishers dodging from tree to tree, or behind logs on the ground, or who occasionally showed their heads above the hastily constructed but remarkably strong rifle-trenches." Confederate resistance had stiffened, and the troops' reliance on improved fieldworks deepened in these operations south of the Etowah River.[32]

In many ways, the terrain south of the Etowah favored Confederate defensive needs more than the terrain north of the river. The high ridges at Dalton and Cassville probably would have been impervious to a Union frontal attack, but those positions could readily be outflanked because the intervening valleys were relatively open to Federal movements. South of the Etowah, the vegetation and comparatively level terrain restricted Union observation and movement a great deal. The landscape enabled the Federals to close in at short range to the Confederate positions, but it also inhibited turning movements. Sherman was bogged down in a wilderness through which his men could move only by great preparation, caution, and exertion.

The tactical situation also led to something akin to siege conditions along the line, with both sides lodged in heavy earthworks at short range. There was "a continual battle" of skirmishers. Many regiments sent out a full company to the skirmish line, loaded with sixty rounds of ammunition per man, and those troops shot away all of their rounds during one shift on the line. On some sectors, one side or the other managed to drive the opposing skirmishers into their main position, creating much-needed breathing space for their comrades. Sharpshooters roamed about on each side of no-man's-land, sniping at any available targets and creating what one officer called "a great annoyance."[33]

Skirmishers dug in deeper for protection. Geary was convinced that more sophisticated defenses lessened his "daily returns of casualties" on the skirmish line. He described them as "log rifle-pits of the V pattern." The historian of the 149th New York pictured these works as "three-sided isolated rifle-pits with top logs to fire under resting on skids extending to the rear to prevent injury to the men when displaced by cannon shot." These works sheltered three to four men who were told not to spare ammunition when on duty. On some parts of the line, the main positions were too close together to allow the Confederates to deploy skirmishers, but they did send out pickets at night to warn of a Union advance. On a typical night, May 29, the 27th Alabama in Thomas M. Scott's Brigade of William W. Loring's Division sent out thirty men to picket the regimental front. They moved quietly in the darkness until they encountered a pile of brush and made noise while negotiating this obstacle. The commotion brought a storm of Union artillery and infantry fire that lasted forty minutes, with the pickets clinging closely to the ground. When it ended, the pickets established their line 100 yards from the Confederate main position and 150 yards from the enemy, each man ten paces apart from the next.[34]

On Polk's sector, some units erected "little bunches of twigs" along the top of their main line parapets to screen the troops more effectively. Thomas Thompson of the 1st Arkansas Mounted Rifles (dismounted) was killed when he took a shot at a Yankee from behind this covering. He waited too long to determine the effect of his round, and a Federal bullet shattered his head, "scattering his brains all around," as Robert H. Dacus remembered.[35]

The close range of the opposing lines gave artillerymen with a clear line of sight to the target many advantages. Alexander A. Greene's 37th Alabama was threatened by a Union battery opposite the left wing of the regiment near New Hope Church. He procured four shovels and two picks, setting his men to work all night of May 26 to strengthen the works. Several twenty-pounder Parrotts in the Union position opened the next morning at a range of only 300 yards. Initially the Federal gunners aimed too high and did little damage, but when they resumed bombarding at 4:00 P.M. it was "with terrible effect." A shell "struck the top of my works and fell over and exploded." It killed and injured four men. The Yankees poured round after round into the position, opening breaches in Greene's parapet. The lieutenant colonel reported the human damage as well: three men were decapitated, another had his shoulder torn off, and still another suffered the loss of both hands. In fact, "scarcely any man in the left wing of my regiment escaped unhurt," Greene reported. Two of his men lost their nerve and ran to the rear, unhurt. Greene deployed snipers but, with old Austrian rifles, they had no effect on the enemy. He asked his brigade commander for help and soon received twenty men from another regiment who possessed Enfield rifles. They harassed the Yankees enough that their artillery rounds began to miss the mark.[36]

The extended stay in temporary earthworks along the New Hope Church, Pickett's Mill, and Dallas Line created uncomfortable living conditions. "Our men were much wearied during these days," reported brigade commander Henry De Lamar Clayton, "as they were forced to lay behind the piles of rails and logs for protection." Cooks prepared food and coffee behind the lines and brought them forward. But whether the men enjoyed their fare is questionable, at least near the New Hope Church battlefield, where the bodies of the May 25 attack lay for days, festering in the hot weather. Many Twentieth Corps troops "were nearly worn out" by their service in the ditches, considering "the anxiety, loss of sleep — and the horrible stench arising from the dead."[37]

"Oh we are so tired of the ditches," complained John Mitchell Davidson of the 39th North Carolina in French's Division. "At times we are the dirtiest and filthyest [sic] looking creatures you ever saw." Davidson felt much better after drawing a clean shirt and underwear and going to the rear to bathe in a creek, but most men on duty in the works had little opportunity for such luxuries. There were different stories as to why the soldiers of both sides called the New Hope Church area the Hell Hole. Among them was the story that twenty-one Federals were shot while occupying one skirmish pit on that sector. But in general, everyone came away from New Hope Church with an abiding memory of the cramped, deadly, and stinky atmosphere of the works that snaked through the tangled vegetation in this area; that was enough to earn the name Hell Hole.[38]

On the Union side of the line near Pickett's Mill, the 96th Illinois of Stanley's division endured the fire of three Confederate batteries focused on the angle of the works the regiment occupied. The Illinoisans strengthened the earthwork and, for the most part, felt secure, but one round nearly buried some comrades when it collapsed a section of the parapet. A solid shot "penetrated the embankment in front of Company A, striking a log and breaking it, severely jarring" three men who had been leaning against the log. A Confederate shell "nearly covered six men up" when it exploded inside the trench occupied by another brigade in Stanley's division.[39]

Near Dallas, the position of both opponents lay along more well-defined terrain features. The Confederate line stretched along a series of hills, some of which were quite large and commanding and appeared very "formidable" to the observant enemy. The Federals at Dallas piled logs and dug a trench behind the pile, throwing dirt to form a parapet. They placed head logs on top supported by the ends of poles, with the other ends resting on the ground behind the trench. Like their counterparts in the Twentieth Corps, Fifteenth Corps troops dug skirmish pits big enough for two or three men and placed them eight to ten rods apart from each other.[40]

Division commander Bate had to admit in his official report that Federal skirmishers and snipers greatly annoyed his men near Dallas. "We could not even stretch our blankets as dog tents," complained Johnny Green of the 9th Kentucky, "but had to just squat in the trenches or behind trees with our blankets wrapped around us & take the rain & catch what sleep we could in this squatting posture." Federal skirmishers "keep a stream of bullets coming over

New Hope Church, Pickett's Mill, and Dallas

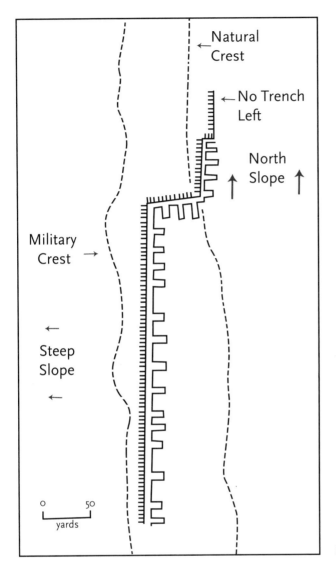

Natural Crest

No Trench Left

North Slope

Military Crest

Steep Slope

0   50
yards

Dallas

the hill all the time," reported John S. Jackman, also of the 9th Kentucky. "There will be a good lead mine down in the valley if we stay here much longer. The bullets are lying around on the ground now, thick as hail stones."[41]

The Federals dominated the skirmish line at New Hope Church, Pickett's Mill, and Dallas more often than did the Confederates. The situation became bad enough that Hardee felt compelled to issue general orders reminding his subordinates how to place a skirmish line and what it was supposed to do. He strongly urged his officers to keep skirmishers out at all times, as far ahead of the main line as possible, with each man no more than five paces from another as a rule. "Skirmish lines must [not] be driven in by skirmishers of the enemy," he lectured. "They will retire only before a line of battle."[42]

Some of the artillery units at Dallas had a rough time of it as well. Rebel gunners managed to explode at least one shell in the embrasure of Charles Gammon's Illinois battery emplacement, showering him with dirt and damaging the earthwork. Capt. Cuthbert H. Slocomb's Fifth Company of the Washington Artillery, in Hardee's Corps, was positioned on top of a "bare rounded ridge" opposite a high, commanding hill covered with trees, which the Federals occupied. "One of the worst positions we were ever in," commented gunner Philip Daingerfield Stephenson. Slocomb lost so many men here that he constructed "sort of a low wicker work of brush and branches of trees" to serve as a covered way to and from the battery position.[43]

On the Federal side at Dallas, the 31st Iowa held a section of the line that was exposed to an enfilade fire by Confederate batteries. Col. William Smyth ordered traverses built for every company, which worked so well that he lost not a man to flank fire. One Confederate shell landed in the trench but failed to explode. The sergeant major "picked it up and threw it over the breast-works."[44]

Life along the lines at New Hope Church, Pickett's Mill, and Dallas leveled all men to a base condition, no matter their rank or the color of their uniform. Everyone's story was nearly the same as that of Sgt. James G. Marston. He kept a detailed account of living conditions in his diary while serving in the 4th Louisiana. "We find the duty very heavy," Marston wrote on June 2. One-third of the men were forced to stay awake all the time, supervised by one commissioned and one noncommissioned officer from each regiment in Randall L. Gibson's Brigade. "The continued whizzing of the enemy's bullets over & around us makes us keep very close to the ditches." Watching Federal troops inch ever closer under cover of new lines of earthworks, Marston felt oppressed by "the never ceasing hideous sound of the balls."[45]

MOVING TO THE LEFT

The siege-like conditions in the trenches did not change as the Federals continued sliding to their left, for they had to remain covered even as they slowly adjusted their position. On June 1, after McPherson's initial move from Dallas, the Fifteenth Corps replaced the Twentieth Corps at New Hope Church, and Hooker took his men to the rear for a short rest. Chauncey Reese guided the two divisions of the Right Wing, Sixteenth Corps, to a refused position where they could protect the army's right flank. Union cavalry took possession of Alla-toona Station, which was unoccupied by the Confederates, and Johnston woke up to the significance of Sherman's move. He began to shift units to extend his right flank eastward.[46]

Hardee's men now had a chance to examine McPherson's old works at Dallas. John S. Jackman of the 9th Kentucky found them "very strong — far superior to our own in construction. The ground in the rear of his trenches was thickly strewn with beef bones and empty hardtack and ammunition boxes." On the other hand, Philip Daingerfield Stephenson thought the Yankee en-trenchments were not as elaborate as the ones his fellow gunners occupied. The Federal trenches were deep enough, he thought, but only fourteen to eigh-teen inches wide, which he believed was big enough only for temporary occu-pation.[47]

When Sherman tried to extend his left eastward by advancing Schofield's corps on June 2, the Federals found that their enemy were one step ahead of them. The cavalry continued to secure the vital rail link up to the town of Ac-worth, enabling work crews to begin rebuilding the track and the bridge across the Etowah River. On the Fifteenth Corps front, Charles W. Wills of the 103rd Illinois had taken position on the New Hope Church battlefield the day before, only ninety yards from the Confederate works. The woods around had been shredded by artillery and rifle fire, "and bloody shoes, clothing and accoutre-ments are thick," he recorded. It was difficult to place pickets at night because the lines were so close, and the regiment moved its skirmish line closer on the night of June 1. Wills took a detail out and dug a new trench for fifty men, sur-prising the Rebels at dawn. "This is getting on the Vicksburg order," he mused.[48]

"Thus far we have had no real battle," Sherman reported to Halleck, "but one universal skirmish extending over a vast surface." He cautioned Thomas not to dig in too promiscuously but fortify only strong points "and keep the troops handy." On the Confederate side, the line of earthworks snaking across the rugged landscape was difficult to grasp completely. French suggested to Polk that Morris make "a correct survey of the lines" of the Army of Mississippi so he could better understand them. French also suffered from an acute short-age of entrenching tools.[49]

The weather by now had turned bad with repeated and heavy rain showers becoming almost a daily occurrence. Union and Confederate trenches filled with water on June 2. Nevertheless, the Federals continued to prepare for fur-ther moves eastward. Reese assigned two engineer officers to construct a four-mile-long military road for McPherson to use to slide toward the railroad.

Battlefield of New Hope Church. Captured by George N. Barnard, this view demonstrates the effect of artillery and small-arms fire on trees and underbrush. The landscape south of the Etowah River was covered with growth through which narrow dirt roads snaked, posing a major environmental obstacle to Sherman's troop movements. *Barnard,* Photographic Views, *no. 27. Courtesy of the Metropolitan Museum of Art.*

Charles Wills lost several men from a work detail that tried to strengthen the regiment's new line, only eighty yards from Confederate rifles, even though the detail was working in the darkest part of the night.[50]

By June 3, Johnston decided to call off further attempts to prevent Sherman from moving his line to the railroad and planned to fall back to another position. Gov. Joseph E. Brown informed Johnston that 3,000 newly raised Georgia militiamen would soon be ready to cooperate with his army, and the general planned to use them as guards for the crossings of the Chattahoochee River. He had also assigned Maj. Gen. Mansfield Lovell to cooperate with Henry C. Wayne, adjutant general of the state government of Georgia, to examine those crossings along a stretch of fifteen miles of the river in order to recommend the placement of defenses.[51]

The Confederates pulled out of the New Hope Church, Pickett's Mill, and Dallas Line after dusk on June 4, as Johnston planned to deploy his army on a wide front facing north and west to cover all the approaches to Marietta. Polk's

New Hope Church, Pickett's Mill, and Dallas

Army of Mississippi moved on three roads toward Lost Mountain, nine miles west of Marietta and about six miles from its present location. Polk's artillery moved first, then most of his infantry pulled out at 11:00 P.M., except two regiments of each division that were left behind to hold the main line for another two hours. The last contingent to leave were the skirmishers, who departed at 3:00 A.M. Engineer officers guided the divisions along their assigned routes of march.[52]

The move was plagued by some of the worst weather yet experienced during the campaign. The rain was "pouring down in torents [sic] all night," reported John Mitchell Davidson of the 39th North Carolina, "and the mud oh you have no ideah [sic] it was like batter & from 3 to 12 inches and no chance to shun it. It was slosh all night." Many Confederates lost their shoes when the adhesive mud pulled them off. Polk's men needed seven hours to move six miles that rainy night. Conditions were bad on the Union side of the old line as well. Members of the 9th Iowa were forced to lie in their trenches all night with guns in hand, enduring the heavy downpour. "We had a rough old night of it," admitted John C. Brown.[53]

When dawn broke on June 5, bringing with it a temporary cessation of rain, many Yankees went out to look at the Confederate works that had confronted them for the past ten days. Charles W. Wills found bodies of Federals who had been killed on May 25 still littering the ground between the lines near New Hope Church. A Twentieth Corps soldier marveled at the immense slashing that fronted the Rebel works farther east of New Hope Church. "We had all we could do to get over as it was, and we never would have done it under fire," he recalled. Everywhere, the Confederate works were in a mess. "The Rebels were awful dirty," Charles Wills reported, "and the smell in their camps dreadful." Irving Bronson of the 107th New York saw a Rebel battery emplacement that "was a hard looking place. Blood and rags etc. all around." About twenty-five stragglers were gathered up in one division sector, and Wills noted that the enemy had torn down the wooden fences enclosing graves in the New Hope Church cemetery "to make beds for themselves."[54]

Sherman optimistically assumed that Johnston would not make another stand until he reached Kennesaw Mountain, but he assured Washington that "I will not run head on his fortifications." He considered the abandoned Rebel works to be formidable and bragged that his men had turned the enemy out of them "with less loss to ourselves than we have inflicted on him."[55]

5

The Mountain Line,
the Gilgal Church Line,
and the Mud Creek Line

By the time Sherman established a position south of the Etowah River, it became necessary for him to pay added attention to the security of his tenuous supply line with the North. Dangling on the end of a single track of rails stretching 350 miles to Louisville, Kentucky, the daily sustenance of Sherman's army group depended on a regular run of trains to the forward line. The Federals had spent an enormous amount of time and resources constructing fortifications to defend the railroad down to Chattanooga, and now they had to extend the system of rail-based supply and its attendant system of field defenses south of that gateway to the Deep South.

RAILROAD DEFENSES

George Stoneman's cavalry division took possession of Allatoona Pass on the late afternoon of June 1, securing a key point of the Western and Atlantic Railroad south of the Etowah River. Stoneman extended his control southward along the rail line until his horsemen had gone all the way to Acworth by June 2. The Federals now controlled the line on both sides of the river and could begin rebuilding the railroad bridge across the Etowah; Johnston had left the rest of the rail line intact when he abandoned the region. Local civilians told the Federals that Georgia governor Joseph E. Brown had been working to fortify the Allatoona Pass since the war began, and two nearby forts testified to the truth of that assertion. A small work was located to cover the north end of the pass, and a larger fort stood three-quarters of a mile from the pass.[1]

Those meager defenses were inadequate to protect the Federal line of communications. Sherman rode to Allatoona on June 6 and issued orders for the construction of new defenses to shield a forward depot of supplies. Seventeenth Corps troops, due to arrive two days later after a long journey from Vicksburg, would provide the garrison. Taking Poe along, Sherman made a quick tour of the terrain and then set out his instructions in a special field order. "Two or more good strong earth redoubts will be located at the eastern [southern] extremity of this pass, and must be constructed by the troops." He assigned Poe to lay the works out, and to visit Kingston and the railroad bridge over the Etowah to survey the ground and lay out additional defenses at those locations. All stragglers were to be arrested and put to work on the fortifications.[2]

Sherman left Poe with Stoneman to oversee the work, and the engineer made a thorough inspection on June 7 and 8, taking along Chauncey Reese and Oscar Malmborg. They concluded that five, not two, redoubts were needed to protect the south end of the pass, and Poe informed Sherman of this decision on June 8. He also recommended another battery be added to the garrison to provide rifled artillery support. Sherman quickly approved all these recommendations and Poe rode off toward Acworth on the evening of June 8, leaving Malmborg to superintend the construction. Only three regiments of the Seventeenth Corps, under the command of Col. George C. Rogers, were yet at Allatoona. They were under strength and few tools were available. Malmborg took three days to stake out the works and get the redoubts started; then he rejoined the bulk of the Seventeenth Corps and left Rogers in charge of the construction. When Poe visited Allatoona on June 16 to gauge progress, the tools he had ordered a week before had still not arrived, but the works were well advanced.[3]

Poe had placed the five redoubts so they would be within artillery range of each other, on average about 500 yards apart, except that No. 5 was 1,200 yards from No. 4 and about a mile and a half from the post headquarters. Thick tree cover surrounded three of the five forts, and Rogers intended to cut it down to clear a field of fire and form a dense slashing. The defense plan at Allatoona would accommodate 800 men and ten guns, but Malmborg planned embrasures only in two forts, with barbette emplacements in the others. He arranged for eighty sandbags to be kept on hand in case embrasures had to be quickly made in the other forts. Rogers's overworked infantrymen nearly finished the redoubts by June 27, although they still had to dig some connecting infantry lines and cut a good deal of timber in front of the forts. Photographs of the de-

Federal defenses at the Etowah River. George N. Barnard exposed this
image of Union fieldworks on the north side of the Etowah River that were
designed to protect the railroad bridge a short distance away. Building timbers
were scavenged from nearby structures to shore up the parapet. *Barnard,*
Photographic Views, *no. 23. Courtesy of the Metropolitan Museum of Art.*

fenses at Allatoona taken after the campaign show deep embrasures and parapets revetted with posts, and saplings that were woven among the posts.[4]

Poe, Reese, and Malmborg also visited the crossing of the Etowah River
on June 7 to inspect the Confederate defenses and plan a new system of works.
The three decided to modify the Rebel fortifications and dig some new trenches
along the river. They planned to station at least two regiments to guard the
bridge. Members of the Pioneer Brigade of the Department of the Cumberland
contributed their labor to the effort as digging continued at least until June 15.
The Pioneers also worked on rebuilding the railroad bridge across the Etowah.
The Federals revetted the parapets with logs and heavy timbers and cut embrasures for artillery positions in the works defending the crossing.[5]

Sherman created a new district to protect his supply line as his men drove
deeper into Georgia. On June 10, the District of the Etowah became a reality, its
boundaries stretching from Bridgeport, Alabama, to Allatoona and from Rome,
Georgia, to Cleveland, Tennessee. Maj. Gen. James B. Steedman was placed

Mountain, Gilgal Church, and Mud Creek Lines

in charge of it, with his primary objective to protect and maintain the railroad and telegraph system that ran through the district. Sherman was shoving more troops into the campaign by mid-June as well. He ordered Brig. Gen. John E. Smith's division of the Fifteenth Corps from Huntsville, Alabama, and nine additional regiments from Kentucky and Tennessee to strengthen Schofield's Twenty-Third Corps. Maj. Gen. Francis P. Blair Jr.'s Seventeenth Corps arrived with 9,000 additional troops after detaching 2,000 men to hold Rome and 1,500 to garrison Allatoona. The railroad bridge over the Etowah was finished by June 12.[6]

North of the Etowah, the Federals were already constructing an extensive system of railroad defenses to guard key points of their supply line. Small fortifications protected bridges, while more elaborate systems of earthworks shielded key towns. The most impressive type of fortification was Merrill's elaborate blockhouse, which consisted of double layers of logs and casemated artillery positions. The typical blockhouse was effective against only guerrilla attacks and small cavalry raids, but Merrill's construction could stand up against artillery.[7]

The garrisons and their commanders were the key to maintaining the security of Sherman's logistics. Maj. Gen. Lovell H. Rousseau, reporting to Thomas as commander of the District of Nashville, was responsible for railroad defense within the Department of the Cumberland. He built new works, maintained the older ones with a system of regular inspections, and supplied the small garrisons to man them. Rousseau also gathered intelligence and was ready to strike out at suspected bands of guerrillas or cavalry concentrations before they got within range of the track. The idea was that each garrison could defend itself for several hours until Rousseau shifted help to their location.[8]

The major cities along the rail line became bastions of defense. Chattanooga had sixteen forts, redoubts, batteries, and lunettes around its perimeter, all of them in various stages of construction by June 1864. Connecting infantry trenches also were in varied stages of construction, as were extensive waterworks and magazines to support the garrison. Federal engineers had redesigned the Chattanooga system of fortifications to make for a smaller area of control compared to the more expansive, emergency system of works thrown up in the wake of the defeat at Chickamauga the previous fall. Work continued on the defenses of Nashville as well during the summer of 1864, although that system of defenses had been under construction since the Federals occupied the Tennessee capital in February 1862. The most expensive and time-consuming aspects of the Nashville defenses were the casemated artillery positions and masonry revetments of Fort Negley. By the time of Sherman's Atlanta campaign, the Federals were spending $70,000 per month on the Nashville works, and there seemed no end in sight. The chief engineer, Richard Delafield, sent an inspector who reported that too much time and effort was being spent on Fort Negley. But a new commander for the post of Nashville, Brig. Gen. Zealous Bates Tower, supported Merrill in his plan and justified the high cost. As a result, the all-too-expensive fortifications of Nashville were finally finished before the end of the war.[9]

The rail lines between Nashville and Chattanooga were studded with fortifications, because this area was the most exposed to cavalry raids and guerrilla activity. Along the Nashville and Chattanooga Railroad, 151 miles long, there were forty-six blockhouses. All but two of them had walls that were one log thick. The two Merrill blockhouses that sported thicker walls were located at Bridgeport, Alabama. Thirty-six block houses, all of them single-log structures, dotted the course of the Nashville and Decatur Railroad, which was 110 miles long. The line from Decatur to Stevenson, Alabama, had thirteen single-log blockhouses and one Merrill structure along its ninety-mile course. As of June 29, three companies of engineer troops were hard at work constructing nine blockhouses along the Western and Atlantic Railroad between Chattanooga and Allatoona, with additional earthwork defenses at Resaca, Kingston, the crossing of the Etowah, and Allatoona Pass.[10]

Lt. John Calvin Hartzell of the 105th Ohio was among the thousands of Union soldiers who guarded Sherman's lifeline during the Atlanta campaign. He exaggerated only a little when writing, "Along the entire line from Louisville to Chattanooga every bridge was covered by a fort and artillery, and stockades filled with soldiers were almost as common as mile-posts, and soldiers patrolled the whole line, at frequent intervals, night and day. The old fighters at the front made light of all this and said the boys who did the guarding at the rear had a soft nap, and called them feather-bed soldiers."[11]

THE MOUNTAIN LINE

Those "old fighters" of Sherman's now had to face more Confederate fieldworks as they resumed the advance toward Atlanta. Soon after Johnston abandoned his position along the line connecting Dallas, New Hope Church, and Pickett's Mill, Sherman felt confident that his opponent would fall back a considerable distance. The now-empty Rebel works seemed enormously strong, and Sherman promised not to attack similar lines when he ran against them. The countryside was ill suited for maneuvering large bodies of troops, for it was densely wooded and the few roads that ran through the trees were in poor shape, especially when the sky dumped unusual amounts of rain on them. The ease with which the enemy could block progress by throwing up even small earthworks frustrated Sherman. "It is a Big Indian War," he complained to his brother. But Sherman remained firm in his resolve to conserve troop strength and use maneuver rather than attack as his mode of operation. "I expect the Enemy to fight us at Kenesaw Mountain near Marietta," he informed Halleck. To his wife, Sherman promised not to "run but headed against any works prepared for us."[12]

A. B. Thornton, a Federal soldier who roamed the area between Allatoona and Atlanta as a scout, reported his findings to Sherman on June 8. The intelligence gave Sherman information about what he could expect as he drove closer to Atlanta. Thornton had been through the area two months before and reported that comparatively little extra work had been done since then, but the Confederates already were improving their ring of earthworks around Atlanta, which now had more artillery in it. Forts and rifle pits extended to both sides of the track, both north and south of the Chattahoochee River, when Thornton most recently passed through that area. Bolstered with information such as this, Sherman continued to express his desire not to lose lives unnecessarily by attacking fortified positions. "We cannot risk the heavy losses of an assault at this distance from our base," he informed Halleck.[13]

Unknown to Sherman, Johnston had no intention of retiring to Kennesaw Mountain just yet. He assumed an expansive position west and northwest of Marietta only a few miles away from his former line linking Dallas, New Hope Church, and Pickett's Mill in order to take advantage of every terrain opportunity and slow down the Federal advance. The Confederates occupied the top of Lost Mountain, nine miles due west of Marietta, on June 5. Then they extended northeastward to an important road junction at Gilgal Church. As the Federals reached out to occupy Allatoona, Johnston was forced to extend his line to encompass Brush Mountain, three miles north of Marietta. He also placed troops in a forward position atop Pine Mountain, six miles northwest of Marietta.[14]

The Mountain Line thus created was impressive for its length and the high peaks it encompassed. At eleven miles long, Johnston's army was stretched nearly to the breaking point to cover the ground. Hood's Corps held the right, which included Brush Mountain at 300 feet high, while Hardee's Corps held the left, anchored on Lost Mountain at 1,520 feet elevation. Polk's Army of Mississippi occupied the center, but Bate's Division of Hardee's Corps held 300-foot-tall Pine Mountain. The Confederate line ran along the high ground that represented the dividing ridge between the drainage area of the Etowah and Chattahoochee Rivers.[15]

Sherman spent several days consolidating his new connection with the railroad before issuing orders for a further advance on June 9. He wanted his subordinates to move forward in columns rather than battle lines, their advance covered by skirmishers. "Intrenched positions will not be attacked without orders," he cautioned. Sherman suggested his commanders use rifled artillery to batter down log and rail barricades along the roads and to dig in whenever they obtained a good position for defense. Expecting not to hit any real opposition until he reached Kennesaw or the Chattahoochee River, Sherman set out on June 10. Thomas, however, encountered Confederate skirmishers only a mile short of Pine Mountain. He ordered his men to stop and fortify. To the right, Schofield halted half a mile north of Gilgal Church along the Sandtown Road, while McPherson, on the Federal left, occupied Big Shanty on the railroad line and continued one mile beyond in the direction of Brush Mountain. As Schofield reported to his superior, there was no doubt that the enemy was ensconced in a strong position north and west of Kennesaw Mountain.[16]

Sherman's left was anchored by the newly arrived Seventeenth Corps, which Blair positioned one and a half miles south of Big Shanty, its right resting on the main road to Marietta. Blair's men dug in along a ridge on the night of June 11, fronted by a large open area and the course of Noonday Creek. They constructed an advanced line about halfway across the open area a few days later, with a fortified skirmish line before it. The Confederates remained in their works near Brush Mountain for several days as Seventeenth Corps troops slowly enlarged their defensive posture east of the Marietta Road.[17]

On the far Confederate left, Lost Mountain towered above the countryside. French's Division of Polk's Army of Mississippi initially held this eminence before shifting farther to the right, and French admired Lost Mountain as it "swells from the plain solitary and lone," offering a wonderful view of the area. The Confederates began to fortify Lost Mountain on June 6, using logs and rocks as the base of their parapet and piling dirt on top of them when tools arrived the next day. The effort tired everyone out, for the ground was rocky. Details of fifty men relieved each other every hour until the work was finished. Then French moved his division to the right on June 7, to a point near the center of the Mountain Line, and began to dig in. Daniel Harris Reynolds's Brigade of Edward C. Walthall's Division "made a splendid line of works" that night, and the next day his men slashed the brush in front of the position to create a field of fire. They also used the cut brush to make arbors to protect themselves from the blazing sun while occupying works that lay in open fields. Troops of Hardee's Corps replaced French at Lost Mountain and finished the construction of field defenses on and near the eminence until they had parapets ten feet wide and at least three feet high. Their trench was more than six feet wide.[18]

Pine Mountain anchored the center of Johnston's Mountain Line. The

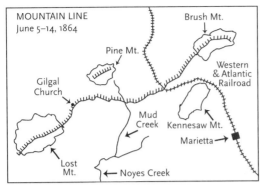

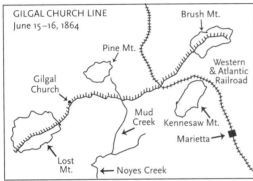

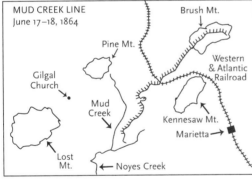

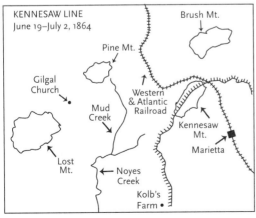

Mountain Line, Gilgal
Church Line, Mud Creek
Line, and Kennesaw Line

eminence rose solitary above the surrounding countryside, its shallow slopes covered with timber. Lewis's Kentucky Brigade of Bate's Division occupied Pine Mountain on June 6 and began to fortify that evening. During the eight days the Confederates occupied the hill, they constructed formidable earthworks. Logs were laid down to compose the base of the parapet, with dirt thrown on top. The parapet was wide and high. An observant Federal veteran who visited the site in 1881 found they were still intact and wide enough for a horse and wagon to pass along on top. Head logs were still in place at that late date, but trees had begun to grow on the parapets. The slashing of cut timber in front of the works still lay in place, with a double row of sharpened stakes just in front of the parapet. There are three one-gun artillery emplacements still intact near the top of Pine Mountain today, with sections of connecting infantry trenches.[19]

To the southwest of Pine Mountain, Samuel French fumed a bit over the shortage of entrenching tools, as his division struggled to make its new line after moving to the area from Lost Mountain on June 7. French called the work staked out by engineer Presstman "a weak, faulty, miserable line." Presstman also ordered French's engineer officer to turn over the division's tools on June 7 when it moved to the right, but the tools lay in a wagon at Polk's headquarters and were doing no one any good. "I cannot construct my line without tools," French sarcastically told one of Polk's staff officers, but in reality his men did work on their entrenchments on the night of June 7 even without implements. They were able to complete them when the tools arrived on the eighth. French's men dug skirmish pits big enough for four to six men located 150 yards in front of their main line and placed the pits ten to fifteen paces apart.[20]

Johnston instructed Polk to cut a military road parallel to his line of works "as much under cover and out of observation of the enemy as possible." The army leader also ordered Col. Moses H. Wright, commander of the post of Atlanta, to use black laborers and available engineer troops to strengthen the fortifications guarding the railroad crossing of the Chattahoochee on June 10. That key crossing lay only thirteen miles south of his current position along the Mountain Line.[21]

As both sides settled in across the Georgia countryside, skirmishers and artillerymen dominated the no-man's-land between them. Members of the 21st Wisconsin in the Fourteenth Corps tore down a small barn and cut the logs into sections eight feet long. The logs, which were at most ten inches wide, were then carried forward to a ridge and used to make V-shaped breastworks for skirmishers, using four logs for each position. They spread fifteen such enclosures along the front of the regiment. The breastworks were about three and a half feet tall, with chinking between the two upper logs for the men to point their

Mountain, Gilgal Church, and Mud Creek Lines

musket barrels through the slit. Each position was about thirty yards from its neighbor and big enough to hold up to ten men. This was an innovative way to protect the skirmish line, as the men could fire right and left oblique with ease.[22]

Along the Sixteenth Corps line, some Union artillerists pushed a couple of pieces forward to a point just behind their own skirmish line and pounded the rail breastworks that shielded the Confederate skirmishers. At times the projectiles managed to upset the rails, forcing the Rebels to run for their lives as Union skirmishers took potshots at them. Close to Lost Mountain, a Federal shell crashed through the parapet held by the 54th Georgia and exploded. Fragments broke Sgt. Clay Elkins's thigh and dug into his back. But Elkins raised himself up and shouted, "They have killed me boys, but don't give up, hold your own." He died a few hours later in the hospital.[23]

Elkins's commander fretted at the long length of the Mountain Line and the exposed position of Bate's Division on Pine Mountain. Johnston's idea was to hold the main line from Gilgal Church to Brush Mountain with as few troops as possible and create a reserve force to either support Bate, protect the army's right flank if the Yankees tried to turn it, or take offensive action if the opportunity arose. Hood reported on June 13 that his sector could be bolstered with more artillery to compensate for reduced infantry strength, and he could hold his corps line with only 5,000 men. On that same day, Johnston asked Polk to offer an opinion on how he could hold the sector assigned his Army of Mississippi with the least number of troops. After a quick consultation with division leaders, Polk reported early that afternoon that he could secure his part of the line with about 5,000 troops, representing one-third of his available strength. That would free up 10,000 men to take the offensive or to act as a reserve for any part of the line. Polk then rode to Johnston's headquarters for further discussion.[24]

Johnston committed himself to the move on the evening of June 13, issuing orders for Polk to extend his line to the right and fill the trenches soon to be vacated by Hood's Corps. Johnston intended to free up Hood's entire command and mass it near the right flank as a reserve. Polk's left flank would remain where it was near Gilgal Church, but the rest of his Army of Mississippi would hold at least half of the Mountain Line. Hardee still worried that Bate was too exposed for comfort, even with a considerable reserve to back him up, so Johnston planned a personal inspection of the position on Pine Mountain early on the morning of June 14 with Polk and Hardee.[25]

It had rained every day since June 8, but the morning of the fourteenth dawned clear and bright. As Johnston, Polk, and Hardee observed the scene from the top of Pine Mountain, Sherman also happened to be riding along the

Union line opposite that height. He was formulating plans to push Thomas's Fourth and Fourteenth Corps through the gap between Pine Mountain and Kennesaw Mountain and break the Mountain Line in one decisive thrust. Sherman noticed the group of gray-clad officers on top of the hill but did not realize who they were. He gave an order for Capt. Peter Simonson's 5th Indiana Battery to fire and rode away as it was being done. Polk was hit as a round went completely through his chest, killing him instantly. William W. Loring temporarily took command of the Army of Mississippi and executed the shift of troop strength later that day as planned. But the inspection, and Polk's gory death, led Johnston to evacuate Pine Mountain as well. There seemed little need to maintain Bate's Division there if the main line to the rear was well protected. The Confederates, many of whom were saddened and disheartened by Polk's death, evacuated the mountain on the night of June 14.[26]

The break in the weather was only temporary, as rain once again became a serious problem for the armies in Georgia. It often was "a steady Cold rain," as Sherman reported to his wife. The downpour "vastly retarded" his attempt to break or push past Johnston's new position on the mountains.[27]

As the armies again became static, siege conditions appeared along the Mountain Line. In the Fourteenth Corps sector, the Federals were lodged too close to the Confederates to send out a skirmish line. They had to make their coffee in the trench because any movement to the rear of the main line brought a bullet. Nevertheless, truces were possible. Lt. John Henry Otto of the 21st Wisconsin reported that all one had to do was place a "rag on a stick, plant the stick on the breastwork and holler: 'Hello Johnny!'" This brought a response: "Hallow Yank! Time for breakfast." The informal cessation of hostilities usually lasted about forty-five minutes and ended with "Hello! Yank, or Johnny! Time is up! Look out."[28]

If truces were not possible, the men just had to endure the fire that came with close proximity to the enemy. Chesley A. Mosman in the Fourth Corps complained on June 12 that "there ain't no fun in eating, sleeping and laying round or walking about all the time and for days and nights together in a fusillade of bullets that are eternally sissing by one, sleeping or waking, and you can't tell what moment you will be in eternity." The next day, Mosman adjusted himself to the situation. "We go right along about our duty or business in camp regardless of the bullets. It seems to be just as safe one place as another."[29]

By mid-June, Johnston's men had dug so many trenches "back and forth across this country until many think we are digging 'our last ditch,' and that here we must fight." Instead of fighting they endured day after day of rain, mud, and misery. The water collected in these freshly dug trenches, turning them into

Mountain, Gilgal Church, and Mud Creek Lines

mud pits. Members of the 27th Alabama became covered with red clay from top to bottom and were "a pitiable spectacle," according to J. P. Cannon. The forced exposure to the elements in unhealthy conditions produced a sharp rise in the number of men reporting sick to the field hospitals of Johnston's army.[30]

THE GILGAL CHURCH LINE

When the Federals ascended the slopes of Pine Mountain early on the morning of June 15 they found Confederate fortifications that were "heavily constructed with flanking works and embrasures for artillery," as division commander Alpheus Williams put it. The occupation of the eminence was an incremental advance for the Yankees, and Gilgal Church now became the focus of operations. Like Pine Mountain, the Confederate position at the church represented a salient in the line, which continued to stretch eastward to Brush Mountain. The Gilgal Church Line was ten miles long. Thomas worked forward carefully until his artillery could obtain a cross fire from the east on Cleburne's Division, which held the church area, and Schofield worked forward in an attempt to turn Cleburne's left. Thomas's chief of staff urged Howard and Hooker to use their artillery on the enemy earthworks "to destroy them, or at least render them untenable." Battery commander Simonson, whose guns had killed Polk on June 14, was in turn killed by a Confederate sharpshooter on June 16.[31]

The Confederate works at Gilgal Church were elaborate because of the exposed nature of the position. The line ran just north of Gilgal Primitive Baptist Church on inferior defensive ground that was lower than the ground occupied by Hooker's Twentieth Corps troops to the north. The Confederates had a field of view only about 100 yards forward. Good troops had to hold well-made defensive works tenaciously to maintain a position like this, which was far less attractive than the one Johnston had abandoned at Cassville nearly a month before.[32]

Extensive archaeological digs of the slight remnants of Cleburne's line at Gilgal Church reveal a good deal about the position. The Confederate trench was six feet wide at the bottom. Along at least one segment of the line, the Rebels had dug a gutter along the floor of the trench toward the bottom of a swale and then run the rainwater through a drain under the parapet to get it out of the trench. The drain was lined with large rocks. A fire step, or banquette, three feet wide also was placed in the trench, and the Confederates dug three steps at one point to take the trench up a steep slope.[33]

The archaeologists discovered no evidence of food consumption in the works at Gilgal Church but they found numerous dropped, unfired bullets, about one every two feet at the highest density. In contrast, they found only two fired bullets, presumably Federal rounds. The archaeologists also uncovered quite a lot of evidence of bullet manufacturing in the trenches in the form of melted slugs of lead. The Confederates also were shaving the soft lead balls, an indication of whittling. A total of twenty-eight "modified" bullets were found, ranging from those that had teeth marks in them to those cut into segments and one that seemed to have been carved into a pig's head. The normal assortment of buckles, hardware from accoutrements, and buttons were also found. The material evidence seems to indicate that Cleburne's men were fastidious eaters, loaded their weapons in the trenches (dropping a lot of ammunition in the process), received comparatively little accurate fire from the Federals, and whiled away their time crouching in their deep trenches whittling musket balls.[34]

Hooker's men also couched low in their works opposite this Confederate position for a couple of days, digging three successive lines of trenches about 300 yards from Gilgal Church. Today these Union works are in relatively poor shape, but distinct enough to show that the forward line was located just north of the crest of a low ridge; the second is only about twenty yards behind and at a diagonal to the first. The third line is about the same distance behind the second and roughly parallel to it. The Federals relied heavily on artillery rather than large-scale infantry action to reduce the Rebel salient at Gilgal Church.[35]

Sherman grew increasingly frustrated at the slow pace of operations. He complained to Halleck that the men "seem timid in these dense forests of stumbling on a hidden breast-work." His chief concern was Thomas's Army of the Cumberland, "which is dreadfully slow. A fresh furrow in a ploughed field will stop the whole column, and all begin to intrench. I have again and again tried to impress on Thomas that we must assail & not defend. We are the offensive, & yet it seems the whole Army of the Cumberland is so habituated to be on the defensive that from its commander down to the lowest private I cannot get it out of their heads."[36]

Sherman was a bit harsh on Thomas and his men, for no other part of his army group worked harder against the stout Confederate works than the Army of the Cumberland. Johnston complained to the authorities in Richmond that the Federals were "approaching by fortifying. I can find no mode of preventing this." Thomas's men, especially Fourth Corps troops, worked assiduously during this phase of the Atlanta campaign to make progress bit by bit. They advanced heavy skirmish lines that at times amounted nearly to a line of battle, lodging the skirmishers as close to the Confederates as possible to acquire an important bit of ground, then moving up more men to hold and consolidate the new position. These men could then deliver oblique fire on other parts of the

Rebel line to help their comrades move up, too. In this way the Federals crept forward in small stages, especially along the Fourth and Twentieth Corps sectors. Thomas was personally involved in this process, probably because he was stung by complaints from Sherman about his army. He offered advice about how to accomplish small advances with minimal losses. After Sherman learned the details, he softened his attitude toward the Cumberland army a bit. "General Sherman is at last very much pleased," Thomas informed his subordinates on June 18. "Our consciences approve of our work, and I hope all will go right."[37]

Geary's division of Hooker's corps lodged troops only fifty yards from the Confederate main line on the evening of June 15, but it was dangerous to build works so close to the enemy. "The sound of an ax was the signal for a volley of bullets and canister," Geary reported, "but by cutting timber some distance in the rear, and carrying it up by the help of old logs, and the creative use of the spade, a tolerable line of irregular intrenchments was thrown up in our front during the night." It was essential to devise some way to protect skirmishers in this close range combat, and Hooker suggested that his subordinates use three logs, about eight and a half feet long and eighteen inches wide, digging one end in the ground to make a ministockade with loopholes cut into it.[38]

A good deal of work involved in this process of moving forward by inches took place at night, and the darkness multiplied the difficulties of maneuvering men and resources. Commanders and their staff members had to work out plans for exactly how, when, and where to make such moves hours beforehand, then filter the details down to their subordinates well before dusk. Fourth Corps troops were instructed to "blaze well the trees, indicating the line of movement and the position to be taken" before a move on the night of June 16. Chesley Mosman led his pioneers as they constructed a new line that night for Fourth Corps skirmishers, located on a hill in open woods only eighty yards from Confederate skirmishers. The men were guided by the sound of chopping and the glint of moonlight off the axes. They cut trees fifteen to twenty-four inches in diameter, making logs from twenty to thirty-five feet long. Using spikes, they then lifted them into a long pile to serve as the base of the parapet. Mosman's pioneers constructed a work 150 yards long and three feet tall that night.[39]

THE MUD CREEK LINE

By the evening of June 16, Thomas and Schofield managed to position their resources to have a good chance of making the Gilgal Church salient untenable, and Johnston ordered the Confederates to evacuate the works. Hardee gave up the entire line from Gilgal Church to Lost Mountain on the night of June 16 and retired to a good position along the east side of Mud Creek, four miles due west of Marietta. Loring's Army of Mississippi held the north-facing line from the creek eastward, with Hood to his right. From Mud Creek to Brush Mountain, the Confederate line remained unchanged.[40]

The next morning offered the Federals an opportunity to examine the works at Gilgal Church. Sherman called the entire position vacated by his enemy "some six miles of as good field-works as I ever saw." Harvey Reid of the 22nd Wisconsin in Hooker's corps termed the Gilgal Church defenses "one vast fort," with parapets of logs and red clay that were six to ten feet thick, adorned with head logs. The parapets "were packed solidly together with dirt and would have resisted a heavy artillery fire," thought another member of Hooker's command. There were sharpened stakes in front of the works. These field fortifications were much stronger than Hooker's men had imagined them to be, and everyone breathed a sigh of relief that they had not been called on to attack. As George F. Cram of the 105th Illinois put it, "Our troops marched on inwardly thanking God, and giving cheer after cheer as they successively filed by the work."[41]

The Confederate pullback greatly altered Johnston's position. Hardee took post along the east bank of Mud Creek, connecting with Loring's line at a point just east of the headwaters of the creek. Unfortunately for the Confederates, this point constituted a very sharp angle in the six-mile-long position, more vulnerable than Pine Mountain and Gilgal Church combined. Samuel French, whose division was responsible for this angle, reported that it was about eighty-five degrees in respect to the two connecting lines, "liable to be enfiladed and taken in reverse." Johnston was worried about this angle, which was the weakest part of any line he had so far assumed during the campaign, and he began to plan for another fallback as soon as possible. Presstman selected a new position to incorporate the peaks of the Kennesaw Mountain range only two miles outside Marietta on June 17. Loring ordered that all the pioneers of the Army of Mississippi who were not already engaged were to be sent to Kennesaw with a couple of engineer officers and tools to begin digging the Kennesaw Line.[42]

The Federals spent two days, June 17 and 18, working up to the Mud Creek Line. Howard accumulated five batteries to fire on the Rebel works for half an hour, beginning at 5:00 P.M. on June 17. He then advanced infantry to capture the enemy skirmish line. That night, his men reversed and strengthened the captured works. The five batteries advanced 700 yards to be closer to the new position. On the night of June 18, Capt. George W. Spencer took the pioneers of Charles Harker's brigade and made artillery emplacements on the captured Confederate skirmish position for four guns of Battery M, 1st Illinois Light Artillery. These pieces were now in place to enfilade nearly a mile of the Mud Creek Line because of the sharp angle in the Rebel works.[43]

Farther east of the angle, Absalom Baird's division of the Fourteenth Corps advanced a heavy skirmish line across open ground, the men crawling as they moved forward. The skirmishers began to dig in on the crest of a rise of ground, "facing directly into the embrasures of the rebel batteries," in Baird's words. Capt. Hubert Dilger's Battery I, 1st Ohio Light Artillery, moved up with the advanced line to provide fire support as the men dug their works 500 yards from the main enemy trench. "I had obtained a magnificent position and lost 40 men in so doing," Baird reported.[44]

Even though the Seventeenth Corps had remained relatively static for days on the far left of Sherman's line, the troops there also continued digging new works whenever there was an opportunity to gain some advantage over the enemy. Pioneers constructed a new redoubt from 10:00 A.M. until dusk on June 17; then Capt. William Z. Clayton moved the guns of his 1st Minnesota Battery into "Clayton's fort" that night. Curtains were constructed to protect the guns from flank fire.[45]

As the rain continued, life within the newly dug trenches became very difficult. The works filled with water, in places up to the top, and the men had to stand in them as best they could because there was no safe place outside. W. L. Truman noted that Federal fire covered the ground for 200 yards to the rear of his battery's works in French's Division.[46]

On the other side of no-man's-land, Joseph W. Kimmel of the 51st Ohio in the Fourth Corps recalled that he and his comrades dug a new trench 300 yards from the Confederates and then "crouched down in the ditch about as close together as sardines in a box, while the rain pelted down filling the ditch with water." By dawn the next day the accumulated water was up to their waists, and by evening the "ditch overflowed." After the rain stopped, conditions in the trench eventually improved as the water soaked down into the earth. When Kimmel and his comrades were relieved, they had spent thirty-six hours in the newly dug earthwork, twenty-four of those standing in water. Upon leaving, Kimmel realized he could not walk because of cramps. He had to crawl along the muddy ground for a while until two comrades picked him up and carried him to the rear.[47]

Conditions were just as bad on the Twentieth Corps sector along the west side of Mud Creek. Geary's skirmishers dug pits on the low bottomland of the stream, with the Rebel main line on high ground east of the water. The Federal main line occupied higher land, but the ground was nearly as soft because of the continual rain. "Our skirmish pits were filled with water," Geary reported, "and the occupants suffered much from cramps." Eventually the bottomland flooded as the creek rose, forcing the skirmishers to retire. Chilly winds made life uncomfortable for everyone along the stream.[48]

Nevertheless, soldiers at various places along the Mud Creek Line were able to arrange informal truces to ease the discomfort for a short while. On the Fourteenth Corps sector, skirmishers on both sides of no-man's-land organized a truce that lasted two days. At times it was so quiet along the line that the Federals could hear Rebel artillery moving some distance away and heard singing at a nearby worship service. Individuals met in small groups halfway between the skirmish lines to talk and trade.[49]

Federal efforts against the salient in the Mud Creek Line intensified on June 18. From the north and west, Fourth Corps and Twentieth Corps troops advanced to capture sections of the Confederate skirmish line and to obtain positions for delivering cross fire of artillery. French's Division fired a total of 43,000 rounds of small-arms ammunition that day while holding the vulnerable salient, compared to 4,390 and 4,000 rounds fired by the other two divisions of Loring's Army of Mississippi. French also lost 215 men that day, with Capt. Henry Guibor's Missouri Battery suffering thirteen casualties. On Hardee's line, Andrew Jackson Neal of Capt. Thomas J. Perry's Florida Battery reported intense skirmish fire that nearly decimated his unit. "To look one moment over the works was to draw a hundred bullets around your head. I am confident I had my cap shot at a thousand times." Perry lost 10 percent of his men in one day of sniping.[50]

The Mud Creek Line seemed untenable so Johnston shifted Stewart's Division to the rear of the angle as a second line of support. He also ordered a pullback on the night of June 18. The Confederates evacuated the Mud Creek Line that night and took position on Presstman's Kennesaw Mountain Line. Early on the morning of June 19, the Federals surveyed the abandoned works and pronounced them to be formidable. Sherman continued to fume at the delay in moving across the Georgia landscape, encountering one strong position after another. "The troops seem timid in these dense forests of stumbling on a hidden breastwork," he complained to Halleck. But his men were doing very well considering the circumstances. Little more could be expected of them, except perhaps an all-out attack, which Sherman was as yet unwilling to sanction.[51]

Mountain, Gilgal Church, and Mud Creek Lines

6

The Kennesaw Line

Johnston took up the ninth fortified position his army constructed during the Atlanta campaign on the night of June 19–20. He placed Loring's Army of Mississippi squarely on the twin-peaked mountain called Kennesaw. Hood's Corps aligned to Loring's right, crossing the vital Western and Atlantic Railroad to the northeast, while Hardee's Corps stretched the position southward from Loring across Noyes Creek.[1]

Kennesaw was a ridge two miles long. Big Kennesaw rose 691 feet from the level of the surrounding area, while Little Kennesaw stood at 400 feet. The much smaller Pigeon Hill, which was connected to the south side of Little Kennesaw, was 200 feet tall. The heights gave Johnston's men a commanding view across the countryside for about twenty miles. The Confederate line was then seven miles long, but later, after it was extended farther south to confront Sherman's attempt to flank the left, it grew to be nine miles long.[2]

The Confederates initially began working on the Kennesaw Line as early as June 17, when they still occupied the Mud Creek Line. Hood sent Stewart's pioneers to the top of the mountain to "cut out a line of battle" through the scattering trees. Presstman marked out the exact location for the trenches, with help from Hardee's engineer, George H. Hazlehurst, and other officers. According to Hazlehurst, black laborers helped to dig the works. They must have been present in very small numbers, for no one else indicated their contribution to what became Johnston's strongest fortified position thus far in the campaign.[3]

In fact, it was impossible to rely on black laborers to construct this line;

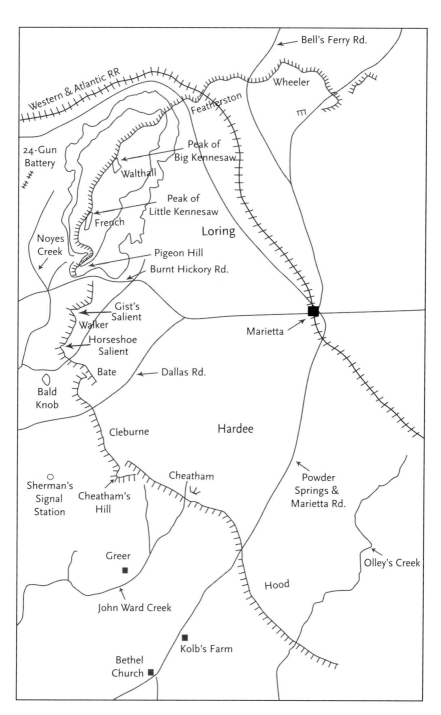

Kennesaw Line

there were far too few of them and far too little time. Johnston also did not have enough engineer troops to dig the works, although Loring dispatched a company of them to help French construct fortifications. The infantrymen and artillerymen themselves had to build the Kennesaw works. French also was in need of more tools, but Loring told him that the other divisions under Brig. Gen. Winfield S. Featherston and Walthall in his Army of Mississippi were equally short of instruments. "Hurry up the defenses along your line" despite the problems, he urged French on June 20.[4]

Loring's men on top of the two Kennesaws used rocks to start their parapet before tools arrived to allow them to dig a trench. The work continued for a couple of days, but French was not satisfied with the line held by Claudius W. Sears's Mississippi Brigade. Sears wrote a long explanation for his commander on June 21, explaining that his men were stretched into a single rank with "wide intervals" between them to cover the long sector assigned his command. The ground on Little Kennesaw was "exceedingly difficult, precipitous, and rocky country." When the tool wagon arrived at French's headquarters, Sears was able to obtain only a handful of spades and shovels, and no axes became available until late afternoon on the twenty-first. His men were unable to work in positions exposed to Federal view except at night. "Officers and men are greatly fatigued," Sears complained, "and in a great measure disabled through want of rest." The exasperated officer concluded that "we were taxed beyond our abilities."[5]

Sears and his men were feeling the strain of six weeks of campaigning, and most other units in the Confederate army felt the same way. The men did the best they could, and Sears would not have written his testy explanation except for French's complaint.

French's gunners were eager for action. Maj. George S. Storrs, who led an artillery battalion, saw Little Kennesaw as a wonderful platform for his guns. He wanted to use the elevated position to harass and disrupt the Federals through long-range fire. Storrs also reasoned that he could drop plunging fire onto Union troop formations and break up any attack directed toward the mountain. The peak of Big Kennesaw offered little room for guns, but the top of Little Kennesaw was more level and could accommodate quite a few pieces.[6]

Storrs initially placed Capt. James A. Hoskins's Mississippi Battery on top of Pigeon Hill, and Capt. Henry Guibor's Missouri Battery and Capt. John J. Ward's Alabama Battery in reserve to the rear of Little Kennesaw. Then he examined Little Kennesaw in company with an engineer and the division inspector general on June 20. The group knew that Johnston's engineers had already pronounced Little Kennesaw unsuitable for artillery because the existing road up the mountain was too steep and too exposed to Federal view. But Storrs believed he could cut a new road up the slope shielded from Federal eyes and pull as many as twenty guns to the top with ropes. French was eager to try the experiment with only one gun; when Storrs accomplished the feat, he authorized his aggressive subordinate to take more. Johnston's artillery chief, Brig. Gen. Francis A. Shoup, refused to send three more batteries when requested, so French had to work only with his division artillery. Storrs prepared to send Guibor and Ward up as French arranged for the infantry to dig works for them on top of Little Kennesaw. The infantrymen asked the gunners to stake out their own positions; then they dug the emplacements and helped the artillerymen carry ammunition up the mountain.[7]

The Federals were in for a rude shock on the morning of June 21 when two batteries of Confederate artillery opened fire from a position 400 feet above the plain. There were no Union guns immediately available to return fire, so Storrs was able to carefully pick his targets. He chased away Union wagon trains, caused the Federals to take down all their tents (because they offered readily viewed targets), and even ran his pieces out of the works and forward down the slope a bit to obtain better positions. When Storrs aimed at the Union earthworks, he found that even at his lowest depression of range he could not hit those near the base of Little Kennesaw. Then his men lessened their powder charge and began to plop shells onto the works.[8]

"It was a genuine field-day for our battalion," Storrs gleefully recalled years later, and he accepted the admiration of many general officers who climbed up to the top of Little Kennesaw to see the show that day. Shoup admitted that he was wrong and offered more guns, but Storrs refused to accept them. He fully understood that the Yankees would concentrate on his position and open a heavy fire the next day, and that is exactly what happened. From that point on, no one dominated the artillery contest near Little Kennesaw Mountain, but Storrs kept about eight guns on the height as long as Johnston held the line.[9]

Elsewhere along the Kennesaw position, opposing artillerists faced off on ground that was more level. Lumsden's Alabama Battery took position on the night of June 19 at a place near a concentration of Union guns. The men worked from midnight until dawn to thicken the parapet and construct good embrasures. They also dug two parallel trenches so that the wheels of the caisson could be lowered into them. In this way, the caisson was close behind the work and somewhat protected. They placed the limber chests loaded with ammunition on the caisson as well as on the ground behind the work. It was a mistake to concentrate so much equipment and ammunition close to the fortification, for the next day a hail of Union fire battered the work. A shell sailed directly through one embrasure, killed a gunner, and set fire to a caisson that had three limber chests resting on it. The battery lost quite a lot of ammunition as a result of the fire.[10]

On the picket line in front of the Confederate works, it was necessary to construct some sort of protection. The men of Bate's Division, located south of Noyes Creek, initially made shelters of rails that were effective in stopping bullets, but artillery rounds shattered the frail structures. As soon as entrenching tools became available, the Confederates dug pits and piled up parapets that were more resistant to cannon fire.[11]

Loring wanted a military road constructed just east of Kennesaw Mountain to connect the different brigades of his command. The looming heights prevented easy transit directly along the trench line, and there was no civilian road conveniently located at the foot of the mountain. Loring instructed his engineer officer to connect the new military road to the line at both ends of the mountain, make it suitable for both wagons and artillery, and cut roads from it up the slope of the eminence to connect with each brigade along the line of the Army of Mississippi.[12]

CHEATHAM'S HILL

The weakest point of Johnston's Kennesaw Line proved to be a sharp salient held by Cheatham's Division of Hardee's Corps. Cheatham was ordered to prolong Cleburne's Division line on June 19 and sent Brig. Gen. Alfred J. Vaughan's Tennessee Brigade to do so. On the night of June 20, Cheatham deployed the rest of his division to continue the line southward from Vaughan's position. Brig. Gen. George Maney's Tennessee Brigade found it necessary to conform to a sharp angle in the line that had been staked out by the engineers. The shallow ridge that the Confederates occupied ended at a branch of John Ward Creek and continued on the other side some distance to the rear. The right wing of Maney's Brigade held the angle thus created; only the four right companies of the 1st and 27th Tennessee (consolidated) faced west, while the remainder of Maney's men faced south. The rest of Cheatham's Division continued the line south of the branch.[13]

There was nothing Cheatham could do but adjust to the difficult segment of his line. Yet, when the light of day dawned on June 21, he realized that the trench was ill placed to protect the rise of ground just north of the branch that would become known as Cheatham's Hill. The engineers had staked out the line in the dark and did not realize that it was placed a bit too far back from the military crest of the slope. The men could not see more than sixty or seventy-five yards ahead before the ground sloped off into another branch of John Ward Creek that ran roughly parallel to the Confederate line. There was, in short, a certain amount of "dead space" in front of Cheatham's Hill not adequately seen or covered by the defender. Union guns already were playing on the position, so Cheatham did not feel comfortable ordering his men to adjust the line forward.[14]

George H. Hazlehurst, the engineer on Hardee's staff, spoke freely about the quality of Johnston's Kennesaw Line to his brother-in-law, James Cooper Nisbet of the 66th Georgia in Walker's Division. "He said it was excellent except at two or three points," Nisbet wrote of Hazlehurst, "where the contour of the ridge was such we were compelled to have salients."[15]

Trouble spots aside, everyone admitted that the Kennesaw Line was the strongest yet seen in the campaign. The engineers chose the ground well and were careful (except at Cheatham's Hill) to stake it out along the military crest wherever possible. The Confederates constructed redoubts on the high ground and connected them with infantry trenches. Interestingly, they built many traverses along the line, connecting them with the trench, to provide flank protection wherever needed. Traverses had appeared as early as the Resaca phase of the Atlanta campaign, but there were many more of them along the Kennesaw Line than at any previous position of Johnston's army. Moreover, an innovation appeared in the Kennesaw works not yet seen previously in the war: the construction of in-trench traverses. These consisted of short segments of filled-in trench to prevent the enemy from firing down the length of the open trench. The presence of many traditionally designed traverses (placed out of the trench and stretching to the rear) plus the innovation of placing traverses within the trench itself resulted from the lengthy occupation of the Kennesaw Line. The men had time to build and experiment. But it also was indicative that the Army of Tennessee was learning how to fortify its positions in a more sophisticated, complex fashion as the campaign progressed.[16]

The Confederates also devoted considerable energy to placing obstacles in front of the Kennesaw Line. Hood issued an order for all his division commanders to make "very formidable" abatis, and Federal troops often reported the presence of sharpened stakes and brush in front of the enemy works. South of the Dallas Road, the men of Brig. Gen. Daniel C. Govan's Arkansas Brigade in Cleburne's Division took advantage of "hundreds of black jack saplings" that stood in front of their line. They used jackknives to cut off the tips of the limbs and then whittled them into points. The result was an obstruction "so sharp and close it would have been an uphill business for a rabbit to creep through." Head logs, which had become common by this point in the campaign, also adorned the Confederate line at Kennesaw.[17]

The Kennesaw Line

When Johnston's men fell back from the Mud Creek Line on June 19, Sherman assumed they were retreating all the way to the Chattahoochee River. It soon became apparent that his assumption was wrong. In fact, reports filtered in that the enemy occupied a stronger line than any yet held in the campaign.[18]

The Federals examined the Mud Creek Line and were amazed at its appearance. Abatis shielded the front, trenches were deep and protected by a thick parapet, and underbrush in many areas contributed to the difficulties of approach. John W. Tuttle of the 3rd Kentucky in the Fourth Corps also noted that one Confederate battery emplacement was "riddled with our balls and a considerable quantity of blood and brains" marked the interior of the work. "They must have had a fine time using their artilery [sic] as we made a lead mine of all their embrasures."[19]

Moving past the Mud Creek defenses, the Federals viewed the Kennesaw Line from a distance and concluded it was a formidable position. Observers noted the good ground and the parapets made of logs, stone, and earth. Howard declared it was "stronger in artificial contrivances and natural features" than the Union position at Gettysburg. Confederate skirmishers opposing Butterfield's division of the Twentieth Corps saucily advanced before the Federals had firmly established their own position opposite the Kennesaw Line, shouting, "Let's drive in the damned Yanks, and not let them fortify to-night." Sherman had pried Johnston out of several weaker positions only to come up against the best one yet, and many Confederates seemed infused with a strong sense of defiance as a result.[20]

The weather continued to make life miserable for both blue and gray around Kennesaw. Chesley Mosman's pioneers dug a new trench through a cornfield in a drenching rain on June 19. "But the mud, it was awful and we had to shovel that mire into a ridge for a breastwork. If a man stood still in one place to shovel he would find himself stuck six inches in the sandy loam of the cornfield." Mosman concluded that too much rain was as bad for his work as it was for a farmer, "and I wish it would 'dry up.'"[21]

With each forward increment, the Federals constructed a new set of earthworks opposite the Confederate position. Seventeenth Corps troops on the far left of Sherman's line made military roads and built bridges across Noonday Creek to allow wagons and troops to move up to and away from their position. Engineer officer Oscar Malmborg estimated that the Seventeenth Corps threw up 2,000 linear feet of parapet from June 11 to 21, in addition to 2,000 feet of corduroy road and 150 feet of bridging. The troops also cut six miles of military roads through the woods to the rear of Blair's position. Along the Fourth Corps sector, the 77th Pennsylvania constructed three lines of works in twenty-four hours as it moved forward in short spurts to follow up Johnston's withdrawal from the Mud Creek Line.[22]

A sharp little fight developed over two hills near the Confederate line along the Fourth Corps sector as the Federals adjusted their position. One of them, which the Yankees called the Bald Knob, was a bare little hill located a few hundred yards in front of the Kennesaw Line and just south of Noyes Creek. It stood near one of the bulges in Johnston's position called the Horseshoe Salient. Stanley reported on the afternoon of June 20 that Confederate possession of both hills threatened his division, and Howard authorized an attack. The Federals bombarded the hills for a short while, and then Walter C. Whitaker's brigade advanced and took the hill located to the north of Bald Knob. Col. Isaac M. Kirby's brigade advanced at the same time and took Bald Knob itself. While Whitaker was trying to dig in, three of Hardee's regiments counterattacked at about 6:00 P.M. Whitaker's men were able to repel the advance, but Kirby, who was positioned on the other side of a marsh from Whitaker, was forced back. The Rebels would not give up, launching several more assaults into the night until Whitaker's men repulsed a total of seven advances. In one of them, some Confederate troops managed to capture a segment of works held by the 35th Indiana, but reinforcements drove them out.[23]

Howard insisted that Kirby advance on June 21 and recapture the ground he had lost. After an artillery bombardment of fifteen minutes, Kirby's men charged at 12:45 P.M., supported by two regiments of Thomas J. Wood's division. According to Howard's account, one of Wood's units, the 15th Ohio, led the attack. Howard was nervous about the success of the operation, and he urged Col. Frank Askew of the 15th forward before Kirby's men started their own advance; as a result, Askew cleared the hill by himself. Despite this success, Whitaker was unable to make a connection with Kirby because of the marshy ravine that separated the two brigades, so Stanley moved William Grose's brigade forward to a position where it could support Kirby.[24]

KOLB'S FARM

A much larger battle developed soon after the fight for control of Bald Knob. Hooker's Twentieth Corps tried to extend Howard's line and possibly flank Hardee's position. Hooker worked hard to stretch his line as far south as the Powder Springs and Marietta Road, with Schofield's Twenty-Third Corps covering his right flank. Johnston acted to protect this important sector as

The Kennesaw Line

soon as word arrived that Schofield had crossed Noyes Creek. Hood's Corps had taken position east of Kennesaw Mountain on June 19, covering the wagon road linking Atlanta with Chattanooga, the Western and Atlantic Railroad, the Bell's Ferry Road, and another, unnamed road farther east before refusing his line a bit for flank protection. The corps was positioned mostly along relatively level ground. Johnston felt he could spare these troops to shore up his vulnerable left flank. When Hood pulled his men out of the trenches early on June 21, Loring extended the Army of Mississippi eastward so that his old division, now led by Brig. Gen. Winfield S. Featherston, stretched at least as far as the Bell's Ferry Road. Maj. Gen. Joseph Wheeler's cavalry filled some of the other trenches Hood vacated. Johnston allowed Hood's men to rest near Marietta on the night of June 21–22 before continuing their march toward Hardee's left.[25]

The morning of June 22 dawned clear, the first dry day in some time. Hooker carefully advanced until his main line reached the vicinity of the Kolb House along the Powder Springs and Marietta Road, only four miles southwest of downtown Marietta. Alpheus Williams's division held the right, but his own right flank did not extend all the way to the road. John W. Geary's division continued the corps line northward with Daniel Butterfield's division connecting to Howard's right flank. A large open field lay before Williams and Geary, and a deep ravine ran parallel to Williams's line. Schofield advanced Milo Hascall's division to join Williams west of the Kolb House, but Cox's division of the Twenty-Third Corps was strung out to the rear to guard the junction of the Powder Springs and Marietta Road with the Sandtown Road, which led farther south. This was a key junction, demarked by the presence of Cheney's House, if Sherman intended to try to continue turning Johnston's left flank. Because there were still several hours of daylight left, Williams and Hascall each sent a regiment ahead to reconnoiter. Williams sent the 123rd New York north of the road and Hascall sent the 14th Kentucky south of the road. Both regiments took the Confederate skirmish line and some prisoners and lodged at the edge of a woods nearly due south of Hardee's left flank.[26]

The advance of these regiments triggered Hood into action. He assumed it presaged a major advance by the Federals and wanted to disrupt the move with a preemptive strike. Hood failed to inform Johnston, much less seek his approval, and threw his men into the advance without adequately scouting the terrain or the exact Union position. Carter L. Stevenson's Division held the left, straddling the Powder Springs and Marietta Road, while Thomas C. Hindman's Division held the right. Alexander P. Stewart's Division remained in reserve to the rear.[27]

When the Confederates advanced at 5:00 P.M., Stevenson did most of the fighting. His left, consisting of two brigades, entered dense underbrush and encountered stiff resistance by the 14th Kentucky, which fired heavily before retiring a short distance and then firing several more rounds at the oncoming enemy. In this way, the terrain and the Kentuckians disarrayed Stevenson's formation, forcing half his men into a slow advance. North of the Powder Springs and Marietta Road, Stevenson's right wing moved across mostly open country and steadily pushed back the 123rd New York. In fact, near the end of its withdrawal, the regiment retired "every man for himself," in the words of Rice C. Bull.[28]

But Stevenson's right wing could not surmount the obstacle posed by Williams's main line. The Federals had carefully posted three batteries on high ground to obtain a cross fire over the open terrain in front of Williams, and they now unleashed the fury of their guns. This was the decisive moment of the battle at Kolb's Farm. The Union artillery broke up Stevenson's formations. As Williams put it, the gunners "rolled them into a confused mass." The Confederates took shelter in the ravine that lay parallel to Williams's line, but the Federal artillery and infantry continued to drop rounds into the ravine for the rest of the day. When Hindman's Division advanced to the north, aiming at Williams's left wing and at Geary's right, the Federal guns had the same effect. "It was a beautiful sight to see their columns shattered and fleeing in confusion," wrote Col. James S. Robinson, the commander of Williams's leftmost brigade.[29]

The battle of Kolb's Farm was decided by the Union guns, although the infantry contributed a great deal to the disorienting fire delivered on Hood's men. It was largely an open field fight, unusual for the Atlanta campaign both in terms of the lack of fieldworks and that most of the action took place in a large cleared area. The Federals were just in the act of fortifying when Hood struck, collecting rails and loose timber when the alarm was sounded. Half the men of Col. Patrick M. Jones's brigade in Geary's division stood ready to receive the enemy, while the rest continued gathering material for the slight breastwork. Because of the Federal guns, none of the improvised and unfinished Union works were tested. When Stevenson's and Hindman's men fell back, many of them after dusk, they threw together breastworks of their own.[30]

Although Hood's ill-advised attack was repulsed, in the end he achieved the basic purpose of preventing the Federals from flanking Johnston's line. Hood settled down, extended the Confederate position south of Hardee's left flank, and blocked Sherman's attempt to enter Marietta. If he had merely assumed position and skirmished instead of attacking, he could have achieved the same result without the loss of 1,000 men. Federal casualties amounted to 250 troops.[31]

Both sides improved their field defenses over the next several days. Stewart's pioneers cut out a line of battle south of the Powder Springs and Marietta Road on June 23. Schofield's men took position along the southern side of that road, facing south to more firmly protect Sherman's right flank from Cheney's House to Kolb's Farm. Members of the 50th Ohio divided responsibilities, with the front rank standing watch as the second rank stacked muskets and went in search of fence rails. Two men of each company were responsible for stacking the rails to make a sort of fence, then leaning more rails against it on the outside. In this way they were able to make a substantial breastwork quickly, and it could be improved as time allowed.[32]

CHEATHAM'S HILL

The weakest part of Johnston's line demanded more work, too. A tall ridge stood only 400 yards away from Cheatham's Hill on the other side of the branch of John Ward Creek. Cheatham placed a skirmish line on that ridge early on the morning of June 21 and sent another regiment out to reinforce the skirmishers the next day. The Federals did not take these moves lightly; they attacked at 5:00 P.M. on June 22 and drove off Cheatham's men, securing the ridge for their own use. After Federal guns took position there, the gunners made life difficult for the Confederates, concentrating their fire especially on the angle held by the 1st and 27th Tennessee on the morning of June 24. The Confederates took this punishment all day, causing Cheatham to fear he might have to abandon the angle and pull back 300 yards to a new position at the base of the salient.[33]

But Cheatham was heartened by evidence that the Federals were unaware they were hurting his men. It seemed as if the Yankee gunners were merely trying to draw out Confederate fire to locate their batteries. Cheatham was determined to stay where he was and continued to position artillery in places where it could support his infantry at the angle. Maj. Llewellyn Hoxton placed Capt. Thomas J. Perry's Florida Battery and Capt. John Phelan's Alabama Battery under Lt. Nathaniel Venable to the south of the angle. This part of the Confederate line was held by Col. John C. Carter's Brigade and Brig. Gen. Otho F. Strahl's Brigade. These eight guns could fire on the right flank of Union troops approaching the angle. To the north, two guns of Capt. John W. Mebane's Tennessee Battery, under Lt. Luke E. Wright, held a large redoubt on Vaughan's right wing. Wright's pieces were sited to fire on the left flank of Union troops approaching the angle. A section of Capt. William B. Turner's Mississippi Battery was placed farther north to add to the converging fire protecting Cheatham's Hill.[34]

As soon as night descended on June 24, Cheatham ordered his men to strengthen their fortifications. He instructed them to work on the outside of the parapet to achieve better results, now that darkness shielded them from view of the Federals on the ridge. The men, especially those Tennesseeans holding the angle, worked with a will, because they had been impressed with the heavy artillery fire that day. The Confederates built up the parapet and constructed traverses for flank protection. Soon they had the trenches deep enough to completely cover a man while he stood straight up, with a firing step to allow him to see over the top of the parapet. They could not construct such impressive works on the skirmish line, which now was located at the foot of the slope on the eastern side of the branch valley. Here, the skirmish pits were big enough for four men each but were not connected to each other.[35]

The reinforced works at Cheatham's Hill secured the position, even though it remained a dangerous place for the rest of Johnston's stay at Kennesaw. The high command sought to bolster the men's spirits at this weakest part of the line. Hardee and Cheatham walked along the angle on June 26, telling the troops to expect an attack at any moment. Cheatham told his boys "that it was a weak place in the line, and that he didn't want a man to leave the ditches." If they were overpowered, the division leader told his men "that he would go with us to prison." After that inspiring talk, Col. George W. Gordon of the 11th Tennessee conferred with his colleagues along the line of Vaughan's Brigade and coordinated plans to have each regiment fire obliquely as well as to their front to support those units that could not see very far forward.[36]

The unfortunate placement of the Confederate trench at Cheatham's Hill could also be mitigated by the construction of obstacles in front of the work. While Maney had no time to place abatis in front of his brigade, Vaughan's men fashioned obstructions along their front. Gordon recalled that Vaughan had an abatis thirty paces deep but the Confederates had also cut many trees much farther away than the abatis. A veteran of the 34th Illinois remembered that timber was slashed for 200 to 300 feet in front of the Confederate line. The larger trees were felled toward the Union position, and the smaller trees and bushes that were left standing had sharply pointed branches. The Confederates placed head logs along Maney's and Vaughan's sectors to protect the heads of the men as they stood ready to deliver fire across the parapet.[37]

At all locations along the Kennesaw Line, men on both sides improved their earthworks at every opportunity. Chesley Mosman directed his pioneers in making revetments for the guns along the line held by William Grose's brigade. They worked at night to take advantage of the cover, piling brush on the outside of the work to have it handy. Then they crowded in the embrasures and weaved the sticks into revetment. This process was difficult and time-consuming, and normally undertaken by the pioneers or the gunners themselves. Farther north, opposite Little Kennesaw Mountain, other Federal troops were busy constructing the largest artillery concentration on either side. Dozens of Federals constructed emplacements for twenty guns on the night of June 22, and the pieces were rolled into the works the next day.[38]

LIFE AND DEATH IN THE TRENCHES

"Well, we are now soldiering in the rough," Col. Samuel Eugene Hunter of the 4th Louisiana informed a friend on June 22. "Lying in the ditches, marching at night in mud knee deep, drenched with rain almost every day, scorched by the sun when not soaked by rain, fed on corn bread and bacon, very dirty and *lousy*, shelled continuously, day after day sleeping when we sleep at all, on the ground wrapped in a wet blanket, these are the luxuries we enjoy, and all for liberty."[39]

Everyone in blue and gray who occupied a place in the developing line of fieldworks sought ways to become both comfortable and secure. On the Confederate side of no-man's-land, the Kentuckians in the Orphan Brigade, stationed with Bate between Noyes Creek and the Dallas Road, built protective shelters. Behind one salient, they dug a "line of sleeping pits down the hill in rear of our main line." But the men were annoyed by enfilading rifle fire even while occupying these pits. The headquarters of the 9th Kentucky also was protected by a separate dugout located just behind the center of the regimental sector. Half the regiment remained on watch at all times, while the other half slept in rotation.[40]

There seemed no place of safety for the men of the 9th Kentucky. "We could not show our heads outside the trenches without having a Minnie ball come whizzing at us," recalled Johnny Green, "but the boys would lay around out side notwithstanding." What Green meant was that many of his comrades became tired of the cramped conditions inside the works and were willing to risk their lives for a little bit of comfort. When Tom Wimms insisted on taking a nap just behind the line, Green admonished him to come back to the trench. "I am sleepy," Wimms replied, "for I was out there on picket all last night & I am going to have a good stretched out sleep, if they kill me for it." In less than ten minutes, Wimms was mortally wounded.[41]

North of Bate's position, division leader W. H. T. Walker constructed a lunette just behind his line for himself to live in. His staff members slept behind trees nearby. They found it relatively safe, except when they had to go to the line and deliver Walker's orders. But, no matter how well planned the works, men were hit by skirmishers, snipers, and artillery on a regular basis along the opposing lines. Absalom Baird reported that his Fourteenth Corps division lost an average of twenty men each day in killed and wounded. They were mostly shot in their camps and outside the works.[42]

SKIRMISHING

Col. Benjamin D. Fearing of the 92nd Ohio in Baird's division called skirmish fighting "the most important feature in this remarkable campaign." He provided detailed information on how his regiment conducted its skirmish operations on one day, June 21, 1864. Fearing detailed 200 men to the skirmish line and placed them under the command of his lieutenant colonel. They operated under explicit orders from brigade and division headquarters not to use their guns unless it was really necessary. Even so, those 200 men fired 24,000 rounds of cartridges during a twenty-four-hour tour of duty in the skirmish pits. The firing continued as heavily during the night as it had during the day. That amounted to 120 rounds per man or five rounds per hour by each skirmisher. Fearing was impressed by these statistics and personally investigated to see if the firing was really needed. All the officers insisted that not a shot was delivered without due cause.[43]

On the Confederate side, John Bell Hood learned a lesson from the debacle at Kolb's Farm on June 22. Two days later, he complained in a circular to his division commanders that the enemy often drove in the Confederate skirmish line and then fortified. This move rarely was the prelude for an attack by the main enemy line. He now instructed his subordinates to respond quickly but in a limited way to this tactic by retaking the skirmish line rather than launching a major attack against the Federals.[44]

Although it often was hard to differentiate between the normal operations of the skirmish line and true sniping, the use of specialized target equipment to zero in at long range was a definite indication of modern-day sniping operations. Col. Ellison Capers of the 24th South Carolina in States R. Gist's Brigade reported that his men captured a Federal who had a unique device on his gun. It was "a small looking glass attached to the butt of his musket, so that he could sit behind his breast-work, perfectly protected, with his back to us, and by looking into his glass, sight along the barrel of his piece."[45]

Artillerists on both sides of the line suffered. Capt. Cuthbert H. Slocomb's Battery, which was the only company of the famed Washington Artillery to serve in the West, took position on a bare, tall hill just north of the Dallas Road along the line of Bate's Division. It was an unpromising place, as far as gunner

Philip Daingerfield Stephenson was concerned. Intense Union artillery fire deteriorated Slocomb's earthworks, with rounds sailing through the embrasures to explode inside the work. Three of Slocomb's four guns were disabled during the time spent there, and two out of three gunners were killed or injured. Those who survived often were deafened by the explosion of enemy shells.[46]

Slocomb's men did all they could to protect the position from this galling fire. They constructed a traverse for each gun as a shield against enfilading rounds from the north. This gave the battery position something "like four little square forts, strung along 'en echelon.'" Open to the rear, these one-gun emplacements "were our homes" for days on end, as Stephenson later put it.[47]

One day the artillery exchange was especially heated, wrecking the saplings used as revetment inside the embrasures. Alex Allain bravely jumped into one embrasure to repair it. A comrade handed him an axe, and Allain "straightened and drove down the upright posts, replaced the saplings behind them," and then shoveled out the extra dirt to clear the embrasure. He did this calmly, his back to the foe in an act of defiance, and called on his comrades to hand him whatever he needed. Miraculously, Allain was not hit.[48]

Along the position held by Stanley's division of the Fourth Corps, the Confederates were so close to the Federals at one point that neither side could place a skirmish line in no-man's-land. Rebel artillery rounds penetrated the Union parapet on occasion as well. Chesley Mosman told his pioneers to stay well to the rear for their own safety, but they sent forward their tools so the infantry could use them to repair damage to the works.[49]

Rotating units in and out of the fortifications could be a tricky business. When Lt. Col. Judson W. Bishop took his 2nd Minnesota of Baird's Fourteenth Corps division to relieve another unit in the works, he did so well after dark on the night of June 22. The sky was clear, however, and the moon shone enough to light up the Yankees. Bishop told his men to "carry the gun-barrels down and under the overcoats or blankets" so the moonlight would not glint on the burnished steel. The Minnesotans moved nearly a mile in safety, but the commander of the regiment to be relieved took no precautions. His men made a good deal of noise while evacuating the works, and this drew Confederate artillery fire. A round hit the head of Bishop's column as it waited for the other unit to get out of the way, killing one man and badly wounding four others. Bishop then rushed his men into the works as fast as possible.[50]

Life along the lines at Kennesaw was not always filled with mortal danger. James Cooper Nisbet of the 66th Georgia in Walker's Division held the Horseshoe Salient between the Burnt Hickory Road and Noyes Creek. His regiment rotated with another to hold the salient in twelve-hour shifts. Nisbet was well served by his black manservant, who was named Isaac. Although Nisbet instructed him not to bring forward his meals to the works if there was artillery fire, Isaac waited until the worst of it was over and then came forward, believing his master was hungry and feeling safer when near him than when away. Isaac was the same age as Nisbet; the two had played together when young and had grown up inseparably in Georgia.[51]

Johnston was frustrated by the Federal method of operating thus far in the campaign. "By his engineering operations (rendered easy by superior numbers and the character of the country, which is densely wooded) the enemy has pressed us back," he informed the authorities in Richmond. Not only were the Yankees pressing forward, they were pressing to the south in an effort to outflank the Kennesaw Line. Johnston was unable "to stop the enemy's progress by gradual approaches."[52]

Col. Josiah Given of the 74th Ohio in the Fourteenth Corps provided a case study in the process of incremental advances, secured by good fortifications. He reported that his men took possession of partially completed works on the night of June 20 near Kennesaw Mountain. They were harassed by musket fire from the Confederate line but completed the construction to their satisfaction. Given lost no troops when Confederate artillery bombarded his position for more than an hour on the afternoon of June 21. He attributed it "to the skillful manner in which the works were built, and the prudence of the men in keeping within the works."[53]

All the digging on both sides of the line at Kennesaw took place under mostly cloudy skies. It had rained for nineteen of the previous twenty-one days, Harvey Reid of the 22nd Wisconsin reported on June 24. A member of Schofield's command announced that he had had no opportunity to wear dry clothing for more than twenty days during this phase of the campaign. A handful of lucky Federals were treated to an issue of beer, courtesy of the U.S. Sanitary Commission. Its agent, H. E. Collins, decided to distribute it to the troops in the trenches. The brew had been meant for use in the field hospitals, but the weather was too warm to keep it very long before it spoiled.[54]

Conditions were trying along the Confederate line as well. Staff officer Robert D. Smith reported that Cleburne's trenches were "becoming very filthy" by June 25, because the men were confined to the works for fear of exposing themselves to Union fire. Parts of the line lay in open fields, and on dry days the sun beat down unmercifully on the troops. The weather was becoming ever warmer as the days passed, and Smith feared that the sick list would grow if the men had no relief. Johnston, in fact, confirmed Smith's fear by June 27.

"Long and cold, wet weather, which ended five days ago, produced a great deal of sickness," he reported to Richmond.[55]

SHERMAN DECIDES TO ATTACK

The stalemate along the lines at Kennesaw lengthened until it became the longest static confrontation of the campaign thus far, and Sherman was unhappy with the lack of progress. The question of whether he should plan a frontal attack as a solution to the stalemate was discussed a great deal. As early as June 15, McPherson informed Dodge that the commander had no plan to assault Johnston's works along the Mud Creek Line. The next day, Sherman informed Halleck that he was "now inclined to feign on both flanks and assault the center. It may cost us dear but in results would surpass an attempt to pass around." He knew the Confederate position was strong but was fascinated by the fact that the Chattahoochee River lay a short distance to Johnston's rear. If the Federals could rupture the Confederate position, the Army of Tennessee might lose very heavily in manpower, supplies, and equipment as the Federals pressed its disorganized fragments against the river. It could "produce a decisive effect," in Sherman's view.[56]

Sherman continued to ponder the situation for several days while relying on incremental advances at minimal cost in lives. "We continue to press forward," he informed Washington, "operating on the principle of an advance against fortified positions. The whole country is one vast fort, and Johnston must have full fifty miles of connected trenches, with abatis and finished batteries. We gain ground daily, fighting all the time." But Sherman also seriously considered a major frontal attack, despite the strength of Johnston's defenses.[57]

A combination of factors led Sherman to order an assault. First, the weather cleared considerably after June 22, making it easier to do everything along the lines. Second, Schofield's effort to extend the Union right south of the Powder Springs and Marietta Road seemed less promising than before. Johnston extended his own line south of the road with cavalry, and there was no guarantee that a successful crossing of Olley's Creek, the next watercourse in Schofield's path, would result in the turning of the Confederate flank. Thomas reported that, at least along the Fourth and Fourteenth Corps fronts, the lines were extended as far as they ought to be. Thinning the ranks anywhere along the line to provide more troops for a flank movement might entice the enemy to strike and possibly gain control of Sherman's vital link with the north, the railroad leading to Chattanooga.[58]

By June 24, Sherman was ready to commit to a frontal effort against the Kennesaw Line. It would be the first time since Resaca that Sherman authorized major attacks against a known Confederate position. He instructed McPherson and Thomas to organize the effort, using a total of 15,000 men in eight brigades. Three points of attack were chosen: three Fifteenth Corps brigades were to hit Pigeon Hill and the saddle between it and Little Kennesaw, three Fourth Corps brigades were to strike Cleburne's Division between Pigeon Hill and Cheatham's Hill, and two Fourteenth Corps brigades were to hit the enemy at Cheatham's Hill. Schofield was instructed to cross Olley's Creek on June 26 in an effort to draw Confederate attention away from the points of attack, and the main assault columns would advance early on the morning of June 27. If successful at breaking the line, the Federals were to move directly toward the railroad and Marietta.[59]

Sherman felt as if the campaign had reached something of a crisis point. Determined to restore mobility to his bogged-down troops and anxious that further delay might tempt Johnston to shift reinforcements to Lee's battered army at Petersburg, he felt the situation called for drastic measures. Seemingly unable to stretch out further and continue flanking, the Federals now should "attack 'fortified lines,' a thing carefully avoided up to that time," Sherman wrote in his memoirs. One more attempt to flank might force the enemy to thin out his line to the point that a frontal attack could succeed. "He is afraid to come at us," Sherman wrote of Johnston to his wife, "and we have been cautious about dashing against his breastworks, that are so difficult to understand in this hilly & wooded Country. . . . Still we are now all ready and I *must* attack direct or turn the position. Both will be attended with loss and difficulty but one or the other must be attempted."[60]

7

June 27

The morning of June 27 dawned clear and warm as Federal officers moved their troops to staging areas for the attack on Johnston's Kennesaw Line. McPherson arrayed three brigades of Maj. Gen. John A Logan's Fifteenth Corps to strike at Pigeon Hill, the southern end of Little Kennesaw, and the open ground south of the hill. Brig. Gen. Charles C. Walcutt's brigade of Harrow's division was on the left, aiming at the area between Little Kennesaw and Pigeon Hill, while Brig. Gen. Giles A. Smith's brigade of Brig. Gen. Morgan L. Smith's division was in the center, aiming directly at Pigeon Hill. Brig. Gen. Joseph A. J. Lightburn's brigade of Smith's division was positioned on the right, south of the Burnt Hickory Road, ready to push forward south of Pigeon Hill into a relatively open and level area. Peter J. Osterhaus's division and the rest of Harrow's division waited in reserve. While French's Division of Loring's Army of Mississippi held the heights (Brig. Gen. Francis M. Cockrell's Missouri Brigade was responsible for Pigeon Hill), Brig. Gen. Hugh W. Mercer's Brigade of Walker's Division in Hardee's Corps held the area south of Pigeon Hill.[1]

THE FIFTEENTH CORPS ATTACK

The shallow stream of Noyes Creek flowed between the lines and offered a considerable obstacle to the Fifteenth Corps advance. Starting about 8:00 A.M. after a short artillery bombardment, Lightburn's brigade moved over an open field in two battle lines, exposed to raking artillery fire, and then plunged into a tangled thicket bordering the creek. Vines and brush tripped up the alignment, preventing Lightburn's men from seeing that the picket line of Mercer's Brigade was dug in at the eastern edge of the jungled mass about 200 yards from the creek. They did not know that Rebel pickets were in their path until they struggled to a point only twenty yards from the pits.[2]

The first Federal line, mostly the 53rd Ohio, engaged in a short but intense fight with Mercer's skirmishers, the 63rd Georgia. Frenzied hand-to-hand combat ensued in and around the pits. "Never did men show more gallantry," boasted Lt. Col. R. A. Fulton of the 53rd Ohio, "mounting the works, shooting the enemy, and beating them over their heads with the butts of their guns." The Federals took forty prisoners and cleared the Rebel skirmish line within a few minutes. The 47th Ohio came up in time to clinch the victory. Walker reported losing more than 100 men on the skirmish line that morning. "They were butted and bayoneted from the pits," he brusquely put it. In fact, at least sixteen members of the 53rd Ohio completely ruined their muskets while using them as clubs in the fight.[3]

Lightburn's men re-formed and moved eastward into an open field that lay immediately south of Pigeon Hill. Marching at least 200 yards from the Confederate skirmish line, the brigade became increasingly isolated and exposed to artillery fire on both flanks. Lightburn's movements were fully in view of the Confederates not only on Pigeon Hill but on Little Kennesaw as well. The Federals halted in the middle of the field, directly south of the crest of Pigeon Hill and about 500 feet west of Mercer's main line, and lay down for cover behind a slight rise in the terrain. Here they stayed for at least ten minutes as the left regiments of Cockrell's Brigade on Pigeon Hill directed fire into the field. French also arranged for some of the artillery on Little Kennesaw to pound targets in the field.[4]

Lightburn was too exposed to accomplish anything, and Giles A. Smith could not keep up with his advance because Pigeon Hill lay directly in his front. After a few minutes lying down in the middle of the open field, Lightburn's officers ordered their troops to pull back. Col. Wells S. Jones told the men of the 53rd Ohio to cheer as they stood up to try to fool the Rebels into thinking they meant to attack. Instead, they rushed back to the captured skirmish line of the 63rd Georgia and took shelter on the west side of the pits, holding for the time at the edge of the woods.[5]

To Lightburn's left, Giles A. Smith moved his brigade to its staging area early on the morning of June 27 and set out at about 8:00 A.M. with his men in two lines. The shallow course of Noyes Creek also interfered with his advance. The Federals struggled through nearly 400 yards of tangled bottomland be-

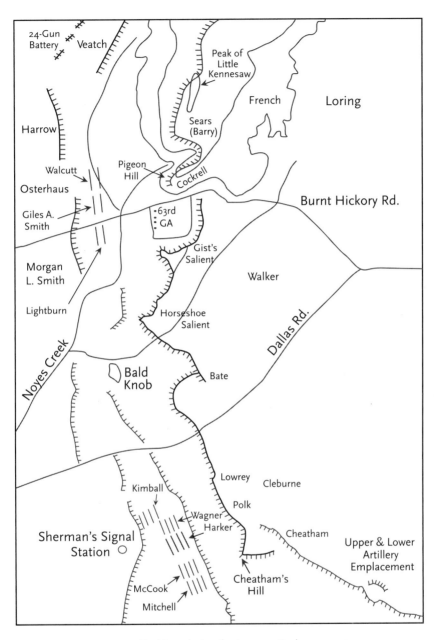

Positions during the June 27 attack

fore emerging into more open country near the west foot of Pigeon Hill. The left wing of Lightburn's brigade had pressured the left flank of Cockrell's skirmish line so much that the Confederate skirmishers began to retire from that flank and bunch up behind the center of the line. Cockrell sent out the rest of his picket reserve to bolster the flank, but then Giles A. Smith's troops hit the front of the Confederate skirmish position and the entire picket line collapsed. Cockrell lost more than forty troops in the process.[6]

Smith's men tried to ascend the rugged slope of Pigeon Hill, which was studded with rocky outcroppings and felled trees. His right wing was forced by the terrain and Confederate fire to halt at the base of the slope, but Col. Americus V. Rice's 57th Ohio in the center moved up through the tangled mass toward the consolidated 3rd and 5th Missouri, which held the center of Cockrell's main line on top of the hill. The Ohioans came to a halt anywhere from twenty-five to eighty yards short of the Confederate earthworks, unable to proceed any farther. As Lt. Col. Samuel R. Mott of the 57th Ohio reported, the felled timber formed "a species of abatis, the difficulties of which to move troops over can never be known, save to those who were there." In addition, as Giles A. Smith wrote, the Confederate fortifications were well placed just on the west side of the natural crest to enable Cockrell's men to cover the entire slope with their rifle fire. Many individuals crawled up close to the Confederate position, but it was impossible to move any considerable body of troops forward to close on Cockrell's men. The loss of officers among Smith's regiments was heavy. Even extricating the men from their advanced position was not an easy task; they were taken away in small groups by the surviving officers. Company A of the 57th Ohio was so close to the Rebel line, and so exposed, that it had to wait for dark to offer cover, and even then the company retired one man at a time.[7]

Smith's attack was blunted by the terrain, the obstructions, and the trenches on Pigeon Hill. The Federal brigade left behind many dead and wounded comrades lying very close to the Confederate works, so close that they could not be removed, and Cockrell's command took in a handful of Yankees who braved all obstacles and made it to their fortified line as prisoners. The 3rd and 5th Missouri bore the brunt of the Federal assault and suffered the heaviest casualties in Cockrell's Brigade. Portions of that consolidated regiment fired off sixty rounds of ammunition per man during the course of the action.[8]

Walcutt's brigade fared little better than Smith's, starting its attack near the left of Osterhaus's division sector in two lines. Like Lightburn's and Smith's, Walcutt's command clawed its way through the jungled mass bordering Noyes Creek and went on to capture the fortified Confederate skirmish line, taking 120 prisoners. The left wing of Walcutt's command headed toward the junction of

Little Kennesaw Mountain and Pigeon Hill, an area defended mainly by Sears's Mississippi Brigade (commanded by Col. William S. Barry). Lt. Col. George W. Wright's 103rd Illinois, on the far left of Walcutt's first line, entered the gorge between the hills with some caution because the vegetation obscured the lay of the land. Finally, the men could look to the right and see that the Confederate line paralleled their axis of advance and was located up the slope of Pigeon Hill. Portions of the 103rd redirected their advance toward the right and crossed a deep ravine before trying to climb up the steep slope toward the enemy.[9]

The 103rd Illinois was stopped by the same obstacle that prevented the rest of Walcutt's brigade from closing with the Rebels: the steepness of the slope and the well-placed Confederate line that was positioned to sweep the approach with fire. Rocks of all sizes protruded from the slope, offering obstacles to the advance as well as some shelter from bullets. Some of Walcutt's units came to ground only fifteen yards short of the objective, but many others stopped much farther away. They remained at their high tide, hugging the ground for as long as forty-five minutes before retiring. Division commander French was chagrined that the Federals lodged so close to his work at all.[10]

Walcutt pulled his men back from their high tide to a point near the start of his attack, about 800 yards from the Confederates, and re-formed the brigade. Then he advanced the command forward a bit and dug a new line of works, remaining there for the rest of the day until Osterhaus sent troops to relieve the command. Walcutt lost 246 men killed and wounded in the futile advance.[11]

THE FOURTH CORPS ATTACK

As difficult as the Fifteenth Corps assault had been, the troops of the Fourth Corps would find even worse conditions. At least most of Logan's men could see the Confederate position atop the high ground, but Howard's men had to advance across more level land that was covered with thick underbrush. As Howard's staff officer Joseph S. Fullerton put it, the "country is so thickly wooded, and the topography is such that it is almost impossible to tell anything about the enemy's works. It cannot be done by a reconnaissance, as such would be almost as fatal as an assault. The works cannot be seen before we can get right upon them." The troops would have to assault blindly and hope for the best.[12]

Howard, Thomas, and Palmer worked hard to plan the attack, selecting the best place they could for the objective point and designating John Newton's division as the attacking force. Howard relied heavily on Newton's advice to pinpoint the area of attack and approved Newton's suggestion that his brigades go forth in columns of regiments. Brig. Gen. Charles G. Harker's brigade was on the right, Brig. Gen. George D. Wagner's brigade was on the left, and Brig. Gen. Nathan Kimball's brigade was positioned on the left to act as a reserve. Newton threw 5,000 troops into this assault, about the same number Logan had used against the high ground to the north. Also like Logan, Newton had a good skirmish line leading the way, with orders to "go smack up to the rebel works and pass over them if possible," as Col. Emerson Opdycke reported. Harker ordered his men to load their muskets but not to cap them, for he did not want any halts to fire along the way. He also instructed his men to fix bayonets.[13]

The Federals were only dimly aware of it, but the shallow course of a branch of John Ward Creek lay directly in their path. It ran parallel to and about fifty yards east of the Union line and also sported a tangled mass of briars and brush. The creek bottom was about twenty feet deep and 200 yards wide, with easy slopes. When Newton's men started their advance at 8:00 A.M., the skirmish line, consisting of the 125th Ohio, made its way through this tangle and came upon the Confederate skirmishers, capturing the line and taking nearly all the Rebel pickets. Then the Ohioans moved forward until they hit a heavy abatis that fronted the Confederate line. Here the regiment lay prone as it waited for the attacking columns to close up. The Confederate line on the other side of the abatis was held by one of Johnston's best divisions, Patrick Cleburne's. Harker aimed at the left wing of Lucius Polk's Brigade and the right end of Alfred J. Vaughan's Brigade of the next division in line, which was commanded by Benjamin Cheatham. Wagner's brigade to Harker's left aimed not only at Polk's Brigade but also at the left of Col. Mark P. Lowrey's Brigade to Polk's right.[14]

Harker's hope that his command could march right over the enemy defenses and achieve a breakthrough was doomed to disappointment. As the brigade cleared the tangled bottomland and entered the cleared area before the abatis, the volume of Confederate fire was so great that the men naturally slowed their advance and began to return fire against orders. They soon took cover on the ground near the 125th Ohio. Harker, who insisted on riding his horse in the attack, tried to get the men started again. Sending a quick message to the rear that the Confederate works were formidable, he rode forward to inspire the troops. Harker was shot while waving his hat, the ball slicing through his left arm and plunging into his side. Col. Luther P. Bradley of the 51st Illinois took charge of the brigade and sent word to the rear concerning Harker's fate. Bradley also reported that the "head of his column is all smashed up and disorganized." There was no possibility of concerted action, although several Federals crawled through the abatis and tried to mount the works only to be shot or taken prisoner. Bradley recalled years later that some Confederate artillery pieces had to traverse so much as the gunners tried to rake the Union position that the cannon blast knocked out sticks from the revetment of the embrasures and sent them flying through the air. His men had the presence of mind to joke that the enemy was running out of ammunition and resorting to firing sticks at them.[15]

After about an hour of such punishment, the remnants of Harker's brigade retreated across the open space that lay between the abatis and the branch of John Ward Creek. It was a dangerous effort, exposed to concentrated enemy fire. The men retreated in haste and confusion, according to John W. Tuttle of the 3rd Kentucky. They "rushed back like an immense herd of infuriated buffaloes running over and trampling each other under foot. I was run over and badly bruised but very glad to get off so well." The brigade lost 231 killed and wounded that day.[16]

Wagner's brigade to Harker's left aimed at the right wing of Polk's line and the left of Lowrey's. It also was massed in a column of regiments, with the 57th Indiana in front as skirmishers. Wagner's troops began to receive enemy fire as soon as they scaled their own works and were pummeled the entire way because the terrain was more open than along Harker's line of advance. For 400 yards the Federals took their punishment as they moved closer to the objective. Wagner's brigade stalled before entering the abatis and, like Harker's command, remained for a while only a few yards from the Confederate line. A Rebel later told a newspaper writer how he felt while taking deadly aim at the approaching Yankees through the narrow slit between the head log and the parapet. "I was glad to see the column retreat. It looked too much like cold blooded murder to kneel there and take dead aim on a man so near that you could see the color of his eyes and hair." After a short halt, Wagner fell back to nearly the main Union line.[17]

Kimball's brigade had formed in a column of regiments to the left and a bit to the rear of Wagner's command, and then waited in reserve. When Opdycke sent word to Newton that a fresh unit could pass through Wagner's stalled brigade and possibly enter the Confederate works, the division commander ordered Kimball to go in. The brigade advanced with fixed bayonets through a tangle of brush and trees, moving to the left of Wagner's more open terrain. When it reached the eastern edge of the thicket, the lead regiment, the 74th Illinois, rushed ahead under heavy canister and rifle fire the entire way. The Illinois regiment "was swept away by it," according to Kimball. The remnants pushed on to the abatis, and the regiment's lieutenant colonel and eleven men managed to reach the Confederate parapet, where Lowrey's troops captured them. Just as the second regiment in the brigade column, the 88th Illinois, reached the edge of the woods, an order came from Newton to call off the attack. Kimball remained where he was to allow Wagner to fall back, and then he pulled his brigade back, too. Although its exposure to enemy fire was brief, Kimball's command lost 194 men killed and wounded.[18]

THE FOURTEENTH CORPS ATTACK

At the same time that Fifteenth Corps and Fourth Corps troops started their assaults, Davis sent two of his Fourteenth Corps brigades into the attack against Cheatham's Hill, just south of Newton's scene of action. The two brigades totaled about 4,000 troops and both formed a column of regiments. Col. Dan McCook's brigade was positioned on the left, its right flank opposite the sharp angle on the summit of the hill, while Col. John G. Mitchell's brigade took post to McCook's right, his left flank hitting the angle. Both brigades deployed a skirmish line of one regiment apiece.[19]

McCook formed behind the main Union line and about 580 yards from Cheatham's Hill. His column crossed the Federal works and descended the western slope of the branch of John Ward Creek into a grassy bottomland that was cleared of trees and brush. The Confederate skirmish line was positioned along the eastern edge of the bottomland in a thin fringe of trees. The skirmishers, the 85th Illinois, easily captured the Rebel skirmish pits and moved up the relatively open eastern slope of the creek, followed by the brigade column moving on the double-quick. Because Cheatham's line had been placed a bit behind the military crest of the shallow slope, his men had difficulty seeing the advancing enemy until blue-coated figures appeared within only a few yards of their main line. Regiments fired obliquely to catch the enemy in a cross fire as sheets of lead sailed down the slope into the head of McCook's column. Maj. James T. Holmes was so impressed by the rush of bullets, he imagined being able to hold up his hand and catch several in midair. A member of the 52nd Ohio, positioned last in the brigade column, suddenly lost his nerve. He turned and tried to go to the rear with an ashen face until Holmes held up his sword and threatened to strike him. Then the man returned to his place in the ranks and kept moving forward.[20]

McCook continued bravely up the slope until the van of his brigade hit the light abatis that lay in front of the parapet. The column then began to collapse because of the physical impediment to its momentum. A break developed in the right wing of each regiment in the column, and as Holmes described it, there was a "melting away of the commands in advance" of the 52nd Ohio. Holmes and other regimental officers managed to maintain the formation of the 52nd and keep moving forward through the scattered remnants of the other regiments. A disorganized mass of men who refused to fall back crowded near the abatis, and many of them tried to find a way through the brushy entanglement and onto the parapet. They suffered from rifle fire delivered on their front but also severe artillery fire raking the line of advance from the right, where Cheatham had placed two batteries to enfilade the approach to the angle.[21]

At this crisis of the attack, McCook tried to lead his men across the enemy works. He made his way through the light abatis and mounted the parapet, calling on his men to follow, but a Confederate soldier shot him in the body at close range. Deflated by the fall of their beloved commander and pelted not only by bullets and canister but rocks thrown onto their heads, the men of McCook's command began to fall back after a few minutes of futile effort to breach the position. They did not fall back to the starting point of the attack, for the Federals quickly realized that the military crest of the slope offered just enough cover to shield them. It was safer than exposing oneself for over 500 yards to reach the Union line. As a result, McCook's brigade tenuously established a new position within 60 to 100 yards of the Confederate works, barely covered by a few inches of red Georgia soil.[22]

Simultaneously to McCook's advance, Mitchell formed his brigade in a column of regiments to the right of McCook's staging area and moved forward, the 34th Illinois deployed as skirmishers. The Illinoisans also took the Confederate skirmish line on the opposite side of the branch and ascended the gentle slope, finding many small trees and saplings that had been cut and "cross-lapped," in the words of a member of the 113th Ohio, the first regiment in Mitchell's column. The plan was for each regiment in the formation to move to the right when near the Confederate works in order to extend the brigade into a battle line, and then to swing most of the line to the left and wrap around the sharp angle on Cheatham's Hill.[23]

The right flank of Maney's Tennessee Brigade held the angle, and the rest of his command extended south. Members of the 1st and 27th Tennessee in the angle saw Mitchell's men approaching and tore down the blankets they had stretched across the trench for shade, clearing the works for action. The angle was thinly held; one occupant recalled that the men were "in single file, about two paces apart." There was only a light abatis in front and some sections of the parapet had no head logs because Union artillery fire had knocked them off.[24]

The only thing that could stop Mitchell's column was stout fighting, and the Federals received heavy fire as they ascended the slope. Not only did bullets sail into the column from the front, but the right flank was exposed to pummeling from the two batteries located on Carter's brigade line to the south.

Mitchell described the fire as "terrific," and most of the musketry was delivered at a range of less than sixty yards because the defending Rebels could not clearly see the advancing Yankees until they had come relatively close to the works.[25]

The Union column nevertheless pushed through this converging fire, its ranks disordered by the exertion, the terrain, and the artillery and rifle rounds. The second regiment in the column, the 121st Ohio, did as instructed and deployed to the right of the 113th Ohio. It closed up on the Confederate works, but the other two regiments in the column failed to duplicate this movement. Mitchell's momentum ground to a halt with his command only half-deployed along one section of the Confederate works as the last two regiments in the column stopped in their tracks and went to ground for cover. The last two regiments were stalled anywhere from 50 to 150 yards from the enemy, while the other two regiments (plus many men of the 34th Illinois who had not gone back to the rear of the column as instructed) were much closer. Many of the troops who were close to the enemy tried to advance through the light abatis and onto the parapet singly or in small groups. Many of them were shot or taken prisoner on the parapet.[26]

For several minutes, Mitchell's men engaged in a furious short-range fight with the Tennesseans. Sam Watkins, one of the outnumbered defenders of the angle, admired the bravery of the Federals as they closed on the works. "It was, verily, a life and death grapple, and the least flicker on our part, would have been sure death to all." Watkins and his comrades held on to the angle with unusual tenacity. "The sun beaming down on our uncovered heads, the thermometer being one hundred and ten degrees in the shade, and a solid line of blazing fire right from the muzzles of the Yankee guns being poured right into our very faces, singeing our hair and clothes, the hot blood of our dead and wounded spurting on us, the blinding smoke and stifling atmosphere filling our eyes and mouths, and the awful concussion causing the blood to gush out of our noses and ears, and above all, the roar of battle, made it a perfect pandemonium. Afterward I heard a soldier express himself by saying that he thought 'Hell had broke loose in Georgia, sure enough.'"[27]

Federal officers were unable to organize a large movement across the works due to the losses they had suffered in the first few minutes of firing and to the natural inclination of most men to seek cover. After a while, Mitchell's troops fell back to take advantage of the military crest of the slope, as McCook's men had done. Col. Henry B. Banning of the 121st Ohio sent a message to Mitchell, who had remained in the rear, informing him of the circumstances. Mitchell sent instructions to refuse his right flank and dig in. Banning assigned half his men to dig and the rest to lay down a covering fire on the Confederate works.

Mitchell's command was roughly in line with and connected to McCook's brigade to the left.[28]

The crisis over, the Confederates in the angle could breathe more easily. "I never saw so many broken down and exhausted men in my life," recalled Sam Watkins of his comrades. "I was as sick as a horse, and as wet with blood and sweat as I could be, and many of our men were vomiting with excessive fatigue, over-exhaustion, and sunstroke; our tongues were parched and cracked for water, and our faces blackened with powder and smoke, and our dead and wounded were piled indiscriminately in the trenches." Two days later, when Watkins undressed to wash, he discovered that his arm was bruised and blistered from shooting an estimated 120 times during the course of the day on June 27. His gun had become so heated and clogged with powder residue that he had to exchange it several times for the weapons left behind by killed and wounded comrades.[29]

Survivors of Mitchell's brigade explained their failure to crack the Confederate line on the heat, the strength of the Rebel works, and the heavy losses incurred in closing on the objective. Mitchell noted in this regard that the 113th Ohio and 121st Ohio each lost nearly half their number in the short fight. As Capt. Toland Jones of the 113th Ohio put it, "We had the melancholy satisfaction of knowing that we failed only because we attempted impossibilities."[30]

The survivors of the Fourteenth Corps attack fortified industriously all day on June 27 within short musket range of the enemy. The front of the new Federal position was anywhere from fifty to seventy yards from the Confederate line. In both brigades, multiple lines appeared, as those in the rear of the column constructed their own works so that at least three trenches constituted a defense in depth. Work on the fortifications was slow because of the need to lie down. The men used bayonets, spoons, tin mess pans, and their hands to construct enough cover within an hour that they could at least raise their heads from the red dust of the slope without fearing that a bullet would find its mark. Their officers could not get entrenching tools to the forward position before dusk, slowing the work even more. When those tools arrived, the men continued improving their trenches all night.[31]

Cheatham decided to accept the presence of two Federal brigades only fifty yards from the weakest part of his division line, for in his extended position, he did not feel strong enough to sally forth and try to drive them away. He counted on the strength of his earthworks and the mettle of his men to hold the hill. The Confederates now vividly saw the ill fruit of the engineering mistake that located their line behind the military crest. The troops were forced to engage in a tedious and stressful confrontation with the enemy at Cheatham's Hill for as long as Johnston chose to remain on the Kennesaw Line.[32]

Many Federals lay wounded in the narrow space of no-man's-land, suffering in the hot sun as both sides fired relentlessly at each other over their heads. Those who could do so tried to crawl back to the new Union position. The Confederates called on a few of the wounded who lay close to the works to crawl in their direction, offering aid. But if the Federals exposed themselves to help their wounded, they often were shot by the Confederates who could not allow anyone to get close to their line. Ironically, Sam Watkins claimed that Federal fire sometimes hit the wounded unintentionally. The lines were close enough that both sides threw rocks at each other, unable to hit their targets with rifle fire because of protecting parapets.[33]

While the opposing sides at Cheatham's Hill refused to let up on their skirmish fire, it was possible to be more lenient on the Fourth Corps sector, because the Federals had fallen back nearly to their old line at the end of the attack. Intense musketry during the assault had set fire to leaves and brush, and the flames began to spread until they threatened the wounded. Lt. Col. Will H. Martin of the 1st Arkansas took it upon himself to call a halt to the firing an hour after the assault and allow the Federals an opportunity to save their men.[34]

THE HIGH COMMAND

Far from the heat, dust, and danger of Cheatham's Hill, Thomas reported to Sherman as early as 10:45 in the morning that the attacks conducted by his army had failed. When Sherman asked him early in the afternoon if he could resume his efforts, Thomas replied that the information given him by his subordinates indicated that was not possible. But Davis suggested planting batteries close to the Confederate position and bombarding it the next day. Thomas added his own suggestion to Sherman that the Federals sap their way across the narrow space of no-man's-land at Cheatham's Hill. Sherman had little faith in either suggestion. He asked Thomas if sapping would prove profitable, given the fact that the enemy could easily construct secondary lines behind the point aimed at in order to hold the position indefinitely. But Thomas reiterated in midafternoon that further assaults were out of the question. "We have already lost heavily to-day without gaining any material advantage; one or two more such assaults would use up this army." He thought that regular siege approaches were the only recourse if Sherman wanted to operate against the front of Johnston's position. He did not convince his commander, who continued to think that siege approaches were too time-consuming and bore too little promise of success.[35]

Thomas had conscientiously asked his subordinates for their advice about the feasibility of attacking again and had received discouraging replies. He instructed Howard therefore to establish a new main line along the captured Confederate skirmish pits in front of the Fourth Corps sector. Hooker also reported that he could find no weak spot in Hood's defenses along the Twentieth Corps sector and that regular approaches or a major flank movement were the only alternatives.[36]

The only glimmer of success on June 27 lay in Schofield's area of operations. Cox's division crossed Olley's Creek early that morning and with comparative ease pushed back Brig. Gen. Lawrence S. Ross's cavalry brigade. Cox advanced a couple of miles to a ridge that separated Olley's Creek from Nickajack Creek. Cox was about three miles from Cheney's House, the current right flank of Sherman's long line, but he had good defensive ground. After hearing of Cox's success, Sherman made up his mind that a major flanking movement was the right course of action. He wanted to move McPherson's entire army to join Schofield in a few days to turn Johnston's left and gain the railroad at Fulton's Station, about seven miles south of Marietta. "Go where we may we will find the breast-works and abatis," he warned Thomas, "unless we move more rapidly than we have heretofore."[37]

Flanking had been Sherman's primary mode of operating thus far in the campaign. After a brief experiment with frontal attacks, he was ready to resort to it again. Federal losses amounted to 3,000 killed, wounded, and missing on June 27, with Davis losing more than Logan or Newton. These were considerable casualties for an attacking force of about 15,000 troops. Confederate losses amounted to about 700 men.[38]

Many Federals tried to explain their failure on June 27. Howard wrote in his memoirs about "the slashings, abatis, and other entanglements, all proving to be greater obstacles than they appeared to our glasses" to account for the bloody repulse of his troops. "We realized now, as never before, the futility of direct assaults upon entrenched lines already well prepared and well manned." Thomas told Sherman that the nature of the Confederate defenses, with parapets seven feet tall and nine feet thick, was a major factor in the repulse. These works were also well manned by veteran troops.[39]

Sherman understood these reasons, but his chief engineer quietly thought differently. Poe reported to his wife that "we made a very feeble attempt to carry the rebel entrenchments by assault." Exactly why he believed the Federals had not thrown their hearts into the attack is difficult to understand. As an experienced engineer, he should have realized the effectiveness of well-made defenses. Even the poorly sited works on Cheatham's Hill withstood the attack of two brigades although the defenders were badly outnumbered.[40]

Sherman continued to justify the decision to attack at Kennesaw Mountain. He lectured Thomas on the advantages that would have fallen into his lap if the attack had succeeded. It "would have been most decisive, but as it is our loss is small, compared with some of those East. It should not in the least discourage us. At times assaults are necessary and inevitable. At Arkansas Post we succeeded; at Vicksburg we failed."[41]

"The assault I made was no mistake; I had to do it," Sherman explained to the Washington authorities on July 9. His men had fallen into the habit of relying on Sherman to work out a scheme to flank the enemy from their heavily fortified lines. These movements pried Johnston out of one line after another but failed to seriously damage the Army of Tennessee. Sherman now echoed Poe's contention by complaining to Halleck about the vigor of the attacks on June 27. "Had the assault been made with one-fourth more vigor, mathematically, I would have put the head of George Thomas' whole army right through Johnston's deployed lines on the best ground for go-ahead, while my entire forces were well in hand on roads conveying to my then object, Marietta." He placed too much emphasis on the fact that Harker and McCook had fallen early in the attacks of their respective brigades, believing that the assaults would have succeeded if they had lived.[42]

Irritated by newspaper criticism, Sherman told his wife, "I was forced to make the effort, and it should have succeeded, but the officers & men have been so used to my avoiding excessive danger and forcing back the Enemy by strategy that they hate to assault, but to assault is sometimes necessary, for its effect on the Enemy." He confided to his wife that the prolonged contact of the campaign was changing his attitude. "I begin to regard the death & mangling of a couple thousand men as a small affair, a kind of morning dash—and it may be well that we become so hardened." Yet he was firmly committed to a campaign of maneuver rather than assault. "I have no idea of besieging Atlanta, but may cross the Chattahoochee & circle round Atlanta breaking up its Roads." Sherman was confident of his army group's ability to handle Johnston in an open battle, but there would be no butting against stout earthworks anymore. "We cannot afford the losses of such terrible assaults as Grant has made" in Virginia.[43]

"We lost nothing in morale by the assault," Sherman told Grant, and he was mostly accurate in assessing the result of his failed effort to crack open Johnston's position at Kennesaw. The most important points were that the losses of June 27 were bearable and Sherman had learned his lesson. The tedious, time-consuming operations of flanking were the order of the day for the rest of the campaign.[44]

8

Flanking the Kennesaw Line

Even though the failed attack of June 27 finally convinced Sherman that flanking was the key to getting Johnston out of the Kennesaw Line, he needed several days to plan and execute the risky move. It meant breaking contact with the railroad once again and moving the bulk of his troops farther away from it, because the Union line already was stretched to the breaking point. The move promised success, but Sherman could not afford to make it without thorough preparation.

CHEATHAM'S HILL

Meanwhile, for nearly a week, the opposing armies remained locked in their earthen homes within easy rifle and artillery range of the enemy. The situation was most tense at Cheatham's Hill, where the troops were within a stone's throw of each other. The Federals mounted an effort to close in even further on the Confederate position, employing siege approaches to crowd the enemy in a face-to-face confrontation. On June 28, Lt. Col. James W. Langley of the 125th Illinois recruited a corporal to help him advance the line on the left center of McCook's position. He and the noncommissioned officer crawled out under cover of night and quietly began digging a new position twenty yards forward of the first line. Langley had the idea of using empty hardtack boxes as temporary shelter while they dug, filling a box with dirt and using it as a shield. It worked, and more men brought forward empty boxes until the new line was long enough for an entire regiment. It was only sixty-eight feet (about twenty-two yards) from the Confederate works. The Federals had moved beyond the military crest of the slope and were "rather too close for comfort," according to a Rebel staff officer.[1]

Both sides maintained what Cheatham called "a continuous and annoying fire" at Cheatham's Hill; it endangered anyone who dared to show a part of his body above the works. The 52nd Ohio fired on average 200 rounds per man every day for the duration of its stay in the advanced works. Stooping inside the trenches did not guarantee safety. Bullets sometimes glanced off the few remaining trees near the works and ricocheted into the ditches.[2]

The Federal works grew in strength to be nearly on the same level as the Confederate trenches. The forward parapet was seven feet tall and twelve feet thick. Both sides erected head logs, propping them up so that a two-inch slit allowed the troops to fire their muskets. The Confederates placed a few sections of chevaux-de-frise in front of their position. Sam Watkins recalled that the three men detailed to place them one night made out their wills before embarking on the work. They managed to place the obstruction about twenty feet in front of the line without mishap.[3]

The Confederates also deployed numerous fireballs made of cotton soaked in turpentine. They lit the balls and threw them into no-man's-land at night whenever a strange noise alerted the videttes to the possibility that the Federals might attempt a night attack.[4]

The lines were close enough that hand grenades could have been used to good effect. Rumor had it that Cheatham tried to get some grenades issued to his troops, but there is no evidence that the weapons ever were used. Sam Watkins claimed that the Federals threw "bomb shells" at the Confederates as a substitute for grenades, and that the Rebels sometimes threw them back if they failed to explode right away. He also noted that the Yankees eventually did throw hand grenades, which either fell short or sailed over the Confederate trench and "were harmless." But there is no supporting evidence from the Union side to indicate that grenades were available to Davis's men.[5]

If grenades were not available, the terrain provided projectiles for throwing. Many soldiers on both sides tossed rocks at the opposing trenches. Engineer Poe thought it was mostly for entertainment. William J. McDill of the 9th Tennessee told his aunt, "We amused ourselves by throwing rocks into the Yankee trenches and shooting every time we could see a piece of a Yank." The rocks sometimes took effect and injured men, seriously at times.[6]

Langley not only devised the cracker-box method of earthwork construction but initiated an effort to mine the angle in the Confederate line on Cheatham's Hill. The mine was started from the most advanced Union position and aimed directly at the angle, which at this point was 105 feet away. Everyone assumed Langley meant to explode it on July 4 as a combination attack and celebration of Independence Day. It was new work for the Federals and they did not have proper mining tools, so their progress was slow at first. They moved the dirt along the trench line until they reached the far left of McCook's position, where they dumped it in a way that it would appear to be an extension of the line. Even though the color of the dirt was only slightly different, James T. Holmes believed the Confederates detected it and correctly assumed that the Yankees were mining. By the time Johnston evacuated the Kennesaw Line, the mine gallery was sixteen feet deep and nearly finished. Langley's crew intended to complete it and already had powder assembled to place in the end of the gallery, according to Holmes.[7]

The Confederates could guess that a gallery was in progress simply by the proximity of the opposing lines. A staff member in Cleburne's Division estimated on June 29 that the Federals could dig a gallery under no-man's-land at the angle in only thirty-six hours. Union veterans recalled that Confederate deserters told them their former comrades suspected the mine was being dug and even used an age-old device to detect signs of its construction. They placed a drum on the ground, put "some pieces of gravel" on the drumhead, and watched for signs of vibration. Word of the Federal mining spread along Confederate lines at least to Walker's Division farther north.[8]

For two days after the failed attack of June 27, dozens of bodies littered the ground between the lines, raising an awful stench. Sam Watkins recalled that the smell was "so sickening as to nauseate the whole of both armies." Hardee's artillery chief affirmed that the dead had assumed "a most revolting appearance, as black as Negroes, enormously swollen, fly blown and emitting an intolerable stench." The problem was most acute on Cheatham's Hill, but scattered dead bodies still lay on the Fourth Corps sector as well. Reportedly Cleburne withdrew his skirmishers because the stench was so terrible they could not stand it. Representatives of both sides worked out the details of a burial truce fronting Newton's division on the evening of June 28. Pioneers roamed the area between the Confederate abatis and the Union line to find bodies, many of which had been so burned and decomposed "that they could not be recognized."[9]

Given the close proximity of the lines on Cheatham's Hill, it was more difficult to work out the details of a burial truce on the Fourteenth Corps sector. The Confederates could not afford to move away from the odor, and Cheatham's men had to stand in their trenches and smell the dead without letup. Both sides finally agreed to terms and the truce began at 9:00 A.M. on June 29.

A line of pickets was sent out from both armies to the midpoint of no-man's-land to prevent anyone from crossing the line to the other side as burial details gathered the dead. Confederate details brought the slain from near their own works to the Union picket line. Given the decomposed state of the dead, they were buried on the Union side of no-man's-land in shallow graves.[10]

As the collection and disposal of the dead continued, men on both sides took the truce as an opportunity to come out of their works. They needed to stretch and feel comfortable in the open, even if for a short time, and there was ample opportunity to talk with the enemy and trade for needed articles. Many men talked with members of the opposing army as if they had been friends and neighbors. James Holmes called it "a cautious, discreet, but good-natured mingling of officers and men in the space between the lines." Brigade and regimental commanders on both sides donned privates' coats and mingled with the crowd to get a better look at enemy defenses. One Confederate soldier challenged any Yankee to a wrestling match, and a recruit of the 52nd Ohio took him up on the call and beat him. A point of contention arose when officers on both sides discussed who had the right to collect the many abandoned rifles that still lay between the lines. Both sides argued that they ought to be allowed to retrieve them, but the Federals suggested leaving the weapons alone until one side or the other secured Cheatham's Hill. When the truce came to an end at 4:00 P.M., everyone returned to their trenches. Holmes remembered that "there was silence for some time. The spirit of the friendly communion lingered over the ground." But after a bit, the sharpshooters resumed their work and the war was on again.[11]

In fact, the war on Cheatham's Hill heated up dramatically that very night. The right flank of Mitchell's brigade was still in the air, despite efforts to dig a flanking work as early as June 27. The 34th Illinois sent out a work detail of three companies on the night of June 29. The men did not work for long before Confederate pickets opened a heavy fire in their direction, soon followed by volleys from the main line and artillery fire from battery emplacements. What followed nearly amounted to a small battle as the fire was taken up by the Federals and soon spread northward along the line to include the Fourth Corps sector. Not only was all sleep destroyed, but tension filled the air as everyone assumed a major attack was underway. The 1st and 27th Tennessee had just been relieved from days of strenuous duty at the angle and were settling down for much needed sleep in a reserve trench to the rear, when the ruckus began. The men were "crazed from loss of sleep. Every one woke up with a start and was dazed to such a degree that we hardly knew where to go." It took some time for the firing to stop completely. As Hardee's artillery chief put it, "The least

Flanking the Kennesaw Line

noise is sufficient to draw someone's fire, and once started, it moves very conta-giously." The Confederates kept fireballs burning the whole night of June 30 as a reaction to the scare of the night before.[12]

The living conditions in the opposing works at Cheatham's Hill were more demanding than on any other portion of the Kennesaw Line. On the Union side, at least there was an opportunity to rotate the units of Mitchell's and McCook's brigades in and out of the forward trench line. McCook's command shifted regiments every twelve hours to give them opportunities to rest in the rear lines. Half of the men in the forward line could sleep at night while the rest remained alert. Even in the rear trenches, at least one member of each company was detailed to remain awake all night. The Confederates could rarely pull units back for rest. They also felt compelled to keep a line of videttes in no-man's-land during the night to sound the alarm in case the Federals tried an attack. It was, of course, far too dangerous to do so during the day. The Federals prepared for a possible Confederate sally by gathering spare guns, loading them, and secur-ing them to the parapet so they could be instantly fired.[13]

The works were imposing but did not offer foolproof safety. "The men in the trenches were cramped for room," recalled Edwin Payne of the 34th Illi-nois, "and were unable to sleep except in the most uncomfortable positions. No one dared show a hand or head above the rifle-pits on either side. The hot sun beat down on them by day, and the dews or rain at night. The trenches became muddy and disgusting. All cooking had to be done in the ravine in rear of all of the lines of breastworks, and then be brought up to the front."[14]

In fact, one member of the 34th Illinois, who was assigned to a cooking detail, became disoriented while delivering a hot pot of coffee to his comrades on the afternoon of June 30. Edward O'Donnell crossed all the rear lines of the works and continued over the forward line as well, moving swiftly across no-man's-land with pot in hand. The Confederates took him in but soon yelled out asking "why we sent that fool over," according to one Federal observer. Despite that comment, many men on both sides thought O'Donnell only pretended to be disoriented. Rumor among the Confederates had it that he had tied a string to his foot so the Yankees could measure exactly the distance between the lines for mining purposes, while rumor among the Federals had it that he was a Southern sympathizer who told the Rebels about the mine at the angle. The truth was that O'Donnell had suffered from sunstroke earlier in the campaign and was, according to Edwin Payne, "scarcely *compos mentis.*" He apparently had no idea what he was doing. The Confederates "enjoyed the coffee and kept the man," Payne reported. O'Donnell was sent to Andersonville, where he died of disease in early September 1864.[15]

With the lines so close to each other, sniping developed into a dangerous reality at Cheatham's Hill. James Holmes became interested in trying his hand with a Henry rifle, perched behind a tree that was incorporated into the parapet of the forward Union line. Holmes became so absorbed in the process of looking for a target that he did not realize he was exposed to enemy fire as well. "Turning my eyes after a time to the right, the whole rebel angle was in sight. The scene made cold chills run over me, for ordinarily it was unsafe to show even a hand to that line." Holmes dropped down for safety and never repeated the experience again. Capt. James I. Hall of the 9th Tennessee recalled that an officer was killed even as he crouched deep inside the Confederate trench because a bullet glanced off the underside of the head log and ricocheted in his direction.[16]

Many Federals used an innovative sighting device to target the Confederates without unduly exposing themselves. As noted in a previous chapter, they attached small mirrors to the stocks of their muskets. Reportedly, a man of the 125th Illinois introduced the device to Cheatham's Hill, although it had been used by the Federals elsewhere along the Kennesaw Line. It allowed a sharpshooter to aim his weapon while sheltering behind the parapet.[17]

Federal sharpshooters, in particular, became adept at eating away the protective elements of the Confederate line because there often was nothing else to shoot at. "The boys practiced billiard tactics on the headlogs," reported Holmes, "and so calculated angles as to have the shots glance downward into the trench and they sometimes killed." Sgt. Washington Ives of the 4th Florida told his father about the Federal sharpshooters who managed to cut a head log ten inches in diameter completely in two during five days of repeated firing at the same spot. The sections of chevaux-de-frise also were splintered by repeated hits.[18]

LIFE ALONG THE KENNESAW LINE

The conditions of trench warfare were more concentrated at Cheatham's Hill than anywhere else along the Kennesaw Line, but its characteristics were duplicated in less intense form at many other sectors. "I always felt a little tenderfooted when getting near the works," admitted Edward Norphlet Brown of the 45th Alabama in Mark P. Lowrey's Brigade. "It is really dangerous to walk about the lines at all." One bullet zinged so close to him "that it made my head dizzy. Another struck a tree just before me & another knocked up the dirt about ten feet behind me." The trench itself offered a large degree of safety from these bullets, but the problem lay in going to the rear. The members of the 76th Ohio in Osterhaus's division had to crawl on their hands and knees toward the rear areas from the trench during the day because they had not constructed covered ways.[19]

Col. Ellison Capers's 24th South Carolina in States R. Gist's Brigade of Walker's Division found its comfort greatly restricted after the failed Union attack of June 27. Before that day, Capers had maintained a skirmish line 300 yards in front of his main position. Even so, bullets often sailed into and over the main line. But after the attack, Capers was unable to maintain a skirmish line at all, and the enemy skirmishers were only 100 yards in his front. The South Carolinians failed to get any rest because the Federals "were constantly firing and watching." During the regiment's thirteen-day stay in the Kennesaw works, it lost a total of fifty-seven men even though it was not engaged in any battle.[20]

For regiments with severely reduced numbers, this sort of loss rate could drain effectiveness in a short while. Hood worried that his men would burrow themselves so deeply in the ground for protection that they might become less aware of what the enemy was doing. "The longer troops remain in the trenches as they now are, the more careless they become. It is enjoined upon Commanding Officers to caution their subordinates to keep a vigilant watch, both day and night to prevent a surprise."[21]

The members of the 4th Louisiana in the Army of Mississippi tried to make their trenches as comfortable and safe as possible. They constructed so many traverses inside the trench that "the various companies were shut off, more or less, from one another." These boxes were something like sixteen to twenty feet long and opened toward the rear so that men could exit and enter without exposing themselves. "For three weeks these little boxes were our homes," recalled John Irwin Kendall. Cooking had to be done at the wagon train well to the rear and food brought forward to the trench. Water was in short supply. It could only be brought forward in canteens, and therefore the men used it sparingly. A few drops to wash their face, none to brush their teeth, with hardly any real towels to keep themselves clean. For entertainment, Kendall's comrades played marbles with canister balls or wrote letters home. They sometimes took a nap on the open ground just to the rear of the works, placing pieces of wood over their heads although the rest of their bodies were exposed. "These were ostrich tactics," admitted Kendall, "yet men did this repeatedly."[22]

Luther P. Bradley grew tired of the lengthy stalemate. "We are still here," he reported to a friend on July 1, "under the shadow of the great Kenesaw." After surviving the costly Fourth Corps attack on June 27, Bradley had no stomach for any more assaults. Federal operations were now "more like a siege than anything else," he concluded. The Federals had "to work them out of the position by slow approaches. Their works are of such strength that we cannot carry them by assault, except at immense cost."[23]

With time on their hands, soldiers on both sides of no-man's-land tinkered with improvements on their works. They placed head logs along sectors that did not have them, or constructed more traverses for flank protection even though sometimes the tired men doing the work thought it was unnecessary. Chesley Mosman's pioneer detachment of the 59th Illinois was busy making embrasures for artillery units and planting abatis made of wood blackened by the fire that erupted from the fighting on June 27. He and his men became covered with the soot every time they handled the material.[24]

For the Confederates on Cheatham's Hill, the close positions of Mitchell's and McCook's brigades demanded a safe way to move from the trench to the rear areas. Cheatham's men constructed a covered way that was roofed with timber and a layer of dirt thrown on top. Elsewhere along the Kennesaw Line, Union artillery fire often knocked down Confederate head logs. Rebel pioneers constructed bombproofs for officers as Hood instructed his division leaders to build more redoubts along the corps line. When Loring heard that one of his division commanders wanted more troops to bolster his position, the temporary commander of the Army of Mississippi told him none were available. Strengthening the works with abatis, along with extra vigilance, was the only recourse.[25]

MANEUVER

The lengthy stalemate would soon come to an end. "Johnston will not come out of his parapets," Sherman informed a correspondent, "and it is difficult to turn his position without abandoning our railroad." But that is exactly what Sherman prepared to do. He intended to break contact with his logistical support and move the entire army group southward along the way pioneered by Schofield, aiming at Fulton's Station about seven miles south of Marietta or perhaps the Chattahoochee River itself. He issued orders to move all spare supplies back to Allatoona Pass, making it the end of the line as far as his communications were concerned, as the troops sallied forth. Sherman sent Poe to inspect the area near Schofield's operations.[26]

Schofield worried about Johnston's reaction to the move. What if the Confederates stayed where they were and constructed a fully enclosed defensive position based on Kennesaw Mountain, with the approaches from the south blocked by heavy earthworks around Marietta? Sherman dismissed the possibility, believing Johnston was too cautious to be trapped like this. Such a sce-

　　　　　　　　　　　　　　　　　　　Flanking the Kennesaw Line

nario would also offer the Federals an opportunity to range as far south as they dared and destroy the Confederate communications line with Atlanta.[27]

After several days spent accumulating supplies for the move, Sherman prepared the way by sending Milo Hascall's division of the Twenty-Third Corps as well as Morgan L. Smith's division of the Fifteenth Corps to advance beyond the forward position Jacob Cox's division had occupied on June 27. By the time Smith's men marched to Schofield's army on July 1, Hascall had moved a couple of miles to a key road junction. From there, the Federals could aim at Fulton and the railroad or directly toward the Chattahoochee River. McPherson moved the Army of the Tennessee out of its trench line early on the night of July 2, but the Confederates alertly realized what was happening soon after the pullout began.[28]

Johnston was ready to evacuate his strong position at Kennesaw; in fact, he had prepared to do so for several days. Schofield's movements alerted him to the need to find a fallback position. Engineer Presstman staked out a new line near Smyrna Station, about five miles south of Marietta. At Little Kennesaw, the Confederates had worked on cutting paths up and down the south side of the mountain to more easily rope the guns down when called on to do so. When the order arrived to pull out, George Storrs quietly withdrew his pieces from their emplacements. He had kept the embrasures covered with brush when not firing so as to be less conspicuous to Federal observers, and now the brush came in handy to shield his withdrawal. Only one section of guns on the mountain had to be pulled out of its emplacements by men crawling on their hands and knees, because it might have been possible to see them if they stood up. The artillery went first, then the infantry, and finally the skirmish line left at about 3:00 A.M., at least on French's part of the line.[29]

Cheatham's men evacuated the hill they had held against great odds that night as well. Maney deployed twelve men to act as videttes; they crawled through the obstructions and settled in a line only ten yards from the Confederate works to keep watch while their comrades fell back. After a while the videttes were all that was left; they crawled back to the trench and left the position at midnight. On Cleburne's sector, the pickets of Granbury's Texas Brigade remained out a couple of hours after the main line evacuated, then fell back one by one into the trench where they all assembled at a designated spot. A guide then took the pickets to the rear and toward their units, which were well on their way to the Smyrna Line.[30]

The Federals, who were lodged only a few yards from the angle on Cheatham's Hill, did not realize the occupants of the opposing trench were gone until they heard a Confederate straggler call out to them, "Say, Yanks; don't shoot, will you? I want to come in, they're all gone." It was 1:00 A.M. and the Yankees sent out a skirmish line to investigate. There was little to do but wait until dawn allowed for a forward movement to follow the retreating enemy.[31]

When ready to move on the morning of July 3, most Union soldiers at Kennesaw crossed no-man's-land and then the opposing trench line. It offered them an opportunity to quickly examine the works that had stalled their advance since June 19. Allen L. Fahnestock of the 86th Illinois was amazed at the strength of the works opposite McCook's position, the caves dug by the Confederates for shelter, and the fact that trees as large as six inches in diameter had been cut down by repeated striking of bullets. "All Our Generals were over to See the Sights," he reported. Other observers noted that the rain of bullets had frazzled head logs and abatis. On the Fourth Corps sector, Chesley Mosman's pioneers cut a path through the Rebel works to let Federal artillery through.[32]

Twentieth Corps troops also were impressed by Hood's earthworks opposite their position. "They were the most complete and strong lines we have come to yet," reported William Clark McLean of the 123rd New York. The work consisted of a parapet twelve feet thick, an ample trench behind it, and two rows of inclined, sharpened stakes that were one yard in length. The inclined palisade consisted of stakes set so close together "that a man could not get through nor over without Injuring himself," according to Fergus Elliott of the 109th Pennsylvania. The stakes were made of fence rails. A Pennsylvania artilleryman "had no idea they were so strongly entrenched till we seen for ourselves." He believed that only 30,000 Confederates could have held the entire Kennesaw Line against the heaviest frontal attack.[33]

Yet Johnston did not intend to hold the Kennesaw Line for any longer than necessary. Maneuver, not attack, pried him out of it and faster and easier than anyone would have guessed. Philip Daingerfield Stephenson of Slocomb's Fifth Company, Washington Artillery, had expected to evacuate the position long before. "We had indeed gotten out of the Kennesaw Line more than we could have hope[d] for," he wrote after the war, "had held it far beyond anticipations. Why the heavy flanking column did not edge us out sooner, I never knew."[34]

9

Crossing the Chattahoochee

Sherman hoped and expected Johnston would cross the Chattahoochee River when the Confederates evacuated the Kennesaw Line on the night of July 2–3, but he was disappointed. The Confederate commander intended to hold every defensible position along the railroad that ran south of Marietta to the last major river confronting Sherman. He had already begun to prepare those positions even before leaving Kennesaw. As a result, the Federal crossing of the Chattahoochee took more time and effort than Sherman imagined, and Johnston conducted the pullbacks and the eventual crossing of his army with such care that his enemy had no opportunity to strike a damaging blow along the way.

THE SMYRNA LINE

Presstman prepared the Smyrna Line for Johnston before the pullout from Kennesaw, laying it out as early as June 26. It was located five miles from the Chattahoochee and stretched for six miles, with both flanks refused. The right flank rested at Rottenwood Creek, and the center crossed the railroad near Smyrna Camp Ground, the location of revival meetings by local Methodists. The left flank ended one and a half miles due east of Ruff's Mill and then headed south for one and a half miles. This refused section of the line utilized the valley of Nickajack Creek, located about one half to one and a half miles in front of the westward-facing line, as an obstruction to a Federal advance. Presstman and his assistants had done nothing more than stake out the new position; it was up to the infantrymen and artillerymen of Johnston's army to do the digging. Manigault's Brigade found the night too dark to work when the men arrived on site at 1:00 A.M., especially since part of his line was in "a thick wood." The men slept until dawn and then began to work. The Federals did not appear in Manigault's front until midday on July 3, and even then the Confederates could see that they were paying more attention to constructing a corresponding line than they were interested in moving against their own for the time being.[1]

On all parts of the Smyrna Line, Confederate troops "fell to work like beavers," as gunner Philip Daingerfield Stephenson put it. Many units worked during the night and had a good earthwork ready at dawn of July 3. In fact, Stephenson claimed that his battery held the only good artillery position it possessed during the entire campaign. His comrades invested a good deal of attention in placing "finishing touches" on their battery emplacement on July 3. "We thought them beautiful, and honestly longed for the enemy." In contrast, when Daniel Harris Reynolds brought his Arkansas brigade to Smyrna, he found that nothing more than skirmish pits had been dug along his sector.[2]

Several commanders were not pleased with the ground on their parts of the line. Manigault thought his brigade position "was a very irregular one," producing "many salient points." Samuel French bluntly called his division's position a bad one and encouraged his men to construct heavy works to compensate for the disadvantage. The men of the Mississippi brigade in French's Division used bayonets as picks and roof shingles from a nearby house as spades because of a dire shortage of entrenching tools. In contrast, the ordnance officer of Polk's Brigade in Cleburne's Division thought Polk had "a splendid position" to defend. On many parts of the line, the Federals came close and opened skirmish fire even as the Confederates were digging their main line on July 3.[3]

When the trench was finished, the Confederates quickly began to build obstructions wherever they had an opportunity to do so. On the far left, they managed to create an abatis of cut brush that stretched for 100 yards in front of their position. The brush was "partly cut off at a height of two or three feet, and the tops bent over and interlaced." Manigault's troops ranged forward to clear-cut the trees in his front, fashion abatis, and erect palisades. The inevitable head logs appeared on top of the Rebel parapet, each one about ten to twelve inches wide. On the far Confederate left, Nickajack Creek presented an obstacle to a Union advance toward the line. The historian of the 6th Iowa recalled that the creek valley was a jungle, with a "density of small growth of timber, canebreak, tangling vines, and rank growth of vegetation." The creek valley also was home to "myriads of insects, venomous worms and reptiles." Confederate pioneers cut military roads through the trees behind Johnston's line to offer easier ac-

cess up to and away from the position. Also, Presstman sent two engineer officers to examine all roads to the Chattahoochee ferry crossings and report their
condition.[4]

Skirmishing and artillery fire began soon after the Federals moved up close
to the line. John Wharton of Guibor's Missouri Battery noted that the Yankee
gunners opposite his position did good execution. One round killed two Confederates and wounded two others. Federal skirmishers drove their gray-clad
counterparts back in front of Guibor's position, and the Missouri gunners returned fire as often as they could during the course of the day. The shock of their
gun's discharges damaged the embrasures, which had to be repaired after dusk.
Federal guns severely shelled several other parts of the Confederate line that day.
Artillery fire punished Hugh W. Mercer's Brigade of Walker's Division before
the men could build anything more than rail breastworks. They "were slaugh-
tered" as a result, in the words of Lt. Hamilton R. Branch of the 54th Georgia.[5]

The Federals cautiously moved forward to develop the new Confederate
position on July 3, but Sherman derived an erroneous view of what lay ahead of
them. Believing that Johnston intended to rush across the Chattahoochee, he
assumed the Smyrna Line was weakly held to retard his progress a few hours.
"No general, such as he, would invite battle with the Chattahoochee behind
him," Sherman told Thomas of his opponent's generalship on the evening of
July 3. "You know what loss would ensue to Johnston if he crosses his bridges
at night in confusion with artillery thundering at random in his rear," he continued. "We will never have such a chance again."[6]

Sherman went to Howard's headquarters early on July 4 and said, in staff
officer Fullerton's words, "There is nothing in front of us but skirmishers; he has
examined the ground and knows there is nothing else there." He told Howard
to move forward and pressure the enemy out of their works. All three division
commanders reinforced their skirmish lines and advanced them across no-
man's-land. Stanley's division rested its right at the railroad and extended the
line east and south to conform to the curved right flank of the Smyrna Line. His
skirmish line easily captured the Confederate skirmishers, who occupied pits
big enough for one to six men and spaced about twenty to thirty yards from
each other.[7]

Stanley intended to strike at the Confederate main line, in a faithful obedi-
ence to orders, but he had already received considerable amounts of small-arms
and artillery fire while taking the skirmish line. One of his brigade commanders
examined the enemy position after making his way to a point 200 yards away
from it and returned to report the position too strong for an attack. All inten-
tions to fulfill Sherman's directive evaporated, and Stanley ordered his men to

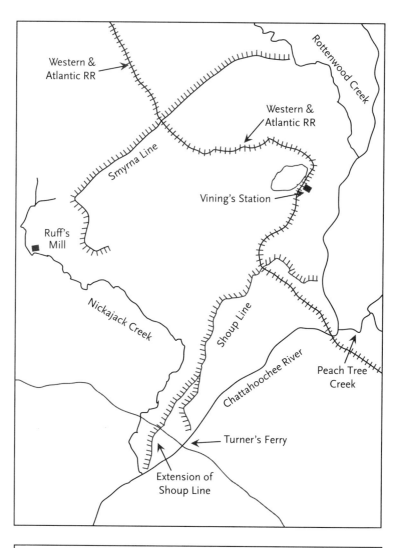

Western &
Atlantic RR

Western &
Atlantic RR

Rottenwood Creek

Smyrna Line

Vining's Station

Ruff's
Mill

Nickajack Creek

Shoup Line

Chattahoochee River

Peach Tree
Creek

Turner's Ferry

Extension of
Shoup Line

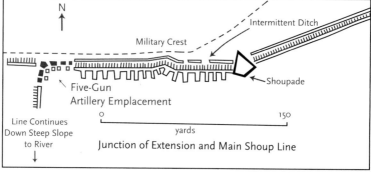

N

Intermittent Ditch

Military Crest

Five-Gun
Artillery Emplacement

Shoupade

Line Continues
Down Steep Slope
to River

0   150
yards

Junction of Extension and Main Shoup Line

Smyrna Line and Chattahoochee River Line

construct a new main line along the Confederate skirmish position. Members of the 59th Illinois found a fence and dismantled it, using rails as the base of their new parapet. Chesley Mosman's pioneers moved in to help the infantry. They were surprised to find a handful of picks and spades left behind by the Confederate skirmishers. While some Federals made new works, others simply reversed conveniently located enemy skirmish pits for their own use. A second Federal line dug in along the former Union skirmish position. Despite the recovery of a few Confederate tools, most Yankees were compelled to use whatever happened to be handy—bayonets and tin cups—to make their works.[8]

Newton and Wood also advanced their skirmishers when Stanley moved forward at about 10:00 A.M., but they did not push as aggressively as their colleague. With Stanley's success, the Confederates pulled back their skirmish line so that both Newton and Wood were able to move their main lines forward to conform to Stanley's. Howard lost ninety-five men and captured eighty-eight prisoners in the day's operation. He could report, in Fullerton's words, that the Confederate main line trenches were "very strong and are full of troops." Howard later recalled the works as "stronger than usual." In fact, a report filtered into Fourth Corps headquarters that the Rebels had even constructed a covered way out from their main line toward their new skirmish line by late that evening. Chesley Mosman had an opportunity to closely examine the Confederate position three months later without any defenders to hinder him. "It would have been madness to have assaulted it as our Brigade started to do," he concluded.[9]

As far as the Confederates were concerned, they assumed Johnston meant to stay at Smyrna as long as possible. John W. Hagan of the 29th Georgia heard that Rebel generals believed Sherman would be forced to attack now, for he could not flank anymore with Johnston's army firmly entrenched to cover the crossings of the river. Hagan did not necessarily believe the enemy would be foolish enough to assault, but his commentary indicates that many Confederates might have believed the Smyrna Line was a better position than Kennesaw had been. They surely noted that the previous line had delayed Sherman for two weeks.[10]

Howard's reconnaissance in force on July 4 finally convinced Sherman that the Smyrna Line was formidable and well manned, and he quickly set about to maneuver Johnston out of it. McPherson was in the best place to accomplish that task. Sixteenth Corps troops moved across Nickajack Creek on July 4 and closed up on the left wing of the Smyrna Line. To McPherson's right, Federal cavalry moved toward Turner's Ferry on the Chattahoochee until coming up against a portion of the Georgia Militia guarding the road.[11]

This militia force represented a small addition to the strength of Johnston's army. Gov. Joseph E. Brown called up the state force and placed Maj. Gen. Gustavus W. Smith in charge of it. Smith moved 2,000 militiamen and a battery northward across the Chattahoochee in late June, and he helped cover the far Confederate left when McPherson and the Federal cavalry advanced on July 4. He held the crest of a ridge near Nickajack Creek, guarding the approach toward Turner's Ferry on the Chattahoochee. Smith found an emplacement for a battery with embrasures that had been previously constructed. In addition, "short lines of trenches for infantry extended on each side, but not enough to give cover to more than five hundred men." His troops improved the works all night. Smith held this position even though it was detached from the Smyrna Line, but McPherson made no attempt to attack or turn it. After dusk, Smith sent a message to Johnston that he intended to withdraw at daylight on July 5, and army headquarters approved.[12]

McPherson was in a position to sail past the left flank of the Smyrna Line, with only a couple of thousand Georgia state troops barring the way. This was enough to convince Johnston to evacuate his entire position at Smyrna. He issued orders to pull out on the night of July 4. The wagons and artillery left first at 9:30 P.M., and the infantry evacuated at 1:30 A.M. The line of skirmishers did not leave until 3:00 A.M. Hood's Corps withdrew later than the other corps; his skirmishers did not leave their pits until dawn.[13]

The Federals had an opportunity to examine the strength of the Smyrna Line early on the morning of July 5. They were surprised that the Confederates had constructed such large, imposing works in so short a time. Poe praised the Confederate engineers for incorporating many salient angles into the system and noted that most artillery emplacements had embrasures. Opposite the Fourth Corps, the Rebels had constructed a second line behind the main one in addition to a new skirmish position in front of it. Opposite the Twentieth Corps sector, the Confederates also had a secondary line of works and had driven stakes in front of both the main line and their skirmish position. John Hill Ferguson of the Fourteenth Corps saw smears of blood in the Rebel works where Union artillery had found human targets. A newspaper correspondent who examined the position found many small shelter pits behind the main line that sported log roofs covered with a thick layer of dirt. "It had become more and more a source of wonder how and when they had built such complete fortifications," remembered Rice C. Bull of the 123rd New York. "They could not have been constructed in the few days that they used them."[14]

Johnston pulled back to yet one more line before crossing the river. According to Francis A. Shoup, his chief of artillery, the commander initially had not intended to make another stand south of Kennesaw Mountain, but cross the river after giving up the position near Marietta. Shoup persuaded him to construct a defensive line just north of the stream. In fact, Shoup had already told Johnston about his idea for creating "a system of works of a somewhat novel character which I wanted to build" when the army assumed its position at Kennesaw Mountain. His plan was to construct a work large enough for the entire army but capable of being held by only one division. This would give Johnston the option of massing most of his force to either strike at an exposed portion of Sherman's host or launch a push against the Federal line of communications. In effect, Shoup envisioned a scenario similar to what Sherman created in late August when he protected the railroad crossing of the Chattahoochee with one corps and took the rest to tear up Confederate rail lines leading into Atlanta from the south. Shoup convinced Johnston and asked only for the use of some engineer officers and black laborers.[15]

Shoup went to work, easily found defensible ground near the crossing, and used Maj. Wilbur Foster and other engineer officers to help him lay out a line that was four miles long and about one mile from the river. Both flanks of the line were anchored on the north bank of the river, with the left ending half a mile upstream from Turner's Ferry. A week after starting the project, Johnston told Shoup to extend the left to the mouth of Nickajack Creek. There also was a reserve line that became part of the complex, a short *tête de pont* near the railroad bridge that had been built much earlier and which could serve as a fallback position.[16]

The only unusual thing about the Chattahoochee River Line, which could be called the Shoup Line to honor the man who designed it, lay in Shoup's effort to make a position four and a half miles long that was defensible by only a few thousand troops. He hoped to do so by constructing a number of self-contained redoubts to serve as strongpoints. Shoup later called his position "not a system of earth works, but a line of detached log redoubts packed with earth." Each redoubt was to be enclosed, capable of holding eighty men, and shaped like a chevron. Log revetments held up the earthen parapets, which were eight feet tall, with front faces that were twelve feet thick and rear faces that were six feet thick. Shoup placed the redoubts about eighty yards from each other and connected them with a stockade made of upright logs, loopholed for infantry fire. Shoup also placed a two-gun artillery emplacement between the redoubts at a reentering angle so its line of fire covered the flank of the neighboring redoubt.[17]

When Gustavus W. Smith saw these structures, he dubbed them "Shoupades" to honor the designer of the line. All told, Shoup constructed thirty-six Shoupades along the River Line, including at least three larger artillery works in addition to numerous two-gun artillery emplacements, or redans. A work for seven guns anchored the left end of the extension near the mouth of Nickajack Creek, and a work for eight guns anchored the right flank. Careful analysis of the remnants of this line by modern researchers has shown that Shoup was unable to place the Shoupades regularly along the line due to variations in terrain. Some of them are much farther than eighty yards apart from each other, and a combination of a Shoupade and two flanking redans on the extension of the line are isolated quite some distance from supporting works.[18]

Johnston authorized Shoup to round up black laborers for the project. He sent responsible men down the railroad to obtain slaves from nearby plantations, along with tools and supplies to feed them. Within three days his energetic agents accumulated about 1,000 blacks. A great many of those laborers were gathered in the city of Atlanta itself, and at least some of them were freemen. Shoup employed these men not only because the soldiers were busy holding the Kennesaw Line, but because he knew farm and plantation workers would be familiar with cribwork from their experience with building cabins. The necessary timber was readily found near the site of the fortification. "The line sprung into existence as by magic," Shoup later wrote. Some of the blacks were still working on the fortification when the Confederates moved to the new line on the morning of July 5. They left as soon as the Yankees approached.[19]

The Federals learned that their opponents had used black laborers to construct the Chattahoochee River Line. Sherman was examining the position from a distance along the Fourteenth Corps sector when a black man appeared from hiding in the abatis and gave himself up to Federal skirmishers on July 5. He accurately told the Federals that 1,000 blacks had worked on the line. Rumors of the man's defection spread rapidly along Union lines, but these rumors also exaggerated the number until everyone believed that 4,000 blacks had built the works now frowning before them. A newspaper correspondent declared as a fact that "the whole able-bodied colored population of Northern Georgia has been pressed for this service."[20]

If nothing else, Shoup had selected good ground for his works. Federal troops often commented on the imposing position, with the tangled valley of Nickajack Creek fronting much of the left wing of the Shoup Line. Henry

Stone, one of Thomas's staff officers, called it "the most difficult position yet encountered" in the campaign.[21]

The Chattahoochee River Line was mostly complete when the Army of Tennessee moved back to it early on the morning of July 5. Everyone noted the Shoupades, which were the unique features of the position. As Capt. Samuel T. Foster of Cleburne's Division wrote, it was "something new in the shape of works to fight behind." The extra labor on this line, combined with the good ground, convinced some members of the Army of Tennessee that Johnston intended to make a firm stand on the Chattahoochee.[22]

But many Confederates either had doubts regarding the line or were openly critical of Shoup's novel features. Ordnance officer Robert D. Smith in Cleburne's Division withheld his opinion for the time being. "I will not say how I like them," he confessed to his diary, "as I have never seen any fighting from the kind of works." John Irwin Kendall did not spare his caustic opinion. "This Shoupades line of defense we hardly took seriously," he wrote after the war. "And I can scarcely believe that Johnston did, either. . . . Among us on the front line, it was the occasion for much fun." Kendall did praise how Shoup had configured the line to take advantage of every twist and turn in the terrain. Philip Daingerfield Stephenson remembered that his colleagues "often laughed as they recalled these Georgia Militia entrenchments." J. L. Hammond considered the Shoupade "a perfect slaughter pen, and in one hour would have been knocked to pieces by Yankee artillery."[23]

Many Confederates set about to rebuild or improve Shoup's line as soon as they reached it on the morning of July 5. Cantey's Brigade occupied a section where "nothing was finished," according to John Irwin Kendall, and "the stockades especially were not half ready for use." Moreover, the connecting line between Shoupades had only been staked out. Kendall's colleagues in the 4th Louisiana "fell to work like beavers digging trenches" and soon realized they occupied "a splendid position." Manigault's Brigade occupied the extreme left, next to Smith's militia. The works were finished there but the South Carolinians labored to make them better. On some parts of the line, the timber used for the stockade was too small, but infantrymen dug a ditch in front and banked the dirt against the weak parts to strengthen them.[24]

Shoup remained sensitive to criticism of the line for the rest of his life. He admitted after the war that the men "were greatly amused and made all sorts of ridiculous remarks about them. The stockades were their chief objects of merriment, and they began to tear them down, and resort to the faithful shovel." The troops of Mercer's Brigade in Walker's Division literally did that; they dismantled the stockade and dug a trench instead. Shoup recalled meeting Cle-

burne on July 6 and listened as the division commander told him how puzzled ·
he was when first assuming the position. Cleburne initially agreed with his men,
but then studied the design and concluded it would work. According to Shoup,
Cleburne then stood on one of the Shoupades and explained to his troops how
the line could be held with converging fields of fire. When they complained that
the log revetment could easily be torn apart by enemy artillery, he told them to
construct casemates or bombproofs inside. Cleburne then showed Shoup how
it was done by laying logs from one parapet to another at an angle to the work
and throwing dirt on them. Cleburne filled the Shoupades with troops and the
artillery redans with guns and camped the rest of his division to the rear.[25]

If Johnston did not fully understand the design features Shoup had incorporated into the Chattahoochee River Line, at least he was willing to trust his
artillery chief. When the army commander heard of the troops' concerns, he
issued a circular on July 7 offering instructions about the unique design features
and urging the men to hold the position to the last. Johnston, with Shoup's help
no doubt, instructed the men to use thick logs as revetment for the redoubts
and construct bombproofs with twelve inches of dirt on the roof. He advo-
cated the use of head logs and the preparation of obstructions in front. Along
the faces of the stockades, Johnston recommended placing a layer of logs inside
and outside at the foot and covering the logs with earth. He suggested that a
parapet inside the stockade might work, too. Johnston also reminded his men
that firing laterally to support the next artillery redan was the key to the defense
of this line. Johnston wanted hand grenades to be distributed to each redoubt
and urged his men to throw fireballs out at night to illuminate no-man's-land. If
those were not available, piles of brush placed 100 yards in front of the redoubt
could be lighted by skirmishers as they retired from a night attack. If the enemy
attempted to mine the position, Johnston recommended digging ditches outside the redoubt to intercept the gallery. Shoup did his part by trying to arrange
for hand grenades and fireballs to be made and delivered.[26]

Shoup received some praise for his design features. Hardee "congratulated
me, and predicted extravagantly, that they would give me fame," he wrote. But
Hood did not agree. Shoup was present at a meeting on July 7 when Hood
argued that the army should fall back across the river. "He did not seem to
understand the design of the works," concluded Shoup, "and I doubt if he ever
stopped to think much about them."[27]

Shoup had made no provisions for obstructions in front of the line, but
the troops readily supplied them. They constructed rows of sharpened stakes,
slanted to catch a man at his chest, each stake three to four inches apart. They
slashed the timber for 100 yards in front of the line to create a field of obstruc-

Crossing the Chattahoochee

tion "so tangled a man could hardly walk through it," according to a Twentieth Corps staff officer. On the Fourteenth Corps front, the Confederates fashioned an abatis consisting of large tree limbs that were trimmed and pinned to the ground close to each other in a line, with sharpened points. The men of Guibor's Missouri Battery cut and collected saplings to fashion abatis.[28]

Sherman had no intention of attacking such a line. His troops moved forward and established positions in front of it. They dug in on July 5 and succeeding days, some regiments using only one pick and two spades, making for slow work. Officers had the luxury of detailing men to construct special little fortifications for their use, and many troops constructed arbors along the trench line to shield them from the hot sun.[29]

The Federals opened their artillery fire as soon as possible, and on some parts of the line they overwhelmed their opponents. Manigault had noticed for some time that, even though many Confederate batteries were very good, others were substandard in their practice and in the morale of the gun crews. He saw an example of that on the Chattahoochee River Line when four Federal batteries concentrated their fire on one artillery emplacement of four Confederate guns on the afternoon of July 5. The Yankee fire blanketed the Rebel position, rounds sailed through the embrasures, and soon the gray-clad offices and gunners "lost their nerve, and almost abandoned their guns, seeking shelter close under the works."[30]

But the Confederates gave a good account of themselves on other parts of the line. On the far right, Federal troops advanced one morning and took the Rebel skirmish line in front of Claudius W. Sears's Mississippi Brigade. French ordered retaliation and the 36th Mississippi sallied forth to recapture the skirmish pits. French lost fifty-two men but captured prisoners from five different Union regiments. Daniel Harris Reynolds held a part of the line that happened to be poorly sited, and he received devastating enfilade fire from Union guns that wounded eight men "in a few minutes." Reynolds had earlier scouted the terrain to his front and thought ground 200 yards forward was better, but his division leader needed time to think about allowing him to move. In the meanwhile, his men fashioned traverses along their line. Reynolds finally obtained permission to move forward and advanced at 2:00 P.M. on July 6. He dug a completely new line, establishing his skirmishers 250 yards in front of it. The new position was better but not safe; it too was enfiladed, so his men worked hard to construct traverses there as well.[31]

Despite these few weaknesses, the Shoup Line presented a formidable obstacle to a frontal attack. It was one of the most impressive examples of Rebel engineering in the war. Johnston justified his defensive strategy to Richmond by arguing that the Army of Tennessee had been "forced back by the operations of a siege, which the enemy's extreme caution and greatly superior numbers have made me unable to prevent. I have found no opportunity for battle except by attacking intrenchments."[32]

The Chattahoochee River Line was vulnerable to flanking, as were all of Johnston's defensive positions during the campaign, and Sherman soon moved troops across the stream to threaten his line of communications. Schofield crossed troops at the mouth of Soap's Creek on July 9 and dug in on the south side of the Chattahoochee. Kenner Garrard's cavalry crossed on the same day at Roswell, supported by Newton's division of the Fourth Corps. When Shoup heard that Johnston ordered the evacuation of his line that night, he was stunned. "I took a long look at the works into which my heart had gone to such a degree, and felt that the days of the Confederacy were numbered." The pull-out and crossing of the river took place that night without trouble. The next day, Johnston called Shoup to a meeting. "He said he was sorry he had been obliged to abandon my works," but he thought it best considering the Union presence south of the river. Shoup had to restrain himself from reminding Johnston that the original purpose of the line had been to guard the crossing with one division while using the rest of the army offensively against the enemy. It was obvious Johnston had no heart for taking the offensive.[33]

The Federals now examined the formidable works that had confronted them for four days. Sherman asked Thomas to make a personal inspection and report to him. Thomas informed Sherman of the "citadels," as he called them, positioned so as to deliver enfilading fire on attackers, and of the immense belt of obstructions in front of the position. Sherman reported to Halleck that the Shoup Line was "the strongest of all" thus far in the campaign and remembered in his memoirs that it was "one of the strongest pieces of field-fortification I ever saw."[34]

The rank and file of Sherman's army group generally agreed with him. Many Federals admired the "precision of engineering skill" evident in the line. "The ditches and the parapets were cut true and smooth," thought Capt. Charles Dana Miller of the 76th Ohio. "I don't think I ever saw better con-structed works." Manning F. Force, a division commander in the Seventeenth Corps, informed a correspondent that "we have been laying siege to a very strong rebel position, finely fortified." Three months later, when he passed by the Shoup Line on his way toward Atlanta to begin the March to the Sea, Force again saw the line and was even more impressed by its strength. Everything was still intact in November 1864, including the field of obstructions.[35]

Crossing the Chattahoochee

Engineer Poe also praised the line. He admired the astute selection of ground and assumed that "good engineers" had been in charge of its construction. But Poe did not like the novel design features Shoup was so proud of, the stockade and the log revetment of the redoubts. "There was nothing in the plan to recommend them to the attention of the engineers," he caustically reported to the chief engineer in Washington. In short, Poe thought that the regular infantry parapet and redoubt would have worked well. The key to the strength of the position lay in the selection of ground and the placement of its component parts so as to allow for thorough fields of converging fire. Other discerning Federals agreed with Poe. George E. Truair, adjutant of the 149th New York, informed his father that the Shoup Line was "formidable only by the nature of the ground." Maj. Abraham J. Seay of the 32nd Missouri called the stockade and log revetment "a clumsy form of defense work."[36]

Ignoring the novel features for the moment, the Chattahoochee River Line was truly a well-planned, well-sited, and well-constructed fieldwork. Josiah C. Williams of the Twentieth Corps carefully examined three miles of it after the Confederates left and said he was so impressed that he would have been ashamed to kill men from behind such protection. A member of the 113th Ohio in the Fourteenth Corps wondered why Johnston left it so early. "It is very strange that they build such strong works and then vacate them without an effort to resist our approach."[37]

The only innovative features of Shoup's design lay in the extensive use of stockades and the log revetment. Shoup's effort to use the age-old principles of converging fire to hold the Chattahoochee River Line with minimal troops involved manning enclosed redoubts that were capable of self-defense and which could be aided by the fire of the artillery redans in between. Shoup planned no connecting infantry trenches because he did not envision stationing troops between the works. The stockade served as a physical obstruction to enemy attackers, and the loopholes were cut in the stockade to serve the infantry if any were to be placed there. In Shoup's conception, the Chattahoochee River Line would have been garrisoned only by eighty infantrymen in each Shoupade, the gun crews in the redans, and some reserve troops drawn from the only division assigned to it. His plan probably would have worked and would have allowed Johnston to mass most of his manpower to attack Sherman. The only advantage of the log revetting for the redoubts was that it allowed the builders to construct a taller earthen parapet with less dirt. When Manning Force saw the line in November, he commented on the "extraordinarily massive block houses [Shoupades], quite elevated."[38]

With Atlanta only six miles south of the Chattahoochee River, Johnston was forced to base his further operations on the city itself. Fortunately for the Confederates an impressive ring of earthworks already circled the place by mid-July. The Atlanta City Line was the handiwork of Capt. Lemuel P. Grant. Born in Maine, Grant had worked as a railroad engineer in Georgia before the war. He accepted a commission in the Confederate Corps of Engineers in late 1862 and repaired railroad bridges and processed salt for the Southern cause. Jeremy F. Gilmer, chief of the Confederate Engineer Bureau, thought very highly of Grant. While trying to persuade him to accept a promotion and transfer to Mississippi in the summer of 1863, Gilmer argued that Grant had a "natural gift of judging promptly of ground." He was certain that the captain possessed all the other attributes necessary to make a fine chief of engineers for any commanding general. Grant seemed, however, not to have possessed the ambition to make military engineering his career.[39]

The captain was therefore available when Gilmer became worried that Federal cavalry raids might threaten Atlanta in the summer of 1863. Federal success in the Tullahoma campaign, which forced the Army of Tennessee to fall back to Chattanooga, betokened a need to provide for the defense of Atlanta and its important arsenal and depots. Grant received his orders on July 15, 1863, and set to work, estimating the city would need a circuit up to twelve miles long, studded with as many as fifteen forts. He also planned works at the railroad crossing of the Chattahoochee River. Black laborers performed much of the hard work at both fortification sites, and Grant had the temporary assistance of engineer Capt. John Morris Wampler of the Army of Tennessee. From July 23 to August 5, Wampler added his considerable expertise to the engineering plan for Atlanta before he was transferred to Charleston, South Carolina. Gilmer transported 500 shovels, 200 picks, and 200 axes to Atlanta on July 27 to facilitate the work.[40]

Gilmer offered Grant general directions concerning the layout of the city defenses. He initially wanted him to place the ring far enough away to avoid a Federal bombardment of the city and urged Grant to begin with detached works, closed in their rear by stockades, on the high points of the terrain. Grant could fill in the intervening spaces later with earthworks for infantrymen. Gilmer urged Grant to construct suitable obstructions in front of the line and advanced $5,000 to finance the beginning of the work. Col. Moses H. Wright, newly appointed commander of the post of Atlanta, requested the detail of a surgeon to take care of the blacks working on the defenses in August. Grant

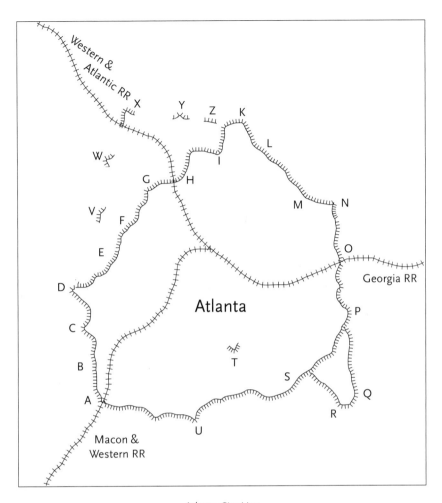

Atlanta City Line

reported to Richmond that he had no difficulty procuring black laborers from the Atlanta area.[41]

By October 1863, the principal forts were advanced enough so that the work of cutting timber to create a field of fire could begin. Gilmer urged Grant to clear-cut an area that would amount to 1,000 cubic yards in front of the works. He even advised Grant to cut the limbs that stood up from the felled timber so that not a shred of cover could be had by the Federals. The engineer chief also told him to select a reliable officer to assess the damages incurred to local landowners. The property owners would be allowed to select their own advocates to work with the officer at assessing a fair sum for compensation by the Confederate government. Gilmer was willing to scrounge up additional entrenching tools if needed, but he hoped that the Army of Tennessee might have captured sufficient tools on the field of its great victory at Chickamauga in late September.[42]

Grant understood the magnitude of his work. "The destruction of forest will be great," he advised Gilmer. In addition to cutting trees, Grant's workers completed the major works by the end of October 1863. Most of the works had five faces, "varying the angles to suit the contour of the hills occupied." Grant had not yet constructed stockades to close the gorge or set up obstructions. Yet, on November 4, he announced that the circuit was seven and a half miles long and an average of one and a quarter miles from the center of Atlanta. The line had nineteen redoubts, with an additional five redoubts located forward of the line along the northwest quadrant. Only one of the twenty-four redoubts still needed some plank laid down for the gun emplacements, but the connecting infantry line was finished. Atlanta was "now well fortified," announced Moses Wright on December 7. A week later, Wright reported that he was placing guns in the redoubts as fast as they became available and had already manned ten forts with the five artillery companies that were in the city. Gilmer visited Atlanta on December 1 to inspect the new works and approved them.[43]

Wright feared for the safety of the city following the defeat of the Army of Tennessee at Chattanooga in late November 1863. Although the army retired safely to Dalton, the enemy had the opportunity of sending mounted raids against Atlanta. Wright could count on only 1,800 troops to guard the assets of the city, and a mere 120 of them were mounted. These men were mostly area mechanics acting as militia and thus of dubious reliability on the battlefield. There were no additional troops to send to Wright.[44]

The Federals first learned details about the Atlanta City Line in early December after the victory at Chattanooga opened up the possibility of a drive into northwestern Georgia. Capt. Lewis L. Carter of the 9th Tennessee (U.S.) had been captured the previous September and was held in Atlanta, among other places. He escaped on November 15 and remained with loyalists in the city for nine days before setting out for Union lines. Carter reported that a ring of earthworks circled Atlanta, and heavy fortifications defended the crossing of the Chattahoochee River. Carter also reported that the Confederates had cut the trees for a great distance in front of the works, "which I think is the greatest obstruction" to entering the place. Several scouts offered similar reports of the Atlanta works in February 1864, along with word that black laborers were used to construct them.[45]

Not long after Joseph E. Johnston assumed command of the Army of Tennessee, he visited Atlanta and inspected the city defenses. By then, Brig. Gen.

Marcus J. Wright had assumed command of the post of Atlanta, and Moses H. Wright continued to manage the arsenal, a job he had done even while commanding the post for many months. Richmond wanted a detailed report on the number and quality of troops constituting the garrison in March 1864, but the number had not appreciably increased since the previous December. Grant also was in need of more black laborers; since the majority of the heavy work had been completed, owners had retrieved their slaves even though much finishing work was yet to be done. Grant requested authority to impress laborers, because many planters refused to answer his call for voluntary contributions. The Engineer Bureau told Grant that a Confederate congressional act passed on February 17, 1864, was authority enough for him to impress laborers. The blacks would be rounded up by the Confederate Conscript Bureau. Grant needed only 200 men to finish the fortifications. He also received help from a draftsman named James J. Davies, who worked in Moses Wright's office. Davies had been trained as a civil engineer before the war and, like Grant, had worked on railroads. Davies became Grant's assistant from January 1 to July 7, 1864, when he received a commission in the 3rd Confederate Engineer regiment.[46]

With adequate labor and engineering expertise, Grant pushed forward to enhance the Atlanta City Line in the spring of 1864 as Sherman's army group prepared for the campaign. In April, Grant reported that the length of the line had increased to just over ten miles and required a garrison of 55,000 troops. Property damage in the construction, thus far, amounted to $250,000. Atlanta was ringed with one of the most extensive systems of city defenses in the South.[47]

Sherman received another detailed report on these works on June 24, three days before throwing his troops into the futile attack at Kennesaw Mountain. A scout named J. Milton Glass traveled around Atlanta and reported his observations. The Confederates were still improving their defenses at the railroad crossing of the Chattahoochee River but had failed to fortify many of the crossings upstream and downstream from that point. Glass saw at least three miles of the circuit around Atlanta and reported that it consisted of large redoubts connected by good infantry parapets. Glass assumed the line continued so as to encircle Atlanta, but he could not detect any signs of an inner line. He estimated that 500 blacks labored on the city defenses as well as on the Chattahoochee works.[48]

When the Army of Tennessee had pulled back to Kennesaw Mountain, Johnston assumed more responsibility for Atlanta's defenses. He ordered Grant to strengthen the works on the north side of town and construct embrasures wherever he had planned barbette gun emplacements. "As soon as the army passed the Chattahoochee," recalled Johnston, "its engineer-officers joined in the work of strengthening the intrenchments of Atlanta with all the negro laborers that could be collected." He assumed Sherman would operate first against the northeastern sector, between the Western and Atlantic Railroad and the Georgia Railroad, so the engineers and workers concentrated their efforts in that area.[49]

On July 10, the day after evacuating the Chattahoochee River Line, Johnston sent Shoup to inspect the city defenses. The artillery chief reported "that the place was enclosed by a rather poor line of rifle pits, with an occasional earthwork of more pretentions," as he later described it. Johnston told him "that was about what he thought." Even Gustavus W. Smith recalled that "Atlanta was not strongly fortified" when the Army of Tennessee moved to its vicinity in mid-July. When Johnston asked Shoup how long it would take him to construct a work similar to the River Line, the artilleryman suggested he could make a line to cover East Point as well. That village, located six miles southwest of Atlanta, was the place where two important rail lines from Macon and Montgomery joined to funnel supplies into Atlanta. At the time, East Point had no defenses. Shoup wanted to make a line long enough to cover East Point in one week, but he needed wagons and laborers, and the latter were now in short supply. The 1,000 blacks who had made the Chattahoochee River Line had dispersed, and Johnston refused to detail men to collect more workers south of Atlanta because his departmental line did not embrace that region. Johnston, according to Shoup, also refused to ask Richmond or the state authorities to help him. When Shoup himself appealed to Governor Brown, he was refused. Brown hinted that a major change in army command was pending. As a result, Shoup was unable to replicate his River Line at East Point or anywhere else.[50]

Neither Johnston, Shoup, nor Smith explained why they thought the city defenses were poorly made, but the reason probably lay with a common disjunction between engineer officers and infantry commanders. Engineers could only select ground, lay out the position, and oversee the basic construction of a defensive line by digging a trench, piling up a parapet, and making artillery emplacements. In this case, Grant also managed to clear-cut the trees in front. Any other smaller embellishments normally were done by the battery men and the line infantrymen, if they were considered necessary. Grant had no combat experience and did not know what, if anything, the troops might desire in the way of further work on the line, even if he had the time and laborers to do it. Traverses usually went in only after troops had held a position awhile and could see where the enemy placed his guns. Ironically, the Atlanta City Line was far more ready for use than any previous position Johnston had held during the

Crossing the Chattahoochee

campaign. It was the citadel, so to speak, the last ditch in the long retreat from Dalton that had begun in May, and it deserved more respect than Johnston, Shoup, and Smith gave it.

Comments by modern historians generally repeat Johnston's view of the line without understanding the explanation offered in the previous paragraph. Thomas Connelly also complained that the works were located too close to Atlanta to prevent the Federals from bombarding the city. That was an unsolvable problem. Given the range of rifled artillery, Grant would have been forced to place the line so far out as to require a garrison far larger than the Army of Tennessee to man the line. Moreover, Grant carefully selected the best hills in the vicinity for his position. One need only visit the location of Mt. Moriah Baptist Church today—near the corner of Ashby Street and Fair Street, west of downtown Atlanta, where Fort D was located—to see that point vividly illustrated. Another key point of the line lay east of downtown Atlanta, where Randolph Avenue runs atop a ridge about thirty feet tall that was also used by Grant for his line. The engineer was constricted by the reality of the terrain and the paucity of resources in planning the defensive line and had to make do with what was available.[51]

Archaeologist Robert Fryman's contention that the Atlanta City Line was not as sophisticated as those that guarded Vicksburg or Richmond also is wrong. The Vicksburg works were meager at best when the Confederates retired into the city following their defeats at Champion Hill and the Big Black River. The men made them into adequate works, but the trenches and parapets never rose above a minimal level for protection, and on many places along the siege lines they were not even adequate. Federal artillery often knocked down sections of the works, forcing tired defenders to repair them on a nightly basis. The Richmond defenses certainly were formidable, but poorly planned and executed. They actually were patched together in stages over several years, winding up with three concentric rings, the first two of which were unnecessary and wasteful. The third, or outer ring, was very effective. By comparison, Grant efficiently carved out an effective line of defense with minimal effort and resources that defended Atlanta as well as the earthworks around Richmond defended the Rebel capital.[52]

The Confederates improved the Atlanta City Line by strengthening parapets, widening trenches, and most important, constructing an impressive spread of obstacles in front of the line. The city defenses reached their fullest form by early September 1864, when the campaign came to an end. Poe offered an assessment of the line's effectiveness when he described the field of obstructions to the engineer chief in Washington. He noted that three or four rows of abatis fronted many parts of the line, along with "rows of pointed stakes, [and] long lines of chevaux-de-frise. In many places rows of palisading were planted along the foot of the exterior slope of the infantry parapet with sufficient opening between the timbers to permit the infantry fire, if carefully delivered, to pass freely through, but not sufficient to permit a person to pass through." The palisades were up to fourteen feet tall. One need only examine the many photographs taken of these obstructions and the line itself to see that Poe's admiration was not ill placed. Careful attention by line officers and the rank and file created this obstruction field from early July to early September; no one could have expected Grant or his black laborers to have done it before the Army of Tennessee crossed the Chattahoochee.[53]

FORTIFIED RIVER CROSSINGS

Johnston had no intention of contesting the Federal crossing of the Chattahoochee River beyond what he had already attempted, which was to temporarily hold the River Line on the north side of the stream. He could not know which of the many crossings Sherman intended to use, and he apparently did not think he had enough troops to disperse units to the southern bank opposite all of those crossings. As a result, getting his army group over the Chattahoochee proved to be easier than Sherman could have imagined. As late as July 6, he assumed that "forts, apparently of long construction," were located at all of the most eligible crossing points, but he was mistaken. There certainly were old works on both the north and south side of the railroad crossing. Maney's Tennessee Brigade of Cheatham's Division constructed more fortifications near that point south of the river on July 8 and 9. Poe noted the existence of Confederate fortifications to cover the railroad bridge from the south in his report to Washington, and a photograph of these works shows that they contained embrasured artillery positions. But most of the feasible crossings either had no defenses or merely small works for skirmishers and pickets.[54]

The Confederates dug many picket pits on the south side of the Chattahoochee at Roswell to contest the crossing of Garrard's cavalry on July 9. The troopers pushed the Rebel pickets aside and established a bridgehead south of the river. The Confederates had managed to burn the covered bridge that rested on stone piers before leaving, but the Federals reconstructed the bridge and moved more troops across. After Chauncey B. Reese and Maj. John R. Hotaling of Logan's staff laid out a system of defense on the south side, Fifteenth Corps troops crossed the stream on July 14 and dug works the next day. The Union line on the south side extended about two and a half miles to cover the

Crossing the Chattahoochee

Roswell Bridge, as well as Shallow Ford farther downstream. Three redoubts, with positions for two guns each, bolstered the line. The left ended on a high river bluff and the right was refused for about 800 feet. In the center, a traverse stretched toward the rear for 1,000 feet to provide protection against enfilade fire, because the line curved in the center to accommodate the course of the river. Careful study by local researchers indicates that about one-fourth of this Union-fortified bridgehead is intact today, and all of it is well mapped. One intact segment located on top of a high ridge is about 200 yards long and well preserved. It has a good ditch in front with a strong parapet, but no trench. There are some Federal picket pits in front and some Confederate picket trenches close to the edge of the river bluff, facing the other way.[55]

SHERMAN CROSSES THE RIVER

When contemplating operations south of the Chattahoochee, Sherman had no intention of attacking the ring of earthworks guarding Atlanta or attempting to lay siege to the city. He instead wanted to range around the circumference of the ring and cut the three rail lines that fed the Army of Tennessee. But first he had to cross all of his divisions over the stream. Fortunately for the Federals, there were at least fifteen viable crossing points up and down the river from the railroad bridge. The Yankees already controlled two of those crossings, at Soap's Creek and Roswell. Sherman preferred to cross upstream of the railroad, however, because that route would offer his host a more direct line of approach to the north side of the city. This line of approach also would make it possible for him to extend his formation southward to snip the Georgia Railroad, which ran into Atlanta from the east. He could then shift troops to the west of Atlanta while still holding north of the city and attempt to reach the much farther lines that lay south of town. To that end, Sherman told Thomas to place more pontoons at Powers' Ferry and Pace's Ferry and arranged for demonstrations at crossing points downstream from the railroad bridge to distract the Confederates.[56]

The Federals prepared for nearly a week to move across the stream after Johnston evacuated the Chattahoochee River Line. In part, the troops needed some rest. "A great many of our officers and men are breaking down from sheer exaustion [sic]," reported Luther Bradley to his mother on July 14. Scurvy began to appear in some units because the heavily burdened railroad could not supply Sherman's army group with a full range of commissary supplies. "Shoes and boots were worn out," recalled John Henry Otto of the 21st Wisconsin, "pants and blouses torn to shreds by brush and briar." Sherman made a supply depot at Marietta for the support of his troops and instructed the commander of the post to convert several buildings into blockhouses for its defense. The courthouse was the main stronghold in town; Sherman told the officer to "barricade and loophole the doors and windows" and make the balustrade on the roof into a parapet. "A few hours' work will convert any good brick or stone house into a citadel," he lectured his subordinate.[57]

Sherman was ready to cross the bulk of his army group on July 17. The Confederates did not oppose the move. McPherson's Army of the Tennessee marched on the left, intending to make a wide sweep southward to gain the Georgia Railroad near Decatur, then move west directly toward Atlanta. Thomas's Army of the Cumberland, to McPherson's right, moved directly south toward the city, while Schofield's Army of the Ohio tried to fill the gap between the other two armies.[58]

THE PEACH TREE CREEK LINE/ CONFEDERATE OUTER LINE

Johnston responded to news of Sherman's crossing by establishing a defensive position outside the Atlanta City Line. He decided not to contest possession of the ground north of Peach Tree Creek, a stream that ran mostly east to west four to five miles north of Atlanta before joining Nancy's Creek and then emptying into the Chattahoochee a short distance upstream from the railroad bridge. His engineers selected a line along the high ground one mile south of the creek. In his report to Richmond, written more than three months later, Johnston stated that he had wanted to attack northward from this line while the Federals were crossing the creek.[59]

The Army of Tennessee took up the Peach Tree Creek Line on July 18. The Army of Mississippi, since July 7 under the command of Alexander P. Stewart, held the left and extended far enough to cover the railroad and wagon road leading into Atlanta from Marietta. Engineer officers pointed out the positions for each of Stewart's divisions. Hardee's Corps took post to Stewart's right. Both corps began to construct works on July 18 and continued the next day until, by the morning of July 20, an artillery officer in Hardee's command could report that he had "good substantial works."[60]

But the job of constructing the Peach Tree Creek Line had barely begun when a dramatic change shook up the Army of Tennessee. Jefferson Davis had long been dissatisfied with Johnston's Fabian policy in the campaign. Davis sent his military advisor, Braxton Bragg, to visit the army's headquarters and report. Bragg indicated that Johnston seemed to have no more intention of attack-

Crossing the Chattahoochee

ing now than he'd had at any point previously in the campaign. Davis felt it was imperative that he be replaced and chose John Bell Hood to do so. Johnston was giving Presstman directions about further work on the city defenses at 10:00 P.M. on July 17, when the telegram arrived informing him that he was relieved. The transfer of authority took place the next day, when the troops were just beginning to dig the Peach Tree Creek Line. While some members of the army were willing to give Hood an opportunity to prove himself, most men were stunned and disturbed by the change. "Whether fighting or retreating the men were satisfied that their Gen knew best," confided Van Buren Oldham of the 9th Tennessee to his diary, "and wherever he led they were willing to follow." Oldham offered the opinion that "Gen Hood will probably teach the army other tactics than fortifying." Word of discontent among the troops filtered quickly into army headquarters, and several units cheered Johnston when they happened to march in his presence on their way toward new positions along the Peach Tree Creek Line.[61]

The change in commanders did not stop the construction of the new position, but it is possible, given his performance thus far in the campaign, that Johnston never had an intention of attacking from it. Hood's Corps, now temporarily under the command of Benjamin F. Cheatham, began to dig in to the right of Hardee's Corps on the morning of July 19. But by the evening of that day, word of McPherson's movement westward along the Georgia Railroad toward Atlanta forced Hood to move Cheatham south, facing east, to block the Federal approach. Cheatham established an extension of the Peach Tree Creek Line on available high ground about two miles east of the city early on July 20, with dismounted cavalry further extending his line southward to cover the railroad. While Manigault reported the line was well constructed, the troops could not have done more than make temporary fieldworks in the short space of time allowed them.[62]

Cheatham's extension of the Peach Tree Creek Line southward to cover the eastern approach to Atlanta took the line away from Peach Tree Creek. The north-facing position continued to be called the Peach Tree Creek Line, but the east-facing was called the Confederate Outer Line. Both Johnston and Hood had had the idea to create the two joint lines to meet the exigencies of Sherman's approach to the city. The ground offered few clear advantages to the Confederates, for it was mostly "broken, thickly covered with forests and undergrowth," as a Southern newspaper correspondent put it. He saw the Confederates digging in on the evening of July 19 "after their own notions." Some units had already erected "bowers of leaves above the works as a shield from sun and rain." Poe praised the Outer Line when he had a chance to examine it after

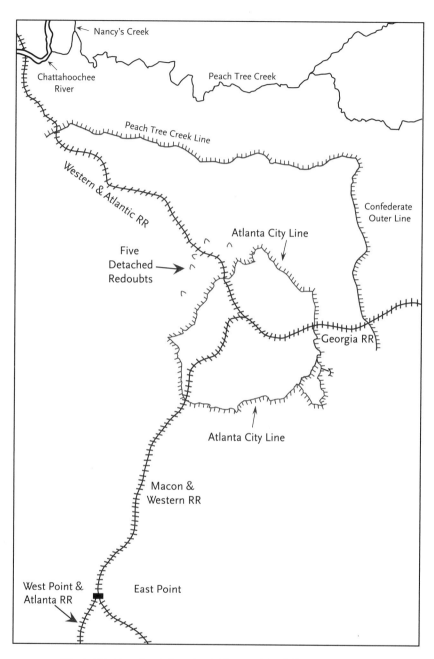

Atlanta City Line, Peach Tree Creek Line, and Confederate Outer Line

the campaign. "This line was well built, and capable of a tolerably good defense. It consisted of a system of open batteries for artillery connected by the usual infantry parapet, with all the accessories of abatis, chevaux-de-frise, &c."[63]

The work that Johnston had ordered Presstman to do at the time that he was relieved involved strengthening the city defenses along the sector that covered the ground between the Western and Atlantic Railroad and the Georgia Railroad. Presstman had a number of black laborers to work with and seven heavy rifled guns recently sent up from Mobile to emplace. Johnston intended to put Smith's militia in this sector, but in October 1864, he also claimed that he intended to attack the left flank of Sherman's line south of the Georgia Railroad if his frontal assault against Thomas at Peach Tree Creek failed to stop the Federals. Whether Johnston genuinely intended to conduct either attack or was just trying to lay claim to the tactics Hood actually employed after he left the army is difficult to tell, but his performance during the Atlanta campaign lends credence to the idea that he had little heart for attacking.[64]

Hood, on the other hand, felt enormous pressure to strike. His experience as an aggressive brigade and division commander in Lee's Army of Northern Virginia in the first half of the war, Davis's frustration with Johnston's defensive strategy, and his own unprecedented elevation to army command with a checkered record as a corps commander all compelled the young officer to risk attacks on Union positions as soon as possible.[65]

10

Peach Tree Creek,
July 22, and Ezra Church

On July 17, the day that his men crossed the Chattahoochee River and began to close in on Atlanta, Sherman instructed all three army commanders to "accept battle on anything like fair terms" with the enemy. He also authorized them to return fire if the Confederates let loose with artillery from the Atlanta City Line, without bothering to request that Johnston evacuate civilians. Sherman also penned a memorandum ordering Thomas to "press close on Atlanta, but not assault real works, but not be deterred by cavalry or light defenses."[1]

PEACH TREE CREEK

Thomas drew the lion's share of attention from Hood as the Army of the Cumberland moved steadily toward the northern sector of the city's perimeter, but first he had to cross Peach Tree Creek. It lay about five miles north of Atlanta and was the last natural barrier to the Federal approach from the north. The water level was low but the banks were rugged. Thomas reached Buck Head, a point about two miles north of the stream, on the evening of July 18, and Schofield generally kept pace with his advance three miles to the east. Portions of the Fourth, Fourteenth, and Twentieth Corps crossed Peach Tree on July 19; only the Fourteenth Corps troops, on Thomas's right, encountered stiff opposition from Confederate skirmishers. Sherman learned on July 19 that Hood had replaced Johnston, but he feared the new commander would more likely attack McPherson than Thomas. The Fifteenth Corps had already reached the Georgia Railroad near Decatur by the evening of July 18 and began to tear up track as McPherson prepared to move westward toward Atlanta.[2]

Hood's intention was to hit Thomas after the bulk of the Army of the Cumberland crossed Peach Tree Creek and was in the act of digging in on the south side. The key to this plan lay in timing. About 55,000 troops occupied the Peach Tree Creek Line; as Stewart on the left and Hardee on the right advanced, Cheatham would hold McPherson on the east of Atlanta. The attackers were told not simply to strike north in their advance but to swing left so as to drive the Federals toward the Chattahoochee River and away from McPherson. Hood meant to divide the Federal host and hoped to defeat it in detail.[3]

Hood wanted the advance to begin at 1:00 P.M. on July 20, but that did not happen. Cavalry commander Wheeler sent a message to army headquarters at 10:00 A.M. indicating that McPherson was approaching sooner than expected and his troopers could not hold him back. Hood was forced to move Cheatham's Corps one mile farther south so the infantry could replace the cavalry straddling the Georgia Railroad. Hardee and Stewart were told to move their lines half a mile farther east. In the process, Cheatham moved his command two miles rather than one, and Hardee and Stewart followed him instead of stopping their lines where originally instructed. By the time the shift ended at 3:00 P.M., Hardee and Stewart had moved farther than anticipated and consumed much valuable time. Hardee had Bate's Division on his far right, east of Clear Creek and the Buck Head and Atlanta Road, and two more divisions on line to the left with one division in reserve. Stewart had three divisions on line but had sent a brigade from each one to the far left to screen that flank. The Confederates had to move through their own slashing in front of the Peach Tree Creek Line when they began their advance. In some places, according to a man in Loring's Division, the cut trees were "lapped and crossed until they presented an almost impassable barrier." After that, they had to penetrate a thicket and cross an irregular and wooded terrain to reach the Federal target.[4]

By noon of July 20, most of Thomas's men had crossed the creek. During that time, John Newton's division of the Fourth Corps screened his left flank while the other two divisions of Howard's command moved farther east to find and connect to Schofield. In Luther P. Bradley's brigade of Newton's division, according to a member of the 51st Illinois, every other man had a spade. Orders went out to construct works and the pioneers began to cut trees, but William D. Hynes of the 42nd Illinois noted that his comrades in Bradley's brigade worked at a leisurely pace, "verry [sic] unconcerned in the matter & did not work with mouch [sic] spirit." Sherman was anxious to press on to the city defenses of Atlanta before the Confederates constructed a new line farther out from those works, not knowing that Johnston had already set the wheels in motion to do just that two days before.[5]

Although the Confederate attack was delayed three hours, Hood's men managed to hit the Federals when he hoped they would, in the act of digging in. At best, some Union units had breastworks and others had literally nothing from which to fight when Hardee started the Rebel advance at 4:00 P.M. Two of Thomas's divisions were not even in their assigned positions yet, and two other Federal divisions had exposed flanks. Moreover, the shift eastward actually placed Hardee in a better position to flank and turn Newton's exposed left and moved Stewart away from the heavily entrenched Fourteenth Corps so that he more squarely faced Hooker's ill-prepared Twentieth Corps.[6]

But because of poor coordination of Rebel efforts and fierce fighting by the Yankees, these Confederate advantages evaporated. The key of the Union defense lay with Newton's division, and those Federals paid the Confederates back for their bloody repulse at Kennesaw Mountain by skillful placement of available troops, supported by effective Union artillery. Bate moved into a cul-de-sac of terrain between Clear Creek and Peach Tree Creek and never made contact with the enemy. Two brigades of Walker's Division drove past Newton's left flank but were repulsed by Bradley's men and a collection of several Federal batteries. Walker's third brigade was decisively stopped in its frontal attack against Newton's left wing, while George Maney's Division, advancing west of the Buck Head and Atlanta Road, stalled some distance short of Newton's right wing.[7]

Hardee's men heard reports that the Federals had no significant earthworks. Even so, as Van Buren Oldham of the 9th Tennessee confided to his diary, "The boys at first did not like the idea of going outside the breastworks, but few failed to go." The report was partly true. William D. Hynes was careful to record the exact state of fortification in Newton's division when the Confederates struck. He learned that Nathan Kimball's brigade "had nothing but piles of rails strung along the line where works were to be built," and John W. Blake's brigade "being more in the timber had logs[,] some regt had on part of their line several logs piled up[,] others only one & in others the timber lay where it was felled." Wilbur F. Goodspeed's Battery A, 1st Ohio Light Artillery, had four guns behind breastworks that had been "formed of timbers from buildings nearby & rails that would protect them verry [sic] well from musket balls." Members of the 40th Indiana in Blake's brigade were gathering logs behind the line and barely had time to retrieve their guns from the stacks and rush to the small breastwork. There they fired on the Confederate skirmish line only twenty-five yards away and managed to blunt the first advance. Whenever a

Rebel attack veered close, the pioneers of Newton's division formed a line to help repel it. Between advances, the infantrymen worked hard to improve their fieldworks.[8]

To the left of Hardee, Stewart's Army of Mississippi advanced against Hooker and won limited gains. Winfield S. Featherston's Brigade approached a gap in the line between Newton and John W. Geary's Twentieth Corps division, a gap created when Hooker failed to push William T. Ward's division forward earlier that day. Ward's men were lounging in the bottomland of Peach Tree Creek, but brigade commanders responded well and mounted a vigorous counterattack that met Featherston's men partway down the bluff slope. Ward's troops fought their way to the top, repelling the Confederates. Thomas M. Scott's Confederate Brigade, advancing to Featherston's left, drove the 33rd New Jersey of Geary's division from an advanced position on a high ridge. Although Geary's men repelled Scott's right wing, the left wing took advantage of another gap to Geary's right, created again by Hooker's lack of attention to pushing Alpheus Williams's division forward to the high ground occupied by Newton and Geary. Scott's left wing tore into Geary's formation and was stopped only by hard fighting. Then Edward A. O'Neal's Confederate Brigade advanced directly into the gap and toward Williams's division but was stopped in heavy firing and compelled to retreat. The Federals continued to improve their defensive position between attacks. Lt. Col. James C. Rogers ordered the rear rank of his 123rd New York to tear down some buildings just behind the regiment after the first assault had been repulsed in order to obtain timber for the breastworks.[9]

The Federals held their advanced position south of Peach Tree Creek despite the assaults by Hardee and Stewart. While many Union troops had some kind of breastwork on the ground at the start of the battle, many others had no protection of any kind. Harvey Reid of the 22nd Wisconsin in Ward's division called Peach Tree Creek "the first field fight of the campaign—the only one in which neither party had the shelter of breastworks." Ward's men had every reason to feel proud of what they did on the afternoon of July 20. The division advanced up a slope hitting the Confederates on the way and shoving them back to gain the height. Then part of each regiment gathered fence rails while the rest fired at the enemy. As Reid put it, "I think it must prove to Mr. Hood that the Yankees can fight as well in the field as in breastworks."[10]

Hood lost 2,500 men at Peach Tree Creek out of about 26,000 engaged, and the Federals suffered 1,900 casualties out of about 20,000 on the field. Prisoners told the Yankees that Hood had assured them "they should fight no more with spades and picks." The work of strengthening the Union line continued after

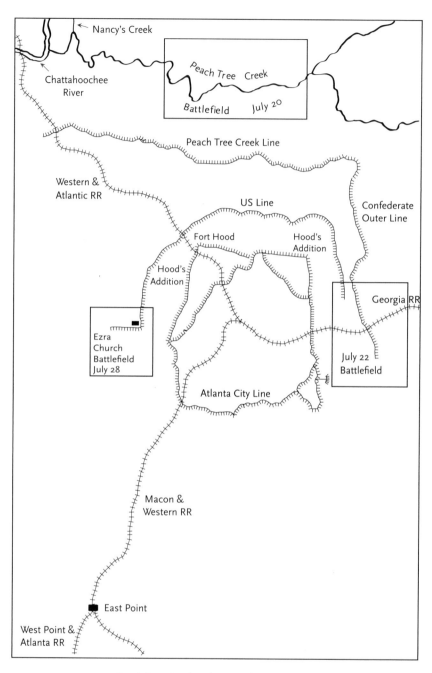

Peach Tree Creek, July 22, and Ezra Church

the battle ended, and any nearby structure suffered as the Federals sought ready supplies of timber and boards.[11]

Stewart was determined to continue the attacks at Peach Tree Creek and convinced Hardee to do likewise, but a dispatch arrived from Hood to send reinforcements to Wheeler. McPherson was pressing the cavalry east of the city, so Hardee dispatched Cleburne's Division that evening. This forced the Confederates to call it quits at Peach Tree. McPherson advanced with caution and was close enough that one of his Fifteenth Corps batteries fired the first Union artillery round into Atlanta at 1:00 P.M. on July 20. He connected his right flank to Schofield's left and extended the Army of the Tennessee southward until the left flank was about a mile south of the Georgia Railroad. Fronting the left wing, Wheeler's men held a prominent height called Bald Hill south of the railroad, but McPherson's advance was so cautious that the Federals could not mount an attack on the hill until the next day.[12]

Sherman was pleased with the results of the battle at Peach Tree Creek but concerned that McPherson was moving too slowly. "We have carried several light lines of rail-pits today all along our lines," he told McPherson on the night of July 20, "but have not followed up quick enough, so that I suppose in the morning we will find the remainder made into good parapets." In a dispatch to Thomas that night, Sherman was already beginning to think of moving McPherson behind the other two armies and shifting his men all the way to the Union right in an effort to reach the rail junction at East Point. He wanted Thomas to advance closer to Atlanta the next day to make McPherson's route shorter.[13]

Peach Tree Creek was the largest tactical offensive conducted by the Army of Tennessee since the battle of Chickamauga ten months before. It also was Hood's second independent battle, the first being Kolb's Farm, and the first test of Hood's new offensive strategy in the Atlanta campaign. Like Kolb's Farm, the attack was conducted with inadequate information about the enemy and the terrain. It also was poorly handled by Hardee and Stewart.[14] Neither corps commander managed to bring all his strength on the target with coordination. As a result, the Confederate assault was conducted mostly by individual brigades with only loose cooperation to right and left. While some of Hardee's brigades veered left according to plan, most of Stewart's brigades failed to do so. The mistake made little difference, for the Federals put up such a good fight that there was no possibility of driving them toward the Chattahoochee River.

Undaunted, Hood determined to attack McPherson as soon as possible, but first he had to ensure the safety of the defensive sector fronting Thomas. Late in the day on July 20, Hood told Presstman to examine the Peach Tree Creek Line and evaluate its usefulness as a defensive position. The engineer returned early on the morning of July 21 with a negative report. He thought it was "located upon too low ground" and therefore "was totally inadequate for the purpose designed," in Hood's words. The army commander then ordered him to locate a better position closer to Atlanta. Presstman decided to stake out a line a short distance in front of Grant's City Line, making what could be termed Hood's Addition to that position. The new line bolstered the city defenses on the northern side of Atlanta. Grant's line was roughly circular in configuration, and Presstman's plan in effect squared the northwest and northeast corners of Grant's perimeter. On the northeast quadrant, it connected to Grant's line and went due north until making a right angle by turning west. The center of Hood's Addition nearly touched the northern curve of Grant's line before continuing west. On the northwest quadrant, Presstman merely connected the five detached redoubts that Grant had constructed to make the left wing of Hood's Addition. Together, the City Line and Hood's Addition now totaled twelve miles of earthworks.[15]

Hood meant to construct and hold this new position with Stewart's Army of Mississippi, freeing up Hardee's Corps for a movement designed to hit McPherson's left flank. Presstman set to work immediately. Young Sarah Huff recalled decades later that early on the morning of July 21, engineer officers "came and laid off a line of battle" between her house and an "old log kitchen that was thirty feet away. They told Mother to leave immediately, as there would be fighting there on the following day." Hood pushed his plan as fast as possible, worried that even a delay of twenty-four hours would give the Federals time to dig in so thoroughly that catching them on the flank would result in defeat. Stewart sent work details to begin digging Hood's Addition during the day of July 21, but completion of the line would have to wait until all his men could fall back to the new position after dusk.[16]

Hood's plan depended on keeping McPherson back for the time it took Hardee to make his long flanking movement, and much of that burden fell on Cleburne's Division. Hardee sent Cleburne to the east side of Atlanta during the night of July 20, and the division took position south of the Georgia Railroad at dawn of July 21, allowing Wheeler's cavalrymen to extend the Confederate line farther south. At 7:00 A.M., Manning F. Force's brigade of Mortimer D.

Leggett's division, Seventeenth Corps, attacked Bald Hill and drove Samuel W. Ferguson's cavalry brigade away from it. Giles A. Smith (only recently transferred to the Seventeenth Corps) led a division forward north of the hill and drove off Alfred Iverson's cavalry brigade. This exposed the right end of Cleburne's infantry line, held by Brig. Gen. James A. Smith's Texas Brigade. Smith launched a counterattack that pushed Giles Smith back for a time, although Leggett continued to hold his advanced position centered on Bald Hill. In fact, the Federals established a battery position on the hill and began firing into Atlanta by midmorning.[17]

The position that Cleburne and Wheeler held on July 21 was anything but good. Staff officer Irving A. Buck called it "weak, ill protected, commanded by higher ground in front, and badly enfiladed by the enemy's artillery on the left." Mark P. Lowrey's Brigade occupied "light works, which had been constructed by the cavalry on ground badly selected." His brigade suffered six killed and forty-two wounded on July 21 even though it was not attacked. James A. Smith reported that a Federal battery 800 yards away "swept my line from left to right, committing dreadful havoc in the ranks. I have never before witnessed such accurate and destructive cannonading." A round fell into the trench and killed or injured seventeen out of eighteen men in one company of the 18th Texas Cavalry (dismounted). W. W. Royal of the 18th was struck on the chest by the severed head of a comrade when another round sailed through the trench. It knocked him down and covered him with blood. By the evening of July 21 "our clothes were sprinkled with blood and men's brains and the bottom of the breastworks was nearly half covered with blood," Royal recalled. The Texans tried to improve their works but had few tools and were fearfully exposed to Union fire.[18]

But the Confederates held on during the long, gory day east of Atlanta to give Hood an opportunity to put his flanking move into operation. When Cleburne informed Hood that his men were hard-pressed, the army commander sent another division from Hardee's Corps to help. George Maney placed his command south of Bald Hill in the early afternoon, leaving Wheeler's dismounted cavalry between Maney and Cleburne. McPherson shifted Giles A. Smith's division from the north side of Bald Hill to the south side to match this extension, as William Harrow's division of the Fifteenth Corps took Giles Smith's place.[19]

When dusk allowed Stewart to pull the Army of Mississippi away from the Peach Tree Creek Line to Presstman's new position near the City Line, many of his subordinates were not pleased with Hood's Addition. Members of the 3rd Maryland Battery found an unfinished redoubt where the line crossed the Buck Head and Atlanta Road that was "circular in form, having a parapet right,

The Ponder House. Built by Ephraim G. Ponder in 1857 outside the city limits of Atlanta, the house was located near Confederate Fort X (often called Fort Hood) on Hood's Addition to the Atlanta City Line. Ponder left his home in 1863 because he had become estranged from his wife, Ellen, who also left, in the spring of 1864. The house was empty during the time when it became prominent as a sharpshooter post for the Confederates during the siege of Atlanta, and it was perforated by Union artillery fire. Ponder owned sixty-five slaves; Henry Flipper, the first African American to graduate from the U.S. Military Academy, was the son of one of those slaves. *Photograph by George N. Barnard. Library of Congress, LC-DIG-cwpb-03415.*

left and rear, with five embrasures." Edward C. Walthall noted that his sector west of the road to Marietta "was naturally weak, much of it being lower than commanding points without held by the enemy, and it was so near the salient at Ponder's House that without heavy traverses to shelter the men from the fire which came from the right it would have been untenable." As Walthall reported, the weakness of the position could only be "cured by constant labor, so bestowed night and day in strengthening the earth-works and obstructing their front that the line became in a few days so strong that it could not have been carried by any force against even a thin line of resolute troops."[20]

Peach Tree Creek, July 22, and Ezra Church

To Walthall's left, French's Division anchored the far left of Hood's Addition, straddling the Turner's Ferry Road. Cockrell's Missouri Brigade, to the right of the road, formed but one rank so as to stretch limited numbers of troops to cover its assigned sector. A short time later, the brigade was ordered to shift more than the length of its own frontage farther to the left and start digging in again. Cockrell's men worked hard for many days constructing "a triple line of picket work, with abatis between each line, in front of the main" position. The Missourians also made "a continuous rifle-pit for the entire skirmish line" with abatis in front. A similarly fortified position was constructed for the skirmish reserve as well. On another part of Stewart's sector, Daniel Harris Reynolds formed his Arkansas troops in one and a half ranks before digging in 1,500 yards west of the railroad. By the morning of July 22, Reynolds had what he called only decent trenches but "good abatis in front of my line and traverses dug to protect against enfilading fire." His men knew the most important components of a defensive position and had concentrated on those elements first, knowing that the trench could more easily be improved over time than any other part of the line.[21]

Thomas followed up Stewart's withdrawal to Hood's Addition with caution on the morning of July 22. Howard had been able to find and connect to Schofield's right flank on July 20, but the right flank of his two-division formation was still detached from Newton's division and Hooker's corps. Stanley's pioneers cut timber across the gap between Howard and Newton in an effort to impede a possible Confederate attempt to exploit that gap. Thomas moved Hooker and Palmer forward on July 22 across the Confederate Peach Tree Creek Line and some two miles beyond it, until they came across Hood's Addition. The Federals now closed the gap and connected Newton with Stanley and Wood. Newton reported seeing head logs on the new Confederate line. The Army of the Cumberland came to rest anywhere from 200 yards to one mile from Stewart and began the process of fortifying.[22]

The Federals could not know it then, but they would occupy these works for more than a month. Members of Frederick Knefler's brigade, Fourth Corps, cut trees and rolled the logs forward on their hands and knees because of the close proximity of the enemy. Then they stacked the logs and dug a trench behind the stack while still on their knees, piling the dirt on the logs until the trench was "deep enough to stand up right." A teamster in Baird's division of the Fourteenth Corps examined a sector of the Peach Tree Creek Line and found "a 'four Square Bull Pen' our Boys call it," which was large enough for perhaps four infantry regiments and several guns. Federal artillery had fired enough at it to tear up the timber revetment on the works.[23]

When Stewart fell back just after dusk on July 21, Cheatham also withdrew from the Confederate Outer Line east of Atlanta to the City Line and Hood's Addition. Wheeler had informed Hood that day that McPherson's left flank was in the air and the Federal wagon trains were parked at Decatur. These dispositions were ideal for Confederate success. Hardee fell back from the Peach Tree Creek Line at dusk and began his flanking march with the initial intention of reaching Decatur to capture the trains and then advancing behind the Army of the Tennessee. Wheeler went along, and Cheatham was slated to attack McPherson's front at an opportune moment. Stewart and the militia were to hold the city. It was a good plan except that the flanking march was long; Hardee started late and his men would have to trudge all night. There was precious little time and limited energy to put the plan into effect.[24]

The Federals were completely unaware of this flanking move. They busied themselves with digging in on the evening of July 21. McPherson warned Francis P. Blair, his Seventeenth Corps commander, to be on the alert for an attack at dawn the next day. "Have the brush and small trees in front of your intrenchments cut down for a distance of 80 or 100 yards, making a sort of abatis." On Bald Hill, Leggett's men worked all night to fortify the open top of the height. The men of Robert K. Scott's brigade built five traverses for each regiment so that two companies could find shelter in the bays that were thus formed. The men of the 12th Wisconsin made their traverses "especially solid and strong." Farther north, on the Fifteenth Corps sector, Capt. Francis De-Gress tried to make the position of his Battery H, 1st Illinois Light Artillery, as strong as possible. It was a poor place for guns, he admitted, located just north of the Georgia Railroad with trees and "thick underbrush in front." His men cut timber as far as their strength and time permitted during the night until he could fire about 200 yards to the front. Still, the undergrowth ran nearly up to his flanks, offering a constricted field of fire.[25]

Sherman seemed at least moderately pleased with his success. Late on July 21, he told Halleck that he intended to shell Atlanta the next day. "I doubt if General Hood will stand a bombardment," he concluded, even though he admitted that the new commander of the Army of Tennessee had shown considerable fight thus far.[26]

On the night of July 21, Bate and Walker led Hardee's march south, then east, to scribe a circuit fifteen miles long before the Confederates could hope to get anywhere near McPherson's flank. Maney, Cleburne, and Wheeler remained in place east of Atlanta until midnight. The delay led Hood to alter his plan a bit, allowing Wheeler to strike at Decatur and the infantry to make a shorter march from the area of Cobb's Mill in order to hit McPherson at dawn.

But it took three hours for the Confederates to evacuate the trenches east of Atlanta. Not until 3:00 A.M. did Maney's Division, at the tail of Hardee's column, leave Atlanta to follow the rest of the corps. In fact, Smith's Texas Brigade left its skirmish line in place until nearly dawn, the men talking loudly and striking the log revetment of their works with sticks to make as much noise as possible and fool the Federals into thinking the line was still manned.[27]

When dawn revealed that the Confederate Outer Line was empty, Sherman initially assumed Hood was in retreat toward East Point and urged McPherson to push the Fifteenth Corps forward in pursuit. That notion was soon dispelled. When Sherman established his headquarters at the Howard House on the extreme right flank of the Army of the Tennessee, he could see that the city defenses were well manned. He reverted to his original thinking, telling McPherson to remain in place for the time but prepare to shift to the west of Atlanta.[28]

McPherson's troops busied themselves with housekeeping chores during the morning of July 22, while Hardee's men continued their exhausting flank march. Chauncey Reese, John Barlow, and Oswald H. Ernst examined the ground in front of McPherson's army in preparation for an advance in case Sherman decided to order one. The troops moved forward enough to occupy the Confederate Outer Line early on July 22 and began to reverse the Rebel works for their own use. Members of the 53rd Ohio used a convenient pile of lumber to revet their sector of the line. In Harrow's division, many men grumbled at yet another order to work on fortifications. Harrow wanted all his guns to be dug in, but the gunners did little more than throw up "a slight parapet ... without embrasures. The work was considered needless by all who expressed themselves in my hearing," commented Capt. Josiah F. Burton of Battery F, 1st Illinois Light Artillery, "with the exception of General Harrow." DeGress moved his battery forward but discovered that a gap of 1,000 yards separated him from Charles R. Woods's division of the Fifteenth Corps to the north, with only a couple of infantry companies as a support.[29]

The Federals pushed their skirmish line as far as possible. Along Woods's front on the Fifteenth Corps sector, the skirmishers established themselves a quarter of a mile ahead of the new main line and began to cut trees to make defenses as Confederate artillery shelled them. On the Seventeenth Corps front, Leggett pushed his skirmishers until they came within long musket range of the city defenses. Here the Federals also dug in, constructing "lunettes of rails with dirt in front," according to Capt. Gilbert D. Munson of the 78th Ohio.[30]

By dawn of July 22, half of Hardee's Corps had not yet reached Cobb's Mill, the point at which Wheeler would strike out for Decatur and the infantry would head directly for McPherson's flank. After the divisions reached the mill, Bate and Walker advanced along Sugar Creek, with Bate to the east of the stream and Walker to the west, in an attempt to skirt the Union flank and strike into the rear. Cleburne advanced east of Flat Shoals Road and Maney west of it to strike the flank directly.[31]

The Confederates hit McPherson shortly after noon, several hours later than Hood had planned. Bate struggled through the wide, tangled bottomland of Sugar Creek. He had no idea of the enemy's position or strength but pushed on in hopes of catching the Federals unaware. To his men's surprise, Bate found Thomas W. Sweeny's division of the Left Wing, Sixteenth Corps, which had just paused for lunch on the highest ground in his front, a commanding position even without breastworks. Bate attacked but his men were repulsed. Walker's Division fared little better. Walker himself was one of the first casualties, a victim of skirmish firing as his division struggled to march past a large mill pond along Sugar Creek. His brigades advanced piecemeal and were repulsed. A Federal counterattack netted some 500 prisoners. Within forty-five minutes, Bate and Walker were out of action. About 5,000 men fought on each side in this fight, and no one was protected by earthworks. The Sixteenth Corps troops had the advantage of terrain. They also were rested and ready for action, and happened to be in the right place at the right time to blunt the threat to McPherson's rear. While this fight had been an open-field contest, the Federals quickly began to dig in as soon as the Confederates retired.[32]

Like Walker, McPherson became a victim of skirmish fire in the battle of July 22. He witnessed Bate's and Walker's attacks on the Sixteenth Corps and then rode toward Blair's command to the west. A large gap existed between Dodge and Blair, and McPherson rode across it just as the skirmishers of James A. Smith's Brigade moved northward through the area. They encountered McPherson and fired when the general refused to give up. Members of the 5th Confederate Infantry, led by Capt. Richard Beard, were responsible for McPherson's death that afternoon.[33]

While Bate's and Walker's divisions made no headway against the opportunely placed men of Dodge, the rest of Hardee's Corps ran right against the poorly refused left flank of the Seventeenth Corps. Hardee was unable to attack with coordination; as a result, individual brigades careered into the Federal position. But these onslaughts produced a fight within the battle of July 22 that chewed up several Federal units, captured a section of enemy earthworks, and came closer to a Confederate tactical victory than any other engagement of the campaign.

Leggett's Third Division held the area around Bald Hill, with Force's brigade to the north of the height and elements of Adam G. Malloy's and Robert K.

Scott's brigades on and immediately south of it. Giles Smith's Fourth Division extended the Union position south of Scott with two brigades, Benjamin F. Potts's on the right and William Hall's on the left. These two brigades occupied an earthwork that slanted from Bald Hill toward the southeast along Flat Shoals Road for a few hundred yards. Hall built a refused line at the far left flank long enough for two regiments and a section of Battery F, 2nd Illinois Light Artillery. The area immediately around Bald Hill was cleared and cultivated, as was the ground in front of Leggett all the way to the City Line. But the area occupied by the flanking line along Flat Shoals Road was thickly wooded, especially toward the rear. The fortifications were little more than temporary fieldworks, with a short cleared space in front of Potts and Hall. The Federals had time enough to cut and bend much of the brush and saplings in front of their line, "leaving the butt or stump two feet high," according to a Confederate who encountered them.[34]

Hardee's confused assault devolved into five discernable attacks on the Seventeenth Corps position. Daniel Govan's Arkansas Brigade advanced astride Flat Shoals Road with Smith's Texas Brigade to its right and Mark P. Lowrey's Alabama and Mississippi Brigade behind Smith. Govan hit Hall's flank and slowed to engage the Federals as most of Smith's Brigade continued northward directly into the huge gap separating Blair from Dodge. This is why Smith's men were able to encounter and kill McPherson. Lowrey lost connection with the other two brigades and stumbled in the forest before launching the third Confederate attack. Smith's command broke up into segments due to the rough terrain, and part of it cooperated with Govan in the first attack.[35]

Govan chewed up the flank of Giles Smith's division line. His left wing hit Hall's trench perpendicularly and the short refused line squarely. Govan's right wing wheeled around to strike the rear of the position. In the process, the Arkansas men crushed most of the 16th Iowa. The Confederates took many prisoners and two guns of Battery F, 2nd Illinois Light Artillery. Many men of Hall's brigade jumped to the west side of their works to fire at Govan's left wing advancing along the main line that ran along Flat Shoals Road, and some men of Scott's brigade farther north also formed west of their works. While they could not save the Iowa regiment, they did contain the damage and hold the Confederates in the lower end (about 300 yards) of the trench line along the road. "Our works were not complete," admitted one Federal, "but they would have afforded considerable shelter had the attack been from the front."[36]

Vaughan's Tennessee Brigade and Strahl's Tennessee Brigade advanced toward the Federals along the west side of the road soon after Govan's success to make the second attack on Blair's position. To confront them, Hall pulled two regiments out of the works and aligned them at a right angle to the parapet, their left touching the works. He kept the rest of his brigade in the trench. Potts performed a similar move, placing his entire brigade west of the line and about seventy-five yards behind Hall's two regiments. The Confederates hit just after the Federals completed this formation, moving forward with "hideous yell-ing," according to an observer. They struck not only the front but the right flank of Hall's two regiments, forcing the Federals back into the protection of their trench. Potts controlled 1,000 troops in his line; he refused the right regiment, the 32nd Ohio, and repelled the enemy.[37]

Five minutes after the repulse of the second Confederate attack, Lowrey's troops found and struck the rear of Blair's position to conduct the third attack. The Alabama and Mississippi men emerged from the thick brush east of Giles A. Smith's Federal division, where the woods came as close as twenty yards to the Union trench. This was the most desperate engagement of the day. Lowrey's command lodged on the east side (rear) of the Union line along Flat Shoals Road and engaged in hand-to-hand combat with the Federals commanded by Hall and Potts. At the height of this desperate encounter, Col. William W. Bel-knap of the 15th Iowa reached out and grabbed Col. Harris D. Lampley of the 45th Alabama by the coat collar and pulled him across the Union work as a prisoner. The thirty-year-old Lampley had been seriously wounded in the right shoulder a short time before, making Belknap's capture easier; he would die of his injury in the Seventeenth Corps general hospital at Marietta little more than a month later.[38]

Lowrey's men held on at the Union work for forty-five minutes before they retired. By this time, it was late afternoon, and Hood ordered Cheatham to ad-vance from the area of Atlanta. Cheatham's advance covered much of the Fif-teenth Corps front as well as that of the Seventeenth Corps, forcing Giles A. Smith's Federals to go back into their trench along Flat Shoals Road. At the same time, Hardee's men continued to punish Smith with artillery and rifle fire as Potts and Hall formed a short refused line extending east from the road a short distance south of Bald Hill. Regiments of Leggett's division (20th and 78th Ohio) pulled out of their works immediately south of Bald Hill to begin forming a second and much longer refused line, extending eastward from the height, on high ground. Any Federals who could be spared from the firing line rushed to the rear to find fence rails for a breastwork along the refused line. They placed the rails on the ground and scooped up dirt with their bayonets and tin cups to make "a very fair protection for men lying on their bellies," re-called an observant artilleryman. Those units, like the 32nd Ohio, which had no opportunity to find fence rails, relied on "the unevenness of the ground" for shelter.[39]

The short refused line held by Potts and Hall received so much enfilade fire from the west that the men were forced to give it up and retire to the longer refused line to the north. Here the Federals had ample manpower to hold a high ridge blocking the Confederate advance northward. Col. Hugo Wangelin's brigade of the Fifteenth Corps came forward to extend the line farther to the east, although not far enough to connect with Dodge's Sixteenth Corps troops, separated from Wangelin by half a mile of timbered landscape.[40]

The fifth Confederate attack by Hardee's men, directed by Vaughan's, Govan's, and Maney's Brigades, with parts of Lowrey's, Gist's, and Smith's in reserve, struck Bald Hill itself and the refused line. The hill was held by the 11th Iowa of Giles A. Smith's division and the 16th Wisconsin of Leggett's division. These regiments held the key height behind their simple fieldworks in the face of Govan's assault, as Wangelin's brigade moved forward to threaten the Confederate right flank and stall the assault on the refused line.[41]

Cheatham's attack from the west produced a temporary and tantalizing success along the Fifteenth Corps sector. Cheatham had already moved his troops forward out of the City Line and positioned them from a point well north of the Georgia Railroad and far enough south to cover Bald Hill before Hood ordered him to go in. Maj. Gen. Henry De Lamar Clayton commanded Stewart's Division on the left, Brig. Gen. John C. Brown led Hindman's Division in the center, and Maj. Gen. Carter L. Stevenson's Division held the right. Seventeenth Corps troops easily repelled Stevenson.[42]

But Brown's men in the center managed to capture a small section of the Union line. Brown had two brigades to the north of the railroad (commanded by Arthur M. Manigault and Jacob H. Sharp) and two south of it. Initially, the Confederates were stopped short of the Federal position, but Manigault's Brigade took cover about 100 yards from the enemy and maintained a heavy fire at the Federals. This helped members of Sharp's Brigade push through a cut along the railroad that was lightly held by the Yankees. They attacked northward to clear the Union line for a few hundred yards.[43]

The Fifteenth Corps position was aligned along the abandoned Confederate Outer Line and thus consisted of a reversed trench. When Manigault moved his brigade forward to occupy the sector cleared by Sharp, he recognized the works as former Confederate fortifications. They "had been much strengthened and altered to fight inwards," he recalled. "The abattis which we had covered our front with had been reversed, and had presented itself as an obstacle to us, but so impetuous was the last rush that many officers and men declared that they were not aware of its existence until some minutes after the contest had ended." There were two trenches, one dug by the Federals on the east side of the parapet for their own use and one on the west of it made by the Confederates.[44]

Capt. Francis DeGress was unable to save the guns of his Battery H, 1st Illinois Light Artillery. Positioned a short distance north of the railroad, he could see comparatively little toward the front but knew that the 30th Ohio, his support to the left, was under great pressure as Sharp's men advanced northward along the line from the tracks. That regiment held on as long as it could to allow DeGress time to evacuate, but the pace of action was too fast. DeGress spiked his pieces and retired when the Confederates were only yards away.[45]

The Federals responded quickly to this rupture of the Fifteenth Corps line. Woods's division, just to the north, refused its left wing to contain the breach and then launched a counterattack. Sherman arranged for Schofield to mass his guns on a convenient height to bombard the sector held by the Confederates, and Logan, who now held temporary command of the Army of the Tennessee, led three regiments of Fifteenth Corps troops plus a brigade sent to him by Dodge on a counterattack. Within a half hour of the rupture, the Federals set into motion four brigades and massed twenty-eight artillery pieces to drive the Confederates away.[46]

Clayton's Division failed to hold Woods's men in place. Clayton assigned Alpheus Baker's Brigade to confront the Federals opposite the Howard House, Sherman's headquarters located on a high, commanding hill. Baker's men advanced to a point only fifteen paces from the Federal trench and held there twenty minutes exchanging rounds with the enemy. Capt. Robert K. Wells of the 42nd Alabama reported that he could see the heads of the Union soldiers above the parapet, but the fire of his men forced most of the enemy to duck frequently. The Union fire was "weak and wild," Wells reported, "most of the bullets passing high in the air." There were no obstructions in front of the line here, and Wells believed he could have taken the trench if allowed to do so. But Baker's troops retired rather than push on.[47]

Clayton led the other three brigades of his division toward the southeast to strike the Federals nearer the railroad. The three lost touch with each other and operated almost independently. Col. Abda Johnson's brigade, formerly commanded by Marcellus Stovall, closed on the Union line just north of the sector held by Sharp and Manigault. It had no support to right or left and received enfilade fire on its flank. Johnson held there at close range for half an hour before retiring.[48]

Cheatham's attack had been conducted with a deplorable lack of coordination, and the tentative breach in the Fifteenth Corps line was only thinly held by the Rebels. As a result, the Federal counterattack quickly achieved its purpose. Converging columns from the north and east soon cleared the Confederates out of the Union works. DeGress went in with the Sixteenth Corps troops and immediately began to unspike his guns. He had lost many of his horses but managed to put most of his pieces back into action within a few hours.[49]

To Cheatham's right, Gustavus Smith and 2,000 Georgia Militia troops tried to help the Confederate attack. Smith's men had strengthened the city defenses during the morning before they advanced east in conjunction with Cheatham to a point about one mile from the Federals. He set up his lone battery within 400 yards of the Union skirmish line. The militia held there during the course of Cheatham's attack but was not engaged, having no orders to go in, when it retired.[50]

Four miles east of the battlefield, Wheeler's cavalry completed its long flank march by striking Decatur from the south. The cavalry outnumbered John W. Sprague's brigade of Sixteenth Corps infantry three to one, but the Federals put up a stout fight to save McPherson's wagon train. The dismounted Confederate cavalrymen pushed the Federals completely out of town in a running fight, but Sprague managed to pull the trains well out of danger while his infantry held them back.[51]

Elsewhere along the circumference of works that surrounded Atlanta, troops of the Fourth Corps advanced to a point within sight of the Confederate City Line on July 22, while the Army of the Tennessee fought its magnificent battle. Stanley moved forward within range of Rebel artillery and dug in his division between the Twentieth Corps and Schofield's army. When Chesley Mosman gazed on the extensive works barring Stanley's approach to the city, he thought the campaign had closed down to "a siege of Atlanta." Then word of the Confederate attack on McPherson filtered along the line. "Hood is initiating Lee's policy of the offensive defensive and we may now look for the Rebels to assault our lines at any time," Mosman commented in his journal. "Well, that is so much better, for, if prepared for such assaults, it is easier to repel an assault than to make it and our generals here in the west know how to prepare for such tactics."[52]

Farther to the right, other Federal soldiers were busy constructing new lines of defense on July 22 rather than repelling enemy attacks. Col. Horace Boughton's brigade of Williams's division, Twentieth Corps, endured constant sniping and artillery fire as it continued to strengthen its earthworks just east of the Western and Atlantic Railroad. The men slashed the timber in front where possible, constructed abatis, and revetted artillery embrasures. To the front, the Confederates in Hood's Addition protected their position by multiplying lines of obstructions.[53]

The 3rd Wisconsin worked to make a parapet eighteen feet thick at the base, four feet tall, and eight feet wide at the top. The berm of natural earth left at the base of the parapet was well placed to serve as a fire step. The men dug their trench twelve feet wide and used posts and fence rails to revet the parapet. They found logs eight to ten inches in diameter to use as head logs and cut them from fifteen to twenty feet long, resting them on blocks three or four inches thick. When time allowed, the Wisconsin men cut pine boughs to create screens supported by poles and crotched sticks to protect them from the sun, but officers soon ordered them to tear the screens down because they would interfere with efforts to defend the trench if the enemy attacked.[54]

Opposite Thomas's men, Stewart's Army of Mississippi was secure in its new position. The men of Matthew D. Ector's Texas Brigade in French's Division worked on a rectangular redoubt designed for infantry beginning on July 22. It measured fifty feet square. They also concentrated on fortifying their skirmish line with a row of abatis consisting of brush with the ends of the limbs sharpened. The Texans planted a row of sharpened stakes "firmly set in the ground in an inclined position," as their brigade commander put it.[55]

Thus was the day of July 22 spent by many troops while the bloody drama played out at the far left of the Union line. Hardee's and Cheatham's attacks ended by dusk, but peace failed to settle across the field. The Confederates lodged in the woods close to Bald Hill and sniped at the Federals all evening. Those who held the refused line that stretched east from the hill were protected only by a hastily thrown up breastwork, and they suffered much from this skirmish fire. Leggett asked for relief to hold the hill itself because his men were exhausted, so a Sixteenth Corps brigade came up in the night. The fieldworks that had existed on the hill during the battle had been severely reduced by shelling. One portion of the parapet was "shot away, razed to the ground by continued battering," thought Gilbert Munson of the 78th Ohio. The Sixteenth Corps troops had to crawl into the fortifications on their hands and knees and then labored throughout the night to strengthen the defenses of the hill that Logan termed "the key-point to my whole position." "Bald Hill was almost a Gibraltar," commented William H. Chamberlin of the Sixteenth Corps. "Its fortification was unique, and though engineered by the men who wielded the shovel, it was complete and invulnerable."[56]

Hardee's men remained where the battle left them and they began to dig in as well. Only at Bald Hill did the opposing trench lines near each other, and there they "almost touched," in Chamberlin's words. Toward the southeast they diverged "at an ever-increasing distance." While no full map of the Confederate works on the battlefield of July 22 exists, there is sketchy information about them as they existed in 1877 in a hand-drawn map made by engineer John R. McGuiness when he was examining the battlefield for the purpose of placing a monument to the slain McPherson.[57]

The battle of July 22, also known as the battle of Atlanta, was the largest and costliest engagement of the campaign. The Federals lost 3,722 men, while Hood suffered 5,500 casualties. Despite their fatigue and lack of coordination, Hardee's men mounted a spirited attack that came closer to success than any other Rebel assault of the campaign. The stubborn defense of their trench line by Seventeenth Corps troops became a subject of wonder among the Federals. "Few troops, with their flank turned in this way by an enveloping force, can ever be kept in position," thought Oliver O. Howard. Yet these men succeeded in "repelling the enemy in two opposite directions with a line in air." The spectacle of Union troops jumping from one side of the works to the other to repel the uncoordinated strikes was unprecedented in Civil War history. Charles E. Smith of the 32nd Ohio in Potts's brigade gave Leggett credit for telling the men to do this. When the enemy came from the rear, "we would just climb over the breastworks and fight them from the other side." Henry O. Dwight of the 20th Ohio argued that Scott's brigade was hit five times within four hours, all from different directions. His comrades fought, "looking for all the world like a long line of these toy-monkeys you see which jump over the end of a stick."[58]

A considerable amount of hand-to-hand combat also took place in this confused melee. "A man was actually well-nigh dismembered," recalled Dwight, "the rebels pulling his feet, to take him prisoner, and our boys pulling his head to save him. Men were bayoneted, knocked down with the butts of muskets, and even fists were used in default of better weapons in that deadly strife." The result after the battle was obvious. When Charles Wills of the 103rd Illinois surveyed the battlefield the next day he found that "dead Rebels lay about as thick on one side of the works as the other, and right up to them."[59]

Even though a failure, Hood's second sortie at Atlanta had an emotional effect on the Federals. The lesson of their narrowly won victory was not lost. Sherman issued an order late on July 22 that all units must dig in more securely and hold back a strong reserve of infantry for all emergencies. The artillery must be protected by good fieldworks as well. If the Confederates attacked the next day, anywhere, all other commanders should strike forward and distract their attention away from the point of assault.[60]

In the Army of the Tennessee that night, there was tension mixed with fatigue and apprehension. "Our suspense was great all night," Maj. Abraham Seay of the 32nd Missouri in Wangelin's brigade admitted, "our line partially shattered and disconnected. We were secure only in the weakness of the enemy and another assault expected at daylight this morning." Henry Dwight noted that his comrades had grumbled a good deal about the labor involved in building earthworks early on July 22, but after the battle they worked hard without complaint. The Seventeenth Corps men "fortified not only the front, but facing the rear and every way," Dwight reported, "so that they could hold out if surrounded." They also gathered spare guns and ammunition from the battlefield and stockpiled them for immediate use. "No grumbling was heard about building the works."[61]

Logan, who continued to command the Army of the Tennessee, visited the Seventeenth Corps soon after the fight. Apparently referring to Leggett's command, he reported to Sherman that one of its divisions was "somewhat despondent." That mood changed with time, but the Seventeenth Corps commander retained the lesson of July 22 for a long time to come. Blair issued an order to his division commanders on August 2 reminding them to "pay the greatest attention to the laying out of field-works, as the direction of a very small portion of the line may decidedly affect the issue of an attack on it."[62]

EZRA CHURCH

Sherman spent much of the day on July 23 examining the entire Union line and informed Logan that the extreme right, held by the Fourteenth Corps, extended to Proctor's Creek to the northwest of Atlanta. At this point, the end of the Union line lay about 1,000 yards from the Confederate position and it was refused to offer protection against a flanking movement. The entire Federal line, which Sherman estimated at five miles long, was well shielded by good earthworks, and he doubted that Hood would be foolish enough to launch another attack on well-prepared positions. "The question now is, What next?"[63]

The question posed to Logan was a rhetorical one, for Sherman had every intention of moving the Army of the Tennessee to the right. He wanted to explain the move in person to Logan, however, for the temporary commander of that field army had not been previously kept informed of Sherman's intent. The move was postponed a few days by a promising cavalry raid launched by Maj. Gen. Lovell H. Rousseau from Tennessee into Alabama for the purpose of disrupting Confederate rail lines. Rousseau brought 2,500 mounted troopers to Sherman's army group, arriving at Marietta on July 22. Sherman then used them to cover his right flank while sending a contingent of his own cavalry under

Kenner Garrard to hit the Georgia Railroad east of Decatur. Sherman waited until Garrard returned from his short trip on July 24, having done limited damage, before preparing the next move.[64]

After Logan's departure from his position east of Atlanta, Schofield's Army of the Ohio would hold the Union left. Sherman hoped to threaten East Point, the junction of two rail lines approaching Atlanta from the south and southwest. He assumed the Confederates would find out about the move in time to shift troops to oppose it, but at least he could force Hood to extend his own line "till he is out of Atlanta."[65]

The cavalry raids gave the Federals an opportunity to prepare for the shift of infantry troops to the right. Sherman told Poe on July 23 that he had no intention of attacking the City Line or of conducting regular siege approaches. The engineer was ordered to plan temporary fieldworks to protect the flank after Logan pulled the Army of the Tennessee away from the left. That meant constructing a long refused line eastward from some point along the current line of Logan's army. Initially, Sherman wanted that refused line to be placed south of the Georgia Railroad to make sure the Confederates did not try to put the rails back into operation. Poe and Chauncey Reese scouted the terrain on July 23 and decided on a spot about 200 yards south of the railroad for the start of the refused line.[66]

Poe then consulted with Sherman and proposed a slight change in the plan. Placing the refused line south of the railroad would force Schofield to stretch his limited manpower even farther, increasing the sector held by the Twenty-Third Corps by several hundred yards. There really was no need to cover the rail line with the refused position; as long as a stretch of track was dismantled and the Federals were within reach of the line, the Confederates could not attempt to use it. Sherman consented to stretching the refused line from Schofield's current left flank, which was located at the Howard House on what is today called Copenhill, a high piece of ground perfectly suited for an important salient in the line and today the site of the Jimmy Carter Presidential Library. Poe and Reese, accompanied by three other engineer officers, laid out this line on the morning of July 24. While Fifteenth Corps troops did the heavy work on this refused line, the chief engineers of each corps in the Army of the Tennessee supervised the effort. Meanwhile, Reese busied himself with scouting the roads needed to take the army toward Sherman's right flank and taking staff officers from each corps headquarters to acquaint them with the routes their commands were to use.[67]

While some of Logan's men constructed the new refused line, others improved fortifications along the front of the Army of the Tennessee. This work continued from July 23 to 26, representing a frenzy of activity induced by the shock of Hood's attack. As the historian of the 2nd Iowa put it, the men "were employed night and day in throwing up fortifications, and, to guard against possible surprise, faced these fortifications towards all points of the compass." Along the sector where Cheatham's men had broken through on July 22, the Federals borrowed axes from Schofield's troops and cut and placed more abatis. They erected head logs, filled in the railroad cut that the enemy had used to break the line, and tore down buildings in front of their position that the Confederates had employed as shelter. They began to build and set up sections of chevaux-de-frise. The men of the 2nd Iowa drew the line when regimental officers told them to dig small pits three feet deep and two feet wide in front of their position. They did not take this seriously and joked about the Confederates falling into these holes so they could bayonet them out like farmers using pitchforks to unload hay. "We posted a man as a look-out, greeting him with the frequent inquiry, 'any rebs in the holes?' to which he always returned the discouraging response, 'nary reb.'" Nevertheless, Poe was impressed by all the activity of Logan's men and thought the army's fieldworks made its position very secure.[68]

Logan's troops were not the only men heavily engaged in earthwork construction after the battle of July 22. Stanley's division of the Fourth Corps also worked on its defenses, particularly the placement of abatis in front of the division line. Thomas H. Ruger's brigade of the Twentieth Corps moved a quarter mile closer to the Confederates on the night of July 24 and constructed a new parapet. Even though covered by darkness, the Federals were fired on by Confederate pickets while chopping down trees to start the new line. The 5th Ohio in Charles Candy's brigade of Geary's division constructed a section of the line that was 1,800 yards long. By July 27, the new position was ready for occupancy. Other Twentieth Corps troops constructed a secondary position 300 feet behind the front line for a layered defense.[69]

Artillery on both sides was active during the several days that followed the battle of July 22. When a Confederate solid shot entered the works held by the 3rd Wisconsin, splattering dirt over William Wallace while he was eating his dinner, his comrades dug it out of the ground and gave it to a nearby battery, which promptly fired it back to the Confederates. Farther along the Twentieth Corps line, the 129th Illinois in Ward's division suffered when a shell hit the works and dumped "a vast amount of ground into the trenches." It covered up several men but fortunately no one was injured by it. This prompted the Illinoisans to work until late at night to improve their protection. Joseph F. Culver thought his comrades were "shell proof unless some of the pieces come straight down" on the works.[70]

Peach Tree Creek, July 22, and Ezra Church

Federal guns continued to shell Atlanta on a sporadic basis if their placement along the line allowed them the range. S. P. Richards, who operated a stationery store in the city, reported that Federal gunnery "scared the women and children and *some* of the *men* pretty badly" on July 23. A round hitting the street threw stones into the windows of one house, forcing the inhabitants to take shelter behind their chimney. The shelling continued on July 24.[71]

Sherman began issuing orders for the transfer of Logan's army to the right on July 26. After the Army of the Tennessee left, Schofield was to shift one of his divisions into the new refused line that stretched east from the Howard House all the way to an abandoned Confederate line of works. This Rebel line had been hastily constructed by Wheeler's cavalrymen upon the initial approach of McPherson's army on July 20. It was little more than a light fieldwork but served as a convenient marker for the end of the refused line.[72]

But Schofield had a different idea and prevailed on Sherman for his approval. Schofield did not want to stretch his manpower too thin, so he planned to construct an entirely new refused line, starting from near the center of his current position and extending back to Wheeler's old line. Jacob Cox's division would occupy this new line upon Logan's departure, and Milo Hascall would extend the extreme left of his division line into it as well. Schofield wanted to improve a section of Wheeler's old line that extended north from the left end of the refused line, long enough to hold two brigades from Stanley's division of the Fourth Corps. This new plan would give Schofield a much shorter, more compact, and more heavily manned position. It also would give him protection on three sides, and he could safely guard his trains in this boxlike position. Schofield planned to use the refused line dug by the Fifteenth Corps to house his skirmishers. The Fifteenth Corps line was a bare trench and parapet, the men having had no time to do more. Cox already had planned to strengthen the parapet and add obstructions in front if he had to use it as a main line. Now that would not be necessary. Sherman had already authorized Schofield to use Wheeler's abandoned line to cover the rear of his army on July 24 and now consented to the new scheme. One could argue that Schofield's plan was excessively cautious, but no one wanted to be caught by surprise if Hood tried another flanking movement.[73]

Just as Logan was about to begin his move, Sherman made a controversial decision to name Oliver O. Howard as permanent commander of the Department and Army of the Tennessee. The decision greatly angered Logan and made of him a bitter enemy of both Sherman and Howard. Sherman told Logan of this decision soon after the troops pulled out early on the morning of July 27. Schofield and Stanley immediately shifted their men into the new flanking positions. Howard wanted to conduct the movement west in a careful manner, placing each division to extend the Union line beyond Proctor's Creek one at a time with a supporting division close behind, beginning on the evening of July 27. The Left Wing, Sixteenth Corps, held the left, then the Seventeenth Corps, and the Fifteenth Corps was held in reserve for the time. The troops "began to prepare the usual cover," as Sherman put it, early the next morning.[74]

As soon as the Federals abandoned the battlefield of July 22, the Confederates opposite that location came forth and examined what was left behind. A group of officers that included Wheeler and Cleburne rode over the battlefield and were amazed by the earthworks they saw. "Their fortifications were like rat holes in a curve and were thrown up on all sides," commented an Arkansas artilleryman named Thomas J. Key. Van Buren Oldham of the 9th Tennessee noted that the Federals had pulled the bodies of several Confederates into "some rifle trenches" as a quick way to bury them. "Several bodies were recognized and re-buried by their friends." The battleground had not changed much when Manning F. Force looked it over in November 1864. Force had been wounded at the height of the engagement on July 22, and this was his first view of Bald Hill since recovering from his injury. He, too, noted that the works were constructed "looking in all directions. Each company was in a little redoubt, and kept ammunition there. Regimental and Brigade head quarters were constructed of circular mounds. The whole ground is dug up. What is not intrenchment, is graves."[75]

Hood discovered Sherman's move soon after it began on the morning of July 27 and reacted to block the extension of the Union line west of Atlanta. He relied on Lt. Gen. Stephen D. Lee, who had arrived from a departmental command in Mississippi on July 26, to take permanent command of his old corps. Lee pulled Brown's and Clayton's divisions out of line northeast of Atlanta and moved them toward the southwest of the city, as Hardee shifted his corps north to replace them. The two divisions reached the Lick Skillet Road by dusk that evening, a few hundred yards south of the position Howard was already beginning to take. Hood wanted Stewart to move Edward C. Walthall's Division and Loring's Division from the northwest side of Atlanta and march out along the Lick Skillet Road past Lee to turn the Federal right flank and attack early on the morning of July 29. The plan was reminiscent of the one that had failed on July 22.[76]

Hood's instructions to his subordinates were explicit: Lee was to hold the Federals' attention as Stewart conducted his flanking march. Hood's chief of staff told Hardee that Lee had orders "not to attack unless the enemy exposes himself in attacking us." Lee merely had to make sure the Federals did not

Peach Tree Creek, July 22, and Ezra Church

touch the Lick Skillet Road, and they were "not to do more fighting than nec-essary." Yet the army commander also told Lee "not to allow the enemy to gain upon you anymore than possible." This last piece of advice was reinforced by a general order Hood had issued to his entire army only three days before. "Ex-perience has proved to you that safety in time of battle consists in getting into close quarters with your enemy," the order read. "Guns and colors are the only unerring indications of victory. . . . If your enemy be allowed to continue the operation of flanking you out of position, our cause is in great peril."[77]

These mixed messages may have contributed to the tragedy that followed on the afternoon of July 28. As Stewart was on his way to the Lick Skillet Road, Lee realized that the Federals were already taking position on good defensive ground just north of the roadway. In late morning of July 28, Logan moved the Fifteenth Corps from its reserve position and extended Blair's Seventeenth Corps line along the low ridge that represented the only decent position in the area. Woods's division faced east like the troops of Blair and Dodge, extend-ing south to a Methodist meeting house called Ezra Church, but Harrow's and Morgan L. Smith's divisions created a long refused line extending westward from the church and only half a mile north from the Lick Skillet Road. Smith held the right wing of this refused line, and Davis's division of the Fourteenth Corps positioned itself to screen Smith's right flank. The Unionists pushed for-ward a strong skirmish line that drove away cavalry troopers opposing them and, in places, reached the Lick Skillet Road.[78]

Lee decided that the Federals already seriously threatened Confederate control of the Lick Skillet Road, and he issued orders to attack. Even though he had only scant information about the enemy and its location, and Stewart's supporting divisions were not yet up to help him, the impetuous commander threw his men into a series of piecemeal attacks along the front of the refused line of Logan's corps.[79]

Poe later deemed the Fifteenth Corps's position on the slight ridge "a most admirable one," but Howard issued orders for the troops to construct defenses as well. Local farmers had partially cleared a field nearby that provided logs and a few fence rails. Each regiment sent details of men to gather this material and pile it high enough to provide some degree of shelter, especially if "kneeling or lying down," Howard noted. "It was too late for intrenching." Sherman rode up to observe the proceedings, catching sight of Logan's men busily "rolling logs and fence-rails, preparing a hasty cover."[80]

Hugo Wangelin, who commanded a brigade in Woods's division, had no tools for his men. They used the benches from Ezra Church, turning them up-side down and filling them with knapsacks, to create a breastwork along one sector of the line. Other members of Wangelin's brigade tore down "an old log schoolhouse" nearby and in half an hour had timber for the breastwork. On yet other sectors of Wangelin's line, the Federals merely used their piled-up knapsacks as shelter.[81]

The troops of Col. John M. Oliver's brigade of Harrow's division went to work "throwing together such poles and chunks as could be found" as Oliver strengthened his skirmish line to offer some protection until the main line could be secured. Oliver wound up sending four companies from each regiment, nearly half his strength, to the skirmish line. Entrenching tools arrived only just before the Confederate attack; as a result, some of Oliver's regiments had virtually no shelter when the battle began. Members of the 99th Indiana, however, managed to scrape together a line of logs with dirt thrown on top by using tin plates and their hands. The 26th Illinois also erected something of a breastwork from available fence rails and rocks before the first attack came.[82]

In Morgan L. Smith's division, the story was similar to that of Harrow's command. Col. James S. Martin's First Brigade erected a line of stones and rails some twenty inches tall. A member of the 127th Illinois reported, however, that his regiment had "no breastworks of any kind." As far as he was concerned, the battle of Ezra Church was "a fair, open, field fight."[83]

Lee began the battle at about noon by sending in three brigades of Brown's Division to hit Morgan L. Smith's division. Brown's men were repelled twice. Col. William F. Brantley's Brigade temporarily took a hill to the west, which offered promise of success, but a Union counterattack reclaimed it. Then Lee sent in Randall L. Gibson's Brigade of Clayton's Division against Harrow. The Louisianans stopped and went to ground short of the Union line and fired for a while before retiring. Then Baker's Brigade advanced to support Gibson but was repelled. Brown resumed his assault by sending Manigault's Brigade against Morgan L. Smith. Twice the South Carolinians advanced, and both times they were driven back.[84]

By this time, Stewart had arrived with one of his divisions, and Lee prevailed on him to join the attack. Walthall sent in his three brigades against Morgan L. Smith at 2:00 P.M. They aimed at the hill Brantley had taken earlier and which now was held by four Federal regiments. Howard also was alert to the danger of losing this slight eminence and had arranged for twenty-six guns to cover that sector. Because Davis's division got lost when it was sent on a mission to flank the Confederate position, it was not within supporting distance. Howard moved ten regiments from Blair's corps and four from Dodge's to the area. Walthall's men swept close to the Union position and held on firing for some time until Loring's Division arrived on the scene. Both Stewart and Loring were now wounded, and a message arrived from Hood. Dated 3:25 P.M., the dispatch warned Lee not to take the offensive unless there was some real advantage to be gained. The battle petered out as Lee called off all further attacks.[85]

The newcomer to the Army of Tennessee had made a bloody mistake. He lost about 3,000 men (compared to only 632 casualties among the Federals) while conducting his uncoordinated assaults, piecemeal, by brigades. Lee had blunted Sherman's effort to extend south for the time, it is true, but the cost was too great. Merely taking position along the Lick Skillet Road and pushing the Union skirmishers away with a heavy skirmish line of his own would have accomplished that goal with only a handful of casualties. Nevertheless, Hood supported Lee's hasty decision to attack and counted the battle of Ezra Church a Rebel victory.[86]

During the course of the fighting, Sixteenth and Seventeenth Corps troops continued to work on their defenses. The Federals piled up rocks and anything else they could find., but the enemy launched no attacks against Dodge or Blair.[87]

Elsewhere along the opposing lines that curved around the northern perimeter of Atlanta, the Federals continued to work on their defenses on July 28. Schofield's Twenty-Third Corps troops were safely ensconced in their three-sided position and skirmished with the Confederates on the other side of no-man's-land. Fourth Corps men concentrated on the obstructions that fronted their sector of the line, erecting chevaux-de-frise, abatis, and stakes. They finished what Chesley Mosman thought was the strongest Federal line he saw during the entire campaign. "Don't see how the Rebels could get through it to the works even if no one was shooting at them," he commented. After slashing the timber for 150 yards in front of the 101st Ohio and placing abatis and sharpened stakes, Capt. Ira Beman Read thought the enemy "would have had a sorry time getting over all that." The skirmishers of Thomas Wood's division of the Fourth Corps pushed their opposing skirmish line back so far that it rested nearly at the Confederate main line.[88]

On the Confederate side, everyone concentrated on holding the defenses while the fighting raged to the southwest of Atlanta. Cleburne's Division of Hardee's Corps had been shifted into the city defenses on July 23, one day after its heavy battle east of town. Cleburne's men busied themselves with erecting head logs and constructing traverses where needed, and stretching brush across sections of trench to screen the men from the hot sun. Initially they lay behind the trench for greater comfort but began to sleep inside the ditch after a few men were killed and wounded by Union artillery fire. "Our works around Atlanta, are now very formidable," wrote John Henry Marsh of Strahl's Brigade staff, "and we are all anxious that, the enemy may be persuaded to charge us. . . . We know absolutely nothing, only to throw up fortifications, and lay in the trenches." When Hardee moved his entire corps into the city defenses after Howard shifted the Army of the Tennessee westward, Cleburne's Division also shifted north for one and a half miles in the line. Now his division could boast of fifty-three guns and three redoubts along its sector.[89]

Life along the lines continued at a normal pace on July 28 as Lee's bloody drama played out near Ezra Church. At headquarters of the Military Division of the Mississippi, however, Sherman felt a sense of satisfaction when news arrived that the Confederates were once again attacking. Maj. James A. Connolly was with his division commander, Baird, at Sherman's side when the word reached headquarters. "'Good' said Sherman, 'that's fine' 'just what I wanted' 'just what I wanted, tell Howard to invite them to attack, it will save us trouble, save us trouble, they'll only beat their own brains out, beat their own brains out.'" Connolly himself wrote to his wife that the Federals "would take it as an easy task to repel an assault anywhere on our lines." Later that day, Sherman told Thomas to fire his artillery into Atlanta all night, a round every fifteen minutes, using Napoleons or twenty-pounder Parrotts.[90]

Confederate commanders tried to put the best face on their dismal defeat. Lee refused to admit he had made a mistake. In his official report, written six months later, he blamed his men for the failure. "I am convinced that if all the troops had displayed equal spirit we would have been successful, as the enemy's works were slight, and besides they had scarcely gotten into position when we made the attack." Hood reported to Richmond that the battles of July 22 and Ezra Church "have checked [Sherman's] extension on both flanks." The army commander now worried about a serious shortage of small-arms ammunition, urging his corps commanders to "use every means to reduce its expenditure. Skirmishers, even, must not fire except in cases of necessity. This is important." This shortage and Hood's instructions impeded the Confederate ability to contend with aggressive Union skirmishing while both sides were locked in static, fortified positions.[91]

Hood had learned his lesson. He wanted, for the time being, to act only on the defensive. His orders to Lee the day after Ezra Church were to "extend the line to the left . . . so that works may be erected by the men." The same instruction was issued to Cheatham, who had temporarily replaced the wounded Stewart. Hood reverted to the same defensive policy that had resulted in Johnston getting fired only ten days before.[92]

Peach Tree Creek, July 22, and Ezra Church

This third battle of Hood's brief tenure as commander of the Army of Tennessee cannot be blamed on him, for Lee was entirely responsible for initiating it. He eerily duplicated Hood's own handling of the Kolb's Farm battle on June 22 by launching poorly coordinated attacks against an enemy whose dispositions he only dimly understood. Ironically, the Confederates had force enough so that, if coordinated, their attacks held a promise of success. The Federals did not have an enormous terrain advantage; their fieldworks were meager at best and nonexistent in front of some regiments. Everywhere along the Fifteenth Corps line, the troops scurried to the rear for more material to improve their breastworks between attacks. Slight as they were, Howard credited the works with reducing the losses he suffered, and Charles Wills of the 103rd Illinois bluntly stated, "The rails saved us." The disparity of casualties suffered in the battle of Ezra Church belied the reality of the fight. The brunt of the Rebel assaults was borne by only six brigades of Yankees, and they barely held on to the low ridge. If the Confederates had conducted the battle with a greater degree of command and control, the result might have been different.[93]

The Confederates held their position along the Lick Skillet Road on the evening of July 28. Daniel Harris Reynolds's Brigade constructed a breastwork of rails on the extreme left of the temporary line. Then at 10:30 P.M., Reynolds evacuated the field and returned to his former position protecting Atlanta. On the Union side, Fifteenth Corps troops "worked all night like ants on our trenches," in the words of a member of the 3rd Missouri in Wangelin's brigade.[94]

Ezra Church had a serious effect on Confederate morale. Arthur M. Manigault thought it was a watershed in the deterioration of hope during the campaign. Despite Lee's complaint, Manigault's troops attacked with "great spirit and bravery" on July 28. "I was much pleased and perfectly satisfied with the manner in which they bore themselves," but he also brooded over "how uselessly and foolishly they had been butchered." Manigault and his men thought Lee had failed to bring all available troops to bear on the lightly entrenched enemy in a coordinated fashion. "The mismanagement in this affair was so patent to the dullest spectator or combatant, that the men lost all confidence in their leaders, and were much dispirited in consequence."[95]

Manigault was not alone in his opinion. "This Battle Discouraged our men Badly as they could never understand why they Should have been Sent in to such a Death Trap to be Butchered up with no hope of gaining any thing," wrote Capt. John W. Lavender of the 4th Arkansas. "We Fell Back to our line in a teriable shattered and Demoralized Condition." Many Confederates who had given Hood a chance to prove himself now pined for the return of Johnston.[96]

The first week and a half of Hood's tenure as commander of the Army of Tennessee initiated an experiment that was drastically different from Johnston's policy. Seeking to reverse Sherman's steady progress, Hood struck with well-intentioned but poorly coordinated assaults on July 20 and 22 and then learned that one of his subordinates had conducted a third offensive without his authority on July 28. All three battles were attempts to hit the Federals before they could fortify positions within striking distance of Atlanta. At Peach Tree Creek and Ezra Church, the Confederates indeed attacked before the Federal line was fully prepared with fieldworks, but stiff fighting by the Yankees and poor coordination by the Rebels prevented the assaults from succeeding. At the battle of July 22, much blame should be laid on the Federals for not taking advantage of the time given them to more heavily fortify their position east of Atlanta. The left flank of Blair's Seventeenth Corps was improperly protected. The slanting line along Flat Shoals Road was inadequate; Blair should have constructed a longer refused line extending eastward from Bald Hill as soon as the eminence was secured, which is exactly what was done under fire and great duress during the course of the battle. McPherson should have made certain these precautions were taken, and there is evidence, already cited, that many members of his army were tired of digging in and did not take such precautions seriously. But again, heroic fighting at the moment of crisis saved the day for Sherman.

11

Utoy Creek and Extending South

After their dismal failure at Ezra Church, the Confederates maintained their position along the Lick Skillet Road for the remainder of July 28, constructing temporary breastworks to secure it. But Lee pulled his men away after dusk. He created a new line to shield the Macon and Western Railroad coming up from the south into Atlanta. It began where the left flank of Hood's Addition touched the City Line due west of town and extended southwest until the works were about two miles west of the rail line. Eventually the fortifications were built to East Point and thus should be termed the East Point Line. John C. Brown placed his division along this new position with its right on the Lick Skillet Road and its left on North Utoy Creek. Having lost about 500 men on July 28, Brown had little more than 2,800 left. He stretched his division across "uneven ground, through woods and open fields, across hills, and over narrow valleys," according to James Patton Anderson, who relieved Brown as the division's commander on July 30. Brown rounded up all the entrenching tools he could find and sent out large labor details. The men worked hard both day and night until "a feeling of security and even defiance pervaded the whole line," according to Anderson.[1]

When the Federals realized their opponents had evacuated the area near Ezra Church, they stayed in place for the time being. The Fifteenth Corps maintained the long refused line that protected Sherman's right flank. Howard issued orders to the Army of the Tennessee to make its earthworks as strong as possible and clear the ground in front. Seventeenth Corps men placed sharpened stakes in front of their growing fieldworks.[2]

Elsewhere along the opposing trench lines, other troops also strengthened their fortifications, sniped, fired artillery at the enemy, and waited for Sherman to devise a plan for the next effort against Atlanta. Twentieth Corps skirmishers intensified their efforts. On July 26, Hooker had ridden through an exposed area along the sector held by Williams's division and received a lot of Confederate sharpshooting, which badly wounded an orderly. The men had suffered from this intense fire, delivered by the skirmishers of Stevenson's Division, for days. In fact, they had constructed communication trenches 100 feet long behind the line to allow for safer movement to and from the position. They could cook their rations and eat in the trenches, but had no shade from the sun. Rice C. Bull of the 123rd New York estimated that one out of every fifty rounds fired by the Rebel sharpshooters hit a man. Hooker became angry at the loss of his orderly and told Williams to clear the Rebels out of their hiding place. The 13th New Jersey advanced and captured the small ridge where they were located, taking thirty-three prisoners. Confederate artillery fire, however, forced the Jerseymen back. An effort by Hooker's line to retake the position on the afternoon of July 28 failed.[3]

But a third effort succeeded. At dawn on July 30, Williams reinforced his division skirmish line and pushed it forward. The Federals took the Confederates by surprise, capturing 135 men, and began to dig in on the ridge. As the infantrymen loosened the dirt with bayonets, Williams's pioneers came forward with shovels and spades to dig while the troops fought off an advance of Confederate skirmishers, taking shelter behind trees to avoid the worst of the Rebel artillery fire. Only by digging good works could the Yankees maintain their exposed position on the ridge. Even so, they lost more than sixty men during the course of the day until those earthworks were large enough to provide adequate shelter.[4]

In the wake of this minibattle between Williams and Stevenson, Hood was concerned that the enemy might become even more active on the northern sector of his line. Francis A. Shoup, Hood's new chief of staff, instructed Stevenson on July 31 to have his skirmishers continue "a slow constant fire" at Federal work parties and to continue strengthening his defenses. Hood also instructed other subordinates to increase the density and size of the obstruction field in front of their positions, "the object being to form an impassable abatis." But Hood also wanted them to leave a few trees standing near the trenches to provide some shade for the men. All along the line, commanders reported making their trenches deeper, their traverses more numerous, and their obstructions thicker.[5]

Utoy Creek and Extending South

But Hood also worried about the somewhat pronounced salient that represented the northwest point of the city defenses, located just east of the road to Marietta. Williams's sortie on July 30, which took place close to the salient, seemed to indicate a possible design to conduct siege approaches against the protruding works. Shoup instructed Stevenson to offer any help to the army's engineers that was necessary as the officers tried to strengthen the salient. Shoup also instructed Col. Robert F. Beckham, the army's new chief of artillery, to employ all the guns in the area against Union work parties near the Marietta Road. "It is of great importance that the enemy do not gain a lodgment in front of that point," Shoup wrote. By August 1, Hood had decided that the best defense was for Presstman to stake off a new line just to the rear of the salient to cut off the apex of the troubled spot. Presstman finished in time for troops of Daniel Harris Reynolds's Brigade to be shifted there and begin digging what Reynolds called "a reserve line." Reynolds maintained this position for the rest of the campaign. His men constructed numerous traverses to protect them from enfilading artillery fire and dug a covered way behind the line so Reynolds could shift troops right or left as needed without undue exposure.[6]

SHIFTING SOUTH

Sherman's next move was to continue shifting troops from his left to his right in order to keep edging southward until it was possible to tap into the rail line supplying Hood's army. If Schofield could move the Twenty-Third Corps to extend Howard's line, the Federals might be able to strike the rails somewhere between White Hall, which was the southwest corner of the Atlanta City Line, and East Point six miles south. Sherman assumed that East Point, where the two rail lines feeding Hood's army from the south formed a junction, was already protected by fortifications, "but there must be a weak point in the long curtain between" that place and White Hall. He told Poe on July 30 to select a new refused line to cover the left flank after Schofield shifted to the west of Atlanta. Poe fully discussed the location of this line with Capt. William J. Twining, Schofield's engineer, and Lt. Henry C. Wharton, Thomas's engineer, before selecting a site for it. He placed it near the Buck Head and Atlanta Road and stretched it almost due north to the Confederate Peach Tree Creek Line. This latest refused position would be held by David S. Stanley's Fourth Corps troops, who already were holding the line from the Buck Head and Atlanta Road south to the Howard House.[7]

Initially, Stanley thought he might have to hold his own corps sector plus Schofield's abandoned sector with his troops, rather than simply fall back on the refused line. He issued instructions for his division leaders to strengthen their works by increasing the size of the obstruction field in front so as to hold them with a thinner line. Stanley offered detailed ideas about how to do this, fastening abatis to the ground with stakes and entangling the brush. He wanted his subordinates to leave a gap in the abatis in front of each regiment wide enough only for one man at a time to pass through so that pickets could be put out and taken in without too much trouble.[8]

But then Thomas told Stanley that his corps would abandon its sector and that of the Twenty-Third Corps and hold only the new refused line. Moreover, the Fourth Corps was responsible for digging the refused line. Stanley issued orders at 2:00 P.M. on July 31 for work details, assigning different units to different sections of the new position. The men started at dawn on August 1 and worked until 7:00 P.M. Schofield began to pull the Twenty-Third Corps away an hour later. Stanley then began to shift his troops south to fill Schofield's old lines. This was part of the overall plan, to hold the Twenty-Third Corps position for only twenty-four hours to hide the fact from watchful Confederate pickets that the shift west was in progress.[9]

But at 12:30 A.M. on August 2, Thomas told Stanley to keep his men in place. At the last minute, the high command decided not to use the newly dug refused line at all and to maintain Schofield's old position. There were some benefits to doing so. In this way, the Federals could continue to be close enough to the Georgia Railroad to discourage the Confederates from trying to repair and use it, and they could force Hood to stretch out his limited manpower on a longer front. Also, by holding this extended position, Stanley could demonstrate along a wider sector anytime it was necessary to divert Confederate attention from more important moves at the extreme right flank of the Union position. These benefits were somewhat offset by the fact that Stanley now had to hold not only his old Fourth Corps sector but Schofield's sector as well, a total of four miles, with no additional manpower.[10]

Schofield moved his Army of the Ohio all night of August 1 and most of the next day toward Sherman's right flank. He reached the right end of the refused Fifteenth Corps line sometime during the afternoon of August 2, and then Logan wheeled his corps to the left at 3:00 P.M. in order to straighten the Union line and face it east, extending the Union position farther south. The men marched directly across the bloody battlefield of July 28 to do so. Poe and other engineer officers helped select a position for Schofield's troops to connect with Logan's right flank, extending the Union line ever farther south. Schofield settled his men in a line that, in part, ran along North Utoy Creek. He held a sector one and a half miles long, with a short refused line at the right flank.

Schofield estimated that the vital railroad was about one and a half miles to the east of his position. When completed, Schofield's shift and Logan's wheel made Sherman's entire line about ten miles long, stretching from near the Georgia Railroad east of Atlanta to a point near the Sandtown Road in the valley of South Utoy Creek west of the city.[11]

Careful reconnaissance revealed that the Confederates already had a solid line of earthworks fronting both Logan and Schofield. It extended southward from White Hall toward East Point some distance west of the railroad. Poe could see enough of the line to report that it was "the same system of batteries, connected by infantry curtains, that we had met before." In other words, it was a well-prepared, well-sited, and strongly built line of earthworks. For nearly a month to come, Sherman was faced with the problem of finding a way to extend far enough south to flank the lengthening Rebel defenses so that he could avoid siege approaches or a frontal attack on them.[12]

While Sherman spent August 3–4 contemplating what to do, his troops busied themselves with small-scale fights along several sectors of the Union line. Logan's men consolidated their new position by pushing forward where the ground seemed to invite a further advance on the enemy. Harrow detailed men from every regiment in his division until he had 1,000 troops available, placing them under Maj. William B. Brown of the 70th Ohio. Brown rushed the Confederate skirmish line on August 3, taking a low ridge and eighty-three prisoners. He secured the position and incorporated it into the Union skirmish line, but Brown was killed and ninety-two Federals were lost in the process.[13]

Stanley, over on the other end of Sherman's line, not only demonstrated to distract the enemy, but his men also wanted to know more about the opposing positions opposite their new sector. As a result, Fourth Corps troops mounted at least two sorties. Col. William H. Gibson advanced his skirmish line on August 2 and could see activity on the main Confederate line as the Rebels hurriedly cleared their trench for action "by throwing down the arbors" they had erected for shade. In places, Gibson's skirmishers lodged within twenty yards of the Confederate skirmish line and in other spots actually mounted the opposing skirmish works. These were untenable positions because Rebel artillery enfiladed the Yankee skirmishers, and rifle fire from the Confederate main line, which lay on higher ground, was punishing. Gibson's men were forced to fall back. They had proved that the enemy had a continuous trench to shield its skirmishers and that there was no good ground for the Federals to lodge close to it, all at the cost of seventeen men.[14]

On August 3, Col. P. Sidney Post's skirmish line advanced and captured a section of the Confederate skirmish position. Post sent his pioneers forward to remodel the pits for Federal use, but supporting skirmishers to right and left failed to come forward. Post's men fought off Confederate counterattacks but were compelled to pull back after dark. They took the time to level the Confederate works before retreating.[15]

UTOY CREEK

Small skirmishes like those on the Fourth Corps front tended to be overshadowed by the big question, extending south from the Union right flank. Sherman planned for a couple of days before attempting to push Schofield farther south. Terrain was a significant problem. "The country in which I am operating is very difficult for a large army," he reported to Grant, "and the defensive positions very strong and hard to circumvent, but perseverance will move mountains." South Utoy Creek, which ran through a comparatively deep, narrow valley toward the west along the Sandtown Road, was the next natural hurdle. Schofield's right flank was close enough to it to launch a crossing, but the Confederates had troops along the southern bank and the territory was relatively unknown to the Federals.[16]

Sherman wanted to shift the entire Fourteenth Corps to help Schofield, giving the Federals close to 30,000 troops with which to operate southward. On August 4, he ordered Schofield and Palmer to move their commands so as to gain the railroad between White Hall and East Point. "If necessary to secure the end ordinary parapets must be charged and carried," Sherman advised, "and every hour's delay enables the enemy to strengthen." Schofield accurately reflected these instructions in his orders to Twenty-Third Corps commanders. He told them to close in on any Confederate works they encountered in the move, scout the position, and if the earthworks were no more than an ordinary parapet and if there were no obstructions in front, they were to attack.[17]

Sherman also told Schofield not to worry too much about the defense of his own position north of South Utoy Creek. "Slash down the timber in the valley of Utoy, and a single battery with a regiment of skirmishers will hold a mile against the whole of Hood's army." He aimed at massing a large force to operate in the open against the Confederate flank, using earthworks and obstructions to maximize defensive potential and minimize the number of men tied down for defense. "If the enemy ever gets a column through our lines," Sherman continued, "we will let go our breast-works and turn on his flanks, and, therefore, I do not care about our line being continuous and uniform."[18]

To support Schofield's move, Howard instructed all three corps leaders in the Army of the Tennessee to double the strength of their skirmish lines and push them forward. He also wanted the main line troops to stand to in the trenches and be ready for anything. Engineer officers also were told to move forward just behind the skirmishers and scout the terrain for the location of a new line, if it became feasible to advance the position.[19]

Sherman's plan to push across South Utoy Creek on August 4 foundered on the thorny issue of interarmy cooperation. When Schofield instructed Palmer to move Baird's division across the Sandtown Road, Palmer refused to comply. He noted that his commission predated Schofield's, was angry at the repeated detachment of his troops to other commands in the past few weeks, and preferred to take orders only from Thomas. Palmer relented only insofar as to send one of Baird's brigades on a reconnaissance eastward. It retired upon meeting the first opposition.[20]

Action along other parts of the opposing lines took place on August 4 as well. Troops of Thomas's army advanced against French's Division, which straddled the Turner's Ferry Road on the northwest sector of the Atlanta defenses. They drove in the line of videttes that fronted the Confederate skirmish position but were stopped by the gray-clad skirmishers. Col. William H. Clark of the 46th Mississippi in Sears's Brigade counterattacked. He advanced both the vidette line and the skirmish line directly behind it forward. Clark's men managed to reach a point only sixty yards from the Federals, who were planted in his old vidette line, but the enemy detected his advance. They fired a volley that mostly sailed over the heads of the Confederates. Then Clark ordered his men to fire and rush forward with a yell. They reclaimed their own vidette line and captured twenty-one prisoners, several rifles (including two Spencer repeaters), and a number of entrenching tools. Clark lost only thirty-seven men out of 420 engaged in this little squabble. Ironically, Hood's chief of staff warned corps commander Lee not to let his men waste ammunition on August 4, "even upon the picket-line." Hood "desires that the firing be discontinued, except in cases of necessity."[21]

Sherman tried to restart his Utoy Creek offensive on August 5. He assured Thomas that he had examined the Federal earthworks and held no fears of a Confederate attack, for the Union line was "well developed" and "generally strengthened by good abatis and parapet, and conforms pretty close to the enemy." Howard and Thomas were instructed to press the enemy on their front to divert attention from the Union moves on the far right.[22]

The Confederate position along the Sandtown Road was clarified by early morning of August 5, based on information gleaned from Confederate prisoners and deserters. The Rebels had constructed a trench stretching from the East Point Line westward along the south side of South Utoy Creek and the

Sandtown Road, held for the most part by dismounted cavalrymen. The works were not strong, a simple trench and parapet. In contrast, the works along the Confederate line that linked White Hall and East Point were "very strong" and thickly held by troops and artillery. Encouraged by news like this, Sherman told Schofield, "I am willing you should be rather rash than prudent in this case."[23]

The program for August 5 was for Cox to push across South Utoy Creek and Baird to push eastward against the East Point Line as a diversion. Cox sent James W. Reilly's brigade over the creek and up the southern bluff. His skirmish line encountered abatis consisting of felled trees and "undergrowth half-cut off and bent downward and interlaced." The Federals managed to work their way through this slashing until they were a few yards short of the enemy parapet, and then they retired. Reilly continued to fall back to the north side of the stream. There seemed to be little desire on the part of Schofield's subordinates for an attack.[24]

Meanwhile, Baird strengthened his division skirmish line and supported it with a reserve consisting of one regiment from each brigade. This large force headed eastward against the stout Confederate defenses that lay west of the railroad. The Federals started with a yell at 10:00 A.M., overran the Confederate skirmish line, and took 140 prisoners. Then the Federals stopped when the main Rebel position loomed ahead. Palmer ordered Baird to remain where he was and construct works. "Our men have dug so much during this campaign that it don't take them long to fortify now," reported James A. Connolly of Baird's staff. The troops had a good fieldwork ready in one hour, even though they labored under heavy artillery fire. Some Confederates had been killed in their skirmish pits so the Federals simply covered them up, "making convenient graves," as an Indiana artillerymen phrased it, and then dug their own works nearby.[25]

At the same time, Davis's division of the Fourteenth Corps took post facing south along South Utoy Creek to support the effort to push across that stream. Johnson's division of the same corps was supposed to move past Davis's right flank and head for the railroad, but apparently Johnson misunderstood his instructions and merely positioned his division to Davis's rear. Davis's troops now were subject to enfilade fire from Confederate guns in the East Point Line. They were compelled to not only dig in but construct traverses for flank protection.[26]

Fourteenth Corps troops received the brunt of criticism for the failed effort of August 5. Schofield expressed his disgust to Sherman in no uncertain terms. "I would prefer to move a rock than to move that corps," Sherman rather rashly told Thomas, the man who had created and led the Fourteenth Corps before his elevation to army command. "On the defensive it would be splendid, but for offensive it is of no use." Sherman blamed it on Palmer and sought a way

Utoy Creek and Extending South

to replace him. Under Palmer's cautious tutelage, the corps had no offensive spirit. "If an enemy can be seen by a spy-glass," as Sherman put it, "the whole corps is halted and intrenched for a siege." Thomas was trying to do all he could to divert Confederate attention, but he reminded Sherman that the Fourth and Twentieth Corps now held the sectors formerly occupied by Schofield and Palmer. He could only skirmish, not form an attack column and hold this extended position at the same time.[27]

The events of August 5 compelled Hood to shift more troops to his left flank. Bate's Division of Hardee's Corps, consisting of only 2,500 men, marched to the Sandtown Road later that day and replaced the dismounted cavalrymen in the light works along the south side of South Utoy Creek. His men improved the defenses on the night of August 5, adding head logs and cutting more abatis. Col. Thomas B. Smith's Brigade was stretched to the breaking point, its men deployed in one rank and at one-yard intervals. The Federals could hear the sound of chopping from their positions on the north side of the creek during the night.[28]

In faraway Richmond, ignorant of the developments of the past two days, Jefferson Davis offered sage advice to his young protégé in Atlanta. "The loss consequent upon attacking him in his intrenchments requires you to avoid that if practicable," Davis warned Hood of the enemy. He liked Hood's suggestion that Confederate cavalry raid Sherman's supply line, an idea that Johnston had also pushed without success throughout the campaign. Hood's men had no need of presidential advice; they knew full well that attacking earthworks was deadly business, and they also knew that digging in ever deeper was the key to surviving defensively. When Union artillery fire began to enfilade Gibson's Brigade in Clayton's Division, Gibson ordered his men to build more traverses to reduce casualties.[29]

Schofield made a more serious effort to cross South Utoy Creek on August 6 than ever before. He instructed Cox to gain a foothold on the other side of the valley, and Cox planned to do so with a strengthened skirmish line followed by Reilly's brigade. Reilly's job was to gain the ridge where Bate's Division was dug in at any place the skirmishers found to be feasible. John S. Casement's brigade was placed to support Reilly, and the rest of Cox's division was nearby to exploit any advantages. Both Sherman and Schofield had given up on using the Fourteenth Corps troops to help their efforts.[30]

Cox's skirmish line succeeded in pushing the Confederate skirmishers back all along the division front, but it failed to discover any particularly weak spot along Bate's extended position. While the Federal skirmishers held on close to the main Confederate line, Cox decided to send Reilly forward near the right center of his division sector, because there a strip of timber extended from the valley up to Bate's position, offering concealment. Reilly's 1,500 men went forward at about 1:00 P.M. but the timber failed to offer them much advantage. The most serious obstacle they encountered was the extensive belt of obstructions fronting Bate. It extended about 100 yards out from the Confederate main line and consisted of undergrowth cut off halfway up and the top bent over, interlaced, to form an almost impenetrable barrier. The Federals struggled through this mass until some reached a point only twenty-five yards from the Confederates, where rifle fire from Smith's Brigade and two of Joseph H. Lewis's Kentucky regiments added to their problems. The attack stalled and the Federals retired soon after.[31]

A group of Reilly's men took shelter behind a convenient fold of ground and sniped at Bate's line. After a while the Confederates launched a sortie and captured thirty Yankees. Reilly's attack failed with casualties amounting to 306 men. Bate suffered a mere twenty losses. The battle of Utoy Creek once again demonstrated the efficacy of well-made obstructions, as well as the usefulness of even a light parapet, for maximizing the defensive power of limited troop strength. Schofield's men were not accustomed to wasting their comrades in frontal assaults on fortifications. Soon after the attack, acting adjutant Henry Clay Weaver of the 16th Kentucky saw Reilly crying over the heavy loss of his men. The next morning, Reilly told the adjutant "it was the last time for a good while that his brigade should go into such a place as that." Schofield reported the results of August 6 to Sherman with less passion, noting that Reilly had attacked "intrenchments of ordinary strength with extensive entanglements in front."[32]

The Federals knew the power of a good barrier field to slow down and even stop an enemy attack. On August 6, Thomas suggested to Sherman that if Stanley's Fourth Corps were assaulted from the south like McPherson had been on July 22, he would prefer that the men fall back to the unused refused line along the Buck Head and Atlanta Road and let the enemy become "well entangled in the abatis before opening fire on him." The Confederates tried to demonstrate on August 6 to divert Federal attention, but they became hung up on well-constructed earthworks, too. French sent a reinforced skirmish line forward on the left wing of his division, which made no headway against the fortified Union skirmish line. French lost forty-three men killed and wounded and gained nothing for his effort.[33]

French's minor failure was dwarfed by one of the few Confederate defensive victories that occurred south of the Chattahoochee River during the Atlanta campaign. Corps commander Lee, who was responsible for Bate's Divi-

Utoy Creek and Extending South

sion at Utoy Creek, issued a congratulatory order praising Bate's men for their victory on August 6 and for capturing a group of Reilly's men, complete with their entrenching tools. Bate's troops used those tools to strengthen their earthworks on the night of August 6.[34]

But Reilly's repulse was quickly followed by news that forced Bate to evacuate the line he had so well defended for twenty-four hours. During the afternoon of August 6, Schofield maneuvered Hascall's division to sweep wide to the west and south of Utoy Post Office, well to the west of Bate's left flank. It was unknown territory, so Hascall took some time to pick his way across the creek and move gingerly toward the supposed position of the Confederates. He drove in the cavalry that screened Bate's left and, after moving a total of two miles, was poised to outflank the Rebel infantry line, when dusk put an end to his movements. Upon learning of this development, Lee and Bate agreed that the division should fall back. The Confederates evacuated their line on the night of August 6 and took post in the East Point Line facing west. The Federals finally won the long struggle for control of Utoy Creek.[35]

On the morning of August 7, Schofield advanced the Twenty-Third Corps across the valley and Reilly's battlefield. He then moved his men southeast along the Sandtown Road, stopping when he encountered the East Point Line. Placing his command to extend the Union line opposite the Confederate position, Schofield found that he still had not reached the end of the enemy earthworks with his right flank. Moreover, his troops were more than two miles from the coveted railroad. Elements of the Fourteenth Corps and Howard's Army of the Tennessee also moved slightly forward on August 7 to consolidate positions closer to the East Point Line, continuing a creeping advance the Federals had been engaged in for several days. The tactic adopted by Howard's troops was to advance a skirmish line to a predetermined point and allow the men to dig pits wherever they could. Then commanders sent forward work details to connect those pits while the skirmishers fired to keep the enemy down, to be followed by more troops as needed once the trench was complete. As a result, according to Poe, the entire Federal line was "as far advanced as the salients had been."[36]

Bate's men fortified their new position along the East Point Line on the night of August 6 and the next day, stretched out in one rank with one-yard intervals between men. Lee urged Bate to make the works as strong as possible as quickly as he could, for the cavalry had reported Schofield's movements toward his position on August 7. Hood fully approved of these defensive measures. Lee also tried to bolster the spirit of his corps following its horrible bloodletting at Ezra Church. He castigated the skirmishers of Baker's Brigade for failing to hold back enemy skirmishers in a sharp little battle on August 3.

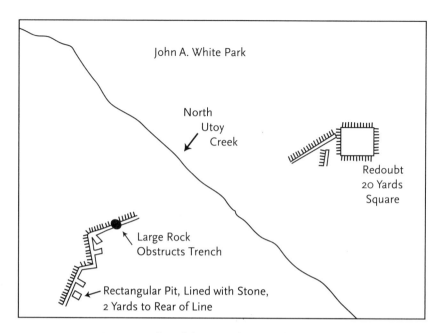

Remnants of Confederate works at North Utoy Creek

Lee thought Baker's command, in the words of Lee's assistant adjutant general, "had lost its picket-lines oftener than any other brigade in the corps and had never retaken them. This he attributes to a want of spirit on the part of the officers and men." Lee also blamed Baker and his officers for lacking a quickness of decision that could allow them to respond rapidly to shifts on the skirmish line. The official criticism must have had an effect. When more skirmish fights developed along corps lines on August 5 and 7, all of the skirmishers of Gibson's Brigade and half of Baker's fought so hard that they lost half their manpower before they retreated. These performances inspired Lee to issue orders congratulating the men for showing greater spirit.[37]

Hood was worried by the Federal success in clearing Utoy Creek and decided to shift troops from Hardee's Corps to extend the East Point Line further southward. His initial orders were for Cleburne to leave one-third of his division to hold his present sector on the north side of the city and take the rest to reinforce Lee. Cleburne moved his men to the far left beginning on the night of August 7. Hood had wanted him to place his troops in reserve behind Lee and Bate, but that was only temporary. Over the next few days, Cleburne stretched his command out to extend the East Point Line. His men, like Bate's, deployed in a single rank and used bayonets to loosen the earth, for there were precious

Utoy Creek and Extending South

few spades and picks available. The ground was "tough cowhide clay land," according to M. L. Wheeler of the 33rd Alabama. "My line is anything but a good one," Cleburne complained, but his command made the best of it. Lowrey's Brigade anchored Cleburne's left only about two miles from East Point, nearly completing the East Point Line.[38]

SHELLING ATLANTA

Sherman began to see the bombardment of Atlanta as a part of his overall strategy by August 7. He had been encouraging his subordinates to periodically shell the city for the past several days, and those subordinates had often taken it upon themselves to pump a few rounds into the place on their own. But this haphazard effort began to become a formal plan by the second week of August. The Fourteenth Corps and the Army of the Tennessee had advanced their lines forward a few yards to snuggle up closer to the Confederate lines. At least for the time being, Sherman wanted them to "push forward daily by parallels." In addition, he would "make the inside of Atlanta too hot to be endured." As far as Sherman was concerned, most of the citizens had evacuated the city and "it is now simply a big Fort." A heavy bombardment might stop "wagon supply trains from coming into town," he told Howard. "One thing is certain, whether we get inside of Atlanta or not, it will be a used-up community by the time we are done with it."[39]

The Federals needed heavier ordnance to accomplish this goal. Sherman instructed Thomas to order two thirty-pounder Parrotts from Chattanooga with 1,000 shells to "knock down the buildings in the town." But the transport of 4.5-inch rifled siege guns from Chattanooga, beginning on August 8, represented a more potent threat to the city. Thomas's people chose a good spot for the 4.5-inch guns on the left of Geary's division line. Two of the rifled siege pieces were in place and firing by August 10. By the end of the campaign, the 4.5-inch battery on Geary's front contained two siege guns plus four thirty-pounders. The embrasures of the gun emplacements were protected with iron mantlets.[40]

Another 4.5-inch gun was placed on the Sixteenth Corps line. Maj. Thomas W. Osborn, Howard's chief of artillery, planted it at John M. Corse's division sector on August 11. It was located 4,000 yards from the city, but Osborn moved the gun 400 yards closer two days later. The crew fired it around the clock, every fifteen minutes during the day and every five minutes during the night. After 700 rounds the vent started to expand, and after 900 rounds

Osborn thought it best to exchange the piece for another 4.5-inch gun on August 23. This new piece, however, fired only two days before a defective trail broke and had to be replaced.[41]

Corse added another element of siege warfare to the bombardment of Atlanta. Blair loaned him a battery of twenty-pounder Parrotts from the Seventeenth Corps, and Dodge's chief of artillery, Maj. William H. Ross, constructed a furnace to heat solid shot. It was made of stone and earth with railroad iron as a grate. The gunners used wet cotton as wadding in the tube to prevent a premature detonation of the powder charge. The battery was located near Proctor's Creek, 3,500 yards from the center of Atlanta. Sherman inspected this location on August 10 and thought it a perfect place for the guns. Cleared ground gave "a fine field of fire," and one could look up the valley nearly to the heart of Atlanta. Two of the Parrotts fired the red-hot rounds into the unfortunate city during the night. "The heating process seemed to expand the shot," Corse reported, "so as to take the rifling more perfectly." In addition, Ross fired hot shot from twelve-pounder smoothbores to reach the outskirts of the city. The crew could see large fires in Atlanta every night, except one, that they used the hot shot. The smoothbore twelve-pounders fired a total of 100 heated rounds and the rifled Parrotts a total of fifty hot shots, although Osborn did not believe the smoothbores did an effective job because the range was too great.[42]

French's Division straddled the Turner's Ferry Road, fronting both Geary's 4.5-inch battery and Corse's hot shot pieces. In fact, French counted a total of thirty Federal artillery pieces on his sector. To counter this fire, he had twenty-five weapons, four of which were thirty-two-pounders, but French could not prevent the Federals from using their siege guns or their hot shot battery at will.[43]

Sherman insisted that the bombardment of Atlanta proceed at a methodical and relentless pace. In addition to the special batteries, he wanted all guns able to bear on the city to open fire. On August 9 alone, 3,000 rounds sailed into Atlanta. He encouraged night firing, as he sought to devastate the city and cripple its logistical support of the Army of Tennessee. "The inhabitants have, of course, got out," he assured Thomas on August 10. "Let us destroy Atlanta and make it a desolation."[44]

But the civilian population was still largely in Atlanta and suffered in the bombardment. The superintendent of the city gas company and his six-year-old daughter were killed, a black barber named Solomon Luckie was mortally wounded, and a young lady also was mortally injured one day while walking toward the car shed located downtown. In addition, a small boy and a Confederate officer were mortally wounded while standing in the front yard of a house. Stationer Samuel P. Richards noted in his diary that by August 21, rumor had it that a total of twenty people had died from the effect of the heavy shelling. "It is like living in the midst of a pestilence," Richards commented. "No one can tell but he may be the next victim.[45]

At least a few Federals came to realize the depth of suffering they caused the civilian population of the city. A group of thirty women came into Twentieth Corps lines as early as July 23, after only a couple of days of sporadic shelling, and told the Federals that they were "tearing the city pretty bad with our shell." One wonders what they would have thought of the concentrated bombardment of mid-August. "You know I was opposed to shelling the place," Orlando Poe quietly told his wife soon after the campaign, "for it did no good at all, and only brought harm to unoffending people."[46]

The citizens quickly learned how to take shelter. They constructed holes in their yards and covered the excavations with timber and dirt. These were civilian counterparts of military bombproofs. "It was painful, yet strange," Hood reported, "to mark how expert grew the old men, women, and children in building their little underground forts, in which to fly for safety during the storm of shell and shot." Some 2,000 to 5,000 civilians still in the city relied on these "dungeons beneath the earth" for the preservation of life and limb. Families who lived in houses that had a cellar did not need to construct bombproofs. Whether in cellars or bombproofs, the citizens often deployed furniture, because they spent many hours waiting out the shells. The worst bombing occurred at night, and at that time, as a newspaper correspondent phrased it, "the whole community may be said to be under ground."[47]

William E. Sloan of the 5th Tennessee Cavalry took time to visit the Lester family of Atlanta and found them hiding in a bombproof dug under their house. A friend of theirs who lived in an adjacent home was eating lunch when a Yankee shell "ploughed through the room she was in, the debris from the wall striking her severely and giving her terrible shock." Sloan thought it was awful to subject civilians to the horrors of war. "That is Brute Sherman's mode of warfare," he commented in his diary.[48]

When the campaign ended and the Federals had leisure to tour the city, many of them became fascinated with these civilian bombproofs because they mimicked the shelters they often dug when locked in static positions along trench lines. John Henry Otto of the 21st Wisconsin heard the citizens call them gopher holes. He noticed dozens of such excavations in yards and in the embankment of the Macon and Western Railroad on the south side of the city.

Civilian bombproof somewhere in Atlanta. Although not specifically identified as a civilian bombproof, this structure most likely was built and used by some of Atlanta's citizens during the Federal bombardment of the city. It does not seem to be located near a military fortification, and the proximity of a house and outbuildings suggests a connection with the civilian population. *Photograph by George N. Barnard. Library of Congress, LC-DIG-cwpb-03457.*

Many houses also had been shattered by artillery fire; some were "almost shot away," according to an officer in the 50th Ohio.[49]

CONTINUING TO EXTEND SOUTH

Following the actions along South Utoy Creek, the Federals took stock of their situation. Schofield reported that the Confederates had easily extended the East Point Line until it once again stretched much farther south than his own

Utoy Creek and Extending South

right flank. On Hascall's division sector, the enemy position was plainly seen on the other side of a valley containing a small branch of South Utoy Creek. There was "a large redoubt resembling those of Atlanta" with connecting infantry parapets. The Rebel line ran along a series of knolls some 400 yards apart from each other, well within effective range for mutually supportive artillery fire. The slopes of these low knolls were cleared. In front of Cox's division, to Hascall's right, the Confederate line bent back so as to face southwest and come nearer the coveted railroad.[50]

Schofield could not move closer to this line without great difficulty, because of the obstacle posed by the branch and its valley. Bypassing the branch would involve cutting loose from the rest of the Union army. Sherman wanted to wait awhile to ponder the right course of action. He was surprised to think that the Confederate line must be fifteen miles long and considered it unwise to extend his own line any further. He continued to seek a weak spot in the Confederate position somewhere, although all previous efforts to do so had failed to detect one. "If we can't do that we must cut loose from our base and go south," he told Schofield on August 9, "a measure almost too rash to undertake, but inevitable unless we can draw Hood out otherwise."[51]

Schofield, who was loath to risk sending one or two divisions alone to the south, proposed a method whereby Sherman could continue to extend. He suggested that the entire Union line shift farther south until the left flank held by Stanley's Fourth Corps rested at Proctor's Creek. This would involve giving up the railroad at least south of the Chattahoochee River and receiving supplies by wagon via Turner's Ferry downstream from the railroad bridge. Schofield's move would also have involved shifting everything the equivalent of Thomas's entire frontage, for the Army of the Cumberland's right flank currently rested at Proctor's Creek. Sherman was not impressed by this suggestion. He thought the Confederates could match the shift with little difficulty. They "can build parapets faster than we march, and it would be the same thing by extending right or left. In a single night we would find ourselves confronted with parapets which we would fear to attack in the morning."[52]

On the same day that Schofield proposed his plan, Sherman consulted with Thomas and Howard about the problem. Howard supported Schofield's suggestion but Thomas seems not to have offered an immediate opinion. Sherman also told Thomas to scout the area around the railroad bridge, with the idea of posting one corps to guard it while the rest of the army operated away from the rail line. After all these consultations, Sherman more strongly favored the idea of cutting loose entirely from his supply line, marching the bulk of his troops to the railroad, and striking it so far south that the enemy could not possibly build works in his path. Late on the evening of August 10, Sherman further explained his idea to Grant. "I may have to leave a corps at the railroad bridge, well intrenched, and cut loose with the balance and make a desolating circle around Atlanta. I do not propose to assault the works, which are too strong, or to proceed by regular approaches."[53]

But it was typical of his careful management style to spend several days contemplating and planning a major move while continuing to explore other options. Between August 10 and 13, Sherman allowed himself to be tempted by the prospect of yet another small-scale, quick move to the railroad. He got the impression from talking with Schofield on the evening of August 9 that such a move might be feasible after all and ordered Schofield to begin organizing the details. The army commander did so, but asked Sherman to clarify exactly what he wanted Hascall to do. Understandably a bit frustrated, Sherman replied with a good deal of force that Hascall ought to hit the railroad and tear it up, with Cox to support him if necessary. "We must act," he lectured Schofield. "We cannot sit down and do nothing because it involves risk. Being on the offensive we must risk, and that is the flank on which we calculated to make the risk." Feeling tied down, Sherman also told his subordinate, "It seems we are more besieged than they."[54]

Although Schofield initially expressed a willingness to try this move, he sent a long dispatch to Sherman at 9:30 P.M. on August 11 explaining why it was very risky. If he had to send help to Hascall, that meant giving up the entire Union right flank position, which had been created through painfully difficult extensions of the line over the past several weeks. He could be cut off from the rest of Sherman's force, at least three miles away from support. When he received this message from his subordinate, Sherman canceled the projected move by Hascall's division.[55]

While Sherman and his commanders pondered their options during the hot days of mid-August, Howard's troops continued to edge forward in their current positions to close still further on the enemy. The result was a series of small movements along narrow sectors of the line, heavy skirmishes and artillery exchanges, and the introduction of something like siege approaches to the military operations in Georgia. Any time one unit moved forward, supporting units to the right and left also had to adjust forward. New works had to be constructed every time a regiment or brigade moved even a few yards ahead. Timber had to be cut, abatis had to be built, and given the close range at which this work took place, much of it had to be done under fire. After one day in their new position, the Federals continued "trimming up and strengthening the work," as brigade commander Lightburn put it of his Fifteenth Corps men. The object

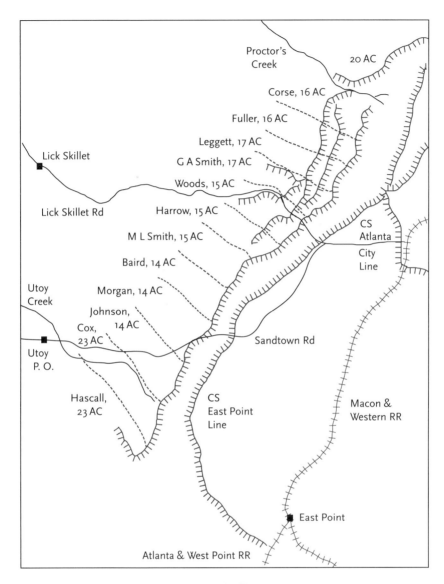

Proctor's
Creek

20 AC

Corse, 16 AC

Fuller, 16 AC

Leggett, 17 AC

Lick Skillet

G A Smith, 17 AC

Woods, 15 AC

Lick Skillet Rd

Harrow, 15 AC

CS
Atlanta

M L Smith, 15 AC

City
Line

Baird, 14 AC

Utoy
Creek

Morgan, 14 AC

Johnson,

Cox,   14 AC

23 AC

Sandtown Rd

Utoy
P. O.

Hascall,
23 AC

CS
East Point
Line

Macon &
Western RR

East Point

Atlanta & West Point RR

East Point Line

of all this labor was to shorten the line as much as possible, hold it with as few men as possible, and be able to extend farther south if Sherman required it. On August 11, Blair reported to Howard's headquarters that the troops of Giles A. Smith's division were so stretched out in one rank that there was barely one man for every two feet of parapet.[56]

On the other end of the long Union line, Stanley's Fourth Corps troops also were stretched to the breaking point. They held the works with only one rank in many places, but compensated for this by making the obstruction belt thicker and deeper, adding sharpened stakes and other obstacles to the abatis. Ironically, the Confederates holding the line opposite Stanley's corps also were doing the same thing. As a result of the constant demonstrations the Federals staged on this flank, the Rebels were worried and compensated for their thin numbers by adding three lines of sharpened stakes in many places along the line and strengthening the abatis.[57]

Sherman could not dally too long in making a decision about the next move, and he wrote to all three of his army commanders on August 13 asking for their formal opinions. In the same dispatch, he briefly outlined his own preference for moving nearly the entire Union force well to the south, cutting off his contact with the railroad. Schofield reiterated his idea of shifting the entire force, one or two corps at a time, from left to right. He thought the Federals could reach the Macon and Western Railroad in three to five days, supplying the army by wagons crossing the Chattahoochee River farther downstream from the railroad. Even if the enemy kept pace, perhaps the Federals could someday attack before the Rebels dug in. Thomas and Howard seem to have acceded to Sherman's idea, for neither offered an alternate proposal of their own.[58]

In fact, Thomas had been busy since August 11 in planning how to station an entire corps to protect the railroad bridge over the Chattahoochee while the rest of the troops were away. His engineer, Henry C. Wharton, selected the location for new works on the south side of the river to protect the bridge. On August 15, Thomas also offered a detailed proposal for moving the troops according to Sherman's ideas. In detailing his proposed move to Halleck, Sherman pointed out that, if unable to regain contact with the railroad bridge over the Chattahoochee, he could tear up miles of track along the Macon and Western Railroad and then move southward to reach St. Marks in Florida or toward the southeast to reach Savannah, Georgia.[59]

"I am more and more satisfied the movement we contemplate is the true one to be made," Sherman told Schofield on August 15. Schofield joined the club and offered a detailed plan for the part to be played by the Army of the Ohio within Sherman's proposal. In fact, probably seeing the writing on the wall, Schofield had since August 14 assured Sherman that he was already beginning to prepare his position to serve as a pivot upon which the rest of the army group could move to the south. His engineer laid out new works by midday on August 15, and Schofield issued orders for the digging to begin that night. Schofield's men worked on this position, a semicircular line of trench, with a good deal of energy. The parapet reportedly was made twelve feet thick at the base. In fact, a

Utoy Creek and Extending South

captain in the 104th Ohio was killed when a tree fell on him during the course of constructing this large earthwork.[60]

Hardee was responsible for holding much of the East Point Line opposite Schofield and Howard, and he was worried that his troops were stretched to the breaking point. The Confederate general was delighted when a Kentucky Federal soldier deserted to the Rebels on August 11 and told Hardee that the Fourteenth Corps was scheduled to attack the Rebel left the next day. "I would like nothing better," he told his wife. But the expected action never developed.[61]

From Hardee's perspective, the Federals had no difficulty extending their line ever southward. "It is easy for him to outflank me and I am apprehensive he may do it at any time." He told Hood he needed another division to protect East Point, but the army commander could not spare it. "My line is very thin," Hardee complained to his wife, "much thinner than that held by any one else, & it is impossible to extend any further."[62]

Hardee tried to compensate by ordering his subordinates to cut trees across roads likely to be used by the Federals in their efforts to approach East Point. Confederate pioneers were kept busy strengthening the works along the East Point Line as well. Presstman's engineer troops, about 600 men, were available to hold sections of the line temporarily. By August 18, the Federals had learned something of the enemy works at East Point through the services of scout J. Milton Glass. Glass reported there were six "strong forts at East Point all ready for artillery." By the end of the campaign, the place was well protected with "a long and well-constructed line of works," according to an observant Union officer who saw them in early September.[63]

The Confederates were stretched thin along the entire length of their line from a point northeast of Atlanta to Hardee's flank well to the southwest of the city. By mid-August, the 40th Alabama in Baker's Brigade of Stevenson's Division, Lee's Corps, was placed in one rank within the trenches, and each man was a yard apart from his comrades to right and left.[64]

By August 16, Sherman reached a decisive point in his thinking. As he put it in his memoirs, "We were held in check by the stubborn defense of the place, and a conviction was forced on my mind that our enemy would hold fast, even though every house in the town should be battered down by our artillery. It was evident that we must decoy him out to fight us on something like equal terms, or else, with the whole army, raise the siege and attack his communications." Sherman set the night of August 18 as the start date for his grand tactical movement, which involved shifting one corps to cover the rail crossing of the Chattahoochee and moving the rest out of their current lines and into a large, sweeping march to hit the railroad well south of East Point.[65]

In issuing his directive to start the movement on August 18, Sherman added a caveat: "unless something occurs in the mean time to mar the plan." Word of a Confederate cavalry raid on his own rail supply intervened to compel Sherman to postpone the movement. Johnston had urged this course of action for some time before his removal from command, but he had been unwilling to employ his own small mounted arm to do it. When Hood suggested that Wheeler conduct an attack on the Federal railroad, Davis approved. Hood instructed his cavalry leader to bypass Sherman's legions and hit the tracks between Marietta and Chattanooga. Then he was to cross the Tennessee River and hit the rail line between Chattanooga and Nashville. Wheeler left on August 10 with close to 6,000 troopers but was unable to inflict crippling damage on the line because of Sherman's defensive preparations. The Federals had been careful to construct earthworks or blockhouses at most of the culverts and bridges, and the major depots such as Allatoona were well prepared to deal with cavalry. Wheeler's men tore up some isolated segments of track between fortified points and occupied the town of Dalton, but they were unable to compel the small garrison there to come out of its fort and surrender. Then the Confederate commander set out to bypass Chattanooga by sweeping widely through East Tennessee, taking most of Hood's mounted arm away from the Army of Tennessee.[66]

Sherman had little to fear from Wheeler's raid, but the enemy move inspired him to try a cavalry strike at the Macon and Western Railroad one last time. Hugh Judson Kilpatrick led 4,700 blue-coated troopers, most of Sherman's available cavalry, to hit both the West Point and Atlanta Railroad to the southwest of East Point and the Macon and Western Railroad near Jonesboro. Hood sent an infantry brigade and a small cavalry force to deal with this raid. Kilpatrick was able to occupy a section of the railroad at Jonesboro for a while, tearing up some track, before he left to avoid the enemy. Despite Kilpatrick's inflated report, his men actually tore up only half a mile of track at Jonesboro and lifted a few rails elsewhere. The line was back in full operation by August 21.[67]

"I do not want to move this vast army and its paraphernalia round Atlanta unless forced to do so," Sherman had told Thomas on August 17. Kilpatrick's raid, along with the limitations of shifting the infantry further along its current lines, proved conclusively that there was no other way to snip the last rail line into Atlanta.[68]

12

Siege

Despite the heavy reliance on fieldworks displayed by both sides in the Atlanta campaign, Sherman had managed to keep up the momentum of the Federal offensive pretty well since early May. When his efforts to extend southward toward the Macon and Western Railroad foundered on distance and effective enemy blocking in early August, however, the campaign developed an increasingly siege-like character. It never really became a siege, for it was impossible for Sherman to invest Hood in the city, and he never had the patience to conduct siege approaches to break open the Confederate defenses. But the opposing soldiers were locked in static positions behind heavy earthworks within rifle shot of each other for up to a month and had to endure conditions similar to those encountered by men engaged in a genuine siege.

THE WORKS

In this stage of the Atlanta campaign, Hood committed himself fully to reliance on heavy earthworks as the key to protecting the city. He issued a circular to his corps commanders on August 13 impressing on them "the absolute necessity of holding the lines they occupy to the very last." Hood expressed his opinion that the heavy field of obstructions combined with effective artillery fire would turn back any Union attack, no matter how large. It also was necessary for the rank and file to hold the trench and use their small arms. "Let every man remember that he is individually responsible for his few feet of line, & that the fate of

Atlanta hangs upon the issue." Copies of this circular disseminated down the chain of command to the regimental level, at least in Lee's Corps.[1]

In Stewart's Corps, temporarily commanded by Cheatham in early August, Brig. Gen. Winfield S. Featherston wrote his own circular to the troops of his Mississippi brigade urging them to make their earthen defenses ever stronger. "By doing so your numbers are virtually increased, and valuable lives are saved." Stewart's Corps held the sector from the Marietta Road southward to the Lick Skillet Road, fronting the northwest approaches to Atlanta. It became evident to many that the Confederates needed to add more embellishments to the fortifications in order to hold their sector with fewer men and continue extending southward to match Sherman's move.[2]

By mid-August, Hood thought that constructing more traverses was one way to achieve the goal of holding the defenses with fewer men. He urged Lee to build traverses "every ten paces if necessary" as a protection from Union artillery fire. Lee passed on that suggestion to his subordinates, urging them in addition to utilize "every means that may suggest themselves" to improve the works.[3]

Arthur M. Manigault settled his brigade of Anderson's Division into its sector one mile south of the Lick Skillet Road and half a mile north of the Sandtown Road on August 1. His men held a section of works that was 450 yards long, stretching across a high open hill with both flanks resting on lower ground. The engineers placed Manigault's parapet on the military crest, about 100 yards down from the natural crest of the hilltop. The ground for 200 yards in front was open and "covered with loose stones and broken rock." Manigault's men built a thick parapet to stop artillery rounds, erected head logs, and planted a "double row of palisades" in front of the position. They further placed abatis in front of the palisades, making the tangled brush 50 to 100 feet deep. Later in the month, after the Federals worked their way closer to this position, one enemy battery enfiladed the entire length of the brigade line, another nearly did so, and two other batteries pounded directly at Manigault's front. He was forced to erect many traverses, "in which the men showed much ingenuity." The troops also dug numerous shelter holes in the ground just behind the works until it "was completely honey-combed," as Manigault put it. Anyone not familiar with the layout of the holes found it dangerous to walk within twenty yards of the line at night.[4]

The Federals also strengthened their works so as to hold them with fewer men and continue their attempts to reach the Macon and Western Railroad. Circulars went out through the command structure of the Sixteenth Corps, for example, to make the parapets proof against artillery rounds. Officers instructed their men to fashion a continuous line of works on the picket line. Fourteenth Corps troops that were exposed to enfilade artillery fire fashioned thick traverses. All of this had to be done at night, and even then the work details often had to drop their tools to avoid volleys from Confederate skirmishers before resuming their labor. The troops soon learned that parapets needed to be about ten to twelve feet wide to adequately protect against artillery fire. Some Seventeenth Corps troops erected a bank of earth just behind the main line to cover them as they cooked and slept, and they dug communication trenches to connect the main line with the skirmishers where the terrain and covering Confederate fire demanded it. Men of the 154th New York in the Twentieth Corps dug a small ditch in front of their works in which to plant a line of sharpened stakes, with three feet of each stake sticking out of the ground, and lay brush in front of the ditch to form an abatis, sharpening the ends of the branches.[5]

Digging in the clay soil of the Georgia Piedmont was not easy. William Wallace of the 3rd Wisconsin in the Twentieth Corps reported that the men always had to dig through roots when doing any large entrenching job. He noted that his regiment had constructed twenty lines since the start of the campaign through mid-August, and the novelty of the experience had long since worn off. The historian of the 3rd Wisconsin remembered very well the quality and consistency of the soil near Atlanta. It was "yellow joint clay, sticky and yielding when wet, but it cracked, disintegrated and became dusty when dry." In some ways this was advantageous to men forced to live in a ditch. "The floor of the trench was of this clay, and under the tramp and wear of so many feet for so many days it became as smoothly even and firm as a cemented cellar floor."[6]

On the skirmish line, there was even more need for protection because the position was so close to enemy lines. In French's Division the men of William H. Young's Brigade made pits for their reserve skirmishers in "the shape of three sides of a hexagon, connected by a substantial ditch, with head-logs on top and a very strong line of stake abatis forty yards in front." The skirmish line also was fronted by abatis. Anderson's Division, stretched south from the Lick Skillet Road, started with a series of "shallow rifle-pits hurriedly dug" when the division took its position right after Ezra Church. They were twenty to fifty paces apart. Then over the next two weeks, the men improved the skirmish defenses at night, connecting the pits and making the skirmish line a continuous work with head logs and loopholes for the sharpshooters. Federal skirmishers pushed their line up until it was only 100 yards away, and in places as close as sixty paces, by the end of the campaign, while the main Union line lay about 200 yards to the rear of the blue-coated skirmishers.[7]

Opposite Anderson's position, members of Harrow's Fifteenth Corps divi-

Head logs on Confederate works. This view depicts a part of the Confederate defenses located just north of the Georgia Railroad on the east side of Atlanta. The head logs consist of building timbers scavenged from nearby structures. George N. Barnard's position enabled him to catch with clarity the head logs, supporting cross timbers across the open trench, and the parapet. *Photograph by George N. Barnard. Library of Congress, LC-USZ62-79792.*

sion constructed zigzag approach trenches forward from their skirmish line to advance it ever closer to Anderson's skirmishers. They rolled logs forward to protect themselves as they crawled and began to dig in. In places, the opposing sides were close enough to hold an "ordinary conversation" with each other. They also dug zigzag communication trenches to connect the Union skirmish line with the main line where needed.[8]

The obstruction field became more important than ever during the "siege" phase of the Atlanta campaign. There was no better way to physically prevent the enemy from attacking the line. All types of barriers were employed by the Confederates, from cut brush to large trees to stakes to chevaux-de-frise. It was important to create deep belts of obstructions with layers of different types. In doing so, the Confederates created the most extensive field of obstructions in front of a fortified position in the western theater of the war. It seemed to Ches-

Siege

ley Mosman, the Fourth Corps pioneer officer, that the forty-yard-wide belt of abatis (termed "tangle foot" by some Confederates) was so thick a man would need two or three hours to pass through it, "even if he had nothing to carry and no one shooting at him." Rows of slanted, sharpened stakes, poised to strike a man a bit above his waist, appeared formidable to observant Union soldiers. Some Confederates called them "haver-sack stealers." Rice C. Bull of the 123rd New York took a long look at such a row of stakes, each one about six inches apart from the next. "From a distance they looked like great hair combs pointing toward us." Presstman's engineer troops planted more of these sharpened stakes in front of the artillery emplacements than before the infantry curtains.[9]

William H. Young, who had taken over Ector's Texas Brigade in French's Division, planted a palisade consisting of upright timbers closely placed together along the entire front of his sector from the Marietta Road to the Turner's Ferry Road. The timbers stood eight feet above the ground. Such a work would have required enormous expenditure of time and labor. In fact, the men did not complete it until September 1, only a few hours before they were ordered to evacuate the position and Atlanta itself at the end of the campaign.[10]

Both Union and Confederate soldiers placed multiple layers of obstructions before their works. Harvey Reid of the 22nd Wisconsin counted six rows of sharpened stakes in front of one Rebel fort, and Chesley Mosman counted eight rows of abatis opposite the Fourth Corps sector. A brigade in Harrow's division placed at least three rows of stakes in front of its fortifications on the west side of Atlanta. The historian of the 96th Illinois in the Fourth Corps carefully documented the layers of obstructions in front of his regiment's defenses. One row of sharpened stakes, each stake six inches from the next, was located close to the parapet. "A few feet in front of the works is another row of sharp sticks, four or five feet long, and three or four inches apart, set at an angle of ninety degrees. These are held in place by logs, dirt being thrown in the spaces." In front of that row there was a line of abatis, consisting of "heavy limbs, or tree tops . . . piled thick and staked down," with the ends of the limbs sharpened. In front of the abatis, the Federals slashed whatever timber was available to create yet another layer of obstructions.[11]

Hood was justifiably proud of his engineer officers and troops, and of the rank and file, for their assiduous work on the layers of obstacles that came to shield the Confederate line by late August. As James Patton Anderson put it, the bristling obstacles gave "confidence to our troops." Arthur M. Manigault echoed this note in his memoirs, stating that his South Carolina troops felt very confident about holding their works with multiple layers of obstacles fronting them.[12]

A Confederate fort south of the Western and Atlantic Railroad. It is difficult to know exactly which fort this view depicts, but George N. Barnard was pointing his camera north—the works are built to defend against an enemy approach from the left. It is possible Barnard stood in Fort V on Hood's Addition to the Atlanta City Line and pointed his camera toward Fort W, the next work north. There is no doubt that Barnard exposed no fewer than four images from this fort, generally looking north. The others can be seen in the appendix and in *Atlas to Accompany the Official Records*, plate 127, no. 7, and plate 128, no. 7. One can see a vertical palisade in front of the line, then an inclined palisade in front of it, and a large field of slashed timber extending quite a distance in front of the latter. Walthall's Division held this sector and invested a lot of time, effort, and material to construct this strong line. *Photograph by George N. Barnard. Library of Congress, LC-DIG-cwpb-02239.*

In addition to multiple layers of obstructions, many unit commanders built multiple lines of defense. The main line remained the main defensive position, and nearly everywhere along the Rebel defenses there was a substantial skirmish line that was well fortified. But in addition to these two basic formations, others sprouted up. French's Division created a second skirmish line behind

Siege

the first, consisting of a continuous trench to hold the skirmish reserve. An interior line located behind the main trench also was constructed, but it was not continuous. French reported that it was dug "at intervals" wherever the ground allowed and the location of the enemy demanded it. At least some of the Confederate units deployed a vidette line in front of their skirmish line. Videttes constituted an early warning line, deployed by Sears's Brigade of French's Division in groups of four men each 500 yards in front of the skirmish line. The skirmish line itself was located 800 yards in front of the brigade's main position. In one rotation, Col. William H. Clark deployed his 46th Mississippi and 120 dismounted cavalrymen to hold the skirmish and vidette lines of the entire brigade, which covered a sector 1,200 yards wide. They had to stretch quite a bit to accomplish this, but the well-developed earthworks on the skirmish line allowed for such a thin deployment.[13]

The Federals did not concentrate so heavily on multiple lines, but their works were also well developed for defense. Harrow's division straddled the Green's Ferry Road and the Lick Skillet Road west of Atlanta. "Heavy and well constructed earthworks were at once built covering the position," wrote the historian of the 6th Iowa, "which extended over uneven ground, through woods and brush, cultivated patches and open fields, orchards and gardens, over hills and across narrow ravines in total disregard of property and homes." The works grew "until a feeling of security from assaults and sallies pervaded along the line."[14]

The soldiers realized that the size and strength of their works far exceeded anything built during the earlier phases of the campaign. Members of the 3rd Wisconsin in the Twentieth Corps had a great deal of time to improve their defenses until the parapet was eighteen feet thick at the base and eight feet wide at the top. It rose four feet from the ground. The regiment constructed a firing step that was three feet wide, located one foot below the natural level of the earth and fifteen inches above the floor of the trench. The trench itself was twelve feet wide, and the men used posts and fence rails as revetment to hold up the interior of the parapet. Their head logs were eight to ten inches wide and fifteen to twenty feet long, raised three or four inches above the top of the parapet.[15]

SIEGE

The works on both sides of no-man's-land outside Atlanta were essentially unassailable, and the question of whether the Federals ought to try siege approaches naturally arose. It seemed a daunting task for many reasons. As Howard's chief of artillery put it, the enemy held "a position which, in this case, has all the elements and advantages of a fortress thus making his force fully equal to ours for all purposes of this semi-siege." Sherman and Poe discussed the possibility of conducting siege approaches to break through the enemy line. "I frequently informed the general commanding that we could easily, at any time, push forward saps and pierce the enemy's lines, yet when we had done so we would have accomplished very little, since the enemy would take the precaution to construct another a few yards in his rear." Even if that were not true, Hood could easily escape Atlanta if his line was irreparably broken, because it was impossible for the Federals to invest the city with their available manpower. Just in case Sherman changed his mind, the Federal pioneers worked from August 8 to 22 to collect and make siege materials. But Sherman had no intention of authorizing siege approaches. He remained fixed on extending southward or breaking contact with his supply line to shift the majority of his manpower onto the Macon and Western Railroad as the most economical way of gaining Atlanta.[16]

Nevertheless, rumors circulated widely among the Confederates that Sherman was conducting a siege. Aggressive pushing by Federal skirmishers led many to believe that the Yankees wanted to gain positions as close as possible to the Rebel line from which they could start digging saps. Rumors that Yankee mining was underway were also passed up and down the Confederate line.[17]

ARTILLERY

Rumors of Union sapping and mining never proved true, but the roar of artillery on both sides of the contested ground outside Atlanta was a constant reality. Life outside the earthworks was dangerous. Along the Sixteenth Corps line west of the city, Confederate guns provided constant annoyance. "There was no safety or security," reported division commander John M. Corse. "Cooks, grooms, clerks at work in their offices, were as subject to being hit by the random shell or shot as men in the extreme front." The same was true along the Fourteenth Corps line farther south. John Hill Ferguson found "there is about as much danger" in the rear as on the skirmish line. A solid shot sailed through the camp of the 10th Illinois, cutting down one tree, boring a hole through a second tree, and decapitating a man. Ferguson was compelled to sink his tent three feet into the ground and build a parapet around it until he felt "perfectly safe." French reported that sometimes the Federal artillery fronting his division fired more than 2,000 rounds per day at his men. "It makes my house an unpleasant residence," he sardonically complained.[18]

Along some sectors of the Union line, the enemy artillery was served very effectively. Lt. Andrew T. Blodgett of Battery H, 1st Missouri Light Artillery, in the Sixteenth Corps, could see four Confederate guns in a fort directly to his front 1,050 yards away. He also spied two more guns to the left at a distance of 1,100 yards, and another fort off to the right was shielded by trees and underbrush. This concentration pummeled his artillery emplacement mercilessly for several days, "their shot penetrating our works and entering the embrasures in several places, and, for a short time, our little fort had the appearance of being demolished." The rounds tore off the revetment holding up the parapet, and shells exploded above the work, killing and wounding gunners. Confederate pieces were equally well served just east of the Marietta Road, where the salient in the Rebel line caused much worry for Hood. Here the gunners also were able to send shot through the Union parapet on many occasions, while sailing other rounds to skim the top of the parapet. It became too dangerous for the Federals to expose themselves, and thus small-arms fire ceased altogether at this location from August 19 to the end of the siege.[19]

The only solution to this problem was to strengthen the works and try to counter enemy fire. Poe reported that all artillery emplacements were finished along Sherman's line by August 20, but of course they demanded constant maintenance and repair. Howard's artillery chief thought that the "average works for the infantry" were strong enough to withstand rounds from twenty-pounder rifles. Whether that proved true in practice is difficult to know, but the Confederates had heavier guns opposing the Federals; they had at least eight thirty-two-pounder rifles in their line. Only by making the works stronger than normal could the Yankees find some protection. According to at least one report, some Federal artillery emplacements had casemates for the guns. These were positions with roofs over the pieces for complete protection, difficult and time-consuming structures to make.[20]

Countering enemy fire was a more effective remedy than digging deeper into the earth, and many Union batteries managed to dominate their opponents at various points of the siege line. Capt. Marco B. Gary had moved his Battery C, 1st Ohio Light Artillery, to a point 700 to 800 yards from an annoying Confederate fort by August 10. At this range, he often "succeeded in battering the embrasures of" the work and stopping its fire for a time. Dodge took an aggressive stand along the Sixteenth Corps front, telling his division commanders to put all their guns as close as possible to the enemy and punish them without mercy. Sixteenth Corps skirmishers also were to target the embrasures of Rebel gun positions to keep down enemy fire.[21]

The Federals opposite Anderson's Division managed to construct a small work for one gun on their skirmish line, only sixty paces from the Confederate skirmishers. The work was located in front of the junction between George D. Johnston's Brigade and William F. Brantley's Brigade. The Federals protected the embrasure with a mantlet. This shield prevented the Rebel skirmishers from firing into the work directly at the gun crew. "Day after day," reported Anderson, "did they use it with damaging effect upon our rifle-pits, only sixty paces from its muzzle, frequently leveling the earth along the line for forty or fifty yards and literally covering our men in the pits with the debris." Some of Brantley's men tried to silence the gun by rolling forward logs and digging a zigzag approach trench until they got near enough "to throw hand-grenades over his breast-works," according to Anderson. But that did not work; only by concentrating the fire of many skirmishers along this sector could the Confederates drop enough bullets into the work to convince the Federals to evacuate it.[22]

Wherever Yankee guns deteriorated Rebel parapets, the defender conducted repairs under cover of night. A shell entered one of the embrasures of Guibor's Battery emplacement and exploded inside one night, but all the men were lying down and miraculously no one was injured. The gunners erected a shield of green bushes in front of the work the next day in an attempt to make themselves a less visible target. In Edward A. O'Neal's Brigade of Edward C. Walthall's Division, the men erected a traverse at the flank of every company to protect themselves from Federal enfilading fire. The men of the 10th Mississippi, in Jacob H. Sharp's Brigade of Anderson's Division, became so familiar with the fire of a particular rifled gun on the Union line near their position that they gave it a name. "This gun is called 'Old Gussy,' by the men in the ditches," reported Isaac Foster.[23]

Manigault's Brigade of Anderson's Division also had an annoying enemy gun planted close to home. It was only 100 yards from Manigault's skirmish line and about 300 yards from his main position. The Federals erected iron mantlets, raised and lowered by means of a lanyard, and Manigault's sharpshooters failed to stop the enemy. "Scarcely a day passed that some of the pits were not filled up by the fire of their artillery," Manigault recalled, "sometimes burying their occupants, who, if not killed or wounded, found it hard to extricate themselves." For ten days, Manigault made a point of living in the trench with his men, sheltered by a traverse. He believed that during this time, at least 1,500 rounds of Union artillery fire landed little more than twenty paces from his home. The bays formed by the placement of traverses along his brigade line were only fifteen paces wide, barely enough to shield Manigault from most of the rounds hitting his section of the line. These rounds often hit the traverses and spread dirt, splinters, rocks, and shell fragments into his bay. This was not only uncomfortable but "far from cleanly," so the brigade leader had a bombproof built for himself 150 yards behind the works in a small woods and inside "a slight gully" that offered him ample protection and comfort.[24]

In the final analysis, it cannot be said that either side thoroughly dominated in the contest of artillery. At some parts of the line, one side or the other achieved at least temporary dominance over the other. On many other parts of the line, neither side achieved anything except protecting themselves well enough to deny the other side any advantages. As Andrew Jackson Neal of the Marion Light Artillery put it, "Where Batteries are as well protected as our & the yankees Batteries before us about as much is made of artillery duels as the sledge hammer makes out of the anvil."[25]

SKIRMISHING

With the lines locked in close proximity of each other for an extended period of time, skirmishing became increasingly important in the campaign. Maj. William H. Chamberlin of the 81st Ohio in the Sixteenth Corps went so far as to say that the "investment of Atlanta from July 22d until late in August, was in the main a gigantic battle of skirmishers." Firing between the opposing skirmish lines "was constant during the day," according to Anderson, "and not unfrequently continued throughout the night." For a week in August, it was so heavy that Lee characterized the skirmishing along Anderson's and Clayton's front as amounting "to almost an engagement."[26]

The siege was a war of videttes as well, for this early warning line became ever more important as a way to safeguard against sudden attacks. On the sector held by William S. Barry's Brigade of French's Division, the skirmish line was located a quarter of a mile from the main line early in August, with the vidette line placed 150 yards in front of the skirmishers. Each vidette post consisted of four men in a hole, and each post was fifteen to twenty yards from the next. Initially, the vidette posts were protected by little more than "flimsey piles of rails or rotting logs, or anything that would stop a bullet," according to Sgt. William Pitt Chambers of the 46th Mississippi. On August 19, the Federals pushed back the 35th Mississippi and captured the vidette position, enabling their skirmishers to "pour a hot fire into our main picket line."[27]

Duty on the skirmish line was hazardous and tense. On Williams's division front along the Twentieth Corps sector, the skirmishers were not allowed to sleep and all talking was done in whispers. The men "sit or stand peering toward the picket line of the enemy, listening as only men listen when their lives depend on their vigilance," according to Rice C. Bull of the 123rd New York. But duty on the vidette line was worse. The New Yorkers placed videttes 100 feet in front of their skirmish line at dusk and held them there all night, sheltering behind trees or other obstacles. It was emotionally and physically draining work. In contrast, duty on the reserve line behind the skirmishers was the easiest to be had forward of the main position. The skirmish reserve was allowed to sleep even though they were prohibited from building campfires. At night they could light a candle only if they were safely placed behind a tree. Duty on the skirmish reserve was comparatively easy, for all the men had to do was "watch and listen," according to Bull.[28]

Many Federal commanders urged their skirmishers to punish and annoy the enemy as much as possible. John Hill Ferguson reported that his twenty-four-hour rotation on the skirmish line resulted in the firing of over 2,000 rounds of ammunition by his company of the 10th Illinois, and other companies fired more than that. A company of the 17th New York in the Sixteenth Corps fired 1,500 rounds during its twenty-four-hour rotation. One-third of the men in the 96th Illinois, a Fourth Corps regiment, went on the skirmish line every day. They fired from 3,000 to 5,000 rounds in each twenty-four-hour period. Many Confederate commanders felt the weight of this aggressive firing and responded by constructing a well-fortified second line for their skirmishers to fall back to in case of need.[29]

Arthur M. Manigault provided detailed information about the skirmish struggle on his brigade sector. Upon taking position between the Lick Skillet Road and the Sandtown Road on August 1, Manigault established a skirmish line consisting of detached pits fifteen paces apart. Each pit was about fifteen feet long and the parapet had a head log. The troops constructed a communication trench that was three feet deep and two and a half feet wide to connect each pit. The communication trench was large enough to allow officers to go from one post to another, shift reinforcements, and let the men take shelter if their pits were damaged by Union artillery fire to the point of uselessness. Most of the labor on this elaborate skirmish position was performed by the skirmishers themselves, although Manigault sometimes sent out work details to help them. All the work to improve the skirmish fortifications was done at night and it never ceased during the entire course of the month. Each soldier going out to the skirmish line for his rotation was required to take along "a forked branch of a tree or young sapling, the leaves all trimmed off and points sharpened," to add to the ever-growing belt of abatis that fronted the skirmishers.[30]

Despite these elaborate defenses, the Federal troops of the Army of the Tennessee pressured Manigault's skirmish line back on two different occasions during the month of August. The first line was located 800 to 825 yards in front of his main line, with dense woods separating it from the Union skirmishers.

The Confederates finally held in their third position, which was located 200 to 250 yards in front of the main line. This was the major reason that Manigault's men had to work on the skirmish defenses for so long; they had to build not one but three fortified positions. To Manigault's left, the skirmishers of Stovall's Brigade were pushed all the way back to their main line. To the right, the Confederates were also pressed back farther than Manigault's third skirmish position, making of his picket line a kind of salient in no-man's-land.[31]

Manigault maintained his skirmish line with 175 men spread along the 450-yard front of his brigade. They fired more than 6,000 rounds of ammunition every day, averaging more than thirty-four rounds per man. In short, during every twenty-four-hour tour of duty on the skirmish line, the troops fired as many rounds as a lot of regiments did at the battle of Stones River or Chickamauga. Manigault arranged it so that everyone could rest for four days before their next tour of skirmish duty occurred because it was such a stressful experience to be in the pits. The firing continued during the night after a lull of a couple of hours at dusk, and at a slower pace than during the day, but there was no real rest for anyone. Bullets fired by the Federal skirmishers often reached back to the Confederate main line. Manigault reported losing ten to eleven men every day during August, and that number rose as high as fifty-five on some days. Ironically, most of the casualties occurred on the main line, for here, despite repeated warnings, the men tended to be careless and became victims of stray balls. Casualties were lighter on the skirmish line because there the men were keyed up and watchful.[32]

This skirmish war in August was grueling, deadly, and destructive. At the end of the month, Manigault examined the environment and reported that head logs "were filled with bullets, much splintered, and in shreds." The last Federal skirmish line in front of his brigade by then was only eighty yards from his third and last skirmish position, and about 280 to 330 yards from his main line. The vegetation in no-man's-land had been wasted by the constant fire. Bushes were gone and trees were decimated. Manigault noted that some pines as wide as a man's leg were so chipped that they fell when the next stiff wind sailed through the area. The landscape had been so destroyed that one could clearly see all the way from Manigault's main line to the Union main line, more than 400 yards away, through groves of scarred tree trunks. Isaac Foster of the 10th Mississippi saw the ground in front of Manigault's Brigade and was impressed by the level of destruction. "Not a single tree or bush . . . escaped untouched while many trees of five or perhaps nine inches" in diameter were cut down. "A more thoroughly ball riddled field is seldom to be seen," Foster concluded.[33]

No one else along the siege lines provided such intimate detail about skir-

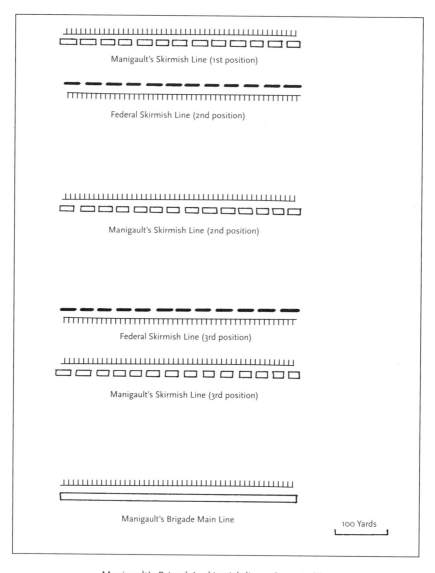

Manigault's Skirmish Line (1st position)

Federal Skirmish Line (2nd position)

Manigault's Skirmish Line (2nd position)

Federal Skirmish Line (3rd position)

Manigault's Skirmish Line (3rd position)

Manigault's Brigade Main Line

100 Yards

Manigault's Brigade's skirmish lines, August 1864

mishing as did Manigault, and his experience gives us a wonderful opportunity to understand the intensity and significance of skirmishing as part of the larger campaign for Atlanta. Daniel Harris Reynolds noted that along his brigade sector in Walthall's Division, improved earthworks enabled him to decrease the number of skirmishers he posted to cover his front. From 100 to 150 for each twenty-four-hour rotation, he reduced it to only sixty-six scattered in eleven pits.[34]

The Federal troops of the Army of the Tennessee aggressively pushed their skirmish line forward as much as possible during the month of August. It became a sore spot for Lee, commander of the Confederate troops opposite much of Howard's line. When skirmishers of Johnston's and Brantley's Brigades demonstrated spunk one day and fought hard to hold their position, Lee praised their stamina in a general order issued to the corps. They "allowed themselves to be bayoneted in the pits rather than be driven back," he proudly wrote. Lee hoped their example would inspire the troops to resist "rather than permit the enemy to approach our main line."[35]

French also was proud of the fact that his skirmishers resisted Union pressure during August, keeping the enemy as far from his main position as possible. It reduced casualties along the main line and allowed his men more freedom of movement, rest, and security. French's skirmish line was more heavily fortified than most. He made a continuous trench for the skirmishers and even placed a stockade along the front of most of the trench. He also constructed a second skirmish line to hold the reserve. His main position also was well dug in, with a double row of sharpened stakes in front and casemated emplacements for his guns. The Federal skirmish line was lodged some 200 yards from his skirmishers, and the fire between those lines was incessant. It killed most of the brush, which dried and withered away during the hot days of August, and killed trees of even moderate size. After the Federals evacuated their lines on August 26, French's men collected 10,000 pounds of expended bullets in no-man's-land and delivered them to the ordnance department. "The ground was literally covered with them," French recalled, "oxidized white like hailstones."[36]

It is possible that the skirmish fighting at Atlanta during August was more intense and deadly than on any other Civil War battlefield, and yet there were a few opportunities for informal truces to take place. Col. Daniel Dustin of the 105th Illinois in Ward's division of the Twentieth Corps reported that his men endured a vicious skirmish fire from their opponents for many days, much of it coming from a couple of small buildings in no-man's-land used as sharpshooting posts. Dustin's troops tried to negotiate with the Confederates to ameliorate the fire, but they refused to talk with them. Dustin finally sent two daring men out on the night of August 18 with combustible material to set the buildings on fire. "The next day," Dustin reported, "picket-firing was amicably adjusted, after which everything was quiet." Before that, the 105th Illinois had lost twenty-one men to heavy Confederate sharpshooting.[37]

With the main line 600 yards away and the skirmish line only fifty yards away in places, life was dangerous along the sector held by Benjamin Harrison's brigade, of which Dustin's Illinois regiment was a part. "Almost every day casualties occurred within my lines," reported Harrison, "and it was in many places impossible to show a head above the works without it being made a target for rebel sharpshooters. The men were compelled to keep continually under cover and suffered great constraint by being kept so continuously in the ditches, which were frequently very wet and muddy. Many casualties occurred while men were sitting in their tents close behind the works, and several were killed while asleep in their bunks."[38]

Confederates opposite the Fourth Corps also punished the Federals during the course of the siege with well-directed sharpshooting. "No one could say any hour that he would be living the next," reported David S. Stanley. "Men were killed in their camps, at their meals, and several cases happened of men struck by musket-balls in their sleep, and passing at once from sleep into eternity. So many men were daily struck in the camp and trenches that men became utterly reckless, passing about where balls were striking as though it was their normal life, and making a joke of a narrow escape, or a noisy whistling ball."[39]

There also was a certain amount of "trench raiding" along the Fourth Corps line. On the night of August 18, the Confederates captured a picket post established by Isaac M. Kirby's brigade. The Federal pickets challenged the Rebels but were taken prisoner. When four men went forward from the skirmish line to investigate the noise, they never returned. James Patton Anderson reported that he regularly sent scouts to penetrate the Union skirmish line on his division's sector to gather intelligence.[40]

Losses in this skirmish war counted for an alarming proportion of total casualties in the campaign. Absalom Baird thought they amounted to the equivalent of those in a large battle. His Fourteenth Corps division had poor ground with several places that were exposed to enemy sharpshooting. His skirmishers were able to create temporary truces at some locations to ease the suffering, but at others "a vicious skirmish would be kept up, and for days the men would be imprisoned in their trenches, not daring to show their heads above the parapet." Baird lost up to thirty men a day in his division to this fire. When Mortimer D. Leggett lost eighteen men in his division of the Seventeenth Corps in one day of skirmishing, he admitted it was but slightly higher than the average for August. On the Confederate side, hospital steward Willis Perry Burt reported that all nineteen men of his regiment who had been shot during the week ending August 14 had been felled by Yankee sharpshooters. French's Division of Stewart's Corps missed the battles of July 22, Ezra Church, and Jonesboro, and had only a marginal role to play at Peach Tree Creek. Yet it suffered the loss of 373 men from July 18 to the end of the campaign. That averages to more than eight men a day. Mercer's Brigade fought in three heavy battles — Peach Tree Creek, July 22, and the second day at Jonesboro — during the same time period. Yet, 23 percent of all its casualties during that period were inflicted by sharpshooting, skirmishing, and artillery fire between battles.[41]

William B. Hazen's brigade of the Fourth Corps held a position on the northeast sector of the lines from July 22 to August 17. He deliberately told his skirmishers to train their muskets at long range and try to drop bullets into the Confederate camps. They fired as many as 5,000 rounds per day for three weeks. After the war, Hazen learned from Confederate sources that three to five men of every regiment were hit by this fire each day, and concluded that perhaps one out of 500 rounds had found a mark. Hazen thought this was an economical way to injure the enemy, given that every 500 cartridges cost the government twenty-five dollars and that, in a pitched battle, the proportion of lead expended to disable one man was far higher than the rate of one per 500 rounds.[42]

A major reason for the heavy earthworks that were built on both sides of no-man's-land was the constant fear of sniping and short-range artillery fire. Locked in static positions, the troops had to protect themselves. As Alpheus Williams put it in a letter home, "One has to be very cautious of sharpshooters and very steady nerved to get into and out of our line of works through the picket bullets and the tornado of artillery missiles." This sort of sniping cost Dodge his command and nearly his life. He was struck on the head by a bullet one day in August while observing the Confederate position. Dodge survived his wound but never returned to the Sixteenth Corps, although he held a departmental command in Missouri later in 1864.[43]

Of course the losses and tension were felt keenly by both sides in this skirmish war. The use of fireballs to light up the darkness of no-man's-land was an expression of the fear and apprehension that arose from the close proximity of enemy troops. While the Federals do not appear to have used them, the Confederates on at least one occasion did what they had done at Kennesaw and what Johnston had recommended they do along the Shoup Line—throw these incendiary devices out when fearful of an enemy advance. Fourth Corps observers saw the Confederates use fireballs from a fort twice on the night of August 16.[44]

Some survivors of the skirmish war thought it had been a useless waste of life. The historian of Company B, 40th Alabama, recalling the heavy losses, wrote, "There is too great a stress put on picket fighting. They are strong lines, but so far away from support that the enemy can carry them by attacking in great force, which they do and our picket lines are sacrificed and no good accomplished."[45]

The intensity of the skirmishing at Atlanta in August was unusual; it caused many men their lives and their health, stressed the participants mercilessly, and reduced the fighting effectiveness of many units. In general, the Federals seem to have gained more than lost in the contest, and many Confederate units lost more than they gained in the struggle. To that extent, it can be said to have been necessary and utilitarian for Sherman's troops to engage in the contest.

LIFE IN THE TRENCHES

"Sun and rain, heat and cold, storm and mud and water, come what may, we took it in the trenches," pungently recalled Philip Daingerfield Stephenson of the Fifth Company, Washington Artillery. Decades after the war, this artilleryman pegged it correctly when he concluded that the "trenches were our home — our beds, our cooking places . . . by day and night." Like any other home, the works provided protection, comfort, and at times a greater-than-usual amount of misery.[46]

"It is oppressively warm in the entrenchments," confided Isaac Foster of the 10th Mississippi to his diary on August 14. Men in the 3rd Wisconsin erected brush arbors resting on forked sticks to shield themselves from the rays, but their officers ordered the structures to be taken down. The officers, Edwin E. Bryant wryly noted, lived in dugouts behind the trenches with brush arbors to protect them, but the trench was a fighting position and arbors got in the way of firing.[47]

"Ditch life has no attraction except for safety," commented Isaac Foster. His sentiment was echoed by Capt. Henry Newton Comey of the 2nd Massachusetts. "This living in holes and under banks is a queer life and is not healthy, but still it is much healthier to live in holes than outside, as anyone here can testify. Now and then some fellow gets tired of keeping cover, shows himself, and is bored by a rebel bullet."[48]

Forced to live in the earth, the men made the best of it. Lt. Col. Daniel F. Griffin of the 38th Indiana in the Fourteenth Corps had a dugout made for himself. It measured twelve by sixteen feet in dimension, and was two feet deep with pine logs to hold up the dirt walls and a parapet around it for further protection. His men lay pine poles on the floor and spread pine boughs on them to "furnish both carpet and bedding." They also stretched tent flies over it for a roof, supported by a ridge pole twelve feet higher than the floor. It made "a large, airy, comfortable, and I might say safe, habitation," Griffin told his wife.[49]

Officers had more opportunities to make the best of a bad situation than did their men. The headquarters of the 7th Iowa in the Sixteenth Corps were located in a dugout fifty yards behind the main line, while the men lived in holes dug just behind the works with logs piled up to protect them. Members of a

Fifteenth Corps regiment, the 70th Ohio, also dug holes behind their works in addition to digging communication trenches stretching from the trench toward the rear to offer some degree of safety in approaching the line. Even so, the regiment lost thirty-six men to enemy sniper and artillery fire in just two weeks. Only in rare cases did enlisted men procure something to make their lives more comfortable in the works. Someone found a stash of chairs near the position of the 101st Ohio, and a number of men took advantage of the opportunity. "You can see them all along the fortifications," Capt. Jay Caldwell Butler told his parents, "sitting down in their high backed chairs."[50]

Surgeon Fielding Sloan of the 50th Alabama in Johnston's Brigade of Anderson's Division wanted his field hospital located as close to the main line as possible. So he had men dig a pit only forty feet behind the trench. It was two feet deep and twelve feet square, with a parapet on the side facing the enemy. The hospital actually was located on higher ground than the main line because of an ascending slope, but Sloan thought it was important to be close to his men.[51]

Exposed to all weather, the troops of both armies endured discomfort whenever it rained. As the skies dropped moisture on the 26th Illinois in Harrow's division of the Fifteenth Corps on the night of August 19, Jesse L. Dozer informed his diary that it was "very disagreeable to sleep in the ditch." The rain continued the next day, creating a slop of muddy earth six inches deep on the floor of the trench. As the rain continued on August 21, Dozer escaped the muddy mess and walked about to the rear of the works, risking exposure to Confederate sharpshooters.[52]

A short distance to the north, William B. Westervelt of the 17th New York in the Sixteenth Corps complained about the rain on August 19. His trench was "half full of water, and sometimes it was a choice whether we would take a bath or a bullet, as it was almost certain death to leave the trenches." Westervelt and his comrades stretched "some poles across" the trench "above high water mark" and "roosted on them until the storm ceased."[53]

Isaac Foster of the 10th Mississippi also had difficulty coping with the mix of water and freshly turned earth outside Atlanta. The men tried to drain water out of the works, but along most stretches of the trench that proved to be impossible. "Rain falls almost every day," he wrote on August 8, "which makes the entrenchments more like hog wallows, than the habitations of men. The men's clothing & even their skin is of a red cast from continued wallowing in the red earth."[54]

Even when it did not rain, many soldiers complained about dirt while living inside the trenches. George S. Lea of the 7th Mississippi thought his comrades "look as bad as a dog just out of a hole after a Rabbit. Instead of being white we are all red." A Georgia militiaman named A. T. Holliday told his Lizzie that "I have lived in the ground until I have turned to be nothing more than a gopher or a mole." The only consolation was that all of his comrades looked the same way, "a nasty dirty set of white men like myself."[55]

In addition to rain and mud, human waste was also an element of trench life. This problem, however, had a solution. Details dug latrines behind the lines and erected brush to provide something of a screen for privacy. Hood issued a circular on July 30, instructing his subordinates to have latrines placed "at convenient and proper places" behind the works. He also ordered all dead animals buried as soon as possible.[56]

Sherman was barely able to maintain an adequate flow of commissary supplies for his men, perched as they were at the end of a rail line 350 miles from their primary base at Louisville, Kentucky. Living in the trenches imposed an additional difficulty when it came to food; it was inconvenient for the men to cook anything while stationed there. Soldiers of the 6th Iowa in the Fifteenth Corps received enough staples such as "hardtack, fat bacon, coffee, and sugar" to keep them going. But the occasional issues of fresh beef and beans "were usually lost to the men serving in the trenches," according to the regimental historian, because of a lack of facilities for preparing them.[57]

Gaining access to clean water was a far worse problem, for the men in both armies had to rely on natural sources that were relatively near the works. As Henry H. Wright of the 6th Iowa put it, the presence of 150,000 men and 50,000 animals "crowded into the space occupied by the two great armies in the siege operations about the city" meant that "all the flowing creeks in the vicinity became badly fouled, so that a drink of good pure water was considered a great luxury." This was a difficulty all soldiers, blue and gray, had to endure near Atlanta. But for those doing a tour of duty on the skirmish line, the difficulty was compounded by enemy bullets. In Manigault's Brigade, the skirmishers solved this problem by loading up one volunteer with all the canteens he could carry, spreading the word down the line as to which pit he would emerge from, and then coordinating their covering fire to keep the Federals down as he sprinted toward the rear. When he was ready to return with loaded canteens, he gave a signal so the same operation could be put into place as he ran back.[58]

Sleep became a problem for many soldiers, given the conditions of living within the works. The intense heat of the Georgia summer made it difficult to nap during the day, and sometimes flies swarmed so thickly during the daylight hours that sleep was impossible for that reason as well. Many times the men could not fall asleep till nearly midnight, but their officers insisted that they awake early in the morning to stand to in the trenches in case the enemy launched a dawn attack. In Ward's division of the Twentieth Corps, the troops awoke at 3:00 A.M. for duty. "This the boys think is a very useless arrangement," reported George F. Cram of the 105th Illinois, and "certainly it is anything but pleasant." By August 12, Stephen D. Lee had decided to wake the men of his corps at 3:45 A.M. instead of 3:00 A.M. and allowed half of them to continue sleeping while the rest stood to in the trenches.[59]

The living conditions in the works contributed to illness. A Georgia militiaman named J. S. Speir told his wife that "being Confined here make our men Sick being Closly Confined & Exposed to the wether." Edward C. Walthall reported much the same thing in his division to the west of Atlanta. He noticed a perceptible weakening of his men's strength and stamina due to constant exposure to the broiling heat and the strain of being under fire twenty-hours a day for weeks on end. "Every day looks more and more like a siege," commented Maj. Abraham J. Seay of the 32nd Missouri, Fifteenth Corps, on August 13. "Sickness increasing and the energies and dash of our men are less vigorous. . . . Nobody spoiling now for a fight."[60]

The health of the men on both sides of no-man's-land was further imperiled by the widespread presence of vermin in the works. "These trenches and breastworks were full of lice," complained a Fifteenth Corps infantryman in the 3rd Missouri named John T. Buegel, and the men did not have the opportunity to take a proper bath or wash their clothes. Before long, "our rags stuck to our skin." In the Confederate lines, Isaac Foster was much impressed by the infestation. "Though we have been troubled with [lice] during nearly the entire campaign," he wrote on August 14, "never before have they been so plentiful. Numbers of them may be seen crawling on the poles supporting our blankets which are spread for shade. Enough may be seen at almost any time to form a strong line of skirmishers." Foster sardonically called them "the soldiers pests." In addition to lice, the men were greatly bothered by "small black flies and musquitoes by the million," as Avington Wayne Simpson of the 5th Missouri (C.S.) wrote in his diary.[61]

At least the lice provided some diversion of a kind for Foster, who also complained of boredom in the trenches. Anytime orders were circulated warning the men to remain in the works for fear of sharpshooters, the boredom intensified. "Time under such circumstances drags slowly by. Sleeping, eating smoking, & chewing tobacco are almost the only passtimes of the men. Newspapers are eagerly sought after, & books are indeed a rare luxury." At times, someone was able to go into town and procure some apples or cakes to distribute to the men, which lifted their spirits for a while. Cakes and fresh fruit were in short supply among the Federals because of the limited carrying capacity of the rail line that linked them with the North. Tobacco also was a luxury among the Yankees, "indulged in only by those who had plenty of money," as Henry Wright of the 6th Iowa put it.[62]

Religion provided some degree of solace and entertainment. Charles D. Gammon, a Fourth Corps gunner in Battery M, 1st Illinois Light Artillery, recorded in his diary that "Elder Raymond preached in the trench" on August 7. Other Federal troops heard indications that a "wave of religious enthusiasm" was sweeping along the opposing Confederate line. Members of the 6th Iowa could clearly hear the "shouting & singing" across no-man's-land, noting that it often continued until late at night.[63]

Few regimental bands were present in either army during the Atlanta campaign, but those that did exist sometimes serenaded the troops. Early in August, the members of Guibor's Battery "were honored again to night with a serenade by the 9th Miss. Band. Their works join our redoubt on the right." In the absence of music, some soldiers created a break from boredom by stirring up trouble. Albert G. Brackett recalled that on the night of August 7, his comrades beat drums and sounded bugles to give the impression that an attack was underway. This caused the Confederates to open a heavy fire of musketry for an hour. The Federals kept low in their works for a long while after the firing ceased, and they "laughed heartily at the discomfiture of the enemy."[64]

An odd form of entertainment for both sides was an occasional visit to the lines by the citizens of Atlanta. According to Irving Bronson of the 107th New York, one could see them nearly every day popping their heads up in a Confederate fort. "The men would bring their wives, and the boys their best girls, and it was no uncommon thing to see all the way from twenty-five to fifty taking us in." Some civilians did more than peek, according to Capt. Jay Caldwell Butler of the 101st Ohio. He heard rumors that a woman was seen in a rifle pit on the skirmish line taking potshots at the Yankees. "It is said the women of Atlanta have expressed determination to help hold the city," he told his parents.[65]

Men on both sides of no-man's-land were forced to adapt their daily lives to the need to shield themselves behind earthworks. If they wanted to communicate with a relative or friend in another unit, they wrote a note and passed it down the line with a request to forward it to the correct unit and person. More than one Confederate survivor of the "siege" recalled this novel way of keeping in touch. Capt. Jacob Ragle of the 80th Indiana in Schofield's army reported making out muster rolls for his regiment on August 4 while the men were still in their trenches. The company commanders "had to work at them in the ditches, for the enemy was shelling our position with great spirit." When a shell landed

Siege

in the trench occupied by Company D, 10th Mississippi, Pvt. R. Eisley threw it out before the thing exploded, saving many lives.[66]

Informal truces held sway on some parts of the line, on some days. The 6th Iowa skirmishers managed to strike up conversations with the Rebels opposite their position, trading coffee for tobacco. Skirmishers of the 15th Kentucky in the Fourteenth Corps engaged in heated exchanges of fire with their counterparts for many days before they managed to arrange a truce on August 6. For days afterward, they were "chatting together quite freely, exchanging papers, tobacco, coffee and other small articles." In fact, one Rebel stayed overnight in the Union lines and returned to his unit the next morning.[67]

The same was true of the 10th Illinois. Its skirmishers kept up a lively fire for days before the men on both sides "got to hollowing" to each other on the night of August 11. As a result, all firing stopped. During the next day, many men felt safe enough to expose themselves at short range to the enemy, and in the afternoon groups began to meet halfway in no-man's-land to talk and trade items. It gave the Federals an opportunity to see their opponents in a human dimension. "The Rebs had huged the riffels pits so close," reported John Hill Ferguson, "that they had become the very collar of the clay and had been mudd all over, but had a chance to dry today."[68]

Officers tried to stop the practice of arranging informal truces. Hood issued a general field order condemning the practice because it provided the enemy an opportunity to gather intelligence about the Rebel works, strength, and position. It also gave an opportunity for wavering Southerners to desert. Hood also urged his officers to keep up picket firing during the night to hinder the possibility of the two sides meeting under cover of darkness. Lee had already anticipated Hood's directive by two days, issuing a circular to his corps condemning the practice. Lee even authorized his artillery officers to fire on his own men if they tried to go into no-man's-land to talk with the enemy without permission.[69]

Confederate officers made sincere efforts to stamp out truces after mid-August. After five days of conviviality, the Confederates opposite the 10th Illinois suddenly refused to talk with a group of Federals who approached their line with a newspaper to trade. "A Rebel lieutennant stood up on the works and told them to go away and stay away or they would be fired on," reported John Hill Ferguson. Members of the 75th Indiana in Baird's division of the Fourteenth Corps had a good relationship with Confederate pickets, talking and trading for several days, when suddenly officers on both sides stopped it. Each side gave a warning to the other before resuming fire.[70]

Even when confined to their skirmish works, under orders to shoot at the enemy, Union and Confederate troops maintained a level of communication with each other that mitigated the dangers of the skirmish war. "All kinds of Jests and Slang phrases are hurled at each other from the Pickets," reported William Bluffton Miller of the 75th Indiana. "But when the Battle begins all Jesting ends."[71]

There existed a commendable spirit of honor among the opposing skirmishers. On Manigault's front, despite the aggressiveness of the Federal pickets, the troops often traded barbs and comments with each other. In this way they came to know something about the character of the men opposing them. If a Confederate was hit, his comrades called out to the Federals, "Cease firing on this pit!" They then placed a white rag on a ramrod, raised it high, and evacuated the wounded man to the rear as the Federals honored the injunction. Firing resumed as soon as he was safe within the main Confederate line.[72]

Even the best of truces, however, could be violated. Ignoring Hood's prohibition of these informal arrangements, Confederates opposite the Third Division of the Twentieth Corps agreed to a truce with their counterparts on August 17. It went smoothly until a member of the 102nd Illinois walked too close to the Confederate line and was shot in the face. He survived the dangerous wound but the incident angered the Federals. "The injury was soon avenged," mysteriously reported the regimental commander, "and all remained quiet thereafter." On the Fifteenth Corps line, Capt. Hiland H. Kendrick of the 6th Iowa allowed two of his men to meet the enemy in no-man's-land to exchange papers on the evening of August 16. This set a precedent and several more men went forth without authorization that night. One of them, Rufus Ready, was taken prisoner by the Confederates.[73]

But there is evidence that many Confederates took Hood's injunction to heart and refused truces when offered them in the latter part of August. Capt. Benjamin Putnam Weaver of the 42nd Georgia in Stovall's Brigade of Clayton's Division informed his parents that a number of Federals sat on their works on the morning of August 18 "and hollored to us to bring them some tobacco — they would give us a pound of coffee for a plug. We sent them an ounce of lead was our only reply."[74]

One of the reasons Hood was adamant about stopping the truces was that it allowed the enemy to better observe conditions in his position. There is little evidence that the Yankees gathered much useful knowledge in truces, because the men normally met partway between the lines, but the Federals did rely heavily on observation to glean whatever they could of their enemy. Signal officers perched on houses trained their binoculars on the Confederate works and reported the number of shelters behind the line, the presence of freshly dug earth on parapets, the erection of new brush in front of artillery emplacements, and newly constructed casemates to cover the guns. Lt. W. W. Hopkins, a signal officer with Thomas's army, observed the effect of Union artillery fire on Confederate lines and on the city of Atlanta. He reported that the Rebels, who normally lounged behind the works, kept snugly within their protected positions all day, and even took horses that normally grazed near the works to safety so they would not be hit by the fire.[75]

But a more fruitful source of intelligence lay in the desertion of Confederate soldiers. They often were willing to tell all they knew of conditions among their former comrades. Whether that information was entirely reliable depended on how intelligent and well informed the deserter happened to be and on the level of trust that developed between him and the Federals. Confederate officers were better informed than enlisted men and could offer many valuable insights to the Unionists.

The story of Capt. John B. Jordan of the 36th Alabama, a regiment in Holtzclaw's Brigade, Clayton's Division, offers a wonderful case in point. Lt. Col. Thomas H. Herndon reported on August 14 that Jordan "failed last night to report with his detail" of pickets. Jordan had a good record as a company commander, but Herndon regretted to admit "that the facts of the case indicate too plainly & painfully that he deliberately and basely deserted his colors and went over to the enemy." Jordan not only deserted but he told the Federals everything he knew: the strength of his regiment and division, the extended nature of Clayton's command, the positions of different brigades, and the fact that Hardee's Corps was stretched so thin it had no reserves at all. He detailed the daily routine in the Confederate trenches, what time the men awoke and prepared for possible attacks, and what kind of obstructions lay in front of the works. He also told the Northerners that ammunition was in short supply in Hood's army.[76]

Jordan also encouraged the Federals to hold their skirmish fire and arrange more truces along the line, for many Confederates were willing to desert if they had a chance. In fact, he had deserted under those conditions. During an informal truce on the night of August 13, Jordan asked the Federal pickets how he would be treated if he gave up and was told he would be allowed to go north rather than be held as a prisoner of war. Rumor had it that deserters were forced to fight in the Union army. Jordan told the Yankees he had "been looking for an opportunity to desert during the whole campaign" and decided to cross the line that night.[77]

But Jordan's is not a simple case of desertion. He took the oath of allegiance to the United States government at Chattanooga on August 22, 1864. Federal authorities transported Jordan to Louisville, where they released him in September on the condition that he stay north of the Ohio River for the duration of the war. Jordan soon grew tired of life in the North and perhaps felt guilty about what he had done. At any rate, by late February 1865, he crossed hostile lines, made his way to Virginia, and tried to rehabilitate his record with Confederate authorities. Jordan wrote a letter claiming that he had been captured on the night of August 13, had escaped from a railroad car on the way to prison in Indiana, and had made his way to Canada. From there, he had sailed to Nassau and run the blockade to enter Wilmington, North Carolina, in early December 1864. Upon going to Richmond, he found himself officially listed as a deserter on the rolls of his regiment. Jordan requested a court of inquiry to clear his name. That court was never convened because Jordan convinced Herndon, his regimental commander, of his story. Herndon bought all of it and allowed Jordan to resume duty with his company because he believed the captain had been "forcibly captured and carried away by the enemy."[78]

Captain Jordan's case is clear. A good Confederate soldier, who had conducted himself responsibly in a position of trust, was worn down by the stress of the Atlanta campaign until he was willing to desert the colors as the only way to find relief. After a period of rest in the North, his optimism and strength returned and he felt guilty about what he had done. The only way to restore his record was to concoct lies about how and why he had left his company and to create an adventure story about how he returned to the fold. His commander needed officers and did not ask probing questions. Jordan served out the remainder of the war, crossing Union lines to take the oath of allegiance (again) on April 19, 1865, in Alabama.[79]

Jordan demonstrated that an otherwise reliable soldier could be so stressed by the prolonged contact with danger on the skirmish line during the Atlanta campaign that his willingness to go on could break. The strain on many Confederate soldiers was noticeable to observers in August. Douglas J. Cater of the 19th Louisiana maintained his spirit and believed that most of his comrades did so as well. But he noticed "a change in the other Brigades of our Division." Benjamin Putnam Weaver of the 42nd Georgia admitted that many Confederates were running away from their units "to see after their families but the most of them have returned." That may have been true, but many Confederates were deserting to the enemy as well.[80]

Opposite the 76th Ohio in the Fifteenth Corps, the skirmishers on both sides maintained good relations for several days in early August before Hood clamped down on informal truces. The Federals learned that the Rebel troops from northern Georgia were demoralized and likely candidates for desertion.

On the afternoon of August 13, they strengthened the skirmish line and made a sudden rush, taking many Rebel skirmishers. A good many of them seemed happy to come over. "They came sweating and panting up to our breastworks," reported Capt. Charles Dana Miller, "and our boys, laughing heartily, gave them a hand to help them over. . . . It looked very much like a preconcerted plan, yet they pretended to be no more than prisoners of war taken in a regular skirmish. One thing was certain; they were willing prisoners. They said that they had been driven back by our armies past their homes in northern Georgia and would go no further."[81]

The emotional effect of being locked in a static, fortified position for weeks on end wore more heavily on the outnumbered Confederates than on the Federals outside Atlanta. There is no evidence of appreciable Union desertion to the Confederates during the siege. Moreover, the Federals maintained their overwhelming confidence in Sherman and in the ultimate success of the campaign. Nothing seemed to shake their belief in either their commander or themselves. Lt. Col. Edward S. Salomon of the 82nd Illinois in the Twentieth Corps might have exaggerated a bit when he claimed in his official report that his men "were in good spirits, they having become so accustomed to the bullets, shells, and solid shot that constantly whizzed and howled by their ears, that they no longer paid any attention to them." But he nevertheless expressed the spirit of optimism that pervaded Union ranks and the fact that the Federals tended to endure the trials of the trenches better than the Confederates. The results of the last movement to end the campaign in late August and early September—the strike toward Jonesboro—also demonstrated that the fighting spirit of Hood's army rapidly deteriorated while that of Sherman's troops remained constant.[82]

13

Jonesboro

Sherman's plan to shift most of his available manpower in a wide flanking maneuver to reach the Macon and Western Railroad demanded complex preparations. It would be as large a movement as Sherman's crossing of the Etowah and his crossing of the Chattahoochee, but with potentially more decisive results.

Thomas was to begin the move on the night of August 25–26 by shifting Stanley's Fourth Corps all the way from the Union left to a location south of Proctor's Creek. Stanley would bivouac near Utoy Creek, well behind the Army of the Tennessee. Williams would take the Twentieth Corps northward to protect the railroad bridge and two other crossings of the Chattahoochee River. Because the Confederates would now be able to move north of Atlanta, Howard had to worry about the security of his left wing, which ended at Proctor's Creek. It would be a problem only for one day, August 26, because he was scheduled to pull out of his own works on the night of the twenty-sixth to twenty-seventh and join Thomas in the move toward the railroad the next morning.

Schofield's Army of the Ohio would serve as the pivot for this movement while holding a newly selected position at the far right flank of the current Union line southwest of Atlanta. Capt. William J. Twining, Schofield's chief engineer, selected a spot for the army's fortified position and Poe inspected it on August 16, pronouncing it "admirably chosen." The day before, Poe had already looked at the ground along Proctor's Creek to see if it was suitable for a refused line to protect Howard's left flank after Thomas pulled the Army of the Cumberland away from its position north of the city. But Proctor's Creek was not suitable; it would have required Howard to move his army northward in order to hold a line along the south side of the stream, breaking his connection with Schofield. Instead, Chauncey B. Reese persuaded the generals to position Howard's left flank farther south, on the battlefield of Ezra Church, after Thomas began to move. Reese thought that refusing the left along the same ridge Logan's Fifteenth Corps had held during the battle of July 28, facing north instead of south, would be the best way to shield the flank. Work on building a line of fortifications along the ridge facing north began on August 24; it would be held by troops of both the Sixteenth and Seventeenth Corps.[1]

Under Sherman's orders, Poe scouted the area around the railroad bridge over the Chattahoochee on August 23 in order to plan a *tête de pont*, or fortified bridgehead, for Williams's Twentieth Corps. Poe then relayed his instructions to Lt. William Ludlow, Williams's chief engineer, who laid out the works and began to construct them. Twentieth Corps pioneers were called into action, and the engineers of all commands scouted the road system as far as they could safely ride to better map out the area soon to be traversed by Sherman's host.[2]

Sherman personally had a hand in much of this work. He visited the Chattahoochee railroad bridge on August 24, the day after Poe had inspected the area, and urged Thomas to begin building the bridgehead before the move started. Sherman worried that Hood might impetuously attack as soon as he learned of the Union withdrawal, assuming the Federals were retreating north, and currently there were but two small redoubts south of the river near the bridge. These were palpably inadequate to protect an entire corps.[3]

Army of the Tennessee troops prepared the new refused flank at Ezra Church but Howard suggested a change of plan. If Thomas could leave the Fourth Corps near his current left flank for a while when the Fourteenth Corps began to move south, he could keep his line intact and not even use the refused line. Sherman liked the idea and told Howard he would order Thomas to leave a division of Stanley's corps near the exposed flank as support. This simplified Howard's movements.[4]

Williams prepared well for his move to the railroad bridge. He sent pioneers and one regiment of each brigade to the proposed position to begin digging in at dawn on August 25. Then he planned to shift his entire corps out of the works on the night of the twenty-fifth, sending his own division plus Harrison's brigade of Ward's division to the railroad bridge. Geary's division would cover Pace's Ferry, while Ward's remaining two brigades would protect Turner's Ferry. Williams planned to mass most of his artillery at the railroad bridge.[5]

As Thomas began his part of the movement on the night of August 25, delays ensued. Stanley needed all night to move, but Howard felt he could not keep his left flank in the air just south of Proctor's Creek all night. He therefore refused his left wing by sending both divisions of the Sixteenth Corps and the Third Division of the Seventeenth Corps into the newly dug line on the Ezra Church battlefield after all. Members of the 15th Iowa on the far left of this refused position that faced north bent the end of the line southward so it came to face west. The lesson of July 22 was still fresh in their minds.[6]

The cautious Schofield had also learned lessons about exposed flanks during the course of the campaign. His fortified pivot position south of Utoy Creek, which he would hold as the rest of Sherman's men moved far away to the south, was "a completely inclosed field-work," in Schofield's words. It was large enough to protect all his wagon trains and was reminiscent of the three-sided position he had created to hold Sherman's left flank after the Army of the Tennessee pulled away from the July 22 battlefield. Schofield recalled that one of his men, while constructing this circular work, commented, "Well, if digging is the way to put down the rebellion, I guess we will have to do it."[7]

The grand movement started on the night of August 25 with Thomas shifting his corps to their assigned locations and Howard refusing his left along the old Ezra Church battle line. Capt. Oscar L. Jackson of the 63rd Ohio in the Sixteenth Corps realized that the ground just behind the works was covered by pits holding up to 100 men each, mounded up because the graves had been dug quite shallow. There even was a shoe and foot still on one leg that was sticking out of a mound. Kenner Garrard's cavalry temporarily occupied a part of Thomas's line on the north side of Atlanta to fool the Confederates into thinking the works were still held, but the Rebels soon realized that a massive shifting of the enemy was in progress. Hood assumed it portended a movement south to reach his railroad, but he could not know for certain or exactly which point along the rail line Sherman aimed to hit.[8]

When Williams's division arrived at the Chattahoochee River railroad bridge, all was bustle and activity. Rice C. Bull of the 123rd New York reached the area at 6:00 A.M. and was assigned a place in the new line, given a shovel, and told to "make [the works] heavy and strong." His comrades "dug in with a will as all felt that if we were to have trouble we wanted good protection." Williams placed a brigade north of the river in old Confederate works to protect the corps train and rear areas. It probably took post in a section of Shoup's Line, although there were some smaller, older Confederate works forming a *tête de pont* immediately north of the bridge that this brigade may have used instead. Williams's line protecting the bridge was two miles long with both flanks resting on the river. It ran along high ground, and the center of the position was half a mile from the bridge itself. Geary's post at Pace's Ferry was designed in a similar way. All Twentieth Corps units slashed timber in front of their new position; the members of Williams's division cut trees for 500 yards forward. Mules were used to drag the tops of felled trees forward to make a formal abatis on some parts of the corps line. Elsewhere, the men let the trees fall where they may "to keep Johnny from coming on to us in too much of a hurry," as William Wallace of the 3rd Wisconsin put it. Artillery was placed in the old Confederate works just south of the bridge. The redoubts however had to be reversed and new embrasures cut in the south faces to fire in the correct direction. Work continued feverishly for two days until the men slowed down and continued puttering on their strong defenses for a few more days.[9]

The movement of Stanley's Fourth Corps to the west of Atlanta was not uneventful. By dawn of August 26, Stanley had positioned his men south and north of Proctor's Creek to rest a bit, and Confederate skirmishers, free to roam about because of the Twentieth Corps withdrawal to the river, found them soon after they stopped. There was a small skirmish with the Federals repulsing the Confederates. Then the corps resumed its march at 9:00 A.M. and safely reached the area of Utoy Creek, well behind Howard's refused left flank at Ezra Church. But when Stanley evacuated Proctor's Creek, Confederate skirmishers roamed south to Howard's new position at Ezra Church and a heavy skirmish ensued that lasted nearly all day on August 26. John Hill Ferguson and his comrades of the 10th Illinois (newly transferred from the Fourteenth to the Sixteenth Corps) began fighting them at 10:00 A.M. The Confederates dug in 300 yards away and then both sides fired and pushed. The Illinois boys obtained a resupply of ammunition just before their forty rounds ran out, but they held the Confederates and helped to protect Howard's refused line.[10]

It was necessary for Sherman to plan a wide flanking movement because, by August 26, Hood had managed to stretch the East Point Line very far south. Lee placed the left flank of his corps at the West Point and Atlanta Railroad three-quarters of a mile south of East Point, and Hardee arrayed his corps to Lee's left. In fact, Hardee had his left flank planted on the Macon and Western Railroad at Rough and Ready, four miles from East Point. It is a testament to the sophistication of Hood's earthwork system that he was able to hold the rest of his threatened line from the northeast of Atlanta to the southwest with only one corps plus a few thousand militiamen, compelling Sherman to cut his connection with his logistical network and move cross-country to bypass the extended Confederate line.[11]

As soon as Thomas and Howard evacuated the works north, northeast, and northwest of Atlanta, the Confederates went out to inspect them. Samuel G. French was appalled at how much filth he found in the Union earthworks, occupied as they had been for more than a month in the sweltering Georgia sun. He and his men found the trenches filled with "'dog' flies" and discarded clothing that crawled with vermin. "I found everything in their works horribly filthy," French later recalled. His men also discovered the brick furnace on Corse's division sector that had been used to heat solid shot for delivery to Atlanta. William Pitt Chambers of the 46th Mississippi in French's Division was amazed at the destruction of undergrowth between the skirmish lines due to constant musket firing. It "had been cut away by bullets about the height of a man's breast almost as evenly as the stubble in a grain field after the grain has been cut." Thomas B. Wilson, a courier at Stevenson's Division headquarters in Lee's Corps, was impressed by the thick layer of obstructions he found fronting the Union works. The Yankees had driven "rows of stakes into the ground and matting brush on small bushes between them." The stakes were three and a half feet tall and two feet apart from each other. "The whole made a mass of stuff that you could not run through nor jump over. They had little zig-zag paths through, or rather between them." In addition, Wilson noted that everything was "covered thick with swarms of flies."[12]

More important than gawking at Union earthworks, the Confederates scouted to find out where the enemy had gone. French moved toward Turner's Ferry with two brigades and skirmished with the Federals to develop their position. Access to the crossing was well protected by two brigades of Ward's division, so French returned to Atlanta. William A. Quarles's Brigade of Walthall's Division advanced along the railroad toward the crossing of the Chattahoochee and reported a large force of Yankees dug in on the south side.[13]

For several days the Confederates had some time on their hands to spend outside the range of enemy guns. Interestingly, work details clear-cut a good deal of timber between the opposing lines along the old Fourth Corps sector northeast of Atlanta. When Chesley Mosman revisited the scene in mid-September, he estimated that the Rebels had cut "about eighty acres of heavy timber," letting the trees fall promiscuously to create a tangled obstruction. Apparently, some Confederate officers feared the enemy might return to their works and wanted to make their own position even stronger by creating an additional layer of obstacles in a spot previously inaccessible to Rebel work crews. But other Confederates took the enemy departure as a rare breathing spell in the campaign. Division leader Henry De Lamar Clayton admitted that his men's spirits had been severely depressed by the results of July 22 and July 28, but they now had a chance to rest and recover their morale. Clayton's troops washed their dirty clothes, something they had had no opportunity to do for more than a month. Their spirits also were bolstered by newspaper reports indicating that the Northern Democratic Party had adopted a peace platform for the coming presidential election, offering the prospect of a negotiated settlement of the war if its candidate won.[14]

Much more than possession of Atlanta seemed to be at stake in Sherman's latest move; many thought that control of the White House might be affected by events outside the city. Whatever its result, Hood certainly was impressed by the carefulness of the Yankee move. "His change of position was made with great secrecy and circumspection," the general reported to Richmond on September 4, "intrenching at each step and sometimes even in advance of his movements." Hood decided to await developments, because to "take the offensive I would have been compelled to have hazarded battle against a labyrinth of field-works over a very broken country, and in any event I could not have hoped for more than a partial success."[15]

The movement continued in earnest on the morning of August 27, after Howard had begun to evacuate the lines held by the Army of the Tennessee the night before. Schofield also shifted his Twenty-Third Corps to its new, circular defensive position at dawn on the morning of the twenty-seventh. Logan moved the Fifteenth Corps to Wolf Creek where he arrayed his three divisions on a ridge to the left of Blair's Corps and began to dig in. Even now with all of his units out of their former positions and poised to head south, Sherman sanctioned the construction of defensive lines to protect his men at every pause in the maneuver. "We shall feel our way carefully," wrote Howard's artillery chief to his brother, "and be ready to stop and entrench at any moment and anywhere to save the men as much as possible." In fact, Lt. Col. Thomas Doan of the 101st Indiana in the Fourteenth Corps reported that his regiment entrenched itself in seven different places during the Jonesboro phase of the Atlanta campaign.[16]

Throughout the course of the day on August 27, as word of Howard's evacuation filtered into army headquarters and Confederate cavalry reported Yankee movement toward the south, Hood knew with certainty that Sherman was not retreating. But he did not know exactly where the Federals would strike and in what numbers. All Hood could do was wait, watch, and be ready to respond as quickly as possible when definite intelligence arrived.[17]

On August 28, what Sherman called "a general left-wheel" transpired, using Schofield's position as the pivot point. Later that day elements of Thomas's army reached the West Point and Atlanta Railroad at Red Oak, and elements of Howard's army did the same at Shadna Church and Fairburn. True to form, about two-thirds of the Federal troops began to construct fieldworks to protect their hold on the rail line while the rest began to tear up track. They continued their work of destruction on August 29, wrecking twelve and a half miles of the road. As Poe reported, this resulted in "every tie being burned and every rail bent." They filled many cuts with dirt, trees, and loaded artillery shells designed to explode when disturbed.[18]

For a day and a half, during the afternoon of August 28 and all day of August 29, the Federals entrenched and destroyed along a stretch of the West Point and Atlanta Railroad. Sherman's attention to this road has elicited some criticism among historians. They point out that the Confederates had come to rely far less heavily on this track than on the Macon and Western Railroad due to previous Union cavalry raids on its exposed line. They also point out that, if Sherman had been willing to divide his strength and send part of his army to the Macon and Western Railroad right away, he probably could have snipped both lines quickly and with comparatively little loss.[19]

Given the high stakes involved in the move, Sherman had no intention of allowing Hood to strike him unless he was concentrated and had all the advantages. He also had worried so long about reaching these rail lines that he was almost obsessed with truly destroying them. Hood's unsuccessful attacks on July 20, 22, and 28 had had a psychological effect by creating an extra sense of caution for Sherman when within attacking range of the Army of Tennessee.

By the evening of August 28, Hood prepared to shift many of his units southward to protect the Macon and Western Railroad, giving up the West Point and Atlanta Railroad as a lost cause. Frank C. Armstrong's cavalry brigade already held Jonesboro, and Hood sent Daniel Harris Reynolds's Brigade and Joseph Lewis's Brigade there as well. He also shifted John C. Brown's Division from East Point to Rough and Ready. Hood instructed all his subordinates to fortify their new positions as soon as they took them up. As Lewis moved south by train, the rest of William B. Bate's Division moved to Rough and Ready to support Brown.[20]

At Jonesboro, Reynolds, Lewis, and an engineer officer scouted the area to see where best to plant their defenses. They then placed their troops at 2:00 P.M. on August 29. Lewis put his Kentucky troops on the right, his right wing crossing the railroad 200 yards north of the depot and his left close to the Fairburn Road. Reynolds extended the line to Lewis's left, with his left flank resting at the railroad south of the depot. The line was barely two miles long, and even at that Lewis had to place his men two paces apart. Reynolds was forced to put up with intervals of up to four paces between his men and dug skirmish pits before his part of the line on the evening of August 29.[21]

Sherman's move veered toward a climax as he started his troops eastward toward Jonesboro on August 30. Howard took the lead, driving Armstrong's and Lawrence S. Ross's brigades of cavalry before him. The Federal van managed to save the bridge across the Flint River, one mile west of town, and continued moving east. Not knowing how many Confederates held Jonesboro, and noting the late hour, Howard positioned the Army of the Tennessee on good defensive ground only a quarter mile west of town. Not more than 2,500 Confederates protected Jonesboro that evening; about half of them were infantrymen.[22]

Thomas needed more time to bring his two corps forward and Schofield also was on the move. The Army of the Ohio left its circular fortification that had served as the pivot of Sherman's movement on the morning of August 30. Schofield pushed his men a few miles until they lodged on the West Point and Atlanta Railroad near Red Oak Station. The men constructed fieldworks, Cox's division straddling the track and facing northeast.[23]

By early afternoon on August 30, Hood assumed the threat to Jonesboro was little more than a small force and the bulk of Sherman's host was much closer to East Point. Thus did Schofield's covering force deceive the Confederate commander. Hood therefore positioned about 10,000 men in the Atlanta City Line and another 10,000 in the East Point Line. An additional 11,000 men shifted to cover the ground between East Point and Mount Gilead Church, located about three miles south of Rough and Ready. This latter force was Hardee's Corps, which constructed a new line extending from East Point toward Rough and Ready on August 30. Yet there still was a gap of about six miles between Hardee's left flank and the threatened town of Jonesboro.[24]

By late afternoon on August 30, indications convinced Hood that the Union threat to Jonesboro was no raiding party but a major force of blue-coated infantrymen. He had to shift a large proportion of his available manpower to the town if he hoped to retain control of the railroad. His chief engineer, Martin L. Smith, already was inspecting the City Line to see how it could be held with an even smaller force, and Hood recommended that fence rails be used to construct more stockades in front of the line. In a conference held in Atlanta at 9:00 P.M., Hood instructed Hardee and Lee to take their two corps to Jonesboro while Stewart held the defenses of the city. Reports indicated that a force of at least three Union corps was on its way to the town. This plan involved abandoning the East Point Line altogether, opening the way for Schofield and elements of Thomas's army to reach the Macon and Western Railroad unopposed if they became aware of their opportunity to do so.[25]

Hood placed Hardee in charge of both his own corps and Lee's men in the move to Jonesboro, but the march proceeded with many vexatious delays. The tail of Hardee's Corps did not leave the area around East Point and Rough and Ready until 11:30 P.M. Although Lee set out immediately after, the van of his column did not reach Rough and Ready until dawn of August 31. James Patton

Anderson reported that the local guides did not know their way properly, and the march was delayed because Lee's men took the wrong roads. After spending the past month locked in fetid trenches, Anderson's troops were in no shape for a rapid march. Many of them were shoeless, and straggling became endemic. Moreover, the head of Hardee's column stumbled upon some Union troops and had to bypass their position. While Hardee made it to Jonesboro early on the morning of August 31, the head of Lee's column got there about 10:00 A.M. and the tail did not come up until 1:30 P.M.[26]

AUGUST 31

Howard planted the Army of the Tennessee only 800 yards from the railroad depot at Jonesboro on the evening of August 30 and strengthened its position the next morning. His guns were close enough to fire on trains traveling along the track. Yet, just as he had done at Ezra Church, Howard intended to act on the defensive to entice the enemy to attack him. The troops used logs and rails as the base of their parapet and scraped dirt over them, even though the "ground was very hard," according to a soldier in the 32nd Ohio. With only tin plates and bayonets available at first, the digging was tough. Even when the 55th Illinois received some shovels and picks, the men had to work for two or three hours on the morning of August 31 to erect a parapet that was "far inferior in height and solidity to those we had become accustomed to construct in the advance upon Atlanta," according to the regimental historian.[27]

To Hardee's infantrymen coming on the ground and assembling for an attack, the Union earthworks looked more daunting than they did to the Federals. Reynolds rode around with Hardee to scout the placement of incoming troops, which gave Hardee an opportunity to observe the Union fieldworks. He described them as formidable. George Maney, who temporarily commanded Cheatham's Division, saw abatis fronting some sectors of Howard's line and a palisade in front of other sectors. The entire position also was fronted by a wide, open, level field.[28]

Hardee was compelled by Hood's instructions and by the force of circumstance to attack this line as soon as possible. Hood's plan had shifted some 20,000 Confederate troops to Jonesboro to oppose about 12,000 Federals dug in on the east side of Flint River, with an additional 7,500 in reserve on the west side of the stream. Francis A. Shoup relayed Hood's sense of urgency in no less than four dispatches to Hardee early on August 31. The message was clear in all of these missives: "The general says you must attack and drive the enemy across the river." Hood wanted Hardee to tell his subordinate officers "that the necessity is imperative," and the men must "go at the enemy with bayonets fixed, determined to drive everything they may come against." Lee positioned his corps to the north, or right, of Hardee. The Confederates dug a new line of works as soon as they arrived, large enough to accommodate the major infusion of manpower compared to Reynolds's and Lewis's Brigades.[29]

Rebel artillery opened at 3:00 P.M. and the skirmishers began to push forward ten minutes later to open Hardee's attack. Cleburne, who temporarily led Hardee's Corps while Hardee controlled the entire force at Jonesboro, pushed his men forward. Granbury's Texas Brigade, on the far left of the Rebel line, diverged from the angle of advance to chase some Federal cavalry across the river, taking a good part of Cleburne's Division along. Farther to the right, Brown's Division was bluntly repelled by John M. Corse's division of the Sixteenth Corps. Maney, whose division occupied a place in the second line, halted rather than go in unsupported. When he asked Cleburne's advice, his superior told him not to attack at all. The men of Lewis's Kentucky Brigade were told to hold their fire until they reached a point only fifty yards from the Federal line. Then they were to let loose a volley and "rush on them with fixed bayonets." But a gulley some ten feet wide and nearly as deep appeared in front of the brigade, and the men sought cover in it. Fortunately for the Kentuckians, the configuration of the gulley allowed them to retire to the starting point of their advance without losing too many men. Hardee's attack fizzled and broke apart without accomplishing anything.[30]

Lee started his advance as soon as the right flank of Hardee's Corps set out, and some of Lee's men made a better effort than Hardee's. Anderson's Division held the front line on Lee's right wing, with Clayton's Division behind as a support and Stevenson's Division to his left. Anderson pushed his men forward vigorously against the Second Division of the Fifteenth Corps, now commanded by William B. Hazen since Morgan L. Smith's sick leave. Anderson advanced over open ground and up a gentle slope until the men came within pistol range of the enemy. There Union fire caused wavering in the ranks and the division lay down for cover only sixty yards from the Federals. Anderson tried to get his men on their feet again to continue forward, but they refused. At least they remained where they were for the time rather than retiring, so Anderson tried to keep his men together and encourage them to return the heavy Union fire. Anderson reported seeing small groups of Jacob H. Sharp's Brigade moving forward at the urging of their officers. Lt. Col. Samuel R. Mott of the 57th Ohio saw them too and ordered his men to fix bayonets and receive the attack. According to Mott, this seemed to take the momentum out of the advance, yet the Confederates did not dare go back to their own line for fear of exposing them-

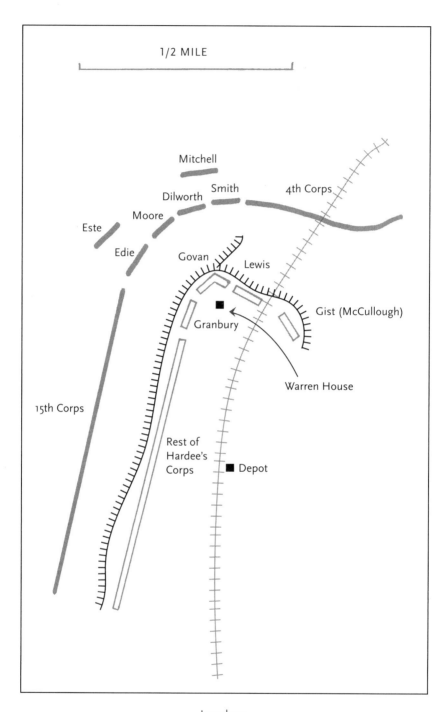

1/2 MILE

Mitchell

Dilworth   Smith   4th Corps

Moore

Este

Edie

Govan

Lewis

Gist (McCullough)

Granbury

Warren House

15th Corps

Rest of
Hardee's
Corps   ■ Depot

Jonesboro

selves to the raging Union fire. Mott twice ceased firing to let them come into his works as prisoners.[31]

At least some units of Anderson's Division broke and fell back, disrupting alignment in Clayton's supporting division. Arthur M. Manigault, whose brigade was behind Anderson's Division, moved his men forward but could not convince them to go any farther than Anderson's position. He brought the troops back until they found an undulation in the terrain that offered some protection about 400 yards from the flaming enemy line. Here the troops erected a "temporary breastwork of rails and such other material as could be found for the purpose" and were joined by other troops falling back from the battle, all of them "to a certain extent demoralized." Anderson rode up and demanded that Manigault attack again; he tried to do so even though it appeared utterly hopeless. Manigault's troops broke and fell back again just as Anderson was shot in the jaw and had to leave the field at about 4:30 P.M.[32]

The rest of Lee's Corps made a poor showing on the field. Randall L. Gibson's Brigade of Clayton's Division advanced across open ground, losing heavily. At least according to Gibson, they attacked with enthusiasm until entering a thicket out of which Federal skirmishers had already been driven by Anderson's men. Here Gibson's troops filled the skirmish pits and began to tear down a fence that stood in their way. When they discovered a resurgence of fire and the advance of fresh Federals toward the thicket, all the fight suddenly went out of Gibson's men. The brigade retired suddenly and with dispatch. Lee also realized it was a lost cause and rode about ordering the troops to retire about 5:00 P.M.[33]

Hood's desperate effort to save his railroad ended in abject failure on August 31. Hardee and Lee suffered a total of 2,200 casualties while inflicting only 172 losses on Howard. The results were reminiscent of the fight at Ezra Church. Anderson reported losing 500 men out of the 2,000 who took part in the battle, while Gibson reportedly lost half his troops. Confederate prisoners told their captors that officers had assured them the Federals were not well dug in.[34]

But it was palpable to everyone in gray that the Confederates had not done their best. "The attack was not made by the troops with that spirit and inflexible determination that would insure success," complained Lee in his report. Instead of rushing to close with the enemy in their "temporary and informidable works," the men halted at the first fire while still in the open within easy musket range, and the advance simply fell apart. "The attack was a feeble one and a failure," Lee concluded.[35]

Many commanders, however, defended the men's action on August 31.

Manigault explained the situation better than most when he recalled the condition of his troops that day. "The long and tedious siege through which they had passed, lying cramped in the trenches, exposed night and day to an harassing fire, badly fed and clothed, added to the fatiguing march [to Jonesboro], had reduced them to a condition by no means satisfactory." Manigault saw unmistakable signs "that there was not much fight" in his men before the battle. Another thing contributing to the "weary, dull, sluggish" condition of his troops was a lack of trust in Hood's judgment. The experiences of July 20, 22, and 28 had created in them a keen awareness of what would happen if they attacked "a complete set of field works."[36]

Col. Bushrod Jones reported that his brigade of Clayton's Division got to a point only forty yards from the Union line, where the Federals had left behind a pile of rails. Here they stopped and simply refused to go farther. "The men seemed possessed of some great horror of charging breast-works, which no power, persuasion, or example could dispel, yet I must say that the officers generally did their duty."[37]

The gloom attending the Confederate attack spread into Stevenson's Division as well. Robert M. Magill survived the advance in the ranks of the 39th Georgia and recalled many years later that "not one in a hundred believed it would accomplish anything." His comrades "moved forward in splendid order through an open field, but just simply run in and out again, at a terrible sacrifice." His company lost eleven out of nineteen men in the attack.[38]

Hood sought culprits for the failure of his effort to save Jonesboro. He blamed Hardee for getting there too late to attack before the enemy had constructed good field defenses. When the army commander noted the low casualty figure for August 31 as proof of a lack of willpower in the troops, Hardee countered the charge by arguing that Hood's overly aggressive tactics since taking command had wasted the vitality and strength of the army. It was not surprising that men "who had for two months been hurled against breast-works only to be repulsed or to gain dear-bought and fruitless victories, should now have moved against the enemy's works with reluctance and distrust."[39]

Hood was incapable of shouldering any responsibility for the failure of his effort to save Atlanta and persisted in blaming either his subordinate officers or his men. His first major dispatch to Richmond following the battle of Jonesboro tried to pin it on the rank and file as well as on his predecessor, Joseph E. Johnston. "It seems the troops had been so long confined to trenches and had been taught to believe that intrenchments cannot be taken, so that they attacked without spirit and retired without proper effect." Hood went so far as to argue that "there is a tacit if not expressed determination among the men of this army, extending to officers as high in some instances as colonel, that they will not attack breast-works."[40]

While Howard repulsed Hardee's and Lee's attacks at Jonesboro, his colleagues decisively cut the Macon and Western Railroad several miles to the north. Jacob Cox's division of the Twenty-Third Corps reached the tracks a mile and a half south of Rough and Ready at 3:00 P.M. on August 31, about the time the Confederates began their offensive at Jonesboro. Fifteen minutes later, the three divisions of Stanley's Fourth Corps joined Cox. At 6:00 P.M., Baird's division of the Fourteenth Corps hit the railroad five miles north of Jonesboro. Cox and Stanley began to dig a fortified position in the shape of a V. Stanley placed his left flank at the track and extended his corps line one and three-quarters miles to the southwest, facing south. Cox placed his right flank at the track touching Stanley's left and extended his division northwest but facing north. Sherman had complained to Howard earlier that afternoon that "I cannot move the troops 100 yards without their stopping to intrench, though I have not seen an enemy." He probably referred to Thomas's men, but at least they were now firmly in control of the vital target of his grand flanking movement.[41]

When a train encountered Schofield's men south of Rough and Ready that afternoon and reported their presence to headquarters, Hood feared that Sherman might attack Atlanta from the south. He ordered Hardee to send Lee's Corps back to the city. Shoup's message to Hardee even urged the general to send a couple of his own brigades if possible and told him to hold out at Jonesboro with what was left as best he could. Lee left Jonesboro a bit after 1:00 A.M. on September 1 and headed north. Hardee was disgusted with this dispersal of his force at the threatened railroad town. Roughly about the same time that Lee left Jonesboro, Hood received Hardee's dispatch announcing his failure to drive Howard away from the railroad on August 31. This led Hood to order the evacuation of Atlanta. Stewart's Corps and Smith's militiamen were to leave their trenches at dusk on September 1, and Hood's chief engineer, Martin L. Smith, rode out into the night to find Lee's Corps en route to Atlanta and post it to cover the withdrawal. Hardee's Corps was left at Jonesboro. Lee's task was to hold the Federals one more day and then join the rest of the Army of Tennessee at Lovejoy's Station, the next defensible position south of Atlanta.[42]

SEPTEMBER 1

Hardee's dangerous task was to hold on for another day against a potentially overwhelming foe at Jonesboro. He had to rely on earthworks to compensate for the danger, yet there was not much time or opportunity to adjust his position and dig better works. He was helped tremendously by Sherman's misjudgment. The Union commander had fretted and worried so much about cutting the last rail line into Atlanta that he became myopically fixated on Cox, Schofield, and Baird tearing up track rather than moving their formidable troops down to Jonesboro, flanking, and overwhelming Hardee's isolated corps. He ordered them to do both — destroy rails and move down to participate in an attack on the enemy, and they could not do both tasks equally well in one day.[43]

Sherman's message to Schofield, that the Confederates were protected by nothing more than "a straight barricade this side of and parallel to the railroad" at Jonesboro, was not far from the truth. When Lee left the town, Hardee had to hold a line two miles long with 12,000 men. Some of his units deployed in one rank with six-foot intervals between men. Lee's troops had had time to do little more than throw up rail breastworks along some parts of the line before launching their attack on the afternoon of August 31, and they had not done much more to improve the defenses that evening before leaving Jonesboro. There was no time to place abatis or any other type of obstruction in front.[44]

"Our new line was not a good one," complained Col. Charles H. Olmstead, commander of Mercer's Brigade. "It was imperfectly laid out and only partially completed." Olmstead lost thirty-three men when he tried to send out a skirmish line in the night to relieve Lee's skirmishers, because the Federals were lodged only 300 paces away. The Federals delayed a long while before taking any offensive action, so the Confederates had some time to dig in. Col. John Weir, who commanded Lowrey's Brigade, managed to construct "very substantial earth-works with a strong abatis in front" during the day. That might have been an exaggeration, for M. L. Wheeler of the 33rd Alabama in Lowrey's Brigade recalled that the men had no axes and could not erect head logs. Most of them dug a trench using their bayonets to break up the "tough clay" soil. On the far left of Hardee's line, the gunners of Slocomb's Washington Artillery company could not properly construct their battery emplacement due to constant Union skirmish fire. It meant death to stand up and try to cut an embrasure or to level off the top of the parapet.[45]

A hasty extension of Hardee's line on the right, and its refusal eastward so as to cross the railroad, created a poorly fortified angle in the Confederate line. Daniel C. Govan's Arkansas Brigade held the far right of Hardee's position, facing west, but the men did not assume their post until dawn of September 1. Because the brigade to the left had difficulty settling in, Govan's men did not begin work on their defenses until nearly 9:00 A.M. By the time they erected a parapet high enough to protect against rifle fire, Hardee discovered indications that the Federals might try to flank his right. He decided to place two more brigades to Govan's right and refuse the line from Govan's position so it would cross the railroad and face northward. Upon examining the ground, Hardee decided that most of Govan's command would also be placed on the refused line, while only his left remained in the original trench, facing west. Govan's men were told to level their old works north of the new angle in the line, but Union artillery fire was so heavy, enfilading this little stretch of trench, that Col. Samuel G. Smith of the 6th Arkansas told his men to stop filling in the work and take cover in the refused line. The new angle in the line rested on a rise of ground about twenty-five feet high in this undulating landscape. The new refused line to the east of the angle was not complete and the old works north of the angle not yet demolished. Govan's men stood in one rank along the refused line.[46]

Lewis's Kentucky Brigade took position to Govan's right and States R. Gist's South Carolina Brigade filled out the rest of the refused line to Lewis's right. Col. James McCullough, who commanded Gist's Brigade, bent his right flank until it was nearly parallel to and east of the railroad track. The troops of Lewis and McCullough laid down rails as a breastwork and used their pocket-knives to cut saplings in front of the line. McCullough's troops tried to pile up traverses every twenty to thirty feet as well.[47]

The Confederates on the refused line encountered major difficulties in constructing their works. A Federal battery in Howard's army already was enfilading Lewis's line even as his men scratched away at the hard clay. Hardee and his staff members rode up to see how Lewis fared, and the general asked Capt. Fayette Hewitt, one of Lewis's staff members, if the Kentucky Brigade could hold its position. Hewitt answered in the affirmative but told Hardee that the new angle held by Govan was the weak spot. Hardee placed a couple of field guns to sweep the new refused line in case the enemy got into it. Lewis's men continued to work with woefully inadequate tools. As Edward Porter Thompson put it, each company had "an old ax, with a rough bit of sapling for a handle, one old shovel," and numerous frying pans to be used for moving dirt. Lewis placed his men in one rank at three-foot intervals. "We cut & piled some logs & dug for dear life," Johnny Green of the 9th Kentucky wrote. His comrades managed to make an earthwork that was meager, to say the least, but it was "better than none," as one of their number later contended.[48]

To Lewis's right, McCullough's men also were arrayed in one rank and finding it difficult to make an adequate fieldwork. The left of Gist's Brigade rested at a railroad cut about ten feet deep, and much of McCullough's line went through a patch of thick woods. Lacking axes, the men climbed up the smaller trees in order to bend them over, then cut them half through their thickness with pocketknives to make an effective obstruction. Other men found rails and logs in the rear and brought them forward to serve as the basis of a parapet. Col. Ellison Capers, whose 24th South Carolina was the second regiment from the left, piled up logs to protect the left flank of his left companies from Howard's enfilading artillery fire. "These proved our salvation," Capers later wrote.[49]

With inadequate time and resources, the Confederates had to face the music by late afternoon. Jefferson C. Davis brought the Fourteenth Corps to Jonesboro and took position only 600 yards north of Hardee's new refused line. The Confederates were still frantically digging when the Federals arrived. Davis launched an attack at 4:00 P.M., sending in two divisions. James Morgan's Second Division moved toward the southeast, aiming at the angle where the refused line joined the west-facing line. Morgan's troops encountered a ravine some 300 yards from their objective, where they took shelter and established a new position rather than continue toward the enemy. William P. Carlin's First Division, to Morgan's left, advanced due south toward the refused line with the only two brigades readily available at the moment. Maj. John R. Edie's brigade was separated from Col. Marshall F. Moore's in a patch of thick vegetation and ascended the undulation upon which the angle was located. The 18th and 19th U.S. Infantry captured some Rebel skirmishers in the partially demolished works but came to a halt only thirty to sixty yards short of the refused line. Moore's brigade also stopped short of Lewis's Brigade because of heavy cross fire and retired. The first Union attack of September 1 only tested Hardee's refused line without damaging it.[50]

The second Union attack of the day threatened to crack the refused line wide open. Davis sent in Col. George P. Este's brigade of Baird's Third Division to relieve Edie's command. Este closed in on the refused line; his right wing went over the incomplete works and overwhelmed Govan's 6th and 7th Arkansas, but his left wing stalled due to vegetation and enfilading fire from Lewis's Brigade. A regiment from Morgan's division moved over to reinforce Este's left, and Morgan restarted the rest of his division for a new push against the angle from the northwest. Morgan's men moved at quick time, then double-quick, without pausing. This combination of Federal moves collapsed Govan's position.[51]

Col. Henry R. Mizner claimed for his 14th Michigan of Morgan's division the honor of being the first Federal regiment into the Rebel works. Govan surrendered to one of Mizner's sergeants as the regiment moved east in the trench. The 14th Michigan also took eight Confederate artillery pieces, bayoneting some of the resisting gunners at their posts. It also captured the flag of the 1st

Arkansas after shooting down the color-bearer and taking the rest of the color guard prisoner.[52]

As more Federal units entered the Rebel position, they hastily formed a line extending south from the trench and began to move eastward along the refused line. Govan's men tried to resist and a good deal of hand-to-hand combat ensued, but many were taken prisoner as the next regiment in line, Col. Peter V. Green's 5th–13th Arkansas, was overwhelmed. The 3rd Confederate Regiment, to Green's right, was confronted by a Union battle line to its front as well as the advancing Yankees from the left, and most of its men were taken prisoner. What was left of Govan's Brigade retired from the refused line to the south.[53]

The Federals found stiff resistance when they tried to do the same to Lewis's Brigade. The Kentuckians had managed to throw up enough traverses so that there were numerous bays twenty to thirty feet wide in the trench line that had to be reduced one by one. Bitter close-range fighting was the result. A Federal soldier who stood up on the parapet called on members of the 9th Kentucky to "surrender, you dam rebels." But Booker Reed replied, "The H--l you say," and shot him down. Johnny Green heard this interchange as he stood up to fire over the works and saw the muzzle of a Yankee musket only six inches from his face. Green moved just as the Federal fired and suffered a flesh wound on his face and neck. The blow knocked him back into "a sitting posture." But Green got up, pushed the muzzle of his gun against the side of the Yankee, and "shot a hole through him big enough to have run my fist through."[54]

"Never give up, boys," Lt. Henry C. Boyd told his men of the 9th Kentucky. But the spirit of fierce resistance could not withstand Federal numbers and position. Pressed in front and badly outflanked, Lewis's Brigade began to crumble. Two hundred members were taken prisoner; one officer became a captive when some Federals pulled him out of a bay "by the hair of his head," according to Edward Porter Thompson. All the officers and twelve men of Company B, 6th Kentucky, fell captive to the Union attack.[55]

The Federals took possession of the refused line west of the railroad, but McCullough's South Carolina troops managed to retain possession of it east of the track, although they endured great stress from both front and flank. To the front, Thomas managed to bring Stanley's Fourth Corps units down to Jonesboro in time to advance against McCullough east of the railroad by about 5:00 P.M., when the Federals launched their successful assault against Govan. By this time, also, Hardee had shifted yet more troops to extend his refused line. Three brigades moved from the unthreatened left to extend McCullough's position farther toward the southeast. Stanley advanced two divisions against this line but the men encountered thick vegetation and a deep ravine. They halted upon nearing the Confederate position and began to dig in.[56]

The Confederates held back the frontal threat pretty easily, but McCullough's left flank nearly succumbed to the flanking attack. A battalion of Georgia sharpshooters was driven out of the railroad cut and replaced by Federal troops of either Baird's or Morgan's Fourteenth Corps divisions. These men fired down the length of the refused line, killing and wounding many Confederates. Those who survived this fire managed to do so by taking shelter behind the numerous traverses McCullough had constructed before the attack. Fourteenth Corps troops advanced against the front of McCullough's left wing also and drove out three companies of Capers's 24th South Carolina. Capers and other officers led a counterattack to reclaim the trench and also counterattacked into the railroad cut to drive the Federals out of it. It was touch and go, but the Confederate refused line east of the railroad held tight.[57]

Moreover, Rebel forces to the left of Govan's embattled brigade also held tight to contain the Union advantage. Granbury's Texans were positioned to Govan's left, entirely in the west-facing line. Granbury's right flank also was attacked by Morgan's division, but the rest of his command was unchallenged. Federal troops lodged no more than forty yards from his brigade when they took Govan's position, and other Federals began to infiltrate the woods that lay to Granbury's rear as well. Granbury began to pull his command out of the trench and form a refused line facing north, its left flank resting at the trench line. He had about finished this movement when Hardee and Lowrey rode up and encouraged him to go back to his original position, as they were sending up reinforcements from the far left to restore Govan's position. Because Howard did not join in the Fourteenth Corps attack, the rest of Hardee's line had no opposition in its front and could shift brigades about as needed.[58]

Before Hardee's reinforcements arrived on the scene, remnants of Govan's shattered brigade made an attempt to reclaim their trench. Col. Peter V. Green took command of what was left of the brigade, gathered men around what was left of the 5th–13th Arkansas, and counterattacked northward. Only the left wing of his hastily organized command reached the Union-occupied trench at a point just to the right of Granbury's position. The rest of Green's men stalled well short of the Union position because of their faulty organization and the strength of the enemy.[59]

The first of Hardee's reinforcements arrived soon after the failure of Green's counterattack. Vaughan's Tennessee Brigade, now led by Col. George W. Gordon, followed one of Cleburne's trusted staff officers. Irving Buck rode ahead to determine where the Tennesseeans were most needed and came back to tell Gordon to reclaim Govan's position. But Gordon's men advanced slanting to the left too much. As a result, three of his left regiments actually entered the westward-facing line already held by Granbury, while only one of Gordon's regiments fully entered the captured works Govan had lost. That regiment managed to throw out the Federals in one small sector at the angle. Moreover, Green rallied his men once again and pushed Govan's troops forward to cooperate with Gordon. This time, Green managed to lodge many of his men in their old trench. He succeeded in extending Gordon's small sector a bit to the east. The result of these hurried Confederate counterattacks was substantial. The refused line west of the railroad was not fully restored, but at least the Federal breakthrough was stalled and thrown back a little. Granbury's position was now secure. Along with the stolid defense of the refused line east of the railroad, Hardee could count his blessings that his position was stabilized.[60]

But Hardee's situation was only temporary. Heavily outnumbered, it was fortunate for the Rebels that dusk provided cover for their retreat from Jonesboro. Govan's Brigade suffered very heavy casualties on September 1, with 26 killed, 68 wounded, and 618 taken prisoner, for a total loss of 712 men. All eight guns of Capt. Charles Swett's Battery (commanded by Lt. Henry N. Steele) and Key's Battery were captured, and all the gunners in each battery, except about two dozen, were taken.[61]

Objectively, what transpired on the afternoon of September 1 was a limited attack by only a portion of Sherman's large concentration of troops at Jonesboro. Why that limited attack was not supported by aggressive moves conducted by Howard's Army of the Tennessee has never really been explained. The Federals did an impressive job of smashing the improvised refused line, but their opponents did an equally impressive job of reacting to the attack and limiting its benefits to Sherman. If the Army of the Tennessee had moved forward at the right moment, or if the Fourth Corps had been up sooner to threaten the right flank, the entire Confederate position at Jonesboro could have been smashed with disastrous results.

The limited benefits derived from the Union success did not prevent the men engaged in the attack from feeling intense pride in and excitement about what they had accomplished. Absalom Baird, whose troops were primarily responsible for creating the success, praised his men in his report. The smashing of Govan's salient was "the first during this campaign in which works upon either side have been assaulted and carried," he wrote with some exaggeration. Baird thought his troops had destroyed "the morale of the boldest and most confident troops in the rebel army."[62]

Maj. James A. Connolly, one of Baird's staff officers, provided the most telling commentary on the emotional release resulting from a successful attack on fieldworks during the campaign. He was on his horse, next to the captured works, weeping tears of joy when the Federals around him raised a cheer of victory. "I could have lain down on that blood stained grass amid the dying and the dead and wept with excess of joy," Connolly told his wife. "I have no language to express the rapture one feels at the moment of victory, but I do know that at such a moment one feels as if the joy were worth risking a hundred lives to attain it. Men at home will read of that battle and be glad of our success, but they can never feel as we felt, standing there quivering with excitement, amid the smoke and blood, and fresh horrors and grand trophies of that battle field."[63]

Despite the emotionally fulfilling experience, the limited Union success of September 1 had little impact on the campaign. Hardee probably would have retired from Jonesboro that night anyway, even if the attack had never taken place. The Confederates pulled away as soon as darkness offered them an opportunity. The Federal troops who still held a large section of the refused line west of the railroad stayed there all night, firing randomly into the darkness toward the south, reforming the works for their own purposes, and gathering spare ammunition from abandoned Confederate cartridge boxes. Col. Moses B. Walker was stunned by the condition of the captured works. He placed members of his Fourteenth Corps brigade in them to relieve the men who had fought on September 1. "Groping my way in the darkness to those bloody trenches, stumbling at almost every step over the dead and dying as I placed fresh lines of men in them, in the midst of other thoughts I shuddered that such was the work of my countrymen."[64]

Losses on September 1 at Jonesboro amounted to about 1,400 Confederates and 1,272 Federals. Hardee counted himself lucky to escape with so little damage. He reported that his position at Jonesboro was a poor one, with no terrain advantages and no time to artificially make it strong. The Federals' mismanagement of their resources spared the Confederates. With ten to twelve divisions at his disposal, opposing only three Confederate divisions, Sherman attacked with only four brigades. When a member of Granbury's Brigade had an opportunity to see the battlefield later that month, he wrote that there was "absolutely nothing to hinder the Yanks from capturing the whole of us on that Occasion."[65]

Hood evacuated Atlanta on the night of September 1 as Hardee moved away from Jonesboro. Not only did Stewart's Corps and Smith's militia troops leave, but Confederate gunners were able to take away all twenty-eight field guns from the City Line. They had to leave behind fourteen twenty-four- and thirty-two-pounders. Many of these heavier guns were mounted in the forts and could not quickly be moved, while others were in storage pending an opportunity to place them in the defenses. By August 27, Henry W. Slocum had arrived from Vicksburg to take command of the Twentieth Corps. His troops easily saw the flames rise into the night sky as the Confederates burned property before leaving. Slocum sent out several units to reconnoiter early on the morning of September 2, only to be greeted by the mayor of Atlanta, who offered them the city.[66]

Slocum's men moved into Atlanta all day on September 2. For Alpheus Williams, who had commanded a division and then a corps while staring at these defenses for more than a month, it felt strange to now march through the layers of obstructions and earthworks. "I rode along full of queer sensations and exciting emotions," Williams told his daughters, "but there was the principal battlement which had caused so much trouble and injury and not a sound came from it. I could hardly realize that its strong and defiant voice had really been silenced."[67]

14

Lovejoy's Station, Palmetto Station, and the Federal Defenses of Atlanta

Even after the Federals occupied Atlanta on September 2, 1864, the opposing armies squared off for another confrontation before the campaign ground to an end. Hood managed to concentrate the Army of Tennessee near Lovejoy's Station, the next defensible position along the Macon and Western Railroad south of Jonesboro. Once again, the Federals and Confederates arrayed in lines heavily protected by strong fieldworks, and Sherman had to decide whether to continue the campaign or stop to rest his men and consolidate his hold on the Gate City.

LOVEJOY'S STATION

Hardee moved five miles from Jonesboro on the night of September 1–2 to take up the new position at Lovejoy's Station by early morning. His men had no opportunity to sleep but they began to dig in by 8:00 A.M. Hardee placed up to 10,000 men in a line about one mile north of the railroad station and on both sides of the tracks. He took advantage of a slight range of hills called Cedar Bluff to place his line. Long talked of locally as the next defensible spot south of Atlanta, this position was shielded from approaches by heavy vegetation and some swampy land. Federal troops did not appear until midafternoon, giving the Rebels several hours in which to make their position secure. Heavy works were necessary because many of Hardee's units could afford to deploy only a single rank of men. In Granbury's Texas Brigade, the men dug a trench four feet deep and placed head logs on top of the parapet.[1]

Sherman left the Fourteenth Corps at Jonesboro to establish a defensive line facing north, in case Confederate forces approached the town directly from Atlanta. He moved the rest of his available manpower south, with Howard west of the railroad and Thomas east of it. Schofield extended Thomas's line eastward. When the Federals arrived, Sherman ordered a forward movement to test the new enemy position. The advance began at nearly 3:30 P.M. and encountered much natural opposition in this rugged, underdeveloped country. Some of Howard's troops took a section of the Confederate picket line west of the track but could go no farther.[2]

Sherman called off the advance at about 4:00 P.M. but word failed to reach Stanley's Fourth Corps in time to prevent two divisions from struggling through tangled brush. Division leaders were told to "take the enemy's works if possible; not to stop for anything trifling," according to Stanley's staff officer Joseph Fullerton. Thomas J. Wood's and Nathan Kimball's divisions finally came within striking range of the Confederate position by 6:00 P.M., where they paused for a second breath. Then three brigades moved forward and took the Confederate skirmish line. A deep ravine choked with thick vegetation stood between them and the main Rebel position. While one of the three brigades continued, only to be repelled by fire from Cleburne's Division, the other two dug in on the Union side of the ravine.[3]

The results of the operations on September 2 indicated that it was too difficult to directly assault the new Confederate line. As Howard's artillery chief put it, "An attack would be attended with difficulties not worth our while to encounter. The loss would be too great for the benefits gained." Sherman was not yet certain that Slocum had occupied Atlanta and he also was impressed by the strength of Hardee's position. "Had we prevented his making intrenchments it would have been well," he informed Howard, "but, as he has a strong line, I do not wish to waste lives by an assault." Howard ordered his subordinates to construct a line of works and make all necessary roads and bridges to the rear so that ammunition and food could be brought forward. In the Fifteenth Corps, the instructions were to make a road leading up to every second regiment in the line. In this tangled, irregular landscape, road and bridge construction would necessarily occupy a lot of time and energy.[4]

The Confederate position east of the railroad probably was stronger than the line west of the track. L. W. Day of the 101st Ohio in Kimball's division later expressed the problem well when he wrote that "the ground itself was against us. Bogs, pools of water, deep trenches that might almost be dignified as ravines, seemed to lie everywhere, and to advance we must climb and clamber, wade and jump, and face the rebel artillery at the same time." Reporting that his men had attempted to move "through a dense jungle ... an almost impassable swamp, through deep ravines, and over steep ridges," Stanley admitted that Hardee's line was stronger than he could have imagined. "I have never seen the enemy take a stronger position, or one of more difficult approach," he reported to Thomas's headquarters. Stanley's men could see the Confederates digging away on their main line, yet Howard found it strange that such a good system of earthworks should suddenly spring up in the middle of nowhere and wondered if Hood's people had previously prepared this position long before the Federals arrived.[5]

With no intention of attacking Hardee, Sherman nevertheless intended to stay at Lovejoy's Station a while to see if he could prevent the junction of Lee's Corps and Stewart's Corps with Hardee. The Federals therefore dug in opposite the Confederate line wherever their advance had left them that day. On the Fourth Corps sector, the task was extremely difficult. As Chesley A. Mosman put it, "We like to broke our necks stumbling round in the dark trying to build our works, cut down trees and hand spike them into line. Work most of the night but our works are poor as we can't see, and it won't do to build fires or carry lanterns for the Rebels to shoot by." On September 3, Sherman instructed Howard to place a division in reserve for each corps, protected by a breastwork. He did not worry about the Confederates turning his right flank because of the swampy nature of the land in that area and urged Howard's troops to rest as much as possible.[6]

Sherman was unable to prevent Hood from bringing the rest of the Army of Tennessee to Lovejoy's Station on September 3. After consulting with Hardee, Lee, and Stewart, Hood came to the assumption that Sherman would "not content himself with Atlanta but will continue offensive movements" toward Macon. In short, the Confederate position at Lovejoy's Station appeared to be the first in a potentially long list of defensible places along the rail line that stretched 100 miles to the next important city in Georgia.[7]

French's Division had covered Stewart's column on the retreat from Atlanta and, soon after arriving at Lovejoy's Station, was sent to relieve the leftmost division of Hardee's Corps after dark. French thought the position was "a miserable line and salient that was enfiladed on either face by the enemy's artillery." At the last minute, his order was postponed, and the men began to work on a new line "to cut off part of the salient, which improved it very much." French relieved Hardee's division in the old line on September 5, "and so completely is the old part of it enfiladed that about 40 men were killed and wounded from shells." Members of Young's Brigade in French's Division nevertheless managed to stake down abatis in front of their line.[8]

While the Confederate position seemed extremely strong to the waiting Federals, there were significant weak sectors. French had discovered one such spot and Hardee's men found some more. Federal skirmishers managed to get close enough, and at an angle to a section of the opposing line, to fire into the main trench held by Granbury's Brigade. That section of the line on top of a segment of Cedar Bluff was so exposed that Granbury's men suffered several casualties on September 3. Granbury set them to work digging a new, secondary line well to the rear that was on less defensible ground but promised to be safer. The brigade commander did not abandon the forward line but used the secondary position to shield most of his men while holding the more exposed position with a minimal number of troops. Elsewhere along the Confederate line, the main trench offered enough safety that no concerns were raised, but the landscape behind much of the line was level. It offered no protection for men coming up to or going back from the main trench. They were "greatly exposed to random bullets from the skirmish line," as staff officer George A. Mercer put it.[9]

The Confederates continued to improve their fortifications for the remainder of the confrontation at Lovejoy's Station. They also managed to exact a penalty on their opponents where the lay of the land gave them an advantage over the Federals. Staff officer Joseph Fullerton noted that Stanley lost forty-two men on the Fourth Corps skirmish line on September 4, which he considered "quite a number." The artillery came into play now and then as well. When Sherman assembled with a group of subordinates in an exposed place, two Confederate batteries opened fire. Sherman wanted the guns silenced, so Howard's chief of artillery coordinated the effort of four Union batteries across a front of a quarter mile and managed to suppress the Rebel guns.[10]

William B. Hazen, who had been given command of Sherman's old division in the Fifteenth Corps only three weeks before, made a science of earthwork construction while at Lovejoy's Station. He issued an order on September 4 detailing how his men should make the reserve line behind the Fifteenth Corps that Sherman had ordered. Hazen wanted his troops to start with the revetment, which could consist of "logs notched into each other, or of rails placed between strong stakes, or of stone, or sods, or any material that may be convenient." Hazen suggested they build up the revetment to a height of two and a half feet, then dig a trench two and a half feet deep behind it. The fire step should be one and a quarter feet tall. "No earth to be broken in front of the works," he recommended. Hazen also suggested the type of obstruction to be placed in front of the line, a row of stakes six feet long located at "point-blank range." He wanted his men to plant the row in a trench two feet deep and slant the stakes at forty-five-degree angles and six inches apart. The row could be stabilized by placing a timber in the trench across the ends, tying it onto the stakes with telegraph wire, and then tamping dirt on top of it. Weaving a withe around the other end of the stakes would complete the obstruction and make it firm. Hazen was certain that his method of earthwork construction would systematize the process and enable troops to provide "a quick and excellent cover against infantry and field artillery. The rapidity with which such lines were made, when the working parties knew precisely what to do, was astonishing."[11]

If the Federals could construct a good earthwork quickly, so could their opponents. Sherman was unable to prevent Hood from concentrating his army and felt uncomfortable continuing the forward movement toward Macon. Wheeler's cavalry was still operating against his supply line and he would be forced to detach garrisons along the way if he continued to penetrate south-ward. "This country is so easily fortified," Sherman informed Halleck on September 4, "that an enemy can stop an army every few miles. All the roads run on ridges, so that a hundred yards of parapet, with abatis, closes it, and gives the wings time to extend as fast as we can reconnoiter and cut roads. Our men will charge the parapet without fear, but they cannot the abatis and entanglements, which catch them at close range." Under all these considerations, Sherman decided to fall back to Atlanta in the near future and rest his men.[12]

While Sherman waited, Hood tried to convince the authorities in Rich-mond that his troops were not demoralized by the loss of the Gate City. "I think the officers and men of this army feel that every effort was made to hold Atlanta to the last," he asserted with no proof to back up his contention. If Sherman tried to flank him at Lovejoy's Station, and Hood assumed his opponent would move west to bypass it, then he would try to "strike him with my entire force on his flank and rear."[13]

For two days, September 4–5, both sides played a waiting game at Love-joy's. The Confederates shifted troops about. Hood wanted Lee to relieve Presstman's engineer troops on the right of the line so they could report to his headquarters for engineer duty instead of holding trenches. Hood also was "much in want of a map of this country," according to Shoup. The chief of staff asked Martin L. Smith, Hood's recently appointed chief engineer, to make one.[14]

Constant sniping and artillery exchanges characterized life along the line at Lovejoy's Station. Casualties began to eat away at troop strength as well. Also, some poor sections of the Confederate line were not improved, even though

Hood's army held the line for three days. When Francis M. Cockrell moved his Missouri Brigade west across the railroad on the night of September 4, he found the spot poorly fortified. The works "were indifferent and exposed to an enfilading, and in some places almost reverse, artillery fire of the enemy's batteries on my left." Cockrell lost seven killed and six wounded on September 5 as a result. Francis P. Blair apparently observed this section of the Rebel line when he reported that the enemy was constructing new works for flank defense in an open field opposite the center of the Fifteenth Corps. The Rebel line here was "perpendicular to the main line."[15]

Sherman worked out the basic components of a drawback to Atlanta on September 4, but told his subordinates to await final word as to the time when it would begin. He wanted Thomas to move all troops of the Army of the Cumberland to the city itself, while Howard stationed the Army of the Tennessee at East Point and Schofield held Decatur with the Army of the Ohio. Sherman explained to Stanton that he was willing to fight a battle with Hood "on his own terms, if he will come outside of his cursed rifle trenches" as he fell back to Atlanta.[16]

After the Federals disengaged at Lovejoy's Station and retired northward on the night of September 5, the Confederates followed up the withdrawal, and skirmishing was the result. French sent Cockrell's Brigade in pursuit, and the Missouri Rebels attacked the Union rear guard which had taken position in skirmish pits south of Jonesboro, driving it away. The Federals fell back to a stronger line of works on the north side of town, which had been converted from the trench held by Hardee's men on September 1. Cockrell's troops drove them out of these works as well, and the Federals fell back to the Union defenses held on August 31 to keep the enemy at bay, then retired to Atlanta. Cockrell lost ten men in this skirmishing. Hood decided not to pursue the Federals north of Jonesboro, sending Hardee's Corps to hold that town while keeping the rest of his army at Lovejoy's Station.[17]

Hood tried to shore up his reputation with Richmond by blaming the rank and file of his army for losing the campaign. "According to all human calculations we should have saved Atlanta had the officers and men of the army done what was expected of them," he complained to Davis on September 6. "It has been God's will for it to be otherwise. I am of good heart and feel that we shall yet succeed." Stephen D. Lee continued to support Hood's line of argument, giving a speech to his men on September 6 castigating them for not showing enough gumption on the battlefield. As Robert Magill of the 39th Georgia wrote, it was a "speech not liked at all by the soldiers."[18]

Hood's plan was to move northward and cut Sherman's line of communications with the north as soon as possible. To that end, he wanted "to strongly fortify Macon" and other cities in Georgia that made up his own communication and supply network. Shoup instructed Martin L. Smith to go to Macon and oversee the defenses of the place. Smith reached the town by September 10 and inspected the works with Lemuel P. Grant, the builder of Atlanta's defensive ring, who had also selected the ground for Macon's earthworks. Smith worked at Macon from September 10 to 18 and then went to Augusta where he spent two days examining the defenses of the city. After that, he had a quick stop at Athens to see the works already erected and went back to Augusta before setting out for Macon on October 1 and then Columbus on October 5.[19]

Sherman settled his troops in defensive positions around Atlanta. Howard placed the Army of the Tennessee near East Point, where the troops either modified the Confederate works or constructed new trenches to protect that important railroad junction. Howard used the 1st Missouri Engineers, the only engineer troops at his disposal, in this effort as well. Schofield marched the Army of the Ohio to Decatur, where the troops built a new system of earthen defenses, laid out by Capt. William J. Twining, the army's chief engineer. Schofield's works were largely finished by September 20. An admiring Union staff officer saw them in mid-November and described the system as "splendid works, with ditch, abattis, etc."[20]

Thomas's Army of the Cumberland was spread out to various places in and around Atlanta. Sherman ordered Poe to evaluate the city's defenses with an eye toward remodeling them to suit Thomas's needs. After scouting around, Poe reported that the line, at twelve miles long, was far too extensive for any garrison the Federals would want to leave in the city. Moreover, members of Slocum's Twentieth Corps found that the Confederate City Line was "dirty and full of vermin." Rice C. Bull of the 123rd New York argued that this was not unusual. "These conditions we found in all the enemy camps we passed through during the campaign. When we could avoid it we never camped on ground that had been used by them. They could make the same criticism about the ground we camped on, for we lived in conditions equally dirty."[21]

Poe used details from the 1st Missouri Engineers to begin making a thorough map of all Confederate defenses in and around Atlanta. This effort was preliminary to proceeding with Sherman's directive to plot a new line of works so the Federals could hold the city with a modest garrison. The engineer chose a line along the high ground that was closest to the center of Atlanta. It was only three miles long but ran through heavily developed parts of the municipality and thus involved the destruction "of a great many buildings," as Poe put it. Meanwhile, Chauncey B. Reese, Howard's chief engineer, began to

Federal Defenses of Atlanta

Federal artillery in a Confederate fort. It is possible that George N. Barnard exposed this view from Fort V looking toward Fort W. If so, it was the fifth photograph he exposed at this location. One can see very well how the Confederates constructed artillery emplacements in Hood's Addition to the City Line. They used thick, wide boards for the gun platform; board and post revetments to hold up a large traverse to the side of the platform; and a combination of board and post mixed with sandbags to hold up the interior slope of the parapet. *Photograph by George N. Barnard. Library of Congress, LC-DIG-cwpb-03401.*

use Seventeenth Corps pioneers to make 500 gabions and 100 fascines for new earthwork construction. The fascines measured eighteen feet long and were bound with telegraph wire.[22]

Sherman's plan was to turn Atlanta into a major Union military post protected by a new line of works. He decided to evacuate the population of the city to make this job easier. The policy elicited an exchange of letters between Sherman and Hood, with the Confederate commander bitterly denouncing the forced migration of thousands of Southern citizens from their homes. Sherman defended his action by telling Hood that the Confederates had torn down fifty houses to make way for their own City Line. Moreover, they had placed their defenses where Union artillery fire inevitably hit inhabited civilian structures within the municipality. Sherman felt it was more humane to remove the citizens beforehand than subject them to this again if the Confederates tried to retake the city.[23]

Sherman could not tell Hood the real reason he wanted to remove the residents, for that would have given his opponent vital clues to his future movements. But Sherman did reveal to Halleck the primary purpose in moving Atlanta's residents from their homes. "My real reasons for this step were, we want all the houses of Atlanta for military storage and occupation. We want to contract the lines of defenses so as to diminish the garrison to the limit necessary to defend its narrow and vital parts instead of embracing, as the lines now do, the vast suburbs. This contraction of the lines, with the necessary citadels and redoubts, will make it necessary to destroy the very houses used by families as residences. Atlanta is a fortified town, was stubbornly defended and fairly captured. As captors we have right to it." Sherman wanted to avoid "a ceaseless wrangle every time we need a house or a site for a battery," as had happened in numerous Southern towns under Yankee occupation, and he did not intend to keep 15,000 men behind to hold the Confederate City Line. Poe's new position would require "less than a sixth part of that number." Unable to tell Hood the real reason for evicting the citizens, he could only focus on the "principle of population evacuation" in responding to the Confederate general's protests.[24]

PALMETTO STATION

Hood remained at Lovejoy's Station for nearly two weeks after Sherman pulled back to Atlanta. He then began to move out on September 18, heading northwest toward Palmetto Station on the Montgomery and West Point Railroad. Palmetto Station was twenty-four miles southwest of Atlanta, and it offered a convenient place to rest the army preparatory to a contemplated move against Sherman's supply line with Chattanooga. The Army of Tennessee constructed a defensive position that straddled the railroad, with its left resting near the Chattahoochee River. Stewart's Corps held the left, Lee's Corps occupied the center, and Hardee's Corps crossed the railroad on the right.[25]

The rank and file, of course, knew nothing of Hood's strategic plans. When the 46th Mississippi marched out on the morning of September 20 to take posi-

Federal Defenses of Atlanta

tion near Palmetto Station and begin to fortify, its members were in the dark as to what lay in their future. "This was done probably as much to keep the men employed as for any other purpose," commented Sgt. William Pitt Chambers, "for it certainly prevented a great deal of promiscuous foraging." Heavy work on the line continued September 20–23, often in considerably rainy and muddy conditions. At least one division constructed two lines rather than one. The Federals obtained reliable information about the position when Pvt. Asbury C. Dale of the 2nd–6th Missouri (C.S.) deserted and told them all he knew. An engineer by profession, the twenty-four-year-old Dale eventually took the oath of allegiance and was released with the understanding that he not travel south of the Ohio River.[26]

Jefferson Davis arrived at Hood's army on September 25 and stayed for four days. The primary purpose of his visit was to consult with Hood about the possibility of striking the railroad between Chattanooga and Atlanta. One day, the president and the general rode along the fortified line to see the troops. In Granbury's Brigade the men were told to "stand in line just in the rear of our works" as the pair rode by. The president was not well received by the troops, who sullenly remained silent as he passed. Hood left Palmetto Station on September 29 to begin his campaign against Sherman's supply link with the North.[27]

FEDERAL DEFENSES OF ATLANTA

The new line of earthworks that Poe laid out to defend Union-occupied Atlanta represented a sharp departure from the line that Lemuel P. Grant had designed to hold the city for the Confederates. While Grant's work had fully encompassed the city in a ring of earth, Poe designed his line only to shield the center of town from a threat coming from the south. Poe's line was about four miles long and in the form of a semicircle. Elements of the 1st Missouri Engineers began initial work on September 28, but the Federals seriously began digging on October 3, after Sherman took most of his available manpower to chase Hood northward and protect his supply line. Poe brought out details of infantrymen amounting to 2,000 men on October 3 to work on the new line.[28]

Slocum's Twentieth Corps, left behind to hold Atlanta, provided the manpower to do most of the digging. James S. Robinson detailed 350 men from his brigade each day for nearly two weeks to work on the fortifications. He took his entire command out on a foraging expedition into the countryside on October 15 but continued to detail 200 men each day after the twenty-first. Three days later, Robinson reduced that detail by half until he was called on to take his en-

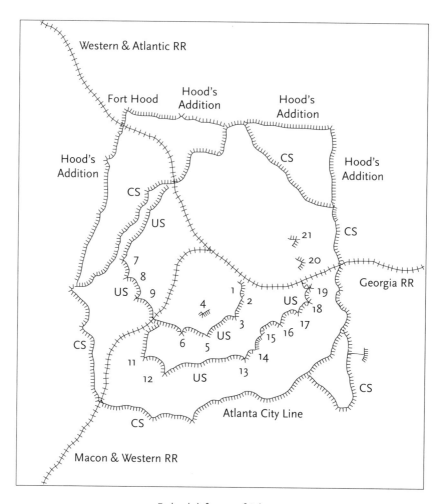

Federal defenses of Atlanta

tire brigade out on a second foraging expedition on October 26. Upon returning to Atlanta three days later, Robinson was told to prepare for a major new movement rather than work anymore on the defenses.[29]

Robinson was not alone in the level of his involvement with the fortifications, for the entire corps provided details for the project. According to Harvey Reid, a brigade commissary in Ward's division, the men were issued double rations and half a gill of whiskey each day that they labored on the works. About seventy Confederate deserters were also put to work on the new line.[30]

Construction of the Federal defenses proceeded at a vigorous pace for the first week following October 3, because Hood's early movements from Palmetto Station portended an attack on Atlanta. Poe argued that by October 5 the

Stakes in ditch of Federal Fort No. 7. George N. Barnard exposed this photographic view in November 1864 to illustrate one of the densest and most dangerous obstructions ever created by a Civil War engineer to protect a fortification. *Photograph by George N. Barnard. Library of Congress, LC-DIG-stereo-1s01402.*

line was defensible along at least a portion of the semicircle. After the first week, Hood had moved so far north that it was apparent Atlanta was not a target, and the Federals finished the line at their leisure. Poe relied on two engineer regiments, the 1st Missouri Engineers (which had reached Sherman's command just in time to take part in the strike against Jonesboro) and the 1st Michigan Engineers and Mechanics (which arrived at Atlanta by late September), to do the fine work on the twenty-two redoubts studding the line. An officer of the 1st Missouri Engineers was hard at work by October 14 making a detailed plan and map of the line.[31]

"Much care had [been] bestowed upon the several redoubts," Poe proudly

Federal Fort No. 9. Taken by George N. Barnard in November 1864, this photograph illustrates the level of professionalism employed in constructing the Federal line of defense at Atlanta. Notice the wide parapet with the top sloping toward the enemy, the board and post revetment of the parapet, and the banquette (firing step designed for infantry) located between the gun emplacements, with sandbags holding up the sides of the embrasures to allow the guns to fire through openings in the parapet. *Photograph by George N. Barnard. Library of Congress, LC-DIG-stereo-1s01408.*

reported to the chief engineer of the U.S. Army, "and the finish put upon each was excellent." He placed mantlets across the embrasures of six redoubts, making this covering out of rope and boiler iron. Each mantlet was shaped so as to completely cover the embrasure when the gun was pulled back. In the ditches of at least a few redoubts work crews carefully planted saplings with sharpened ends sticking up. The tops of these stakes reached to within a foot of the ground level. Such an obstruction could not have been seen by attacking infantrymen until they were at the edge of the ditch. Manning F. Force, a brigade commander in the Seventeenth Corps, was impressed by this unique obstruction. "It is a most repelling sight, and would be troublesome to a storming party."[32]

The Federal defenses of Atlanta were actually tested in a small fight that occurred on November 9. Artillery fire was heard that morning southeast of the city as a brigade of Confederate cavalry led by Alfred Iverson approached Atlanta. The Rebels opened fire with two guns and shelled the camp of the 85th Indiana of Ward's division. Maj. Jefferson E. Brant deployed the 85th "along the works from the Augusta railroad to the fort on the right," but the Confederates did not launch an attack.[33]

Poe's Atlanta line became superfluous as soon as Sherman decided to change his plans in the wake of Hood's attempt to cut his supply line with the city. The Confederates failed to take the huge Union depot at Allatoona Station on October 5 and briefly captured Dalton shortly thereafter, but Hood soon veered off into north Alabama because he intended to strike into Union-occupied Middle Tennessee. Hood's north Georgia campaign demonstrated the difficulties of maintaining a Union garrison in Atlanta, and Sherman had no intention of chasing the Confederates back to Nashville. He dispatched sufficient forces to take care of Hood and organized the rest, some 60,000 hardened veterans of the western campaigns, for a strategic move toward the sea and ultimately to Petersburg to reinforce Grant's efforts to deal with Lee's Army of Northern Virginia. Sherman intended to abandon Atlanta altogether, rendering Poe's hard work on the Federal defenses of that city unnecessary.[34]

Yet, those Federal defenses of Atlanta were a model of their kind. "They are the most beautiful earthworks I have ever seen," commented Manning F. Force when he saw them on November 14, just before the start of the March to the Sea. "I have built the finest line, here in all the Southwest," wrote Poe to his wife, "and I take a great deal of professional pride in it. My line is nearly four miles long and the work and finish is most beautiful." Fortunately, we have a set of photographs of this line to serve as a resource to study the works. They were taken by George N. Barnard, a civilian photographer working on contract for the government, who exposed numerous views of Atlanta, its facilities, and the Union and Confederate earthworks around the city before Sherman abandoned the prize capture of his four-month-long campaign.[35]

Conclusion

When the 1st Missouri Engineers moved south to join Sherman's army group operating about Atlanta in mid-August, Horace B. Hooker was amazed at Federal progress. "It seems perfectly wonderful to me that Sherman has been able to work his way so far down into the heart of the rebellion, through so many positions that seem almost impregnable, and if the rebels cannot hold such a country as this through which we have already passed they might as well give it up altogether."[1]

One of several reasons that Sherman was able to penetrate Georgia was the widespread use of fieldworks by his men. "Fortifying is all the rage now," commented James Carnahan of the 86th Indiana in his diary. "Just as soon as we stop in front of the enemy, the boys at once go to building breastworks." Protecting their forward positions with earthen defenses, the Federals could not be dislodged. While Carnahan called it a "rage," Lt. Henry O. Dwight of the 20th Ohio more properly described it as "a principle with us" to use earthworks to "resist the tremendous attacks in mass of the enemy." Rice C. Bull of the 123rd New York preferred to call the practice of consistently fortifying "almost a habit with us as soon as we halted close to the enemy." Each man "would dig in as though his life depended on his work. In many cases it did." More than one of Sherman's veterans commented on the significance of entrenching tools in the Atlanta campaign. "The axe, the pick and shovel have done more to bring us success in this campaign than have the rifle and cannon," wrote James Carnahan, while the historian of the 75th Indiana concluded that "the spade and the gun were inseparable companions in practical warfare on the Atlanta campaign."[2]

The Confederates also adopted the habit or principle of repeatedly entrenching in attempts to stop Sherman's advance. John Irwin Kendall of the 4th Louisiana recalled jokes about the Army of Tennessee and its impressive string of fortified positions in the campaign. It had been "a current gibe that we never fought in the open, but always behind cover. It is quite true that in the Georgia campaign we never halted half an hour without throwing up some kind of earthwork."[3]

LEADERSHIP

It is logical to think that the generals in charge of the campaign were responsible for the use of fieldworks, but that assumption is not true. On the Confederate side, Joseph E. Johnston's innate caution and reliance on the defensive certainly contributed to extensive fortifying. In fact, Capt. Andrew H. Buchanan, an engineer officer with the Army of Tennessee, praised Johnston in a postwar article for his understanding of military engineering and his ability to survey terrain and adapt his plans to take advantage of it. Whether Johnston really deserved the hero-worshipping terms Buchanan used in his article is open to question. Stephen W. Presstman, Johnston's chief engineer, was primarily responsible for most of the fortified positions the Confederates built during the campaign.[4]

Sherman's role in his men's use of fieldworks has been more accurately assessed because Sherman provided more commentary on the subject than did Johnston. The Federal commander had never been a devotee of field fortifications; most of what was done by his army group during the campaign came from lower-ranking officers and at times from the common soldier as well. Yet Sherman deserves credit for adapting his mode of operations to the evolving use of fieldworks in a very effectual way to achieve his strategic goals. Arthur Wagner, who became a major military writer by the late nineteenth century, exaggerated when he gave Sherman credit "for first adopting a strategic use for hasty entrenchments thoroughly in accord with the genius of modern war." Wagner referred specifically to the practice of entrenching part of his army group for defensive purposes while maneuvering the rest to flank a strongly fortified position. Such a use of fieldworks was not a secret; Robert E. Lee had used it at Chancellorsville, to name one prior instance. It is true, however, that Sherman used field fortifications as an offensive tool, both on the strategic and tactical level, "with more imagination and skill than any other Civil War general," as historian Edward Hagerman has put it. Grant, of course, used fieldworks in a similar way during the Overland and Petersburg campaigns, but the result of his operations often involved horrendous casualties and lack of success.[5]

For Sherman this use of fieldworks always was a matter of pragmatism. He adopted it through necessity only, because he never truly succumbed to the temptation to rely on fieldworks in every confrontation with the enemy. Sherman worried about how the excessive use of fortifications could impair the spirit of his troops, because he always tried to achieve and maintain a morale advantage over the enemy. He allowed his troops to dig in extensively during the Atlanta campaign because the Confederates were already doing so, and it was necessary to protect his close position to their works with fortifications of his own. When Union skirmishers also dug in, Sherman admitted, "I cannot say that it worked a bad effect; so that, as a rule, it may safely be left to the men themselves" to decide whether to seek protection in the earth. This hands-off policy allowed lower-ranking officers and the rank and file great latitude in decisions about field fortification during the campaign, and they typically chose far more often to dig in than not.[6]

As a result, the reliance on fieldworks evolved during the course of the campaign from roots centered in the division, brigade, and regimental command structure and sometimes from the privates. The first confrontation at Dalton resulted in only light works, in large part due to the imposing, angled, and rocky terrain of the ground. In the next confrontation, at Resaca, Sherman launched several major attacks on the Confederates. Johnston's men had better works here than at Dalton, but they still were light, hasty entrenchments compared to what they would soon dig farther south, and many Confederates suffered unnecessary losses as a result. Resaca was an important turning point for the defending Rebels; they learned to deepen their trenches, add head logs, and fortify their skirmish lines after that battle.

Charles Fennell of the Kentucky Orphan Brigade wrote an article about this theme for the *Confederate Veteran* after the war. His comrades had not heeded their colonel's warning to dig in properly when they took position outside Resaca, and the men paid for it on May 14 by losing one-third of their comrades to heavy Union artillery fire and several strident infantry assaults by the Federals. The Kentuckians feverishly dug in that night and retained the lesson for the duration of the campaign.[7]

Most of the troops Polk brought from Mississippi to join Johnston's army in late May had had little if any experience at hasty entrenchments on the battlefield. W. L. Truman of Guibor's Missouri Battery noted that when his comrades took their position on the night of May 19 near Cassville, they were ordered to dig in for the first time in their war experience on an open battlefield.[8]

The pace of field fortifying picked up when Sherman crossed the Etowah River. It was during the New Hope Church, Pickett's Mill, and Dallas phase of the campaign that operations settled down to conditions that eerily resembled siege warfare, with opposing lines planted very close to each other, constant sniping and artillery fire, and a narrow strip of disputed ground between the opponents. These conditions encouraged ever-deeper digging as the armies continued to move south. The 98th Ohio, for example, was engaged in "building works whenever our brigade commander thought it proper and necessary to do so for our safety," wrote Lt. Col. John S. Pearce in his official report. Eventually the fieldworks of the Atlanta campaign came to resemble semipermanent earthworks that ringed major cities like Washington, D.C., and Richmond. Given latitude by both Johnston and Sherman, officers and men on both sides chose to protect themselves as much as possible and rely on their commanders to institute plans to avoid tactical and strategic stalemates on the Union side, and efforts to save Atlanta on the other side.[9]

As Maj. Abraham J. Seay of the 32nd Missouri put it in early August, his men had learned "long since by sad experience that bullets do not so much damage to dirt as flesh." The desire for protection was so great that the men learned to dig in upon taking a new position even if there was yet no enemy within striking distance. "This is a duty now required of us," commented W. L. Truman, "whenever we form a new line of battle."[10]

Johnston never worried about the effect of this extreme practice of fortifying on his men's morale, for he had little intention of launching tactical offensives against the Federals anyway. But Sherman had to be concerned about maintaining an aggressive edge over his opponent or possibly see his offensive grind to a halt well short of its goal. Of course, a similar tendency to dig in occurred in the Virginia campaign that ran concurrently with Sherman's drive. One reason Grant launched several major attacks on Lee's fortifications was to instill a sense of aggression in the Army of the Potomac, a spirit of confident offense that the men of this army had never displayed in such abundance as did the western troops Grant commanded before coming to Virginia. But the Virginia offensive resulted in horrific Union casualties; while Sherman applauded Grant's spirit and his effort to teach the Army of the Potomac not to fear the enemy, he also came to realize that using up the army in massive assaults that resulted in little tactical gain was counterproductive. Sherman learned from the attacks at Resaca to conduct the rest of his campaign with more caution. For him, it became a matter of balancing the need to conserve troop strength and keeping an offensive edge on his army group that would facilitate the need to keep moving south.[11]

"Grant's Battles in Virginia are fearful but necessary," Sherman told his wife, Ellen, on May 20. "Immense slaughter is necessary to prove that our northern armies can & will fight. That once impressed will be an immense moral power." On June 12, he told Ellen that "Grant will give Lee all the fighting he wants until he [is] sick of the word." Sherman was convinced that the Army of the Potomac needed lessons in how to dominate the enemy with fighting spirit, something that the western Union armies had already achieved over their opponents. "Out here," he wrote to Stanton on May 23, "the enemy knows we can and will fight like the devil; therefore he maneuvers for advantage of ground." Yet, after the failed assault on Kennesaw Mountain, Sherman admitted to Ellen that "at this distance from home we cannot afford the losses of such terrible assaults as Grant has made" in Virginia.[12]

Therefore, Sherman's handling of operations in Georgia followed a fairly consistent and wise pattern. He sought to avoid major attacks on well-fortified positions, concentrated on flanking, and kept tabs on the men's morale so that they did not fall into the habit of keeping their heads down and missing opportunities to punish the Confederates. Sherman's argument that his attack on June 27 was motivated in part by a desire to prove to his men that the old man could mix assaults with flanking, to keep their offensive spirit up, was not just a post-event justification for a failed assault. Sherman genuinely worried that his men might lose their offensive edge. He certainly complained a lot about the Fourteenth Corps and its slowness, its tendency to halt at the mere mention of the Rebels in the vicinity. "I cannot move the troops 100 yards without their stopping to intrench, though I have not seen an enemy," he complained to Howard on August 31, just before the Confederates launched their attack at Jonesboro.[13]

In contrast, Johnston spelled out his tactical and strategic plan during the Atlanta campaign in October 1864, long after he was relieved as commander of the Army of Tennessee. It was to act on the passive defensive at least as long as the army was operating north of the Chattahoochee River. The reason was weak; if Johnston attacked and succeeded, Sherman could always fall back on his base at Chattanooga and escape. If he attacked and lost, the Army of Tennessee would have to cross the river and retire to Atlanta. Now, if the first alternative happened, that would have been acclaimed as a major victory by all Confederates and something that Lee had been unable to force Grant to do in Virginia. If the latter alternative transpired, it would have been nothing less than what actually did happen under Johnston's passive leadership. Sherman's operations provided for all contingencies; the Federals were ready to take on a Confederate attack from behind their earthworks, and they were equally ready to take the offensive by flanking Johnston out of his well-fortified positions. By acting on the defensive nearly the entire time that he commanded the Army of Tennessee, Johnston made it easier for Sherman to advance as quickly as he did across nearly 100 miles of Southern territory in less than two months.[14]

The reversal of Johnston's policy by his replacement, John Bell Hood, astonished the Federals and nearly succeeded in causing their army group much damage, especially on July 22, but it did not effect a reversal of the campaign. Indeed, even Hood stopped his active defense of Atlanta pretty quickly and reverted to Johnston's passive defense. The period of attacks lasted only from July 20 to 28, costing Hood at least 11,000 losses. The result was that the Federals, especially those serving in the Army of the Tennessee, dug in more assiduously than ever before and became a bit warier of surprise attacks, but they never lost their self-confidence or faith in their commander. The battles slowed Sherman's efforts to cut Hood's supply lines, but no more than Johnston's passive defensive measures had slowed Sherman in earlier phases of the campaign. The failed attacks of those nine days, however, had an enormously depressing effect on Hood's army that weakened it far more than the numerical loss of manpower. Hood began his tenure as commander of the Army of Tennessee under a dark cloud because of the affection his men felt for Johnston, and he worsened the situation because of these failed attacks. Within a remarkably short time, the effectiveness of the Army of Tennessee had plummeted both morally and physically.[15]

Hood's failure to save Atlanta by taking the offensive haunted him for the rest of his life and deepened the rift between him and Johnston. Hood tried very hard to blame his former commander's passive policy for his failure to roll back Sherman's army group. He recalled being "deeply concerned and perplexed" as to why the Confederates failed to damage Thomas's army more seriously at Peach Tree Creek. Stewart's Army of Mississippi did well, but Hardee's Corps seemed to attack with no spirit or enthusiasm. About a week later, Cleburne visited Hood and the two men talked about the events of July 20. Cleburne, according to Hood, claimed that Hardee had ridden along the line just before the corps advanced and, in Hood's words, "cautioned him to be on the lookout for breastworks." Cleburne implied that the troops would have attacked with more spirit without this warning. In contrast, Stewart encouraged his men to ignore and overrun temporary works. Hood thought this injunction proved that even in Polk's former command a fear of earthworks had developed by the time he took charge of the army. Hood concluded that Hardee's men did almost nothing at Peach Tree Creek "when they discovered that they had come into contact with breastworks," but rather "lay down" and failed to support Stewart.[16]

Hardee passed away before the publication of Hood's memoirs, which contained the most damaging criticism of Hardee's role in the Atlanta campaign, but his staff officer and son-in-law, Thomas B. Roy, vigorously denied Hood's accusations. Roy published an article in the *Southern Historical Society Papers* in which he assembled letters by several men who argued that Hardee never warned his troops about encountering earthworks just before the attack. Roy also wondered how Cleburne or his men, who were the best soldiers in the army, could be cowed by such a warning, especially when they performed so well against McPherson's fortified position on July 22.[17]

Hood persisted in blaming Johnston as well as Hardee, claiming that the Army of Tennessee was in good spirits at the start of the campaign but had become timid and depressed by the time it crossed the Chattahoochee River due to Johnston's handling of the troops. The men had "been so long habituated to security behind breastworks that they had become wedded to the 'timid defensive' policy," he wrote. This was a theme that Hood had initiated in February 1865, when he penned his long overdue report of the Atlanta campaign to Samuel Cooper. "Daily temporary works were thrown up," he contended of Johnston, "behind which it was never intended to fight. The men became travelers by night and laborers by day. They were ceasing to be soldiers by the disuse of military duty." Hood continued in his report to assert that "this constant digging and retreating from Dalton to Atlanta" weakened the spirit of the army, and "hope had almost left it."[18]

The results of the engagement at Jonesboro became another element in Hood's argument. "To let you know what a disgraceful effort was made by our men" in their attempt to shove back Howard on August 31, Hood reported to Bragg that Hardee lost only 539 and Lee only 946 wounded. The killed represented "a very small number."[19]

Lee took up Hood's cause and voiced supportive views. He had justified his own failure at Ezra Church by blaming his men and was even more desperate to shield his failure at Jonesboro by the same method. "I consider it a great misfortune to any army to have to resort to entrenchments," he wrote to Hood in 1874. "Its *morale* is necessarily impaired from their constant use." Lee approved of the occasional use of fieldworks whenever they served a real purpose, "but the habitual use of entrenchment" not only "impairs the boldness of attack" but caused campaigns to devolve into quasi sieges that created casualties from daily sniping and artillery barrages equal to pitched battles, and with no possibility of a quick or decisive victory. "To attack entrenchments," Lee concluded, "give me troops who have never served behind them."[20]

Not surprisingly, Johnston was critical of Hood's plan to save Jonesboro and the last railroad link into Atlanta. Long after the war, he told John M. Schofield that dividing the Army of Tennessee was a mistake. He claimed to have anticipated Sherman's movement and prepared for it by planning to construct a series of artillery redoubts along the rail line, designed for self-defense. His engineers could link them with infantry parapets if needed, but Johnston hoped to stretch his line all the way to Jonesboro in this method, stockpile supplies in Atlanta, and outlast any movement by Sherman without taking the offensive against his overwhelming numbers. Whether this plan was workable, or had any better chances of success than the one Hood adopted, is highly questionable, but Johnston's comments further highlighted his defensive policy and contrasted it with Hood's willingness to close with the enemy.[21]

Hood had, ironically enough, a fairly balanced view of the use of field-works. He was critical of their overuse, not their judicious use, and looked at Robert E. Lee's campaigns to prove his point. Lee never utilized fortifications except where necessary. "He well knew that the constant use of breastworks would teach his soldiers to look and depend upon such protection as an indispensable source of strength," until they magnified enemy works into "a wall ten feet high and a mile in length" in their imaginations. Hood wanted each soldier to rely "solely upon his own valor" in battle rather than on a ditch.[22]

Richard McMurry, Hood's best biographer, argues that Hood never sought to frontally attack Union earthworks. Instead, he tried to hit the Federals before they could dig in, as at Peach Tree Creek, or strike them on an unprotected flank, as on July 22. Hood cannot be blamed for the attacks at Ezra Church on July 28, for they were launched at Stephen D. Lee's order. Even then, Lee sought to hit the Fifteenth Corps before the Federals could dig in. The concepts supporting all three actions were soundly worked out by Hood, but the execution of each one left much to be desired. In part this was due to the creaky workings of the Army of Tennessee, and in part to Hood's desire to implement complex movements in short spurts of time. As McMurry puts it, "Hood's plans may have been unrealistic in terms of how far battle-weary men could march in a given time, but they did not call for suicide assaults on fortified positions." Instead, McMurry sees Hood as striving "to seize the initiative and maneuver aggressively for tactical and strategic advantages rather than simply to react to Federal moves."[23]

McMurry's assessment of Hood's handling of the Army of Tennessee is fair and balanced, but Hood left a good deal to be desired as commander of one of Johnston's corps before July 18. In many ways, he was out of his element as a corps commander and contributed to the many withdrawals Johnston conducted from Dalton to the Chattahoochee River. Hardee made a point of this as early as August 4, when he urged his wife to remind Johnston how many times Hood had failed to take advantage of opportunities to attack the enemy. "Tell Genl Johnston when he writes the history of the campaign from Dalton not to forget that he gave Hood three opportunities of the enemy in flank, at Resaca, New Hope Church, and Kennesaw & on each occasion he failed." Hardee himself wrote about these incidents in more detail when corresponding with Johnston in 1867. Moreover, Hardee reminded Johnston that Hood had on more than one occasion insisted that the army abandon strongly fortified positions and fall back. "No position subsequently occupied by the army between Cassville and Atlanta was abandoned previous to Genl Hood's recommendation to that effect," he told Johnston, "and in some instances, as at the New Hope Church and Kennesaw Mountain lines the recommendation was of the most earnest and pressing character, and was urged for several days prior to their abandonment."[24]

Hood conveniently ignored his own role in forcing the continual policy of withdrawal during Sherman's approach to Atlanta, preferring to paint the campaign as dominated entirely by Johnston's timidity rather than his own. To his credit he grew in his thinking when given command of the army and planned feasible operations, but he was unable to effectively manage the army to execute them properly. One of his worst failures as army commander was in blaming his own men for the lack of success evident in his operations, and blaming his subordinates and his predecessor, whose legacy as commander of the army deserved better at the hands of the man who succeeded him. Hood's attempt to blame everyone but himself for the loss of Atlanta, covering up his own serious flaws as corps commander, was sordid in the extreme.

THE ATLANTA CAMPAIGN AS OPERATIONAL HISTORY

The Atlanta campaign highlighted some aspects of Civil War operations because it was conducted along a string of earthworks that lay in serrated fashion across more than 100 miles of Georgia landscape. The extensive use of fieldworks imparted a semistatic nature to the campaigning, especially south of the Etowah River, pinning the armies close to each other for extended periods of time. This situation gave skirmishers, snipers, and artillerymen a venue to practice their military craft on an intensive scale. Arthur M. Manigault noted that, during the course of the four-month campaign, he was under fire for all but twelve days. The skirmishers, snipers, and artillerymen did their work so well that the opposing side was forced to dig in ever deeper for greater protection. Semi-siege conditions ensued but never stalled the armies permanently in one place; maneuver combined with extensive digging made the Atlanta campaign a rare example of balance, compared to the tragic stalemate of the western front in World War I.[25]

Participants in the campaign asserted that no other engagements of the war allowed skirmishers to shine as they did in Sherman's drive toward Atlanta. "That campaign might properly be termed the skirmishers' war," stated Samuel W. Price of the 21st Kentucky. Oliver O. Howard asserted that the Federals strengthened their skirmish lines as the campaign progressed, doubling the number of men to increase the confidence of the troops and to put more pressure on enemy picket lines.[26]

The skirmish war heated up considerably when the armies operated between the Etowah River and the Chattahoochee River. One could see a perceptible increase of aggressive skirmishing along the Mountain Line, the Gilgal Church Line, the Mud Creek Line, and the Kennesaw Line. In part this was due to episodic mistakes made by one side or the other. When Alpheus Baker placed his picket line from half a mile to three-quarters of a mile in front of his brigade, he soon came to understand that it was "too far to be either supported or withdrawn in case of sudden attack." When the Federals advanced, Baker lost 130 men as they engulfed the position. Many of those lost served in the 40th Alabama, "who stood their ground and fired till the enemy swarmed all over their rifle pits."[27]

But the main reason that the skirmish war in the Atlanta campaign seemed hot and heavy was because of aggressive leadership on the part of many Union leaders. Chesley Mosman noticed that his brigade commander, William Grose, was ever vigilant to push the skirmish line forward. "Grose is a daisy," Mosman admitted in his journal. "If Rebel pickets cease firing at night it seems to waken him at once and he is so darned inquisitive that he starts his line right out to learn what is the trouble with them." When the Confederates evacuated the Kennesaw Line, the brigade moved forward immediately and with energy. "Old Grose shoves things," Mosman wrote.[28]

The skirmishers became adept at improvising protection on the skirmish lines. Fourteenth Corps troops used cracker boxes filled with dirt to shield their heads by pushing the boxes forward as they crawled closer to Johnston's Kennesaw Line. A month earlier they had carried fence rails with them as they advanced to find a new Confederate position, piling up the rails in a snap when encountering enemy resistance.[29]

The Federal skirmishers dominated their opponents during the Atlanta campaign, and increased their edge over the gray-clad skirmishers as the campaign veered to a close in August. Henry Stone, an officer on Thomas's staff, estimated that the Army of the Cumberland expended 200,000 rounds of small-arms ammunition every day during the months of May and June, most of it on the skirmish line. Chesley Mosman heard a report that skirmishers of the Fourth Corps alone fired 150,000 rounds every twenty-four hours, double that when ordered to do intense work. In contrast, the Confederates suffered a serious shortage of small-arms ammunition during most of the campaign. Loring was forced to warn his division leaders in the Army of Mississippi to be careful of expenditure early in the Kennesaw Mountain phase of the campaign. "The question of ammunition is very important. Please do your utmost to enforce economy in its use — especially by skirmishers."[30]

Losses suffered on the skirmish line, with so much firing taking place, amounted to a considerable portion of the campaign's total casualties. Col. Samuel W. Price of the 21st Kentucky believed these casualties amounted to half of all losses suffered by the Federals during the course of the campaign, while an officer on Stewart's division staff asserted the same thing in relation to the Army of Tennessee.[31]

Sniping also became a deadly fact of life during the struggle for Atlanta. It had occurred in previous campaigns, but the semistatic nature of operations in northwest Georgia gave more ample play for the practice than any other campaign in the west except the siege of Vicksburg. "Sharp-shooters play an important part in the operations of our army," asserted Henry O. Dwight of the 20th Ohio. They were allowed the freedom to choose their positions, dig in for protection, and fire at any target of opportunity for extended periods of time. "Nothing short of an actual attack in force will dislodge these sharp-shooters," claimed Dwight, "and it is rarely that one of them is killed." It took a special kind of man to excel at this trade, a loner who had a natural aptitude for judging distance, taking cover, and calmly waiting for opportunities to develop. "They take the same pride in their duty that a hunter does in the chase," continued Dwight, "and tally their victims in three separate columns — the 'certainly,' the 'probably,' and the 'possibly' killed — thinking no more of it than if it were not men they hunt so diligently."[32]

Artillery played a prominent role in the semi-siege conditions south of the Etowah River. At the very least, the long arm expended a good deal of ammunition, even if much of it merely degraded earthen parapets rather than found targets in the opposing lines. Henry Stone estimated that Thomas's guns expended 1,200 rounds per day during the months of May and June. Battery I, 2nd Illinois

Light Artillery, which served in Baird's division of the Fourteenth Corps, fired a total of 6,766 rounds of ordnance over the length of the campaign. Most of it was shell and case shot; the battery fired canister only once, during the Dallas phase of the campaign. The battery's expenditure amounted to an average of fifty-six rounds per day, divided between the six guns of the company. Ironically, casualty statistics indicate that artillery accounted for a very low proportion of the wounded while the armies were stuck in earthworks. For the 308 men who were treated in Fifteenth Corps hospitals during the Dallas phase of the Atlanta campaign, conical balls accounted for 94.1 percent of the battlefield injuries. Artillery rounds accounted for only 3.8 percent of the wounds.[33]

Many observers were impressed by the siege characteristics inherent in Sherman's operations from the Etowah River south to Atlanta, but they were aware that the campaign really never devolved into a true siege. Sherman called his operations "a quasi siege," and at one point referred to the Union position as "our line of circumvallation." Howard also used the term "a partial siege" of Atlanta, similar to George McClellan's operations against the Confederate line at Yorktown on the Peninsula.[34]

Many of Sherman's subordinates wrote about this odd combination of siege tactics and mobile, though slow, operations as the huge Union army group moved south in stages. "In a protracted attack like that on Petersburg or Atlanta," commented Henry O. Dwight, "although not actually a siege, still the operations have to be carried on more or less after the principles of one. The works are more solid, more substantial, than mere field-works." One of Stewart's staff members commented soon after the war that "both armies may almost be said to have moved behind breast works," imparting the elements of siege approaches to the effort to snuggle up closer to the enemy position. Union soldiers at times used head logs or pork barrels filled with dirt as sap rollers when they tried to advance the skirmish line across no-man's-land, rolling the improvised protection ahead as they crawled forward to shield themselves.[35]

Yet, as Howard's artillery chief accurately put it soon after the campaign, "Sherman never attempted to take Atlanta by a siege proper. He made several approaches by establishing one line in advance of another, but did not go beyond this in siege operations proper." Sherman himself summed up the issue in his memoirs by asserting that "sieges, such as characterized the wars of the last century, are too slow for this period of the world . . . but earth-forts, and especially field-works, will hereafter play an important part in wars, because they enable a minor force to hold a superior one in check for a *time*, and time is a most valuable element in all wars. It was one of Prof. Mahan's maxims that the spade was as useful in war as the musket, and to this I will add the axe."[36]

Most of Sherman's men fully understood his basic tactic during the course of the campaign—to hold a forward position with earthworks and then maneuver the enemy out of his own works with minimal loss. Josiah C. Williams, a member of Ruger's brigade staff in the Twentieth Corps, called this basic tactic "the main feature and beauty of this campaign." Every time Sherman had a chance to examine one of the strong earthworks Johnston evacuated, his commitment to this basic tactic deepened.[37]

While the majority of Union troops understood and appreciated Sherman's mode of operation, some of the less intelligent among them grumbled at the major work expended on building field fortifications that they never used to repel an attack. It seemed to be labor lost. Many Confederates also complained at the immense amount of work expended on their own fortification systems, and they seldom had a chance to use them in repelling the enemy. The Rebels also complained about building a good work and then being compelled to give it up to another unit as the army shifted right or left. The colonel of the 9th Kentucky in the Orphan Brigade had enough when told to give his entrenchment to a battery of Parrott rifles. "The Colonel would not fortify any more," recalled John S. Jackman. "He said he had given way for batteries long enough, and that if a fight came off his reg't could simply take it 'straight.'"[38]

At times, men on both sides expressed a desire for a good open battle fight with the enemy. Ario Pardee Jr. of the 147th Pennsylvania confessed that he was not "particularly anxious for a fight," but he had to admit that merely flanking the Rebels out of one fortified position and into another was not enough. "It would be better if we could flank them and whip them beside, which would tend to demoralize them." Sherman's tactics were comparatively safe, for they did not expose the majority of his soldiers unnecessarily, but it nevertheless was a long, tedious, and difficult process to work large units around Johnston's flanks through the hilly, thickly wooded terrain of northwest Georgia. "An open field fight would be almost a luxury," commented a soldier in the 86th Indiana.[39]

Achieving what Ario Pardee wanted—flanking combined with an attack on the enemy before he could dig in—would have been ideal, but it also was extremely difficult to arrange that combination. Sherman attempted it several times and never succeeded. Schofield ascribed the failure to the rapidity with which the Confederates could fortify, the difficulties of moving troops fast enough to catch them before they were shielded, and to a degree, to the men's reluctance to attack if the enemy had even a minor breastwork. Schofield argued that the rank and file helped to stymie this effort by deliberately marching slowly so they would not be up in time to launch an attack on an enemy they assumed would be ready for them anyway.[40]

Conclusion

Any reluctance on the part of men in either army to dig protective works evaporated when the enemy launched an attack. Bate's assault on the Fifteenth Corps at Dallas on May 28 was the first time that these Federals repulsed a charge from behind earthworks. "For two years we had been digging intrench-ments," wrote Alonzo Abernethy of the 9th Iowa, "and since the beginning of the present campaign, incessantly day and night. . . . So far we had only dug to go forward and leave our works in the rear. Now, suddenly, we had our reward for all this labor." Abernethy understood the wisdom of Sherman's tactics. "That few moments' experience behind breastworks had taught us, and the whole Fifteenth Army Corps, such a lesson as was never forgotten; the lesson that no number of men could have driven them that day, nor ever afterwards, from be-hind a line of earthworks."[41]

Union soldier morale was very high throughout the Atlanta campaign, pri-marily because Sherman had proven to his men that he could continue mov-ing forward without wasting their lives. Every time the Federals passed safely through a line of extremely strong Confederate works, recently evacuated with-out a battle, their confidence soared. "Our soldiers think the world and all of Sherman," wrote Andrew J. Johnson of the 70th Indiana to the "Folks at Home" in late July. "He believes in using the Spade and then flanking." Charles W. Wills of the 103rd Illinois explained that the men were content and patient. "Every man feels that we have 'a goodly thing' and is content to work and wait. I never heard less complaining, or saw troops in better spirits. If we get to Atlanta in a week all right; if it takes us two months you won't hear this army grumble. We know that 'Pap' is running the machine and our confidence in him is un-bounded." Even the repulse of June 27 at Kennesaw Mountain created only a momentary flutter among the Federals. James A. Connolly, a member of Baird's division staff, stated that the repulse "didn't make half as much impression on this army as two days steady rain would have made." For Henry Wright of the 6th Iowa, the crossing of the Chattahoochee River with so little loss was the turning point in everyone's growing confidence in Sherman. Most of the Fed-erals felt their army group could not be whipped, and they were sure of success. Federal pickets sometimes joked with their Rebel counterparts that "Atlanta is ours, and we won't be Hood-winked out of it."[42]

Confederate morale told a different story. It is true that most of the sol-diers' comments about Johnston's Fabian strategy in the campaign indicate that Confederate morale remained fairly high despite the constant falling back. The majority of Rebel soldiers loved Johnston and retained faith in him de-spite the fact that he gave up huge swaths of Confederate territory. But a mi-nority of Rebels had lost all faith in the Confederate war effort, and Johnston's retreats gave them opportunities to stay behind until the Federals advanced and "captured" them. Charles Wills noted that twenty-eight men and four officers deserted from Confederate lines on the night of June 13. Three days later, eighty-three Confederates came into Union lines. Wills thought half of them were deserters and "the rest figured to get captured."[43]

Johnston's constant withdrawals had an effect on both Union and Confederate soldiers, but the extent to which they had that effect is difficult to estimate. There is no doubt that Federal soldiers interpreted the enemy's fallbacks positively. When he had a chance to see the high, commanding ridge that Johnston gave up at Cassville on May 19, Federal brigade leader James Sidney Robinson was convinced the opposing commander had no heart for a real fight. "His retreat from this place, after fortifying it very strongly, shows that he is afraid to risk another engagement," Robinson told a friend.[44]

Some observant Confederates read conflicting evidence when looking at the earthworks they were told to dig. Lt. William Harvey Berryhill of the 43rd Mississippi was convinced that the heavy earthworks constructed along the Kennesaw Line by July 1 could only mean that Johnston was "going to make a death struggle here." But when the Army of Tennessee pulled away from those earthworks, the heart began to go out of some men. "I have almost desponded of our ever doing anything in this Army but ditch and spade," lamented Thomas L. Clayton, an engineer officer on Hood's corps staff. "The men are almost wore out with work and falling back." Clayton admitted to his wife that "I came near giving up in despair when we fell back from Marietta. . . . God grant that Gen Johnston may be right in all these movements."[45]

Johnston left, Hood took over, and Confederate morale plummeted all across the Army of Tennessee after the bloody failures of July 20, 22, and 28. Especially for those Rebels who survived the last of those days' action, the battle of Ezra Church was the breaking point in their willingness to give Hood a chance to prove himself. Ezra Church "swept away every trace of any lingering defense of Hood in our army," wrote Philip Daingerfield Stephenson of Slocomb's Battery. "Many, especially the humbler and more ignorant of the men, became demoralized. They looked upon Hood with a sort of dread, as though he were almost a madman." Weeks of grueling duty in the trenches under a hot August sun further demoralized and physically drained the troops, so that at Jonesboro the Army of Tennessee did not fight at its best. Capt. Staunton H. Dent of Dent's Alabama Battery in Lee's Corps was shocked by the lack of spirit displayed in the attack of August 31. "I feel badly over the result of that fight," he wrote home. "It is a new thing for our men to refuse to fight or what is the same thing to fight with no spirit."[46]

Both armies were strained by constant duty in the trenches. The ditches in fact were more than fighting positions; they were the soldiers' homes for months, exposed to all kinds of weather, cramped, dirty, and sometimes filled with vermin and deep mud. "The trenches were our home," wrote Philip Daingerfield Stephenson, "our beds, our cooking places (when we could get fire to warm our rations), by day and night." Stephenson and his comrades tried to make the works as comfortable as possible, widening the trench and stretching blankets across it with sticks to ward off the sun and rain when officers allowed them to do so. More often than not, however, soldiers on both sides had to make do with very uncomfortable conditions, looking forward to a chance to get out of the trench now and then to stretch and recover from the stress of living in a hole. The worst phase of the campaign in this regard lay in August. The Confederates survived those weeks in the trenches with far less energy and confidence than did the Federals, and it told in their lack of spirit at Jonesboro.[47]

SUMMING UP

Both sides used fieldworks extensively in the Atlanta campaign, but differently, too. The Confederates, under both Johnston and Hood, concentrated on defensive works for the most part, making them so strong and sophisticated as to render the fortified positions impervious to attack. This merely compelled the Federals to avoid attacking them and to seek alternate ways to keep moving south. Simply building good earthworks and failing to devise a way to prevent Sherman from flanking them was a recipe for disaster, as far as Confederate hopes were concerned. Whether Johnston or Hood could have found a formula to stymie Sherman's flanking moves, given the wide latitude the Federals had to find routes and their preponderance of numbers, is doubtful.

But one thing is certain: the Federals made better use of fortifications to achieve their strategic goals than did the Confederates. They used fieldworks offensively very well. Closing on the heavy Rebel earthworks, skirmishing, sniping, using artillery in forward positions to harass and draw Confederate attention, and then moving large columns in wide flanking marches to threaten either Johnston's or Hood's line of communications spelled success for Sherman from the first move of the campaign down to the very last.

The terrain and vegetation of northwest Georgia cooperated with the armies in several ways. The lay of the land north of the Etowah River facilitated Sherman's tactics by offering him wide valleys protected by long, high ridges to conduct flanking movements. The Federals took full advantage of these opportunities. Between the Etowah and the Chattahoochee Rivers, however, the more level and heavily vegetated landscape offered Johnston defensive advantages. The Confederate general used those opportunities. One can see a growing doggedness in his tactics: retreating shorter distances, digging in more securely, and slowing the Federal advance to a crawl. Once across the Chattahoochee, however, Sherman again had more open and level country suited to large troop movements.

For both contending armies in northwest Georgia, the environment at times helped and at other times hindered their operations. Pine forests could either hide fortified lines and strengthen defensive power, or mask approaching troops bent on attacking the enemy. The environment provided a tree that was in many ways perfect for the needs of Union and Confederate soldiers. Because of its soft wood fiber, they could easily cut the pine tree into poles for revetments and fashion head logs out of them. Millions of trees of all kinds were cut down during the course of this long campaign across a heavily forested landscape. Much of this timber destruction involved clear-cutting all trees and bushes for hundreds of yards in front of fortified lines. The resulting felled timber changed environmental patterns in dozens of mini-ecosystems along the former infantry lines for decades to come.

Armies come and go but the landscape and the vegetation remain, even if altered by the presence of war. A great deal of the trench systems that sheltered men also remained, although deteriorating over time, and the tactics remain a source of endless study for interested students of the Civil War.

appendix

Fortifying during the Atlanta Campaign

Jacob D. Cox, who struggled through the drive toward Atlanta as a division leader in the Twenty-Third Corps, also wrote a short but perceptive book about Sherman's operations nearly twenty years later. "No clear understanding of this remarkable campaign can be had," he concluded of the terrain and earthworks, "unless the difficult character of the country and the formidable nature of these artificial defences are remembered."[1]

The most complicated part of the combination of tactics, terrain, and trenches is the art of fortifying in the field, and that is the primary topic of this appendix. The process of digging in for both Union and Confederate soldiers was essentially the same. As Arthur M. Manigault put it, the men remained in line where the engineer officers had staked out the position, and tool wagons came up to distribute their loads before the regiments broke ranks. Then they were divided up into work details because there never were enough shovels for everyone, with details being relieved every hour. As soon as the trench was deep enough to serve the basic needs in case of attack, only as many men were assigned to finish it as the number of tools that were available. Improvements on the fortifications continued as long as the army held that position, and skirmishers also worked hard to protect their forward, exposed position in front of the main line.[2]

Many Federals recorded the details of earthwork construction for posterity. Some of them had a habit of cutting brush and piling it in front of the new positions to screen their activity from Confederate pickets. They normally started the fortification by cutting trees and piling the trunks in a line on the ground to make what Theodore F. Upson called "a solid straight fence 3 feet high." They then dug a trench about four feet wide and two feet deep, piling the dirt on top of the logs. If time and opportunity permitted, they also dug a ditch in front of the log pile to make the parapet higher with the loose dirt. Head logs with notches cut on the underside at each end to accommodate cross poles that stretched across the trench completed the defensive arrangement of the parapet.[3]

Sherman noted in his memoirs that the head log normally was about twelve to twenty inches in diameter "at the butt," making for a stout protection for the head. It, of course, had to be manhandled into position and thus could not be much larger than those dimensions. The pine trees that covered northern Georgia were mostly yellow pine and Virginia pine, and they made ideal head logs. These trees are straight and light enough to manhandle, and the soft fiber is easy to chop. A minié ball could penetrate a pine log about six inches at a range of 500 yards, according to postwar trials, and thus a medium-sized log would suffice as a head log. It took about forty to fifty years to grow a pine tree that was about eight inches in diameter, but several more years to make a tree as large as the one Sherman indicated was typical for head logs. Placing a support, or skid, about every six to eight feet to hold the log if it was knocked off the parapet was sufficient. If logs were not available, the men of Granbury's Brigade used fence rails as a substitute for head logs. The rank and file invested a good deal of time and thought to the head log, which they called "the top log." When members of the 14th Wisconsin had to move forward across a field and dig a new line, they carried their head logs from the old position so they would not need to make new ones.[4]

While the head logs had to be carefully chosen, the logs used as the foundation of the parapet could be as large and long as possible. Lt. John Henry Otto of the 21st Wisconsin noted that the longer and thicker they were, the better. On comparatively rare occasions, stones or cotton bales (if the latter were available) also were used to supplement logs in the parapet. At least on the Federal side, there rarely was a ditch in front of the work. Chesley Mosman, the pioneer officer, understood that this was a departure from the fortification manuals, but he also understood that these temporary fieldworks really did not need a proper ditch. When the Federals dug ditches in front, it was primarily to obtain more dirt to strengthen the parapet. Traverses were a common feature of both Union and Confederate trench systems to protect the men from enfilading fire. They often were placed at the flanks of each company and at angles in the trench line.[5]

Clearing the ground for some distance in front of the works was an essential part of preparing the fortified position. Sherman thought 100 yards was typical, while Henry Dwight reported the distance as fifty yards. This clear field denied an attacker cover and exposed him to defending fire within close range. The trees and brush thus cut down served as an effective obstruction to an attack, slowing down the enemy close to the defender and making them extremely vulnerable to small-arms fire. Simply letting the vegetation lie where it fell made a good obstruction, usually termed a "slashing," but fashioning the tree branches and brush into an organized line was called an "abatis." This demanded much more time and labor, of course, and it was a way to make sure that all the ground was covered by an obstruction, whereas the slashing could leave some holes in the defensive arrangement. Charles H. Olmstead noted that wire often was used to tie brush together and strengthen the abatis in front of the Atlanta City Line, but wire was never used by the Confederates in the field because it was not readily available.[6]

Clear-cutting the ground in front of an earthwork, especially at night, could be hazardous. George A. Newton of the 129th Illinois recalled that when creating a slashing in the darkness, he and his comrades "could scarcely see to strike two licks in the same place with our axes, and as the trees were falling around us, some one would cry, 'Look out!' and down would come a giant of the forest alongside of one." One night a man of the 102nd Illinois "was killed by a tree falling on him."[7]

The array of obstructions that appeared along the trail of Sherman's drive to Atlanta included stakes driven into the ground. Capt. Samuel T. Foster of the 24th Texas Cavalry (dismounted) recorded the use of fence rails driven in a line about forty feet in front of the works and slanted at a forty-five-degree angle. The soldiers sharpened the ends, too, aiming the tops to strike a man at his chest. Another man-made obstruction was the chevaux-de-frise, an elaborate but portable fence "made something like a horse rack," according to pioneer Hiram Smith Williams. Apparently only the Confederates deployed these obstructions, which raised comment from every Yankee who saw them. George F. Cram of the 105th Illinois called it "an infernal machine similar to a hay rack with stakes sharp pointed, and so arranged that it would have rolled over and over us as we tried to get through just as a porcupine defends itself by rolling onto a ball and thrusting its quills out." The chevaux-de-frise, which a member of the 3rd Confederate Engineers spelled "Shiverdefrieze," made their appearance along the Kennesaw Mountain Line and sporadically after that along other Confederate defensive positions, especially at the Atlanta City Line.[8]

The landscape of northwest Georgia was well suited to the widespread use of obstructions. It was, as Alpheus S. Williams put it, "all woods, deep ravines, muddy creeks, and steep hills, the most defensible positions by nature I have ever seen." He praised the Confederates for bringing "art to aid nature. Rods

View of a Confederate fort from the Federal perspective. Unlike most of his other images, George N. Barnard took this photograph to demonstrate the view of a Confederate fort from the perspective of the attacker rather than the defender. In the foreground, one can see a clear view of chevaux-de-frise, and farther on there is a small abatis (cut tree limbs arrayed in a line) and a stout vertical palisade. This photograph also demonstrates the wisdom of Lemuel P. Grant in selecting knolls on which to locate his forts in the Atlanta defenses. *Photograph by George N. Barnard. Library of Congress, LC-DIG-cwpb-03301.*

and rods of abatis, trees, and bushes cut down and intertwined in front, and chevaux-de-frise of strong pointed stakes, fastened firmly in the ground in the midst of the abatis, making a network through which a man could hardly crawl in an hour." In devising obstructions, more than in any other area of earthwork construction, the rank and file devised ingenious ways of strengthening their positions. The historian of the 96th Illinois noted that the obstructions "were

Appendix

often as novel in material and construction as can well be imagined." As Williams indicated, a well-made line fronted by an array of different kinds of well-made obstructions was impregnable to frontal assault. Henry Dwight stated it bluntly: "An attack on fortified lines must cost a fearful price, and should be well weighed whether the cost exceed not the gain. This, then, is what an assault means—a slaughter-pen, a charnel-house, and an array of weeping mothers and sisters at home. It is inevitable."[9]

Compared to those for infantry positions, emplacements for field artillery required specialized attention. James Robert Maxwell of Lumsden's Alabama Battery noted that at Dalton his comrades merely "piled up a few logs, perhaps twenty feet long, to a height of the muzzle of our guns, which at that commencement of campaign, we considered ample protection." That style of fortifying proved inadequate later in the fight for Atlanta. Soon gunners and pioneers learned to make the parapets of artillery emplacements heavier than the infantry parapets until they were from ten to fourteen feet thick. They also made them as high as feasible in order to protect the full body of each crew member. The embrasures had to be done just right, and often the gunners reserved that weighty responsibility for themselves alone. The opening normally was eighteen inches wide at the near end and eight feet wide at the far end to give the piece ample lateral play on targets. If the narrow opening was too wide, it could expose the gunners to enemy sharpshooters. If too narrow, the crew could not work the gun properly. The science of fortifying an artillery emplacement was to provide maximum cover without inhibiting the artillerymen's ability to deliver fire, and that could be worked out only through a process of trial and error.[10]

During the Atlanta campaign, even skirmish and picket lines were fortified. They often consisted of individual pits arranged in a line, each pit large enough for four or more men with fence rails formed into a chevron on the enemy side of the hole. Thoughtful men even cut leaves from nearby trees and spread them around on the freshly dug earth to hide the telltale red clay from enemy skirmishers, practicing an early kind of forest camouflage.[11]

Fortified positions in heavily wooded areas demanded a good deal of work behind the lines as well. Military roads often had to be cut through the forest to allow men and artillery easier access up to and back from the trenches. Often these special roads were constructed laterally along the trench line so commanders could be connected with neighboring units more readily. As a result, there was no end of heavy labor to be performed by pioneers and detailed infantrymen, especially when the armies stayed in one fortified position for unusually long periods of time.[12]

Revetment of a parapet possibly in Confederate Fort V. For this photograph, Barnard stood where he could not only take in the long-distance view of the connecting line but obtain a richly detailed image of the revetment holding up the main parapet of the fort he was standing on, which likely was Fort V on Hood's Addition to the Atlanta City Line. The Confederates used wattle and post (with the horizontal pieces woven around the posts) as well as timber and post (constructed like a fence) to hold up the dirt of these massive parapets designed to protect artillery emplacements. Barnard exposed three other photographs from this site; see the photograph of head logs on Confederate works in this book and *Atlas to Accompany the Official Records*, plate 127, no. 7, and plate 128, no. 7. *Photograph by George N. Barnard. Library of Congress, LC-DIG-cwpb-03417.*

On rare occasions the Confederates employed fireballs to light up the dark nights immediately in front of their position. There is no evidence that the Federals did this, but their enemy, who more often acted strictly on the defensive, now and then nervously threw these lighted cotton balls into the darkness when they suspected the Yankees were approaching.[13]

Union troops occupying a Confederate fort in the Atlanta City Line. This photograph displays an interesting assortment of varied materials used for revetting a work. The Confederates relied heavily on boards supported by posts with many sandbags lining the top of the parapet and the embrasure. The camera was trained along the parapet of the connecting line between this fort and the next, and a few traverses are clearly visible on the left of this connecting line, quite near the fort the photographer occupies. *Photograph by George N. Barnard. Library of Congress, LC-DIG-cwpb-03357.*

THE EXTENT OF FORTIFYING

The participants of the Atlanta campaign did a prodigious amount of digging. Because nearly every regimental commander in Sherman's army group filed a campaign report, we have a good deal of information about unit construction. Even the 8th Kansas, which joined Sherman only on June 28 from its veteran furlough, helped to construct nine lines of works before the end of the campaign. The 92nd Ohio made twelve lines of complete fieldworks and two incomplete lines. In addition, the Ohio men remodeled many works "that in the shifting of the lines we have occupied and found incomplete," according to Col. Benjamin D. Fearing. In the Fourth Corps, Col. Alexander M. Stout's 17th Kentucky "made twenty-seven lines of strong defensive works and many slight lines and barricades, without counting those made by our skirmishers." Perhaps the 85th Indiana in the Twentieth Corps held the record, with a total of thirty-six lines of works, according to Jefferson E. Brant.[14]

Unit reports for the Army of Tennessee are far less numerous than for the Federal side, limiting our understanding of the number of fortified lines any regiment in gray worked on during the campaign. W. L. Truman of Guibor's Missouri Battery noted that his comrades occupied thirteen redoubts from late May to late August.[15]

The length of any line of fieldworks in the campaign can be estimated to provide an understanding of the extent of these positions. Postwar army officers who studied the campaign concluded that the Federals dug between twenty-five and thirty miles of works along the New Hope Church, Pickett's Mill, and Dallas Line. Henry Stone, one of Thomas's staff officers, argued that Union and Confederate soldiers dug 400 to 500 miles of earthworks in six weeks of campaigning from New Hope Church down to the Chattahoochee River. But Lt. F. Halsey Wigfall, an officer on Hood's staff, believed the Army of Tennessee had opened up 200 miles of earthworks from Dalton down to Atlanta by early August. Poe estimated that the Federals constructed fifty miles of infantry parapet and a similar length of artillery emplacements from the Chattahoochee River down to Jonesboro. Sherman was compelled to use vague language in his memoirs, stating that "hundreds if not thousands of miles" of works were dug during the campaign by both sides.[16]

Even if the more conservative estimates are taken for granted, that means the landscape of northwest Georgia was scarred for many miles on both sides of the Western and Atlantic Railroad and the Macon and Western Railroad, all the way from near Chattanooga down to Lovejoy's Station. Gazing from the summit of Kennesaw Mountain, Col. Samuel E. Hunter of the 4th Louisiana was struck by the sight of the piles of freshly turned earth that stretched across the landscape "within a few hundred yards of each other, looking like two lines drawn in red for miles and miles." Sherman was keenly aware of the volume of earthwork construction when he confronted the Smyrna Line by July 5. "The extent of the enemy's parallels already taken is wonderful, and much of the same sort confronts us yet, and is seen beyond the Chattahoochee."[17]

A newspaper correspondent for the *Cincinnati Commercial* was astounded by the sight of field fortifications when he visited Sherman's army in early July. "Imagine all the country between the Allatoona mountains and the Chattahoochie river ploughed into huge ridges," he advised his readers. Each position lay about five miles behind the other and consisted of "continuous cribs built of rails and poles, or oftener of huge logs, twelve miles long, filled with dirt wrenched out from the clenched roots of a Georgia forest, four feet high and six feet wide, running through the thickest woods and cleared fields alike, always two, oftener three, and sometimes five miles deep, and all finished perfectly and polished, the trenches cut down, square and true, and the parapets shaped as if with the square and plummet."[18]

Philip Daingerfield Stephenson, a gunner in the Fifth Company of the Washington Artillery, had an opportunity to see the successive lines of fieldworks when Hood launched his raid northward against Sherman's rail line in October. Stephenson saw many of the fortified lines, from south to north, and was astounded. "The whole country between Dalton and Atlanta seemed literally dug up! Dug up into parallel lines of entrenchments, zigzag in actual construction but parallel in general trend, in intervals of four to ten miles, and in length anywhere from five to fifteen. The effect of the sight of them, lying there silent and desolate was awe inspiring. Frowning and threatening they seemed. We stood amazed at their dimensions and could hardly believe our own eyes. Then did we realize as never before that our toil and struggle in that campaign had been literally gigantic."[19]

There were very few antecedents in the prior experience of Sherman's or Johnston's/Hood's men for this scale of digging. The siege of Vicksburg was one of the few previous experiences that came close to comparison. The Fifteenth and Seventeenth Corps had conducted much of the earthwork construction during the siege, but even Federal troops who had not participated in the Vicksburg operation used it as a counterpoint to their own fortifying in the Atlanta campaign. Edwin W. Payne of the 34th Illinois in the Fourteenth Corps bragged to his wife that "we carry spades now and fortify. I think we will be as good at 'Gophering' as the Vicksburg boys after a while." On the Confederate side, many regiments had experienced the strain of enduring siege operations at Vicksburg. William Anderson Stephens informed his wife that "we have better ditches hear to fite in than we had at Vicksburg . . . [and] if I have to fite I want ditches to fight in."[20]

The older units in Thomas's Army of the Cumberland had constructed heavy earthworks at Murfreesboro (Fortress Rosecrans) following the battle of Stones River, as well as extensive works to protect their fragile possession of Chattanooga following the battle of Chickamauga. In both cases, those works were semipermanent systems for the protection of a fixed asset. During the Atlanta campaign, Thomas's men had to learn how to construct temporary works in difficult terrain and often far away from any fixed asset. Peter B. Kellenberger of the 10th Indiana informed a friend in late August that "very little was known in this army about entrenching . . . but certainly, no one who travels over the Battle ground from Ringgold to Atlanta, will Say, that any thing has been left undone in that line."[21]

The units comprising two divisions of the Twentieth Corps had hard experience in the eastern theater before they joined Sherman's army group. The old Twelfth Corps units, in particular, had done a good deal of temporary fieldwork construction at Chancellorsville and Gettysburg. John W. Geary noted the significance of his division's work in this way on Culp's Hill at the latter conflict. "The efficiency of our intrenchments was clearly demonstrated from an early period in the action," Geary reported. Although consisting of slight parapets of logs and rocks, the works protected his men from Rebel artillery and reduced his casualties. They also enabled his troops to hold their position against terrific attacks by Lee's veterans on July 2 and 3.[22]

Yet no amount of prior experience in fieldwork construction was sufficient for the demands of the Atlanta campaign. All of Sherman's men had to learn and adapt to the terrain of northwest Georgia, to the threat posed by the Army of Tennessee, and to the extended duty that stretched out into four months of grueling work through hot summer months. Daniel Butterfield's Third Division of the Twentieth Corps consisted mostly of western regiments with little more than garrison duty as their fund of experience before the campaign. Butterfield was dissatisfied with a line of works the men of his Second Brigade built near Rocky Face Ridge. "It is not well constructed for want of tools and inexperience on the part of the troops," he reported to Hooker.[23]

Experience led to skill among those Federals who had had little in their prior service to guide them, even among the more experienced members of Sherman's army group. William Clark McLean of the 123rd New York, who had dug earthworks at Chancellorsville and Gettysburg, learned something from looking at Confederate earthworks by the time Johnston evacuated the Kennesaw and Smyrna Lines. "The boys pattern after the rebs in building them by digging a ditch behind them to protect them from the shells." McLean, in other words, indicated that his comrades had a habit of digging a ditch in front of the work in conformity with fortification manuals instead of a trench behind it, but they were learning from the example of their enemy.[24]

It was evident in both armies that experience led to skill, for the fortified lines became stronger, more elaborate, and more extensive as the campaign continued. The rank and file became experts at smaller details that added to the protection of their bodies and, collectively, they could erect immense fortifications almost overnight. When the 71st Ohio joined the Fourth Corps in late August after doing garrison duty at Decherd, Tennessee, the hardened veterans who watched as the green troops dug in were amused. "It is a brand new work for them and they all seem to be bosses, at least all gave orders." Chesley Mosman assumed that the Ohioans must have felt how different campaigning was compared to garrison duty. The 71st Ohio was large and superbly disciplined, but utterly green as to how to take care of itself on campaign.[25]

Those who had invested months of hard work fighting for Atlanta came to be so expert in fortifying that they sometimes could estimate the age of an abandoned Confederate work. Oliver O. Howard was certain a Rebel trench his Fourth Corps troops occupied on July 21 was "probably five or six weeks" old, which he considered a long time as far as the history of earthworks during the Atlanta campaign was concerned.[26]

Many men probably would have agreed with Luther P. Bradley, a Fourth Corps regimental and brigade commander, when he mused on his experiences only two weeks after the campaign ended. In an extended sentence to his sister, Bradley wrote of "the long marches, the miles upon miles of earth works built, the battles and daily skirmishes equal to old fashioned battles, the night fights, surprises and repulses, the fording of streams and bridging those that couldn't be forded, often under fire, building roads through swamps, and cutting them through forests: all these so indelibly impressed on our minds. The real work of the campaign, the incidents and dangers, exceed all my former service put together. I think I have been under fire at least a hundred times this summer."[27]

WORKING ON THE DITCHES

The end result, dozens of impressive lines of fieldworks stretching in serrated formation across the countryside, came about through a great deal of hard, physical labor. But not every soldier was adept at using the pick and spade. Albert Theodore Goodloe of the 35th Alabama recalled that some men were particularly good at it. While those individuals were not exactly cowards in battle, they "were somewhat famous for finding and making hiding places from bullets." Goodloe also recalled that other men "seemed to have no talent or energy or care for the work of fortifying, and would only go at it like some citizens work roads, because they were ordered to do so."[28]

While entire units were often compelled to work on a new line to get it ready for action, Union and Confederate officers preferred to detail men to finish construction so as not to fatigue entire units. The size of these work details varied according to need. Lt. Col. Orrin Hurd of the 30th Indiana sent groups of fifty men led by two commissioned officers for each relief while repairing earthworks along the Fourth Corps line at Kennesaw Mountain. Will M. Mc-Lain of the 32nd Ohio identified the typical work detail as 300 men. He was assigned to be a "boss of fatigue parties" along the Kennesaw line by his regimental commander. McLain was responsible for superintending each relief, working mostly at night. As the moon was full in the last two weeks of June, the landscape was lit up uncomfortably when the night sky was clear, making Mc-Lain's work much more dangerous. Even though he had no engineering training or experience, McLain was in effect a regimental engineer. "I'm so used to ditches and ditching, to scarps and counterscarps, lunettes, salients, and re-entrant angles, bastions and lines of crests, that I expect when the war is over, I'll have to employ three hundred Irishmen . . . and go about ditching farms by the wholesale!"[29]

With experience, soldiers were throwing together works at rapid speed. A captain in the 63rd Indiana of Schofield's corps noted that his comrades could tear down a house in only twenty minutes that had required weeks to build, and they could use the timbers to make the foundation of a parapet. Alpheus Williams praised the men of his Twentieth Corps division for making a breastwork in thirty minutes that was "very formidable-looking." Howard witnessed troops who could use axes and shovels well enough to build a work that would provide good protection against both artillery and small-arms fire in only half an hour. Confederate officer John Irwin Kendall noted that collecting tree trunks, digging a trench three feet deep, and making a parapet three feet tall and four feet thick with head logs was a matter of two hours' labor for his men. As a soldier of the 96th Illinois told a correspondent, "Many hands make light work."[30]

Jacob D. Cox carefully observed as the men of his Twenty-Third Corps division dug in on August 30 near East Point. There were plenty of signs that the Confederates might attack without warning, so the men apparently did their best digging of the campaign. "Giving the order to make the light trench of the rifle-pit class," Cox later wrote, "where the earth is thrown outward and the men stand in the ditch they dig," he timed them. It took only fifteen minutes to create enough cover so that Cox felt certain they could repel an infantry attack.[31]

SITING, DESIGNING, AND BUILDING

A good deal of discussion about exactly who was responsible for siting and building earthworks during the Atlanta campaign has taken place. One strain of this theme has it that the rank and file increasingly took charge not only of siting earthworks but designing their features and constructing them. Henry Dwight contributed to this theme in his *Harper's Monthly* article, published in 1864, when he asserted that "every man is to some extent his own engineer." While officers sited the location, the infantrymen handled everything else. The historian of the 59th Illinois believed the common soldier regarded fieldworks as something like "his personal armor" and wanted to make certain it provided all the protection possible. This theme has been taken up by modern historians who have made rather extravagant claims that common soldiers in effect were in charge of all aspects of fieldwork construction in the 1864 campaign.[32]

These claims are exaggerations of a significant kernel of reality. It was certainly true that common soldiers played a large and important role; they provided the bulk of the hard labor to construct earthworks during the Atlanta campaign, and they very often tinkered with details such as providing traverses for flank protection and obstructions in front of the works. But the common infantrymen never were responsible for locating a fortified line or deciding where to put artillery emplacements. Engineer officers performed that important duty, while decisions by middle- and lower-level officers played a large role in directing and overseeing earthwork construction. Common soldiers and their company and regimental officers could, on occasion, tear down and remodel the earthworks constructed by a different unit if the fortification did not suit them when they were assigned to it, but the larger issues associated with field fortifications during the campaign lay in the hands of higher-ranking officers and engineers. Control of the design and construction of fieldworks during the drive toward Atlanta was a collaborative affair with responsibilities divided among all ranks in both armies.[33]

It appears that artillerymen had greater latitude in placing and designing their fortified positions than did infantrymen. Philip Daingerfield Stephenson of the Washington Artillery recalled that "much was left to the discretion of subordinate officers, of necessity, even to battery officers, and in a company like ours, every man became an engineer." The specialized, technical nature of their service made artillerymen a special kind of soldier who, through experience, often knew more about their needs than did engineer officers. W. L. Truman of Guibor's Missouri Battery asserted in early August that "we lay off our own works and build them to suit ourselves, and make such improvements from day to day, as we find necessary."[34]

The engineer officers on both sides have never been given their due for the role they played in the campaign. Andrew Hickenlooper, who served as McPherson's engineer, praised his counterparts in gray for designing a series of fortified positions that forced Sherman to crawl forward an average of only one mile per day during the campaign. Logan's chief of artillery praised Capt. Herman Klostermann, the chief engineer of the Fifteenth Corps, for his ability to site and construct gun emplacements. Even so, engineers in general received scant notice by the public or in the work of modern historians.[35]

Infantry officers of all ranks played a role in making earthworks. F. M. McAdams of the 113th Ohio in the Fourteenth Corps noted on June 23 that "some of the left companies strengthened their works during the night." If one looks closely at some of the well-preserved earthwork remnants at Kennesaw Mountain, for example, it becomes evident that some small design feature appears along a short length of the work comparable to a company line and does not appear elsewhere. All this indicates that some company commanders were more inventive and attentive to the need for protecting their men than others. On the brigade level, Col. Benjamin Harrison included a statement in his official report to make it clear that he was responsible for at least one feature of his command's defenses: "I planned and constructed a lunette" on the left of his line for four guns in mid-August. Even army-level officers at times offered detailed instructions for earthwork construction. Schofield mandated that Hascall should dig in along a ridge in mid-July but be sure to leave gaps in the works to allow movement along the road that intersected with the works along the top of the ridge.[36]

It also would be a mistake to ignore the enormous labor performed by pioneer officers and their men. They especially were important in fashioning embrasures for artillery positions, at least in the Union army. Confederate pioneers were often assigned the more difficult tasks associated with placing wood as revetment along the interior slope of parapets, reserving the hard labor of shoveling dirt to infantry details. Pioneers were detailed soldiers, so they retained their weapons and combat skills. When Hood attacked Thomas at Peach Tree Creek, the pioneers of Wagner's brigade of Newton's division stopped working on the breastworks and formed line to help cover Newton's left flank. They continued working on the defenses between attacks.[37]

Many Federals were convinced that a large corps of Southern blacks contributed to the mix of labor in constructing Confederate defenses during the Atlanta campaign. This idea appeared in accounts as early as June 17, when a report circulated that the Confederates maintained a force of 30,000 blacks to dig earthworks for them. Reports such as these rarely specified whether the black laborers were slaves or freemen, but we can assume that most of them were in fact slaves contributed by their owners for short-term work with the Confederate army. The rumors that Johnston employed a large force of black laborers increased when he evacuated the Kennesaw Line and moved to Smyrna Station. Johnston had used "an army of negroes," as Hickenlooper put it, to construct nearly every fortified position thus far in the campaign. Sherman reported this news as fact when writing to Grant in mid-July. To a limited extent, the rumors were true, although they tended to be greatly exaggerated. We know that blacks worked on the Atlanta City Line and on Shoup's Line north of the Chatta-hoochee River, but probably at no other Confederate fortified line.[38]

Thomas wanted to make sure that Union deserters also contributed to the mix of labor in earthwork construction. Until court-martial proceedings could be arranged for them, he ordered that deserters should be put to work on the most forward element of the army's defenses, skirmish pits. Whether this direc-tive was ever carried out is uncertain. Thomas mandated that proper guards be placed to watch the men, which would have been an unusual drain on reliable manpower, and the chances for deserting to the enemy on the skirmish line were such that the scheme seems unworkable.[39]

TOOLS

Finding the tools needed for proper entrenching during the campaign was not an easy matter. Of 600 wagons supporting the movement of Fourth Corps troops early in the campaign, six were reserved to carry entrenching tools. In contrast, 150 wagons conveyed ammunition, and 422 carried food for men and forage for animals. Some units packed the tools on mules when entering par-ticularly rugged territory, such as the area immediately south of the Etowah River.[40]

Federal commanders often had to deal with significant shortages of tools. Oscar Malmborg complained that from the start of the Seventeenth Corps's participation in the campaign he had fewer than six entrenching tools per regi-ment. This forced him to keep those implements busy day and night by deploy-ing details on a rotating basis along the Kennesaw Line. Malmborg received a large shipment of 600 spades, 600 axes, and 300 picks on June 20. He distrib-uted them equally among the two divisions in the corps, putting commanders of pioneer companies and regimental quartermasters in charge of the tools. That amounted to two and a half spades for each of the 240 companies in the corps. Most of those tools were still in use a month later. Hosea Rood reported that each company of the 12th Wisconsin had one or two spades available as of July 21.[41]

Repeated requisitions for more tools streamed to the rear as the campaign lengthened. Quartermaster Edward L. Hartz handled these requests from his office in Chattanooga. They included an urgent order for 500 picks, 1,000 spades, 1,000 shovels, and 1,000 axes for the Army of the Tennessee on June 10. "The army is badly in need of them," affirmed the quartermaster of the Left Wing, Sixteenth Corps. In similar fashion, the Fourteenth Corps needed 1,000 axes, 500 shovels, 250 spades, and 300 picks by mid-June, and Twentieth Corps troops required 448 axes, 80 picks, 100 spades, and 110 shovels by the time of the Kennesaw phase of the campaign. When the Third Division of the Fifteenth Corps arrived on the scene and was assigned garrison duties at Allatoona and elsewhere, it required an infusion of 100 spades, 100 axes, and 50 picks for the heavy fortifying that took place in the area. Hartz was quick to supply all requisitions. When a quartermaster in the field filed a request on July 8, Hartz assured him he had shipped the tools from his Chattanooga depot the very next day.[42]

At times, tool shortages occurred because of enemy action. Blair's men lost many tools during the battle of July 22 because the Confederates took them while holding Seventeenth Corps earthworks. This led to problems in terms of fortifying properly on July 28 when the battle of Ezra Church began. But Blair's problems did not compare with Schofield's. John Humphrey's company of the 50th Ohio in the Twenty-Third Corps had no axes or spades at all from the start of the campaign. One day Humphrey captured a Confederate axe and a comrade captured a Confederate spade. From then on, "when we go to work, we keep them running till they are hot, for every man has an interest to get some place to get his head behind to save it."[43]

Unit commanders often had to borrow tools. Maj. Levin T. Miller of the 33rd Indiana managed to obtain twelve shovels, seven picks, and six axes from Capt. Alphonso G. Kellam, the provost marshal on John Coburn's brigade staff, who had scrounged them up from some source. Miller had to return the tools by dusk the same day, but he obtained a few more from the brigade pioneer corps only to return them in a few hours. Meanwhile, his men made good use of the tools.[44]

The pioneers received priority when it came time to distribute tools. As a result, pioneer officer Chesley Mosman often was besieged by requests to borrow his implements. On June 2, he loaned all his tools to the 59th Illinois, but when told to construct roads the next day, he had to wait for the regiment to return them. The commander of the 59th Illinois "eternally wants to borrow axes and won't take care of them," Mosman complained. He again loaned his tools on June 20, this time to the 30th Indiana so it could secure its exposed position. The commander returned the implements by dusk. Mosman noted that this was common practice, for he had to keep the limited number of tools busy twenty-four hours a day. The axes must have nearly worn out, for Mosman re-quested a new supply on June 23 and received them the next day.[45]

Thomas B. Byron of the 70th Ohio, an officer detailed to pioneer duty in the Fifteenth Corps, spent the entire morning of May 31 collecting entrench-ing tools he had loaned to several units "to build themselves breastworks." The units were located all along the division line, thus the length of time and trouble in collecting them. Tragically, a member of his corps was killed by Confederate sharpshooters while he was in the process of hunting up tools loaned to other units on June 3.[46]

Now and then, soldiers used axes as weapons in the heat of battle. Charles Wills of the 103rd Illinois saw a wounded Federal in the recaptured works of the Seventeenth Corps, who had been shot in the thigh on July 22. A Confederate had taken an axe and cut him in three places about his face. The Federal man-aged to save himself and bayonet the Rebel.[47]

Axes, spades, and picks constituted the basic entrenching tools of the Civil War, but John Henry Otto of the 21st Wisconsin thought the army could have used another tool. It was a cant hook, a metal device attached to a wooden handle so that men could more easily move logs. It was commonly used in tim-bering and sawmilling and would have been useful in piling up logs to make the foundation of a parapet. The regimental quartermaster "promised to order some but they never came," Otto recalled years after the war.[48]

The Confederates suffered a more serious problem in shortages of tools than did their opponents and often resorted to extraordinary measures to com-pensate. In early January 1864, Army of Tennessee headquarters mandated that quartermasters throughout the chain of command should gather all tools pos-sible by pressing them from local civilians, offering compensation for them. Each brigade was allowed to carry its tools in one two-horse wagon, with the brigade quartermaster in charge of it and two men detailed to take care of the wagon and its contents. The brigade quartermaster also was charged with the tedious task of issuing the tools, keeping detailed records of who received them and whether they were returned, and reporting on his work to the brigade commander every week. Headquarters intended to stop the pay of anyone who failed to return implements. In addition to pressing tools and keeping strict accounts of their use, the Confederates were careful to return broken tools to their quartermasters for repair.[49]

Polk mandated that division leaders in the Army of Mississippi inspect all tools held by their troops, engineer units as well as line units, and report the re-sults to their inspector generals. In short, keeping up with the inventory was important. The entire 4th Louisiana had only two axes, and "they had to be passed from company to company," according to John Irwin Kendall. French had no entrenching tools at all in his division. Ector planned to ambush the Federals on July 8 as they advanced toward the Shoup Line in order to take tools from them. The plan worked, according to French, and the result was a small supply of picks, spades, and steel axes. French noted that Confederate axes were normally made of cast iron, so the Yankee implement was doubly appreciated.[50]

Arthur Manigault provided detailed information on tool management during the Atlanta campaign. He recalled that each brigade had at least one wagon to haul implements, with a commissioned officer and a couple of detailed men to take charge of them. The tools were distributed normally at the end of the day so they could be used to construct works during the night. Receipts documented how many went to which command, and the implements had to be returned the next morning. "Such tools as were required were very expensive, scarce, and could hardly be replaced," Manigault recalled. "Our success and means of defense in a great measure depended during the last year of the war in preserving our supply." He reserved the best wagon available to haul the tools. Manigault remembered that one such tool wagon was loaded at the start of the campaign with "100 shovels, 35 picks, 60 axes, 12 froes, 4 wedges, 2 cross cut saws, 3 hand saws, [and] 4 or 5 augers, and a few other tools." This was considered enough for 1,500 men and represented a balance between the needs of the campaign and the necessity of streamlining transportation to keep the army mobile.[51]

"The tool wagon became an institution and a necessity," Manigault continued in his memoirs, "nearly as important to us as those used for ammunition." But regimental commanders and the rank and file did not always honor that institution. It was quite common for them not to return all tools, forcing the responsible officer to undergo difficult and often fruitless efforts to locate them. The statistics Manigault cited for the number of tools for his brigade amounted to about the same proportion as Malmborg gave the Seventeenth Corps (roughly two spades per company). But that proportion would have declined steadily during the course of the campaign due to attrition.[52]

Confederate requests for more entrenching tools during the course of the campaign worried at least one officer. Maj. Samuel Henry Lockett served as chief engineer of Polk's Department of Mississippi and East Louisiana, but he remained at Meridian, Mississippi, when Polk took his available troops to join Johnston in Georgia. Lockett was puzzled by the continual falling back of the army and the repeated calls for more tools. Perhaps recalling his experience at Vicksburg, where he served as John C. Pemberton's chief engineer during the siege, Lockett thought Johnston should have offered battle early in the campaign for Atlanta. "I don't much like the heavy call they are making for entrenching tools up in that Army," he told his wife on June 12. "It looks more like dig than fight, and the Yankees notoriously can beat us at the first."[53]

COMPARING UNION AND CONFEDERATE WORKS

There were many opportunities for both sides to examine the earthworks constructed by their enemy during the course of the campaign and soon after its end. Artillerist Philip Daingerfield Stephenson found the Federal earthworks at Dallas to be less elaborate than his own. "They were trenches that could only be occupied by men for a brief time," he concluded. They were deep enough for protection, but only fourteen to eighteen inches wide, "barely wide enough for men to stand," not to live comfortably in. He fondly remembered that his comrades made the trench "broad enough to sit in with our backs to the embankment and our legs stretched out to full length, and, if possible, wide enough to lie down in." When Stephenson saw some Union works near Lost Mountain in October, during Hood's north Georgia campaign, he thought they were peculiar. "They would dig traverses and little pits and trenches for every conceivable purpose. The interior of their lines looked like a cemetery robbed of its dead."[54]

Federals normally were astonished at the depth of trenches, the thickness of parapets, and the extensive obstructions that fronted Confederate works, especially from the Kennesaw Line down to Atlanta. Gottfried Rentschler of the 6th Kentucky (U.S.) concluded that the Confederates learned quickly how to dig in securely by the time the campaign reached Kennesaw. "Earlier ours were much stronger by far than those of the Rebels. They have exceeded us during this campaign in this highly important skill." Everyone seemed to understand that attacking such works as the Rebels made from Kennesaw southward amounted almost to murder.[55]

It is true that the Confederates became more adept at building earthwork systems during the last half of the campaign, but then they had to do so because of their defensive purpose. The Federals had less fear of attack, at least until Hood launched his assaults at Peach Tree Creek, on July 22, and at Ezra Church, and thus tended to construct lighter works. Even though lighter, the Union fortifications were normally strong enough and sited properly enough to protect their occupants. Even Stephenson concluded upon further examination of Union earthworks while marching northward with Hood's army in

October that, in general, both armies built their works well. The difference between the two was only a matter of degree, not a difference between skill and incompetence.[56]

The red clay of northwest Georgia helped to preserve the earthworks of the Atlanta campaign for a long time to come. In late October 1864, when George F. Cram of the 105th Illinois visited the old lines his Twentieth Corps regiment had held for nearly a month just north of Atlanta, he found that "the very head log of the breastwork which I had helped to lift there was unmolested." Improvements on the Western and Atlantic Railroad had obliterated many earthworks lying near the tracks by the summer of 1880, when Charles O. Brown visited the sites associated with the campaign. But Brown found that a short walk into the countryside on either side of the railroad revealed that most of the trenches located in the woods were intact. Only when the ditches stretched across cleared land had local farmers demolished them to put their farms back into operation.[57]

When Stephen Pierson of the 33rd New Jersey visited Pine Mountain in September 1881, he was amazed that this place was undisturbed. The head logs still adorned the wide Confederate parapet. New trees had begun to grow on the works, but the abatis felled by the Rebels in front of them still lay intact. "Immediately in front of their line was what was left of a double row of abatis, that is, stakes driven into the ground close together in rows, inclined forward at an acute angle, the ends of the stakes sharpened to a point." Pierson collected one of the stakes to take home as a souvenir.[58]

Many local citizens scavenged whatever they could find of use from the abandoned earthworks, including usable planks and timber. The people living near Marietta reportedly collected more than 200,000 pounds of lead by digging up spent balls and selling them.[59]

But the remaining earthworks also became a major instructional feature with the developing professionalism of the U.S. Army by the late nineteenth century. Staff education led the army to use the Atlanta campaign as a case study in operations, and many staff rides were conducted along the route taken by Sherman's army group. The staff ride of 1906 led officers to conclude that the Confederate earthworks were usually "much more massive and elaborate" than the Federal works because Rebel engineers had an opportunity to choose the best sites for them and build them with a bit more leisure. The Federals had to construct their lines in conformity with the Confederate works and often had to make do with poor ground. As a result, the students and teachers of the 1906 staff ride concluded that the Federals were more inventive in their design of earthworks, "as regards the accidents of the terrain." They also concluded that "trenches built under fire and by the troops that are to occupy them are generally superior from tactical standpoints to those laid out at some previous time."[60]

The field fortifications came to define, to a large extent, the nature of the Atlanta campaign. In no other continuous field operation of the western theater had temporary fieldworks been employed to such a degree and for such a long time. The Union and Confederate soldiers who constructed them, lived in and fought from them, were keenly aware of this unique aspect of their tremendous efforts to take or save Atlanta.

notes

ABBREVIATIONS

ADAH	Alabama Department of Archives and History, Montgomery, Alabama
AHC	Atlanta History Center, Atlanta, Georgia
ALPL	Abraham Lincoln Presidential Library, Springfield, Illinois
CHM	Chicago History Museum, Chicago, Illinois
CWM	College of William and Mary, Manuscripts and Rare Books Department, Williamsburg, Virginia
DU	Duke University, David M. Rubenstein Rare Book and Manuscript Library, Durham, North Carolina
EU	Emory University, Manuscript, Archives, and Rare Book Library, Atlanta, Georgia
IHS	Indiana Historical Society, Indianapolis, Indiana
ISL	Indiana State Library, Indianapolis, Indiana
JBC	Judy Beal Collection, Harrogate, Tennessee
LC	Library of Congress, Manuscript Division, Washington, D.C.
LMU	Lincoln Memorial University, Abraham Lincoln Library and Museum, Harrogate, Tennessee
LSU	Louisiana State University, Louisiana and Lower Mississippi Valley Collections, Baton Rouge, Louisiana
Mary-HS	Maryland Historical Society, Baltimore, Maryland
MDAH	Mississippi Department of Archives and History, Jackson, Mississippi
MHM	Missouri History Museum, St. Louis, Missouri
MOC	Museum of the Confederacy, Richmond, Virginia
Mohi-HS	Mohican Historical Society, Loudonville, Ohio
NARA	National Archives and Records Administration, Washington, D.C.

NYSL New York State Library, Albany, New York

OR *War of the Rebellion: A Compilation of the Official Records of the Union and Confederate Armies.* 70 vols. in 128. Washington, D.C.: Government Printing Office, 1880–1901. Unless otherwise cited, all references are to series 1.

PMSHS Pickett's Mill State Historic Site, Dallas, Georgia

RU Rice University, Woodson Research Center, Houston, Texas

SOR *Supplement to the Official Records of the Union and Confederate Armies.* 100 vols. Wilmington, N.C.: Broadfoot, 1993–2000. Unless otherwise cited, all references are to part 1, volume 7.

TC The Citadel, Archives and Museum, Charleston, South Carolina

TSLA Tennessee State Library and Archives, Nashville, Tennessee

UAF University of Arkansas, Special Collections, Fayetteville, Arkansas

UGA University of Georgia, Hargrett Rare Book and Manuscript Library, Athens, Georgia

UK University of Kentucky, Audio-Visual Archives, Lexington, Kentucky

UM University of Mississippi, Archives and Special Collections, Oxford, Mississippi

UNC University of North Carolina, Southern Historical Collection, Chapel Hill, North Carolina

UO University of Oklahoma, Western History Collections, Norman, Oklahoma

US University of the South, Archives and Special Collections, Sewanee, Tennessee

USAMHI U.S. Army Military History Institute, Carlisle, Pennsylvania

UTA University of Texas, Center for American History, Austin, Texas

UTK University of Tennessee, Special Collections, Knoxville, Tennessee

UTM University of Tennessee, Special Collections, Martin, Tennessee

UW University of Washington, Special Collections, Seattle, Washington

VT Virginia Polytechnic Institute and State University, Special Collections, Blacksburg, Virginia

WCL-UM University of Michigan, William L. Clements Library, Ann Arbor, Michigan

PREFACE

1. Hess, *Trench Warfare*, 205–53; Hess, *In the Trenches*, 280–316.

2. Connelly, *Autumn of Glory*, 361–90, 429–40; Stephen Davis, *Atlanta Will Fall*, ix–x; McMurry, "Policy So Disastrous," 223–48; McMurry, *John Bell Hood*, 118, 121, 123; McMurry, *Atlanta*, 49, 65, 180–89; McMurry, "Confederate Morale," 226–43; McNeill, "Survey of Confederate Soldier Morale," 1–25; Daniel, *Soldiering in the Army*, 140–46.

3. Hess, *Kennesaw Mountain*, 215–61; Hess, *Battle of Ezra Church*, 194–207.

CHAPTER 1

1. Castel, *Decision in the West*, 111–12.

2. Hess, *Civil War Infantry Tactics*, xx–xxi.

3. Ibid., 81–87, 103–61.

4. Ibid., xx–xxi.

5. Hess, *Kennesaw Mountain*, 1–27; Hess, *Battle of Ezra Church*, 1–10.

6. Hess, *Trench Warfare*, 205–16; Hess, *In the Trenches*, 280–85.

7. Timothy B. Smith, *Corinth, 1862*, 49–62.

8. Meadows, *Modern Georgia*, 1–3.

9. Poe to [Delafield], October 8, 1865, *OR*, 38(1):128–37.

10. W. E. Merrill, "Block-Houses," 456–58.

11. Foster, "Battle Field Maps," 369–70; Kundahl, *Confederate Engineer*, 302–3n; Nichols, *Confederate Engineers*, 88.

12. Mahan, *Treatise on Field Fortification*, 1–89; Hess, *Field Armies and Fortifications*, 1–11.

13. Taylor, *Orlando M. Poe*, 6–18, 31–129; Shiman, "Engineering Sherman's March," 281–82, 284, 288.

14. Poe to [Delafield], October 8, 1865, *OR*, 38(1):128; Shiman, "Engineering Sherman's March," 268n, 320.

15. Shiman, "Engineering Sherman's March," 244, 275; Gilbert Thompson, *Engineer Battalion*, 4, 43; J. C. Woodruff to W. P. Trowbridge, September 5, 1863, Letters Sent by the Chief of Engineers, NARA; Hickenlooper, "Our Volunteer Engineers," 304; Reese to Poe, September 14, 1864, *OR*, 38(3):67; returns, muster rolls, and company descriptive book, James R. Percy Service Record, NARA; Poe to [Delafield], October 8, 1865, *OR*, 38(1):128.

16. General Orders No. 10, Seventeenth Corps, August 2, 1864, *OR*, 38(5):338–39.

17. Reese to Poe, September 14, 1864, *OR*, 38(3):64–65, 68; diary, May 10, 1864, and Poe to wife, May 15, 1864, Orlando Metcalfe Poe Papers, LC; William Kossak Journal, June 16–19, 29, August 14, September 4, 12, 1864, WCL-UM; Table of Organization, Military Division of the Mississippi, and Poe to [Delafield], October 8, 1865, *OR*, 38(1):100, 128.

18. Poe to [Delafield], October 8, 1865, *OR*, 38(1):127–28.

19. Table of Organization, Department of the Cumberland, *OR*, 20(1):214–15; Table of Organization, Department of the Cumberland, *OR*, 30(1):169; Table of Organization, Department of the Cumberland, *OR*, 31(2):21; Shiman, "Engineering Sherman's March," 271–72; Table of Organization, Department of the Cumberland, *OR*, 32(3):550, 559.

20. Thomas to Stanton, June 1, 1864; Stanton to Thomas, June 2, 1864; and Special Field Orders No. 152, Headquarters, Department of the Cumberland, June 4, 1864, *OR*, 38(4):377, 385, 407; Circular, Headquarters, Department of the Cumberland, June 10, 1864, in *Nashville Daily Times and True Union*, July 27, 1864; Thienel, "Engineers in the Union Army," pt. 1, 37, and pt. 3, 115.

21. Neal, *Illustrated History*, 9, 142–45; Shiman, "Army Engineers," 36; Shiman, "Engineering Sherman's March," 244; Howard to Sherman, August 31, 1864, *OR*, 38(5):728.

22. Shiman, "Engineering Sherman's March," 278, 302; Shiman, "Sherman's Pioneers," 258–59; Table of Organization, Military Division of the Mississippi, *OR*, 38(1):111; Richard Delafield to C. W. Bennett, July 29, 1865, Letters Sent by the Chief of Engineers, NARA.

23. Sherman, *Memoirs*, 2:55, 400; Sherman to Thomas, June 26, 1864, in Simpson and Berlin, *Sherman's Civil War*, 658.

24. Shiman, "Sherman's Pioneers," 252, 254, 259.

25. Ibid., 256–57.

26. Gates, *Rough Side of War*, 191, 218, 242, 248; John K. Ely Diary, May 31, June 23, 30, 1864, JBC.

27. Shiman, "Sherman's Pioneers," 254–56; Hickenlooper, "Our Volunteer Engineers," 304; Reese to Poe, September 14, 1864, and Corse to Barnes, September 8, 1864, *OR*, 38(3):64, 408.

28. Shiman, "Engineering Sherman's March," 390.

29. Stewart, *Dan McCook's Regiment*, 101; White to Immell, September 9, 1864, and Goodspeed to Immell, September 7, 1864, *OR*, 38(1):495, 499; diary, June 23, 1864, Osterhaus Family Papers, MHM.

30. Bennett and Tillery, *Struggle for the Life*, 169; Dodge, "Reminiscences of Engineering Work," 457; William Kossak Journal, June 24, 1864, WCL-UM; Shiman, "Sherman's Pioneers," 265.

31. Shiman, "Sherman's Pioneers," 259–60; Cox to Schofield, May 26, 1864, *OR*, 38(4):320.

32. Willett, *Rambling Recollections*, 5; W. E. Merrill, "Block-Houses," 441, 443–47.

33. Orders No. 28, Headquarters, District of Tennessee, Office of Inspector of Fortifications, June 27, 1863, in *Nashville Daily Times and True Union*, July 27, 1864; W. E. Merrill, "Block-Houses," 452–53.

34. Kundahl, *Alexandria Goes to War*, 197–99; A. L. Rives to James A. Seddon, April 1, 1864, Letters and Telegrams, NARA.

35. Special Orders No. 170, Adjutant and Inspector General's Office, July 20, 1864, *OR*, 38(5):898; Warner, *Generals in Gray*, 282–83.

36. Martin L. Smith Diary, July 20–21, 28, August 1–2, 1864, Mary-HS; Special Field Orders No. 64, Army of Tennessee, August 1, 1864, *OR*, 38(5):940.

37. Shoup, "Dalton Campaign," 262.

38. E. A. Nisbet to Leroy P. Walker, April 23, 1861, George H. Hazlehurst Service Record, and summary of service, Thaddeus Coleman Service Record, NARA; Wiley, *Four Years*, 146, 198; Circular, Hood's Corps, June 28, 1864, *OR*, 38(4):805; Hood to Bragg, August 1, 1864, *OR*, 38(5):937; Kundahl, *Confederate Engineer*, 197, 199.

39. Special Orders No. 106, Adjutant and Inspector General's Office, May 6, 1864, *OR*, 38(4):671; Special Orders No. 183, Adjutant and Inspector General's Office, August 4, 1864, *OR*, 38(5):945; A. L. Rives to Stephen W. Presstman, May 23, 1864; A. L. Rives to D. W. Currie, May 23, 1864; A. L. Rives to Thomas E. Marble, May 24, 1864; A. L. Rives to Samuel Cooper, July 13, 1864; Jeremy F. Gilmer to Simon B. Buckner, August 6, 1864; and J. H. Alexander to Wilbur F. Foster, August 6, 1864, Letters and Telegrams, NARA.

40. Thomas M. Jack to James Cantey, June 5, 1864, Special Orders from May 9th 1864 to June 19th 1864, NARA; Jeremy F. Gilmer to Martin L. Smith, August 13, 1864, Letters and Telegrams, NARA.

41. Jeremy F. Gilmer to Stephen W. Presstman, June 19, 1863, and A. L. Rives to Stephen W. Presstman, September 9, 1863, May 24, July 16, 1864, Letters and Telegrams NARA; abstract of returns, Army of Tennessee, December 10, 1863, *OR*, 31(2):657; John Green to mother, June 28, 1864, Benjamin and John Green Letters, University of Virginia, Special Collections, Charlottesville, Virginia; Nichols, *Confederate Engineers*, 94–95, 97;

Robinson, "Confederate Engineers," 411; record of events, Companies A, D, E, Service Records of 3rd Confederate Engineers, NARA; Kundahl, *Confederate Engineer*, 161; Table of Organization, Army of Tennessee, and abstract of returns, Army of Tennessee, *OR*, 38(3):644, 675–76, 678–82.

42. A. L. Rives to Jeremy F. Gilmer, April 5, 1864, Letters and Telegrams, NARA.

43. [Shoup] to Conscript Authorities at Macon, July 29, 1864, *OR*, 38(5):930; R. H. Griffin to A. L. Rives, July 28, 1864, Letters and Telegrams, NARA.

44. Granbury to Milner, September 5, 1864, *OR*, 38(3):743–44; muster rolls, Mathew E. Ezell Service Record, NARA; Johnston, *Narrative of Military Operations*, 577.

45. Special Orders No. 96, Headquarters, Brown's Brigade, January 8, 1864, Orders and Circulars, NARA; Stewart to Ratchford, June 5, 1864, *OR*, 38(3):816; Wynne and Taylor, *This War So Horrible*, 34, 74; French, *Two Wars*, 201.

46. Isaac W. Smith to L. G. Gardner, May 4, 1864; Smith to George P. Macmurdo, May 31, 1864; A. L. Rives to Gardner, June 2, 1864; and Rives to J. W. Glenn, July 1, 1864, Letters and Telegrams, NARA.

47. Braley, "Battle of Gilgal Church," 36.

CHAPTER 2

1. Grant to Thomas, January 19, 1864, in Simon, *Papers of Ulysses S. Grant*, 10:46.

2. Grant to Halleck, February 12, 1864, and Grant to Thomas, February 12, 13, 24, 1864, in Simon, *Papers of Ulysses S. Grant*, 10:109, 115, 119, 151.

3. Johnston to Cooper, October 20, 1864, *OR*, 38(3):613; Castel, *Decision in the West*, 50.

4. Davis to [Norton], March 22, 1864, and Stewart to Wilson, February 28, 1864, *OR*, 32(1):456, 479; J. C. Thompson to A. P. Stewart, December 8, 1867, Joseph E. Johnston Papers, CWM; John S. Jackman Journal, February 23, 1864, LC.

5. Davis to [Norton], March 22, 1864; Cumming to Reeve, February 28, 1864; Pettus to Reeve, February 25, 1864; and Reynolds to Reeve, February 25, 1864, *OR*, 32(1):456–57, 482–83.

6. Johnston to Cooper, October 20, 1864, *OR*, 38(3):613; Stewart to Wilson, February 28, 1864, *OR*, 32(1):479; Castel, *Decision in the West*, 54; Stephen Davis, *Atlanta Will Fall*, 35; Connelly, *Autumn of Glory*, 327.

7. Castel, *Decision in the West*, 52.

8. Cruft to Norton, March 2, 1864; Kilgour to Preston, March 1, 1864; and Hurd to Preston, February 28, 1864, *OR*, 32(1):426, 437–38, 440; J. C. Thompson to A. P. Stewart, December 8, 1867, Joseph E. Johnston Papers, CWM.

9. Thomas's journal, April 7, 1864, *OR*, 32(3):282; "Autobiography of Edwin Hansford Rennolds, Sr.," 23, UTK; Stevenson to Ratchford, May 30, 1864, *OR*, 38(3):811; Norman D. Brown, *One of Cleburne's Command*, 71.

10. Sherman, *Memoirs*, 2:32; Castel, *Decision in the West*, 121, 123, 125.

11. Stephen Davis, *Atlanta Will Fall*, 34–35; field visit to Rocky Face Ridge, January 4, 1993; Claiborne diary, May 2, 1864, *SOR*, 116.

12. Castel, *Decision in the West*, 130.

13. Greene to Loughborough, June 2, 1864, *OR*, 38(3):847; Ferrell, *Holding the Line*, 183; William C. Davis, *Diary of a Confederate Soldier*, 119.

14. Byrne, *Uncommon Soldiers*, 137, 140.

15. Longacre and Haas, *To Battle for God*, 171; Sherman to Schofield, May 8, 1864, *OR*, 38(4):84; Partridge, *History of the Ninety-Sixth*, 307–8, 310; William C. Davis, *Diary of a Confederate Soldier*, 120; Castel, *Decision in the West*, 131, 140; field visit to Rocky Face Ridge, November 30, 1986.

16. Albert Smith statement, May 8, 1864, and Butterfield to Sherman, May 8, 1864, *OR*, 38(4):71–72, 79; J. C. Thompson to A. P. Stewart, December 8, 1867, Joseph E. Johnston Papers, CWM; Stewart to Ratchford, June 5, 1864, *OR*, 38(3):816; Wynne and Taylor, *This War So Horrible*, 34, 40, 57–58; Cate, *Two Soldiers*, 73.

17. Palmer to Thomas, May 9, 1864, *OR*, 38(4):91; Wynne and Taylor, *This War So Horrible*, 62.

18. Hood to Stewart, May 6, 1864, General Orders and Circulars, Hood's Corps, MOC; Stewart to Ratchford, June 5, 1864, *OR*, 38(3):816; Sherman to Ellen, May 22, 1864, in Simpson and Berlin, *Sherman's Civil War*, 638. For a modern photograph showing the profile of Mill Creek Gap, see Kelly, *Kennesaw Mountain*, 13.

19. Stevenson to Ratchford, May 30, 1864, *OR*, 38(3):811; Sherman to Schofield, May 9, 1864, and Schofield to Sherman, May 9, 1864, *OR*, 38(4):98–99; Cox, *Military Reminiscences*, 2:215–16; Castel, *Decision in the West*, 140.

20. Castel, *Decision in the West*, 132–34. For a modern photograph of Dug Gap, see McMurry, "Atlanta Campaign," 16.

21. Geary to Perkins, May 9, 1864, *OR*, 38(4):93–94; Bushbeck to Elliott, May 14, 1864; Jackson to Brown, May 9, 1864; and Warner to Mindil, September 8, 1864, *OR*, 38(2):203, 238, 246; Pierson, "From Chattanooga to Atlanta," 334; George G. Truair to father, May 9, 1864, Truair Family Papers, UTA.

22. Cleburne to Hardee, August 16, 1864, and Lester to Whitehead, May 30, 1864, *OR*, 38(3):721, 829; Norman D. Brown, *One of Cleburne's Command*, 72; Breckinridge, "Opening of the Atlanta Campaign," 278; Geary to Perkins, May 10, 1864, *OR*, 38(4):116; field visits to Dug Gap, November 30, 1986, and January 4, 1993. For a modern photograph of the rock breastworks at Dug Gap, probably the reconstructed segment, see McMurry, "Atlanta Campaign," 10. Harvard archaeologist Philip E. Smith studied the rock breastworks at Dug Gap in 1956, ignored local reports that they had been constructed during the Civil War, and even argued that they were not military artifacts of any kind. He stated that their construction in the war was "not corroborated by historical sources," but the *OR* offers indisputable proof that the Confederates built them on the evening of May 8. See Smith, "Aboriginal Stone Constructions," 20.

23. Sherman to McPherson, May 10, 1864, *OR*, 38(4):125; Hickenlooper, "Reminiscences," 48, USAMHI; Castel, *Decision in the West*, 135–38; field visit to Snake Creek Gap, January 5, 1993.

24. McPherson to Sherman, May 9, 1864, *OR*, 38(4):106; Hickenlooper, "Reminiscences," 49, USAMHI; Castel, *Decision in the West*, 141–44.

25. Sherman to McPherson, May 10, 1864; McPherson to Sherman, May 10, 1864; and Special Field Orders Nos. 5 and 6, Headquarters, Department and Army of the Tennessee, May 10, 11, 1864, *OR*, 38(4):125–26, 132, 145; Reese to Poe, September 14, 1864, *OR*, 38(3):64; Hickenlooper, "Reminiscences," 49–50, USAMHI.

26. Whipple to Palmer, May 10, 1864, and Circular, Headquarters, Third Division, Twentieth Corps, May 11, 1864, *OR*, 38(4):115, 145; Byrne, *Uncommon Soldiers*, 143; Holzhueter, "William Wallace's Civil War Letters," 94; Sherman, *Memoirs*, 2:34.

27. Castel, *Decision in the West*, 145–51; Elmore to parents, June 1, 1864, Day Elmore Letters, CHM; John K. Ely Diary, May 13, 1864, JBC; Gates, *Rough Side of War*, 198; Reinhart, *Two Germans*, 109; John H. Tilford Diary, May 13, 1864, Filson Historical Society, Louisville, Kentucky; diary, May 13, 1864, Daniel Wait Howe Papers, IHS; Sherman to Howard, May 13, 1864, *OR*, 38(4):163.

28. Mackall to Cantey, May 10, 1864, *OR*, 38(4):687, 702–3; West to Loring and Cantey, May 12, 1864, Special Orders from May 9th 1864 to June 19th 1864, NARA; field visit to Resaca, May 12, 2006.

29. Loring to West, June 1, 1864, *OR*, 38(3):874–75; Crowson and Brogden, *Bloody Banners*, 65; Bate to not stated, [July] 30, 1864, *SOR*, 92; Hall, "History of Company C," in Fleming, *Band of Brothers*, 64; "Autobiography of Edwin Hansford Rennolds, Sr.," UTK; Jill K. Garrett, *Confederate Diary*, 63.

30. Castel, *Decision in the West*, 152, 154, 156; Special Field Orders No. 7, Headquarters, Department and Army of the Tennessee, May 12, 1864, *OR*, 38(4):160.

31. William C. Davis, *Diary of a Confederate Soldier*, 122–23; Ed Porter Thompson, *History of the Orphan Brigade*, 245; journal of operations, Army of Tennessee, *OR*, 38(3):979.

32. Walthall to Wilson, June 2, 1864, *OR*, 38(3):795–96.

33. Castel, *Decision in the West*, 156, 159–62; Bate to not stated, [July] 30, 1864, *SOR*, 92–93; Walthall to Wilson, June 2, 1864, *OR*, 38(3):796; Secrist, *Battle of Resaca*, 25–26; Joyce, "A Hot May-Day at Resaca," 500.

34. McKelvaine to Sykes, [May 19, 1864], *OR*, 38(3):801; Ed Porter Thompson, *History of the Orphan Brigade*, 245; Archie Livingston to sisters, May 29, 1864, MOC; Inglis to cousin, May 28, 1864, MOC.

35. Walthall to Wilson, June 2, 1864; Brantley to Sykes, May 30, 1864; and Benton to Sykes, May 30, 1864, *OR*, 38(3):796–97, 805, 809; Secrist, *Battle of Resaca*, 28; William C. Davis, *Diary of a Confederate Soldier*, 124; McMurry, "Atlanta Campaign," 48, 51.

36. Walthall to Wilson, June 2, 1864, and Benton to Sykes, May 30, 1864, *OR*, 38(3):796, 809; William C. Davis, *Diary of a Confederate Soldier*, 124.

37. Castel, *Decision in the West*, 163–66; Stevenson to Ratchford, May 30, 1864, and Welch to Macon, May 29, 1864, *OR*, 38(3):812, 839; C. J. H. account in *Memphis Daily Appeal*, May 25, 1864, *SOR*, 112–13; Simonson to Bridges, June 9, 1864, *OR*, 38(1):488–89.

38. Castel, *Decision in the West*, 166–68, 173; Secrist, *Battle of Resaca*, 19; Reese to Poe, September 14, 1864; Smith to Smith, May 22, 1864; and Rice quoted in Mott to assistant adjutant general, First Brigade, Second Division, Fifteenth Corps, September 9, 1864, *OR*, 38(3):64, 191, 214.

39. Hall, "History of Company C," in Fleming, *Band of Brothers*, 66.

40. "Autobiography of Edwin Hansford Rennolds, Sr.," 24, UTK; William C. Davis, *Diary of a Confederate Soldier*, 124; Walthall to Wilson, June 2, 1864, *OR*, 38(3):797.

41. Sherman to Halleck, May 14, 1864; Butterfield to Wood, May 14, 1864; and Sherman to Thomas, May 15, 1864, *OR*, 38(4):173, 179, 190; Castel, *Decision in the West*, 181.

42. Castel, *Decision in the West*, 169.

43. Bate to not stated, [July] 30, 1864, *SOR*, 92–93; William C. Davis, *Diary of a Confederate Soldier*, 124; Kirwan, *Johnny Green*, 129; Hall, "History of Company C," in Fleming, *Band of Brothers*, 67.

44. Walthall to Wilson, June 2, 1864, and McKelvaine to Sykes, [May 19, 1864], *OR*, 38(3):797, 801–2.

45. Castel, *Decision in the West*, 173–74.

46. Johnston, *Narrative of Military Operations*, 313; Hood to Johnston, no date, 1864, and Stevenson to Ratchford, May 30, 1864, *OR*, 38(3):761, 812; Secrist, *Battle of Resaca*, 58; Cobham to Elliott, May 21, 1864, and Case to Grubbs, September 22, 1864, *OR*, 38(2):277, 366; C. J. H. account in *Memphis Daily Appeal*, May 25, 1864, *SOR*, 113; field visit to Resaca, May 12, 2006. While Johnston reported that the Cherokee Battery was positioned eighty yards in front of the Confederate line, Federal reports noted that it was about thirty yards. The emplacement is well preserved on private land today, and a field visit by the author confirmed that it was about thirty yards in front of the main line.

47. Barnum to Forbes, September 11, 1864; Cobham to Elliott, May 21, 1864; Case to Grubbs, September 22, 1864; and Harrison to Ward, May 20, 1864, *OR*, 38(2):272, 277, 366, 371; Reyburn and Wilson, *"Jottings from Dixie,"* 214–15; C. J. H. account in *Memphis Daily Appeal*, May 25, 1864, *SOR*, 113; Castel, *Decision in the West*, 175.

48. C. J. H. account in *Memphis Daily Appeal*, May 25, 1864, *SOR*, 113; Stevenson to Ratchford, May 30, 1864, *OR*, 38(3):812.

49. Stewart to Ratchford, June 5, 1864, *OR*, 38(3):817; Castel, *Decision in the West*, 176–78.

50. Stevenson to Ratchford, May 30, 1864, *OR*, 38(3):813.

51. Buckingham to Speed, July 31, 1864, and Shirer to Cobham, May 20, 1864, *OR*, 38(2):165, 456; Buckingham to wife, May 22, 1864, Philo Beecher Buckingham Papers, American Antiquarian Society, Worcester, Massachusetts; Fenton, "From the Rapidan to Atlanta," 496; Kilpatrick, "Fifth Ohio Infantry," 249–51; field visit to Resaca, May 12, 2006.

52. Warner to Mendil, September 8, 1864, and Riedt to Brown, May 22, 1864, *OR*, 38(2):248, 255; Kilpatrick, "Fifth Ohio Infantry," 251–52.

53. Buckingham to wife, May 19, 22, 1864, Philo Beecher Buckingham Papers, American Antiquarian Society, Worcester, Massachusetts; Castel, *Decision in the West*, 179; Bailey, *Battles for Atlanta*, 47.

54. Morgan, "Home Letters," 208, AHC.

55. Reese to Poe, September 14, 1864, *OR*, 38(3):64.

56. Hood to Johnston, no date, 1864, and Stevenson to Ratchford, May 30, 1864, *OR*, 38(3):761, 813; Castel, *Decision in the West*, 179; William C. Davis, *Diary of a Confederate Soldier*, 125.

57. Castel, *Decision in the West*, 188; Walthall to Wilson, June 2, 1864, and Loring to West, June 1, 1864, *OR*, 38(3):797, 875.

58. Nichol to father, May 21, 1864, David Nichol Papers, USAMHI; diary, May 16, 1864, Daniel Wait Howe Papers, IHS; Josiah C. Williams diary, May 16, 1864, Worthington Williams Papers, IHS.

59. Sherman to Halleck, May 16, 1864, *OR*, 38(4):201; Johnston, "Opposing Sherman's Advance," 266; Haughton, *Training, Tactics and Leadership*, 151. One Federal observer later reported seeing abatis, palisades, a bombproof, and a bastioned fort in the Confederate line at Resaca, but there is no concurring evidence to support this contention. See Gould and Kennedy, *Memoirs of a Dutch Mudsill*, 246.

60. Geary to Perkins, September 15, 1864, *OR*, 38(2):118.

CHAPTER 3

1. Connelly, *Autumn of Glory*, 344–45; field visit to Calhoun, Adairsville, Kingston, and Cassville, April 14, 1994; William C. Davis, *Diary of a Confederate Soldier*, 126; Wynne and Taylor, *This War So Horrible*, 72, 74.

2. Castel, *Decision in the West*, 192, 194, 196; Cunyus, *History of Bartow County*, 221; Cleburne to Hardee, August 16, 1864, *OR*, 38(3):723.

3. Cleburne to Hardee, August 16, 1864, *OR*, 38(3):723; Connelly, *Autumn of Glory*, 344; Castel, *Decision in the West*, 195.

4. Dodge to Rawlins, February 26, 1864, *OR*, 32(2):476–77; Davis to McClurg, September, no date, 1864, *OR*, 38(1):628; Castel, *Decision in the West*, 198.

5. Kirwan, *Johnny Green*, 130; Thomas B. Mackall journal (McMurry transcript), May 19, 1864, Joseph E. Johnston Papers, CWM; General Orders, Headquarters, Army of Tennessee, May 19, 1864, *OR*, 38(4):728; William C. Davis, *Diary of a Confederate Soldier*, 127; Journal of Operations, Army of Tennessee, May 19, 1864, *OR*, 38(3):984.

6. Castel, *Decision in the West*, 200–202; Scaife, "Waltz between the Rivers," 284–86; Thomas B. Mackall journal (McMurry transcript), May 19, 1864, Joseph E. Johnston Papers, CWM.

7. Thomas B. Mackall journal (McMurry transcript), May 19, 1864, Joseph E. Johnston Papers, CWM; Castel, *Decision in the West*, 203; Connelly, *Autumn of Glory*, 345, 348; Johnston, *Narrative of Military Operations*, 322; Johnston to Cooper, October 20, 1864, *OR*, 38(3):616.

8. Johnston, *Narrative of Military Operations*, 322; Cunyus, *History of Bartow County*, 228–29, 233; field visit to Cassville, November 27, 1992; "Map Showing Approximate Position," NARA; Cartersville and White West Quadrant Map, U.S. Department of the Interior; *Atlas to Accompany the Official Records*, plate 62, no. 7.

9. Cleburne to Hardee, August 16, 1864, and Benton to Sykes, May 30, 1864, *OR*, 38(3):723, 810; Anderson, *Memoirs*, 388; Wynne and Taylor, *This War So Horrible*, 74; J. C. Thompson to A. P. Stewart, December 8, 1867, Joseph E. Johnston Papers, CWM; Tower, *Carolinian Goes to War*, 186; W. H. Brooker Diary, May 19, 1864, RU; French, *Two Wars*, 371; Johnston, *Narrative of Military Operations*, 322.

10. Cartersville and White West Quadrant Map, U.S. Department of the Interior; French, *Two Wars*, 196, 379–80; Walter J. Morris to William W. Polk, June 25, 1878, Leonidas Polk Papers, US; Hood, *Advance and Retreat*, 112. Wilbur G. Kurtz has argued that Hood's left wing actually went forward rather than to the rear compared to Polk's line, but there is no support for that contention. See Cunyus, *History of Bartow County*, 230, 233, and McMurry, "Cassville," 9.

11. Hood to Cooper, February 15, 1865, *OR*, 38(3):635; Johnston, *Narrative of Military Operations*, 323; McMurry, "Cassville," 45; Scaife, "Waltz between the Rivers," map between 284 and 285, 288, 293. In his memoirs, Hood contended that he told Johnston that as much as a quarter of a mile of his corps line was dangerously enfiladed by the Federal guns. Johnston, according to Hood, responded "that the troops could not hope to be always sheltered from fire, and that they must make the best of it by traversing." See Hood, *Advance and Retreat*, 105.

12. Walter J. Morris to William W. Polk, June 25, 1878, Leonidas Polk Papers, US.

13. Returns: Alfred L. Rives to Samuel Cooper, November 18, 1863; and James Nocquet

to Jeremy F. Gilmer, March 12, 1863, Walter J. Morris Service Record, NARA; Alfred L. Rives to Leonidas Polk, February 2, 1864, Letters and Telegrams, NARA.

14. Walter J. Morris to William W. Polk, June 25, 1878, Leonidas Polk Papers, US. Morris's letter has also been printed in several venues. See Polk, *Leonidas Polk*, 2:376–82; Hood *Advance and Retreat*, 110–16; and *SOR*, 133–39.

15. Cartersville and White West Quadrant Map, U.S. Department of the Interior. For the Morris map see *Atlas to Accompany the Official Records*, plate 62, no. 7; and Hood, *Advance and Retreat*, between 112 and 113.

16. Sherman, *Memoirs*, 2:38; Padgett, "With Sherman through Georgia," 291; Thomas B. Mackall journal (McMurry transcript), May 19, 1864, Joseph E. Johnston Papers, CWM; Scaife, "Waltz between the Rivers," 287.

17. Field visit to Cassville, November 27, 1992; Scaife, "Waltz between the Rivers," 287.

18. Scaife, "Waltz between the Rivers," map between 284 and 285; French, *Two Wars*, 196; Simonson to Bridges, June 9, 1864, and White to Immell, September 9, 1864, *OR*, 38(1):489, 495; Castel, *Decision in the West*, 203–4.

19. Hood, *Advance and Retreat*, 105–6; McMurry, "Cassville," 45; Tower, *Carolinian Goes to War*, 186–87; French, *Two Wars*, 379; French to Polk, May 31, 1864, *OR*, 38(3):899.

20. Polk, *Leonidas Polk*, 2:356–57; Johnston, *Narrative of Military Operations*, 323–24; Walter J. Morris to William W. Polk, June 25, 1878, Leonidas Polk Papers, US; French, *Two Wars*, 198; Hood, *Advance and Retreat*, 106, 108; Johnston to Cooper, October 20, 1864, and Hood to Cooper, February 15, 1865, *OR*, 38(3):616, 635. The anonymous author of an article published in the New Orleans *Picayune* in October 1893 annoyed French by trying to fix the blame for the retreat from Cassville on him. See French, *Two Wars*, 198, 367–70, 372–75, 378–80.

21. French, *Two Wars*, 198, 375.

22. Tower, *Carolinian Goes to War*, 187; Hafendorfer, *Civil War Journal*, 148; diary, May 20, 1864, Daniel Harris Reynolds Papers, UAF; Walter J. Morris to William W. Polk, June 25, 1878, Leonidas Polk Papers, US; French, *Two Wars*, 198; Castel, *Decision in the West*, 206, 208.

23. Poe diary, May 21, 1864, Orlando Metcalfe Poe Papers, LC; Thomas to Sherman, May 20, 1864, *OR*, 38(4):263; Quaife, *From the Cannon's Mouth*, 311; Partridge, *History of the Ninety-Sixth*, 339; Padgett, "With Sherman through Georgia," 291.

24. Sherman, *Memoirs*, 2:39–41.

25. Castel, *Decision in the West*, 204–6, 590n; McMurry, *Atlanta*, 82–83; Hood, *Advance and Retreat*, 106–8; McMurry, "Atlanta Campaign," 56; McMurry, "Cassville," 47–48.

26. Polk, *Leonidas Polk*, 2:357; Johnston to Cooper, October 20, 1864, *OR*, 38(3):616; French, *Two Wars*, 381.

27. Cleburne to Hardee, August 16, 1864, *OR*, 38(3):724. I found faint remnants of Confederate works on top of the ridge, just south of the junction of Hood's and Polk's commands. The trench was on the natural crest of the ridgetop, atop the middle peak of three that lay between Mac Johnson Road on the north and Jewell Road on the south. This line ran only a short distance down the northern side of the middle peak, and it had a refused segment on the right extending about ten yards to the rear. Field visit to Cassville, July 8, 1987.

28. Thomas B. Mackall journal (McMurry transcript), May 20, 1864, Joseph E. Johnston Papers, CWM; "Personal Biography of Major General Grenville Mellen Dodge 1831–1870,"

1:211, Grenville Mellen Dodge Papers, State Historical Society of Iowa, Des Moines, Iowa; field visit to Cassville and Cartersville, April 14, 1994; Connelly, *Autumn of Glory*, 353.

29. Reese to Poe, September 14, 1864, *OR*, 38(3):64; Special Field Orders No. 11, Headquarters, Military Division of the Mississippi, May 22, 1864, *OR*, 38(4):288.

30. Field visit to Allatoona, April 14, 1994; Sherman to Ellen, May 20, 22, 1864, in Simpson and Berlin, *Sherman's Civil War*, 638–39.

CHAPTER 4

1. Castel, *Decision in the West*, 217–18.

2. Sherman, *Memoirs*, 2:42; Sherman to Grant, July 12, 1864, *OR*, 38(5):123; Speed to parents, June 5, 1864, Thomas Speed Papers, Filson Historical Society, Louisville, Kentucky; Howard, *Autobiography*, 1:542–43; Howard, "Struggle for Atlanta," 306; William Alan Blair, *Politician Goes to War*, 185. Connelly argues in *Autumn of Glory* (353–54) that the terrain south of the Etowah favored Sherman because the road system tended to allow him lines of advance to bypass Confederate positions. But the road system favored Sherman in this way everywhere during the Atlanta campaign; moving large masses of troops along roads through a terrain with lots of choking vegetation was the real problem.

3. Castel, *Decision in the West*, 219–21.

4. Stewart to Ratchford, June 5, 1864; Thomas to Whitehead, May 29, 1864; Clayton to Hatcher, May 29, 1864; Wemyss to [Clayton], June, no date, 1864; Welch to Macon, May 29, 1864; and Greene to Loughborough, June 2, 1864, *OR*, 38(3):818, 828, 833, 838, 840, 848; Stewart to A. J. Kellar, May 31, 1864, Alexander Peter Stewart Letter, UGA; Johnston, *Narrative of Military Operations*, 328; Castel, *Decision in the West*, 221; Blomquist and Taylor, *This Cruel War*, 252; J. C. Thompson to A. P. Stewart, December 8, 1867, Joseph E. Johnston Papers, CWM.

5. Tower, *Carolinian Goes to War*, 188–89.

6. Castel, *Decision in the West*, 223, 225–26; Howard, *Autobiography*, 1:545, 548; J. C. Thompson to A. P. Stewart, December 8, 1867, Joseph E. Johnston Papers, CWM; Quaife, *From the Cannon's Mouth*, 312; Bohrnstedt, *Soldiering with Sherman*, 100; Ario Pardee Jr. to Pa, June 8, 1864, Pardee-Robison Family Papers, USAMHI; Stewart to Ratchford, June 5, 1864, and Welch to Macon, May 29, 1864, *OR*, 38(3):818, 840.

7. Rogers to Palmer, September 7, 1864; Kilpatrick to Creigh, June 9, 1864; and White to Creigh, September 8, 1864, *OR*, 38(2):48, 167, 182; Pierson, "From Chattanooga to Atlanta," 340; Bauer, *Soldiering*, 118; Merrell, "Personal Memoirs of the Civil War," LMU.

8. Wemyss to [Clayton], June, no date, 1864, and Greene to Loughborough, June 2, 1864, *OR*, 38(3):838, 848; Little and Maxwell, *History of Lumsden's Battery*, 39–40.

9. Castel, *Decision in the West*, 229.

10. Cleburne to Hardee, August 16, 1864, *OR*, 38(3):724; Jill K. Garrett, *Confederate Diary*, 65; Howard, *Autobiography*, 1:551; Castel, *Decision in the West*, 229.

11. Howard, *Autobiography*, 1:553; J. Litton Bostick to sister, June 14, 1864, Bostick Papers, TSLA; Cleburne to Hardee, August 16, 1864, *OR*, 38(3):724; Hazen, *Narrative of Military Service*, 257; Castel, *Decision in the West*, 233, 235, 237.

12. Norman D. Brown, *One of Cleburne's Command*, 85; Cleburne to Hardee, August 16, 1864, *OR*, 38(3):724; Ridley Wills, *Old Enough to Die*, 125; B. F. Grady to editor, February 20, 1902, B. F. Grady Letter, DU.

13. J. Litton Bostick to Bettie, May 31, 1864, Bostick Papers, TSLA; Cleburne to Hardee, August 16, 1864, *OR*, 38(3):725; Buck, *Cleburne and His Command*, 219.

14. Bierce, "Crime at Pickett's Mill," 291; Dean, "Forgotten 'Hell Hole,'" 360–61; Hazen, *Narrative of Military Service*, 257–58.

15. Sherman to Schofield, May 27, 1864, *OR*, 38(4):326; Howard, *Autobiography*, 1:551; Dean, "Forgotten 'Hell Hole,'" 369, 371; Castel, *Decision in the West*, 239.

16. Dean, "Forgotten 'Hell Hole,'" 362, 366, 371; Noe, *Southern Boy in Blue*, 292; Wagner, "Recollections of an Enlistee," 123, USAMHI; Castel, *Decision in the West*, 239.

17. Dean, "Forgotten 'Hell Hole,'" 362; Cleburne to Hardee, August 16, 1864, *OR*, 38(3):725; Castel, *Decision in the West*, 237.

18. Gates, *Rough Side of War*, 205; Partridge, *History of the Ninety-Sixth*, 346–47.

19. Partridge, *History of the Ninety-Sixth*, 347–48.

20. Geary to Perkins, May 27, 1864, and Butterfield to Hooker, May 27, 1864, *OR*, 38(4):325; W. H. Brooker Diary, May 27, 1864, RU.

21. Cleburne to Hardee, August 16, 1864, *OR*, 38(3):725–26; Norman D. Brown, *One of Cleburne's Command*, 85–86; Noe, *Southern Boy in Blue*, 293; Dean, "Forgotten 'Hell Hole,'" 364.

22. Cleburne to Hardee, August 16, 1864, *OR*, 38(3):726; Castel, *Decision in the West*, 241; J. Litton Bostick to Bettie, May 31, 1864, and Bostick to sister, June 14, 1864, Bostick Papers, TSLA; Norman D. Brown, *One of Cleburne's Command*, 88.

23. Sherman, *Memoirs*, 2:43; Sherman to McPherson, May 27, 1864, and McPherson to Sherman, May 27, 1864, *OR*, 38(4):326–27.

24. Special Field Orders No. 8, Headquarters, Left Wing, Sixteenth Corps, May 27, 1864, *OR*, 38(4):330; Hardee to Joseph E. Johnston, April 10, 1867, Hardee Family Papers, ADAH; Castel, *Decision in the West*, 242–43.

25. Bate to not stated, [July] 30, 1864, *SOR*, 95, 97; Castel, *Decision in the West*, 243–44.

26. J. A. Bigger Memoir, May 28, 1864, UM; Bate to not stated, [July] 30, 1864, *SOR*, 95–98; Castel, *Decision in the West*, 244–46.

27. Bate to not stated, [July] 30, 1864, *SOR*, 95–98; J. D. account, May 31, 1864, in *Memphis Daily Appeal*, June 9, 1864, *SOR*, 96, 109–10; William C. Davis, *Diary of a Confederate Soldier*, 132–33; Ed Porter Thompson, *History of the Orphan Brigade*, 255; Bennett and Tillery, *Struggle for the Life*, 164; diary, May 28, 1864, Abraham J. Seay Collection, UO; Capron, "War Diary," 381; Sherman to Halleck, May 29, 1864, *OR*, 38(4):343.

28. Thomas B. Mackall journal (McMurry transcript), May 31, 1864, Joseph E. Johnston Papers, CWM; Bennett and Tillery, *Struggle for the Life*, 164; Castel, *Decision in the West*, 246–47.

29. Hickenlooper, "Reminiscences" 52, USAMHI. Special Field Orders No. 9, Headquarters, Left Wing, Sixteenth Corps, May 28, 1864, *OR*, 38(4):342.

30. Reese to Poe, September 14, 1864, *OR*, 38(3):65; Bennett and Tillery, *Struggle for the Life*, 165; William C. Davis, *Diary of a Confederate Soldier*, 133–34; Jill K. Garrett, *Confederate Diary*, 66; Kirwan, *Johnny Green*, 134; Bate to not stated, [July] 30, 1864, *SOR*, 99; Castel, *Decision in the West*, 250.

31. Reese to Poe, September 14, 1864, *OR*, 38(3):65; Castel, *Decision in the West*, 251; Hickenlooper, "Reminiscences," 52, USAMHI.

32. Castel, *Decision in the West*, 247; Sherman, *Memoirs*, 2:45.

33. Sherman, *Memoirs*, 2:45; Padgett, "With Sherman through Georgia," 292; Pierson, "From Chattanooga to Atlanta," 340; Reyburn and Wilson, "*Jottings from Dixie*," 220; Ario Pardee Jr. to Pa, June 8, 1864, Pardee-Robison Family Papers, USAMHI; Cobham to Elliott, June 8, 1864, *OR*, 38(2):280; Fergus Elliott Diary, May 31, 1864, USAMHI; Wemyss to [Clayton], June, no date, 1864, *OR*, 38(3):838.

34. Geary to Perkins, September 15, 1864, *OR*, 38(2):124–25; Collins, *Memoirs of the 149th Regiment*, 260; Crowson and Brogden, *Bloody Banners*, 70–71.

35. Merrell, "Personal Memoirs of the Civil War," LMU; Dacus, *Reminiscences*, not paginated.

36. Greene to Loughborough, June 2, 1864, *OR*, 38(3):848–49.

37. Clayton diary, May 26–27, 1864, Henry De Lamar Clayton Papers, University of Alabama, William Stanley Hoole Special Collections, Tuscaloosa, Alabama; Pierson, "From Chattanooga to Atlanta," 340–41; Ario Pardee Jr. to Pa, June 8, 1864, Pardee-Robison Family Papers, USAMHI.

38. John Mitchell Davidson to Julia, June 4, 1864, Davidson Family Collection, AHC; French, *Two Wars*, 199.

39. Partridge, *History of the Ninety-Sixth*, 348–49; Gates, *Rough Side of War*, 205–6.

40. Little to Lizzie, June 7, 1864, Alexander C. Little Papers, CHM; field visits to Dallas, November 23, 1990, and April 14, 1994; Winther, *With Sherman to the Sea*, 109–10.

41. Bate to not stated, [July] 30, 1864, *SOR*, 99; Kirwan, *Johnny Green*, 134; William C. Davis, *Diary of a Confederate Soldier*, 132, 134.

42. General Field Orders, Headquarters, Hardee's Corps, May 31, 1864, *OR*, 38(4):751.

43. Hughes, *Civil War Memoir*, 182–83; Charles D. Gammon Diary, June 1, 1864, EU.

44. Smyth to Shields, June 6, 1864, *OR*, 38(3):162–63.

45. James G. Marston Diary, May 31, June 1–4, 1864, LSU.

46. Reese to Poe, September 14, 1864, *OR*, 38(3):65; Castel, *Decision in the West*, 251–52, 255–56.

47. Jackman, "From Dalton to Atlanta," 452; Hughes, *Civil War Memoir*, 185.

48. Charles W. Wills, *Army Life*, 253–54; Winther, *With Sherman to the Sea*, 112; Castel, *Decision in the West*, 256–57.

49. Sherman to Halleck, June 2, 1864; Sherman to Thomas, June 2, 1864; and French to Polk, June 2, 1864, *OR*, 38(4):385–86, 755.

50. Crowson and Brogden, *Bloody Banners*, 72; French, *Two Wars*, 201; Reese to Poe, September 14, 1864, *OR*, 38(3):65; Charles W. Wills, *Army Life*, 254.

51. Lovell to Johnston, May 31, 1864, and Johnston to Brown, June 4, 1864, *OR*, 38(4):749, 758; Castel, *Decision in the West*, 257–58.

52. Reese to Poe, September 14, 1864, *OR*, 38(3):65; Circular, Headquarters, Army of the Mississippi, June 4, 1864; and Special Orders, Headquarters, French's Division, June 4, 1864, *OR*, 38(4):758–59; Castel, *Decision in the West*, 259.

53. John Mitchell Davidson to Julia, June 4–6, 1864, Davidson Family Collection, AHC; French, *Two Wars*, 201; Walter A. Rorer to cousin, June 9, 1864, James M. Willcox Papers, DU; James G. Marston Diary, June 4–5, 1864, LSU; John C. Brown Diary, June 5, 1864, University of Iowa, Special Collections, Iowa City, Iowa.

54. Charles W. Wills, *Army Life*, 254–55; Bronson, "Recollections," 40, TC.

55. Sherman to Halleck, June 5, 1864, *OR*, 38(4):408.

CHAPTER 5

1. Castel, *Decision in the West*, 255, 257; Padgett, "With Sherman through Georgia," 292; Robert and Company, "Allatoona Battlefield Master Preservation Plan," 26.

2. Sherman, *Memoirs*, 2:50–51; Special Field Orders No. 20, Headquarters, Military Division of the Mississippi, June 6, 1864, *OR*, 38(4):427.

3. Poe diary, June 7–8, 1864, Orlando Metcalfe Poe Papers, LC; Poe to [Sherman], June 8, 1864, *OR*, 38(4):433–34; Malmborg to Cox, June 21, 1864, *OR*, 38(3):559.

4. Malmborg to Cox, June 21, 1864, *OR*, 38(3):559; Rogers to Cadle, June 27, 1864, *OR*, 38(4):624; Barnard, *Photographic Views*, nos. 28, 29.

5. Malmborg to Cox, June 21, 1864, *OR*, 38(3):559; Hobart L. Morris, *One Year at War*, 89–91; Barnard, *Photographic Views*, nos. 23, 24.

6. Alexander to Gresham, June 6, 1864; McPherson to Blair, June 7, 1864; and Special Field Orders No. 22, Headquarters, Military Division of the Mississippi, June 10, 1864, *OR*, 38(4):425, 431, 453; Jenkin Lloyd Jones, *Artilleryman's Diary*, 229–30; Castel, *Decision in the West*, 214, 264–66.

7. Shiman, "Engineering Sherman's March," 506–39.

8. Rousseau to Whipple, May 12, 13, 1864, *OR*, 38(4):154–55, 167–68; Shiman, "Engineering Sherman's March," 522–24.

9. Burroughs to Whipple, June 29, 1864, *OR*, 38(4):639–40; Shiman, "Engineering Sherman's March," 339, 341, 344.

10. Burroughs to Whipple, June 29, 1864, *OR*, 38(4):640.

11. Switzer, *Ohio Volunteer*, 173.

12. Sherman to Ellen, June 9, 1864; Sherman to Halleck, June 5, 1864; and Sherman to John Sherman, June 9, 1864, in Simpson and Berlin, *Sherman's Civil War*, 643, 644n, 645.

13. Thornton report, June 8, 1864, and Sherman to Halleck, June 13, 1864, *OR*, 38(4):437, 466.

14. Castel, *Decision in the West*, 267.

15. Ibid., 267, 269, 273; Braley, "Battle of Gilgal Church," 6; Johnson and Hartshorn, "Development of Field Fortification," 593. In *Atlanta* (103), Richard McMurry calls the Mountain Line the First Kennesaw Line.

16. Special Field Orders No. 21, Headquarters, Military Division of the Mississippi, June 9, 1864, and Schofield to Sherman, June 10, 1864, *OR*, 38(4):445, 451; Sherman to John Sherman, June 9, 1864, in Simpson and Berlin, *Sherman's Civil War*, 645; Castel, *Decision in the West*, 267.

17. Malmborg to Cox, June 21, 1864, *OR*, 38(3):559–60.

18. Field visits to Lost Mountain, January 31, 1987, and April 15, 1994; French, *Two Wars*, 201; James G. Marston diary, June 6–7, 1864, Henry Marston Family Papers, LSU; diary, June 6–8, 1864, Daniel Harris Reynolds Papers, UAF; Fryman, "Fortifying the Landscape," 54.

19. Bate to not stated, [July] 30, 1864, *SOR*, 99; Johnston, *Narrative of Military Operations*, 336; Gates, *Rough Side of War*, 288; William C. Davis, *Diary of a Confederate Soldier*, 137; Barnard, *Photographic Views*, no. 30; Pierson, "From Chattanooga to Atlanta," 345; field visit to Pine Mountain, January 30, 1987.

20. French, *Two Wars*, 201; French to Jack, June 8, 1864, *OR*, 38(4):764; Anderson, *Memoirs*, 388.

21. Thomas J. Jack to W. J. Morris, June 9, 1864, Special Orders from May 9th 1864 to June 19 1864, NARA; Mackall to Wright, June 10, 1864, *OR*, 38(4):767.

22. Gould and Kennedy, *Memoirs of a Dutch Mudsill*, 258–59.

23. Jackson, *Colonel's Diary*, 130; Little and Maxwell, *History of Lumsden's Battery*, 41; Hamilton M. Branch to mother, June 16, 1864, Branch Family Papers, UGA.

24. Johnston to Polk, June 13, 1864, and Polk to Johnston, June 13, 1864, *OR*, 38(4):772–73; Polk, *Leonidas Polk*, 2:370–71; Polk to Johnston, June 13, 1864, Special Orders from May 9th 1864 to June 19th 1864, NARA.

25. Mackall to Polk, June 13, 1864, *OR*, 38(4):773; Thomas B. Mackall journal (McMurry transcript), June 13–15, 1864, Joseph E. Johnston Papers, CWM; Circular, Headquarters, Army of the Mississippi, June 13, 1864, Special Orders from May 9th 1864 to June 19th 1864, NARA.

26. Hampton journal, *OR*, 38(3):707–8; Castel, *Decision in the West*, 275–76, 278; Polk, *Leonidas Polk*, 2:372–74; James G. Marston diary, June 14, 1864, Henry Marston Family Papers, LSU.

27. Sherman to Ellen, June 12, 1864, and Sherman to Grant, June 18, 1864, in Simpson and Berlin, *Sherman's Civil War*, 646, 655.

28. Gould and Kennedy, *Memoirs of a Dutch Mudsill*, 262–63.

29. Gates, *Rough Side of War*, 212.

30. Walter A. Rorer to cousin, June 9, 1864, James M. Willcox Papers, DU; Crowson and Brogden, *Bloody Banners*, 73; Castel, *Decision in the West*, 275.

31. Quaife, *From the Cannon's Mouth*, 321; Johnson and Hartshorn, "Development of Field Fortification," 593; Whipple to Howard and Hooker, June 15, 1864, *OR*, 38(4):483; Castel, *Decision in the West*, 280–81.

32. The Gilgal Church location is today called the Due West Community. Field visits to Gilgal Church, January 31, July 8, 1987.

33. Braley, "Battle of Gilgal Church," 25–27.

34. Ibid., 29, 33–34, 37, 42, 50, 53; field visit to Gilgal Church, November 27, 1992. I thank Steve Acker for sharing information with me about a project he and fellow reenactors conducted in 2009. They constructed a fieldwork in Wisconsin and fired minié balls from it, and toward it. One of their conclusions is that a battle line firing in a cramped environment often led to a considerable number of dropped rounds littering the floor of the trench. Conversation with Steve Acker, June 24, 2010.

35. Kerksis, "Action at Gilgal Church," 837; field visit to Gilgal Church, July 8, 1987.

36. Sherman to Halleck, June 17, 1864, *OR*, 38(4):498; Sherman to Grant, June 18, 1864, in Simpson and Berlin, *Sherman's Civil War*, 655.

37. Howard to Thomas, June 16, 1864; Thomas to Howard, June 18, 1864; and Johnston to Bragg, June 16, 1864, *OR*, 38(4):493, 513, 777; Fullerton journal, *OR*, 38(1):879–84.

38. Geary to Perkins, September 15, 1864, *OR*, 38(2):128; Perkins to Williams, June 16, 1864, *OR*, 38(4):493.

39. Fullerton to Newton, June 16, 1864, *OR*, 38(4):493; Gates, *Rough Side of War*, 217.

40. Castel, *Decision in the West*, 281.

41. Sherman to Halleck, June 17, 1864, *OR*, 38(4):498; Byrne, *Uncommon Soldiers*, 162; Bohrnstedt, *Soldiering with Sherman*, 109; Reyburn and Wilson, "Jottings from Dixie," 226.

42. Thomas B. Mackall journal (McMurry transcript), June 16, 1864, Joseph E. Johnston Papers, CWM; field visit to Mud Creek, January 31, 1987; French, *Two Wars*, 203; Johnston,

Narrative of Military Operations, 338; Johnson and Hartshorn, "Development of Field Fortification," 593; [Thomas M. Jack] to French, Cantey, and Featherston, June 17, 1864, Special Orders from May 9th 1864 to June 19th 1864, NARA. In *Atlanta* (103), McMurry calls the Mud Creek Line the Second Kennesaw Line.

43. Bridges to Fullerton, September 9, 1864, *OR*, 38(1):482; Howard, *Autobiography*, 1:566; Castel, *Decision in the West*, 282–83.

44. Baird to McClurg, September 7, 1864, *OR*, 38(1):738; Howard, *Autobiography*, 1:567.

45. Edward Spear Diary, June 17, 1864, Kennesaw Mountain National Battlefield Park, Kennesaw, Georgia.

46. W. L. Truman Memoirs, June 18, 1864, www.cedarcroft.com; Ervin, "Genius and Heroism," 497.

47. Joseph W. Kimmel Memoir, 23–24, TSLA.

48. Geary to Perkins, September 15, 1864, *OR*, 38(2):131.

49. Barnhart, "Hoosier Invades the Confederacy," 188.

50. French, *Two Wars*, 203; Circular, Headquarters, Army of Mississippi, June 24, 1864, Featherston Order Book, Winfield Scott Featherston Collection, UM; Neal to Ra, June 20, 1864, Andrew Jackson Neal Letters, EU.

51. Sherman to Halleck, June 17, 1864; Butterfield to Perkins, June 19, 1864; and Mackall to not stated, June 18, 1864, *OR*, 38(4):498, 526, 780; Blair to Clark, September 12, 1864, *OR*, 38(3):552; Force to Mr. Soule, June 26–28, 1864, M. F. Force Papers, UW; Thomas B. Mackall journal (McMurry transcript), June 18, 1864, Joseph E. Johnston Papers, CWM; McMurry, *Atlanta*, 103.

CHAPTER 6

1. Castel, *Decision in the West*, 285. For a detailed discussion of operations leading to the Federal assault of June 27, see Hess, *Kennesaw Mountain*, 1–70.

2. Hess, *Kennesaw Mountain*, 51–53; Johnson and Hartshorn, "Development of Field Fortification," 593; McMurry, *Atlanta*, 100–101, 104; Stephen Davis, *Atlanta Will Fall*, 81; Connelly, *Autumn of Glory*, 358; French, *Two Wars*, 203.

3. Wynne and Taylor, *This War So Horrible*, 90; Johnston, "Opposing Sherman's Advance," 271; Wiley, *Four Years*, 198.

4. Loring to French, June 20, 1864, *OR*, 38(4):782.

5. Diary, June 18–20, 1864, Daniel Harris Reynolds Papers, UAF; Sears to Sanders, June 21, 1864, *OR*, 38(4):784.

6. Storrs, "Kennesaw Mountain," 138. For a modern photograph showing the view from the top of Big Kennesaw, see Kelly, "Atlanta Campaign," 10.

7. Storrs, "Kennesaw Mountain," 136–37; Castel, *Decision in the West*, 287.

8. Storrs, "Kennesaw Mountain," 137–38.

9. Ibid., 138–39.

10. Little and Maxwell, *History of Lumsden's Battery*, 42–43.

11. Kirwan, *Johnny Green*, 137.

12. [Thomas M. Jack] to W. J. Morris, June 19, 1864, Special Orders from May 9th 1864 to June 19th 1864, NARA.

13. Cheatham journal, *SOR*, 143; "Battle of Kennesaw Mountain," 110; Losson, *Tennessee's Forgotten Warriors*, 152–53.

14. Cheatham journal, *SOR*, 145; Eleazer, "Fight at Dead Angle," 312; "Battle of Kennesaw Mountain," 110.

15. Wiley, *Four Years*, 198.

16. Field visit to Kennesaw Mountain, December 19, 1986.

17. Circular, Headquarters, Hood's Corps, June 26, 1864, General Orders, MOC; John K. Ely Diary, June 27, 1864, JBC; Barnes, "Incident of Kenesaw Mountain," 49; Capers to Smith, September 10, 1864, *OR*, 38(3):716.

18. Sherman, *Memoirs*, 2:56.

19. Jackson, *Colonel's Diary*, 133; John W. Tuttle Diary, June 19, 1864, UK.

20. Josiah C. Williams diary, June 19, 1864, Worthington Williams Papers, IHS; Howard, "Struggle for Atlanta," 310; Butterfield to Hooker, June 19, 1864, *OR*, 38(4):526.

21. Gates, *Rough Side of War*, 219–20.

22. Malmborg to Cox, June 21, 1864, *OR*, 38(3):559–60; Rose to [Lawton], September 14, 1864, *OR*, 38(1):287.

23. Yates, *Historical Guide*, 21; Fullerton journal, *OR*, 38(1):883; Partridge, *History of the Ninety-Sixth*, 360–66.

24. Fullerton journal, *OR*, 38(1):884; Howard, *Autobiography*, 1:568–70.

25. Castel, *Decision in the West*, 289–90; Leggett to Alexander, June 28, 1864, *OR*, 38(3):563; *Atlas to Accompany the Official Records*, plate 59, no. 3; Marietta Quadrant Map, U.S. Department of the Interior.

26. Peter J. Osterhaus diary, June 22, 1864, Osterhaus Family Papers, MHM; D. P. Conyagham dispatch, June 22, 1864, in *New York Herald*, July 4, 1864; Hooker to Whipple, June 22, 1864; Williams to Perkins, September 12, 1864; and Gallup to not stated, August 11, 1864, *OR*, 38(2):15, 31, 655; Toombs, *Reminiscences of the War*, 141; Bauer, *Soldiering*, 129–33; Tower, *Carolinian Goes to War*, 193; Castel, *Decision in the West*, 290–92; McMurry, "Affair at Kolb's Farm," 21, 25.

27. McMurry, *Atlanta*, 105; McMurry, "Affair at Kolb's Farm," 21.

28. W. H. Brooker Diary, June 22, 1864, RU; Stevenson to [Ratchford], August 19, 1864, *OR*, 38(3):815; Gallup to not stated, August 11, 1864, *OR*, 38(2):655; Bauer, *Soldiering*, 133–34; Castel, *Decision in the West*, 294–95.

29. Williams to Perkins, September 12, 1864, *OR*, 38(2):32; Quaife, *From the Cannon's Mouth*, 328; Merrell, "Personal Memoirs of the Civil War," LMU; Robinson to Hunt, June 24, 1864, James Sidney Robinson Papers, Ohio Historical Society, Archives/Library, Columbus, Ohio; Castel, *Decision in the West*, 295.

30. Merrell, "Personal Memoirs of the Civil War," LMU; William Walton, *Civil War Courtship*, 89; Quaife, *From the Cannon's Mouth*, 328–29; Marvin, *Fifth Regiment Connecticut*, 315; Jones to Forbes, August 1, 1864, *OR*, 38(2):211; Tower, *Carolinian Goes to War*, 193.

31. Castel, *Decision in the West*, 295.

32. Wynne and Taylor, *This War So Horrible*, 97; Thoburn, *My Experiences*, 98.

33. J. T. Bowden to editor, December 15, 1903, J. T. Bowden Letter, DU; Cheatham journal, *SOR*, 143–44; Losson, *Tennessee's Forgotten Warriors*, 153–54.

34. M., "Battle of Dead Angle," 71; Losson, *Tennessee's Forgotten Warriors*, 152, 154.

35. Cheatham journal, *SOR*, 144; Maney, "Battle of Dead Angle," 159; Eleazer, "Fight at Dead Angle," 312; J. L. W. Blair, "Fight at Dead Angle," 533; Payne, *History of the Thirty-Fourth*, 128.

36. J. T. Bowden to editor, December 15, 1903, J. T. Bowden Letter, DU.

37. "Battle of Kennesaw Mountain," 113, 116; J. T. Bowden to editor, December 15, 1903, J. T. Bowden Letter, DU; Payne, *History of the Thirty-Fourth*, 128–29; Demoret, *Brief History*, 43.

38. Gates, *Rough Side of War*, 225; Thaddeus S. C. Brown, Murphy, and Putney, *Behind the Guns*, 96–97.

39. Samuel Eugene Hunter to D. C. Hardee, June 22, 1864, Samuel Eugene Hunter Letters, LSU.

40. Kirwan, *Johnny Green*, 138–39.

41. Ibid., 135, 138.

42. Cumming reminiscences, 57–58, Joseph B. Cumming Papers, UNC; Baird to McClurg, September 7, 1864, *OR*, 38(1):739.

43. Fearing to Curtis, August 16, 1864, *OR*, 38(1):786.

44. Circular, Headquarters, Hood's Corps, June 24, 1864, *OR*, 38(4):789.

45. Capers to Smith, September 10, 1864, *OR*, 38(3):716.

46. Hughes, *Civil War Memoir*, 198–99.

47. Ibid., 196.

48. Ibid., 197–98.

49. Gates, *Rough Side of War*, 221–22.

50. Bircher, *Drummer-Boy's Diary*, 120–21.

51. Wiley, *Four Years*, 198–99, 202–3.

52. Johnston to Bragg, June 27, 1864, *OR*, 38(4):795–96.

53. Given to Montague, September 5, 1864, *OR*, 38(1):615.

54. Byrne, *Uncommon Soldiers*, 163; James M. Merrill and Marshall, "Georgia through Kentucky Eyes," 330; H. E. Collins to James E. Yeatman, June 24, 1864, in *St. Louis Daily Missouri Democrat*, July 4, 1864.

55. Jill K. Garrett, *Confederate Diary*, 71; Johnston to Bragg, June 27, 1864, *OR*, 38(4):795.

56. McPherson to Dodge, June 15, 1864: Sherman to Halleck, June 16, 1864, *OR*, 38(4):490, 492.

57. Sherman to Halleck, June 21, 23, 1864, *OR*, 38(4):544, 572–73.

58. Thomas to Sherman, June 24, 1864, *OR*, 38(4):581; Castel, *Decision in the West*, 300–301.

59. Special Field Orders No. 28, Headquarters, Military Division of the Mississippi, June 24, 1864, *OR*, 38(4):588; Castel, *Decision in the West*, 303–5, 320.

60. Sherman, *Memoirs*, 2:60; Sherman to Halleck, June 25, 1864, *OR*, 38(4):589; Sherman to Ellen, June 26, 1864, in Simpson and Berlin, *Sherman's Civil War*, 657.

CHAPTER 7

1. Castel, *Decision in the West*, 307, 309. For a detailed discussion of the fighting on June 27, see Hess, *Kennesaw Mountain*, 71–164.

2. Lightburn to Lofland, June 28, 1864; Jones to Lofland, September 12, 1864; and Taylor to Fish, September 10, 1864, *OR*, 38(3):222, 226–27, 244.

3. Fulton to Fisk, September 8, 1864, *OR*, 38(3):253; Walker to French, June 28, 1864, *OR*, 38(4):802; Duke, *History of the Fifty-Third*, 146.

4. Lightburn to Lofland, June 28, 1864; Jones to Lofland, September 12, 1864; Fulton to Fisk, September 8, 1864; French to Loring, June 28, 1864; Young to Todhunter, June 28, 1864; and Cockrell to Sanders, June 27, 1864, *OR*, 38(3):222, 227, 253, 900, 913, 915; Storrs, "Kennesaw Mountain," 138; Duke, *History of the Fifty-Third*, 146.

5. Duke, *History of the Fifty-Third*, 146.

6. Giles A. Smith to Morgan L. Smith, June 28, 1864; Mott to assistant adjutant general, First Brigade, Second Division, Fifteenth Corps, September 9, 1864; French to Loring, June 28, 1864; and Cockrell to Sanders, June 27, 1864, *OR*, 38(3):194, 216, 900, 914; Capron, "War Diary," 384.

7. Giles A. Smith to Morgan L. Smith, June 28, 1864; Mott to assistant adjutant general, First Brigade, Second Division, Fifteenth Corps, September 9, 1864; and Cockrell to Sanders, June 27, 1864, *OR*, 38(3):194, 216, 915; Capron, "War Diary," 384.

8. Cockrell to Sanders, June 27, 1864, *OR*, 38(3):915.

9. Walcutt to Wilkinson, August 10, 1864; Willison to Upton, September 9, 1864; and French to Loring, June 28, 1864, *OR*, 38(3):318, 326, 900–901; Charles W. Wills, *Army Life*, 269–70.

10. Walcutt to Wilkinson, August 10, 1864; Willison to Upton, September 9, 1864; Alexander to not stated, September 12, 1864; French to Loring, June 28, 1864; and Cockrell to Sanders, June 27, 1864, *OR*, 38(3):318, 326, 337, 901, 915.

11. Walcutt to Wilkinson, August 10, 1864, and Willison to Upton, September 9, 1864, *OR*, 38(3):318, 326; Charles W. Wills, *Army Life*, 271.

12. Fullerton journal, *OR*, 38(1):887.

13. Howard, *Autobiography*, 1:582; Castel, *Decision in the West*, 307; Longacre and Haas, *To Battle for God*, 189; John W. Tuttle Diary, June 27, 1864, UK.

14. Moore to Waterman, September 12, 1864, *OR*, 38(1):371; field visit to Kennesaw Mountain, December 16, 1986.

15. John W. Tuttle Diary, June 27, 1864, UK; Moore to Waterman, September 12, 1864, and Fullerton journal, *OR*, 38(1):371, 887–88; Longacre and Haas, *To Battle for God*, 189–90; Bradley memoirs, Luther P. Bradley Papers, USAMHI.

16. John W. Tuttle Diary, June 27, 1864, UK.

17. Wagner to Lee, September 10, 1864, and Blanch to Cox, September 15, 1864, *OR*, 38(1):335–36, 346; unidentified Confederate soldier quoted in McAdams, *Every-Day Soldier Life*, 90.

18. Kimball to assistant adjutant general, Second Division, Fourth Corps, August 4, 1864, and Fullerton journal, *OR*, 38(1):304, 888.

19. Castel, *Decision in the West*, 314; Langley to Wiseman, September 9, 1864, and Holmes to Swift, September 7, 1864, *OR*, 38(1):710, 729; James, "McCook's Brigade," 257; Holmes, *52d O.V.I.*, 178.

20. Work, "Map of the 'Dead Angle,'" 1902, DU; Holmes, *52d O.V.I.*, 178–79; Langley to Wiseman, September 9, 1864, *OR*, 38(1):710; James, "McCook's Brigade," 258–59.

21. Holmes, *52d O.V.I.*, 181–82; Holmes to Swift, September 7, 1864, *OR*, 38(1):729; Barnhart, "Hoosier Invades the Confederacy," 190; James, "McCook's Brigade," 261.

22. James, "McCook's Brigade," 259–60; Langley to Wiseman, September 9, 1864, *OR*, 38(1):710–11; Barnhart, "Hoosier Invades the Confederacy," 190.

23. Mitchell to Wiseman, September 4, 1864; Van Tassell to Wilson, September 5, 1864;

Pearce to Wilson, September 9, 1864; and Banning to Wilson, September 9, 1864, *OR*, 38(1):680, 685–86, 692, 703; McAdams, *Every-Day Soldier Life*, 87.

24. "Battle of Kennesaw Mountain," 110, 112; J. L. W. Blair, "Fight at Dead Angle," 533; M., "Battle of Dead Angle," 71; Watkins, "*Co. Aytch*," 162.

25. Mitchell to Wiseman, September 4, 1864, and Jones to Wilson, September 10, 1864, *OR*, 38(1):680, 697; W. J. McDill to aunt, July 9, 1864, W. J. McDill Letter, Kennesaw Mountain National Battlefield Park, Kennesaw, Georgia; Smith journal, and Cheatham journal, *SOR*, 78, 144–45.

26. Mitchell to Wiseman, September 4, 1864; Jones to Wilson, September 10, 1864; and Banning to Wilson, September 9, 1864, *OR*, 38(1):680, 698, 703; Payne, *History of the Thirty-Fourth*, 128.

27. Watkins, "*Co. Aytch*," 158, 160.

28. Mitchell to Wiseman, September 4, 1864, and Banning to Wilson, September 9, 1864, *OR*, 38(1):680, 703–4.

29. Watkins, "*Co. Aytch*," 159–60.

30. Mitchell to Wiseman, September 4, 1864, and Jones to Wilson, September 10, 1864, *OR*, 38(1):680, 698.

31. James, "McCook's Brigade," 261–62; Payne, *History of the Thirty-Fourth*, 129, 131, 133; J. T. Bowden to editor, December 15, 1903, J. T. Bowden Letter, DU; Stewart, *Dan McCook's Regiment*, 122–23; Pearce to Wilson, September 9, 1864, *OR*, 38(1):693; Cabaniss, *Civil War Journal and Letters*, 67.

32. Smith journal, and Cheatham journal, *SOR*, 78, 145.

33. Stewart, *Dan McCook's Regiment*, 119–20, 124; Banning to Wilson, September 9, 1864, *OR*, 38(1):704; Watkins, "*Co. Aytch*," 160–63; Palmer endorsement in Davis to Palmer, June 27, 1864, *OR*, 38(4):614.

34. Barnes, "Incident of Kenesaw Mountain," 49; Jill K. Garrett, *Confederate Diary*, 71–72.

35. Thomas to Sherman, June 27, 1864, 10:45 A.M., 1:40 P.M., [no time], and Sherman to Thomas, June 27, 1864, 1:30 P.M., 2:25 P.M., 4:10 P.M., *OR*, 38(4):609–10; Castel, *Decision in the West*, 317.

36. Howard to Thomas, June 27, 1864; Newton to Fullerton, June 27, 1864; and Hooker to Whipple, June 27, 1864, *OR*, 38(4):612–14; Fullerton journal, *OR*, 38(1):888.

37. Castel, *Decision in the West*, 317; Sherman to Thomas, June 27, 1864, *OR*, 38(4):612.

38. Castel, *Decision in the West*, 317, 320.

39. Howard, *Autobiography*, 1:582–83; Howard, "Struggle for Atlanta," 311; Thomas to Sherman, June 27, 1864, 1:40 P.M., 6:00 P.M., *OR*, 38(4):609–11.

40. Poe to wife, June 28, 1864, Orlando Metcalfe Poe Papers, LC.

41. Sherman to Halleck, June 27, 1864, in Simpson and Berlin, *Sherman's Civil War*, 659; Sherman to Thomas, June 27, 1864, *OR*, 38(4):611.

42. Sherman to Halleck, July 9, 1864, and Sherman to Grant, July 12, 1864, *OR*, 38(5):91, 123.

43. Sherman to Ellen, June 30, July 9, 1864, in Simpson and Berlin, *Sherman's Civil War*, 660, 663–64.

44. Sherman to Grant, July 12, 1864, *OR*, 38(5):123.

CHAPTER 8

1. Rogers, *125th Regiment Illinois*, 98; Work, "Map of the 'Dead Angle,'" 1902, DU; Jill K. Garrett, *Confederate Diary*, 72; Cheatham journal, *SOR*, 145; Nelson, "Dead Angle," 321. For a detailed discussion of operations leading to the Confederate abandonment of the Kennesaw Line, see Hess, *Kennesaw Mountain*, 165–226.

2. Cheatham journal, *SOR*, 145; Stewart, *Dan McCook's Regiment*, 128; Holmes, *52d O.V.I.*, 185; Payne, *History of the Thirty-Fourth*, 135.

3. Stewart, *Dan McCook's Regiment*, 129; Holmes, *52d O.V.I.*, 185–86, 197; J. T. Bowden to editor, December 15, 1903, J. T. Bowden Letter, DU; Watkins, *"Co. Aytch,"* 161; "Battle of Kennesaw Mountain," 115.

4. J. T. Bowden to editor, December 15, 1903, J. T. Bowden Letter, DU; Cabaniss, *Civil War Journal and Letters*, 67; Hall, "History of Company C," and McDill quoted in Fleming, *Band of Brothers*, 71, 118; Aten, *History of the Eighty-Fifth*, 189; A. L. Jordan, "'Dead Angle' Tunneled," 601; Harmon, "Dead Angle," 219.

5. Nelson, "Dead Angle," 321; Watkins, *"Co. Aytch,"* 160–61.

6. Poe to wife, July 1, 1864, Orlando Metcalfe Poe Papers, LC; McDill quoted in Fleming, *Band of Brothers*, 118; Stewart, *Dan McCook's Regiment*, 126; Grimshaw, "The Charge at Kenesaw."

7. Rogers, *125th Regiment Illinois*, 98; Morgan, "Home Letters," 225, AHC; Work, "Map of the 'Dead Angle,'" 1902, DU; Aten, *History of the Eighty-Fifth*, 190; Holmes, *52d O.V.I.*, 187; A. L. Jordan, "'Dead Angle' Tunneled," 601; J. T. Bowden to editor, December 15, 1903, J. T. Bowden Letter, DU; diary, July 3, 1864, Allen L. Fahnestock Papers, ALPL.

8. Jill K. Garrett, *Confederate Diary*, 72; Rogers, *125th Regiment Illinois*, 98–99; Stewart, *Dan McCook's Regiment*, 128; Wiley, *Four Years*, 200.

9. Watkins, *"Co. Aytch,"* 159; Smith journal, *SOR*, 78; Ellison, *On to Atlanta*, 56; John K. Ely Diary, June 28, 1864, JBC; Jill K. Garrett, *Confederate Diary*, 72; Kimball to assistant adjutant general, Second Division, Fourth Corps, August 4, 1864, *OR*, 38(1):304; John W. Tuttle Diary, June 29, 1864, UK.

10. Briant to not stated, no date, *OR*, 38(1):542; M., "Battle of Dead Angle," 72; James, "McCook's Brigade," 263; Payne, *History of the Thirty-Fourth*, 133; J. T. Bowden to editor, December 15, 1903, J. T. Bowden Letter, DU; Cheatham journal, *SOR*, 145; Holmes, *52d O.V.I.*, 197.

11. Payne, *History of the Thirty-Fourth*, 134; Holmes, *52d O.V.I.*, 187; Ellison, *On to Atlanta*, 55; Jill K. Garrett, *Confederate Diary*, 72; Stewart, *Dan McCook's Regiment*, 127; Rogers, *125th Regiment Illinois*, 99.

12. Payne, *History of the Thirty-Fourth*, 133; Smith journal, and Cheatham journal, *SOR*, 78–79, 146; James, "McCook's Brigade," 263, 265; Gates, *Rough Side of War*, 229; M., "Battle of Dead Angle," 72–73.

13. James, "McCook's Brigade," 262, 265; Maney, "Battle of Dead Angle," 159; Nelson, "Dead Angle," 321.

14. Payne, *History of the Thirty-Fourth*, 134.

15. J. T. Bowden to editor, December 15, 1903, J. T. Bowden Letter, DU; Stewart, *Dan McCook's Regiment*, 128; "Rash Deed at Dead Angle," 394; Payne, *History of the Thirty-Fourth*, 134.

16. Holmes, *52d O.V.I.*, 186; Fleming, *Band of Brothers*, 72.

17. Langley to Wiseman, September 9, 1864, *OR*, 38(1):711; Stewart, *Dan McCook's Regiment*, 127; Watkins, "*Co. Aytch*," 164.

18. Holmes, *52d O.V.I.*, 183, 187; Cabaniss, *Civil War Journal and Letters*, 67.

19. Brown to Fannie, July 2, 1864, Edward Norphlet Brown Letters, ADAH; Bennett and Tillery, *Struggle for the Life*, 173.

20. Capers to Smith, September 10, 1864, *OR*, 38(3):716–17.

21. Circular, June 30, 1864, General Orders and Circulars, MOC.

22. Kendall, "Recollections of a Confederate Officer," 1162, 1164–65.

23. Bradley to Buel, July 1, 1864, Luther P. Bradley Papers, USAMHI.

24. Fergus Elliott Diary, July 2, 1864, USAMHI; Charles D. Gammon Diary, July 4, 1864, EU; Gates, *Rough Side of War*, 231.

25. Harmon, "Dead Angle," 219; Gates, *Rough Side of War*, 231; Wynne and Taylor, *This War So Horrible*, 103; Circular, June 28, 1864, General Orders and Circulars, MOC; West to French, June 28, 1864, *OR*, 38(4):802.

26. Sherman, *Memoirs*, 2:61; Sherman to Webster, June 28, 1864, *OR*, 38(4):629; Sherman to Halleck, July 1, 1864, *OR*, 38(5):3; diary, June 28, 1864, Orlando Metcalfe Poe Papers, LC.

27. Schofield to Sherman, June 30, 1864, and Sherman to Schofield, June 30, 1864, *OR*, 38(4):643–44.

28. Sherman, *Memoirs*, 2:62; Castel, *Decision in the West*, 324–25, 327, 329.

29. Johnston, *Narrative of Military Operations*, 345; Storrs, "Kennesaw Mountain," 139; French, *Two Wars*, 215.

30. M., "Battle of Dead Angle," 73; Norman D. Brown, *One of Cleburne's Command*, 99; John S. Lightfoot Diary, July 3, 1864, EU.

31. James, "McCook's Brigade," 265–66; Stewart, *Dan McCook's Regiment*, 129.

32. Diary, July 3, 1864, Allen L. Fahnestock Papers, ALPL; Gates, *Rough Side of War*, 233.

33. William Clark McLean diary, July 3, 1864, and McLean to Father, July 4, 1864, McLean Family Papers, NYSL; Fergus Elliott Diary, July 3, 1864, USAMHI; Johnston to Folks, July 12, 1864, Andrew J. Johnson Papers, IHS; Nichol to father, July 8, 1864, David Nichol Papers, USAMHI.

34. Hughes, *Civil War Memoir*, 202.

CHAPTER 9

1. Johnston, "Opposing Sherman's Advance," 273; Poe to [Delafield], October 8, 1865, *OR*, 38(1):129; Scaife and Erquitt, *Chattahoochee River Line*, map between 8 and 9; Castel, *Decision in the West*, 330; McMurry, *Atlanta*, 113; Hughes, *Civil War Memoir*, 202; Mary Miles Jones and Martin, *Gentle Rebel*, 37–39; Tower, *Carolinian Goes to War*, 194.

2. Hughes, *Civil War Memoir*, 202–3; diary, July 3, 1864, Daniel Harris Reynolds Papers, UAF.

3. Tower, *Carolinian Goes to War*, 194; French, *Two Wars*, 215; Capers to Smith, September 10, 1864, *OR*, 38(3):717; Jill K. Garrett, *Confederate Diary*, 73.

4. Chamberlin, "Skirmish Line," 190; Norman D. Brown, *One of Cleburne's Command*, 100; Tower, *Carolinian Goes to War*, 194; Henry H. Wright, *History of the Sixth Iowa*, 299; Jill K. Garrett, *Confederate Diary*, 73; Order No. 2, Headquarters, Army of Mississippi, July 4, 1864, D. Wintter Service Record, NARA.

5. Diary, July 3–4, 1864, John Wharton Papers, MHM; record of events, Company A, 4th Louisiana, *SOR*, pt. 2, 23:781; Hamilton R. Branch to mother, July 4, 1864, Branch Family Papers, UGA.

6. Sherman, *Memoirs*, 2:62, 65; Sherman to Thomas, July 3, 1864, *OR*, 38(5):30–31; Castel, *Decision in the West*, 331.

7. Fullerton journal, *OR*, 38(1):892; Howard to Thomas, July 4, 1864, *OR*, 38(5):43; Howard, "Battles about Atlanta," 386; Howard, *Autobiography*, 1:594.

8. Gates, *Rough Side of War*, 234–37; Fullerton journal, *OR*, 38(1):892; Howard to Thomas, July 4, 1864, *OR*, 38(5):43.

9. Howard, *Autobiography*, 1:594; Fullerton journal, *OR*, 38(1):892; Gates, *Rough Side of War*, 286.

10. Wiley, "Confederate Letters," 282.

11. Castel, *Decision in the West*, 332.

12. Gustavus W. Smith, "Georgia Militia," 332–33; Head to Sallie, July 7, 1864, Thomas J. Head Letters, Earl J. Hess Collection, Knoxville, Tennessee.

13. Castel, *Decision in the West*, 332; McMurry, *Atlanta*, 114; Thomas B. Mackall journal (McMurry transcript), July 5, 1864, Joseph E. Johnston Papers, CWM; Hamilton M. Branch to mother, July 4, 1864, Branch Family Papers, UGA; Capers to Smith, September 10, 1864, *OR*, 38(3):717.

14. Quaife, *From the Cannon's Mouth*, 323; Poe to [Delafield], October 8, 1865, *OR*, 38(1):129; Fullerton journal, *OR*, 38(1):893; Holzhueter, "William Wallace's Civil War Letters," 101; Ellison, *On to Atlanta*, 58; William Clark McLean diary, July 5, 1864, McLean Family Papers, NYSL; correspondence in *Cincinnati Commercial*, July 8, 1864, reprinted in *Washington Daily National Intelligencer*, July 20, 1864; Bauer, *Soldiering*, 139.

15. Johnston, *Narrative of Military Operations*, 346; Johnston, "Opposing Sherman's Advance," 273; Shoup, "Dalton Campaign," 262–63.

16. Shoup, "Dalton Campaign," 263; Scaife and Erquitt, *Chattahoochee River Line*, map between 32 and 33, 36.

17. Shoup, "Dalton Campaign," 263; Poe to [Delafield], October 8, 1865, *OR*, 38(1):129; Fryman, "Fortifying the Landscape," 54. For differing information about the distances between Shoupades and other measurements of the Chattahoochee River Line, see Scaife and Erquitt, *Chattahoochee River Line*, 3, and William C. Brown, *One of Cleburne's Command*, 102. Jill K. Garrett, *Confederate Diary*, 73; Josiah C. Williams to Edistina, July 12, 1864, Worthington Williams Papers, IHS; R. L. Dixon to wife, July 2, 1864, Harry St. John Dixon Papers, UNC.

18. Shoup, "Dalton Campaign," 263; Scaife and Erquitt, *Chattahoochee River Line*, 33, 37; Poe to [Delafield], October 8, 1865, *OR*, 38(1):129.

19. Shoup, "Dalton Campaign," 263; William C. Brown, *One of Cleburne's Command*, 103; Bell to wife, June 24, 1864, Alfred W. Bell Papers, DU; R. L. Dixon to wife, July 2, 1864, Harry St. John Dixon Papers, UNC.

20. Sherman, *Memoirs*, 2:66–67; Davis to wife, July 7, 1864, Leander E. Davis Letters, NYSL; correspondence in *Chicago Daily Tribune*, July 3, 1864.

21. Stone, "From the Oostanaula to the Chattahoochee," 424.

22. Johnston to Bragg, July 5, 1864, *OR*, 38(5):865; John S. Lightfoot Diary, July 5, 1864, EU; R. L. Dixon to wife, July 2, 1864, Harry St. John Dixon Papers, UNC.

23. Jill K. Garrett, *Confederate Diary*, 73; Kendall, "Recollections of a Confederate

Officer," 1171–72; Hughes, *Civil War Memories*, 203–4; Norrell, "Memo Book," 77; J. L. Hammond to sister, July 7, 1864, quoted in Haughton, *Training, Tactics and Leadership*, 154.

24. Kendall, "Recollections of a Confederate Officer," 1170–72; Tower, *Carolinian Goes to War*, 195; Norrell, "Memo Book," 77; R. L. Dixon to wife, July 2, 1864, Harry St. John Dixon Papers, UNC.

25. Shoup, "Dalton Campaign," 263–64; George Anderson Mercer Diary, July 5–6, 1864, UNC; Hamilton M. Branch to mother, July 6, 1864, Branch Family Papers, UGA; Josiah C. Williams diary, July 11, 1864, Worthington Williams Papers, IHS.

26. Shoup, "Dalton Campaign," 263; Thomas B. Mackall journal (McMurry transcript), July 7, 1864, Joseph E. Johnston Papers, CWM; Shoup to Oladowski, July 4, 1864, Francis A. Shoup Service Record, NARA; circular, July 7, 1864, Headquarters, Army of Tennessee, George S. Storrs Papers, Augusta State University, Special Collections, Augusta, Georgia.

27. Shoup, "Dalton Campaign," 263–64.

28. Josiah C. Williams to Edistina, July 12, 1864, Worthington Williams Papers, IHS; William Clark McLean to father, July 6, 1864, McLean Family Papers, NYSL; Ellison, *On to Atlanta*, 60; diary, July 8, 1864, John Wharton Papers, MHM.

29. Sherman to McPherson, July 9, 1864, *OR*, 38(5):98; Ellison, *On to Atlanta*, 59; diary, July 9, 1864, Abraham J. Seay Collection, UO.

30. Tower, *Carolinian Goes to War*, 196.

31. French, *Two Wars*, 215–16; diary, July 5–7, 1864, Daniel Harris Reynolds Papers, UAF.

32. Johnston to Davis, July 8, 1864, *OR*, 38(5):869.

33. Sherman, *Memoirs*, 2:68–70; Sherman to Thomas, July 9, 1864, *OR*, 38(5):93; Shoup, "Dalton Campaign," 264; Castel, *Decision in the West*, 336.

34. Sherman to Thomas, July 10, 1864; Thomas to Sherman, July 10, 1864; and Sherman to Halleck, July 11, 1864, *OR*, 38(5):103, 114; Sherman, *Memoirs*, 2:66.

35. Bennett and Tillery, *Struggle for the Life*, 176; *Story of the Fifty-Fifth Regiment*, 332; Henry H. Wright, *History of the Sixth Iowa*, 299; Ellison, *On to Atlanta*, 60; Force to Mr. Kebler, July 9, 1864, and journal and letter book, November 13, 1864, M. F. Force Papers, UW.

36. Poe to [Delafield], October 8, 1865, *OR*, 38(1):129–30; Harry Stanley Diary, July 16, 1864, AHC; George E. Truair to father, July 10, 1864, Truair Family Papers, UTA; diary, July 10, 1864, Abraham J. Seay Collection, UO.

37. Josiah C. Williams to Edistina, July 12, 1864, Worthington Williams Papers, IHS; McAdams, *Every-Day Soldier Life*, 93.

38. Journal and letter book, November 13, 1864, M. F. Force Papers, UW. A detailed study and tour guide relating to the remnants of the Shoup Line can be found in Scaife and Erquitt, *Chattahoochee River Line*, 32–37. Dickey, "Johnston's River Line," 26–29, also offers a tour guide to the remnants of the line. Biggs, "'Shoupade' Redoubts," 85, 90, is also a study of the works. I do not agree, however, with these authors' claims of the brilliance of Shoup's design features.

39. Julian, "Atlanta's Defenses," 23; Fryman, "Fortifying the Landscape," 49; Jeremy F. Gilmer to L. P. Grant, January 5, October 22, [1863], and A. L. Rives to Gill Shorter, January 29, 1863, Letters and Telegrams, NARA; Jeremy F. Gilmer to L. P. Grant, June 23, 1863, L. P. Grant Papers, AHC.

40. Jeremy F. Gilmer to Samuel Cooper, July 14, 1863; Gilmer to L. P. Grant, July 15, 1863; Gilmer to George Hull, July 15, 1863; Gilmer to Braxton Bragg, July 27, 1863; and Gilmer to John Morris Wampler, July 27, 1863, Letters and Telegrams, NARA; Julian, "Atlanta's Defenses," 24; Kundahl, *Confederate Engineer*, 231-33; Fryman, "Fortifying the Landscape," 49-50.

41. Rhodes, "Jeremy Gilmer," 146-47; Jeremy Gilmer to Grant, August 11, 1863, L. P. Grant Papers, AHC; Moses H. Wright to Engineer Bureau, August 19, 1863, and A. L. Rives to L. P. Grant, September 22, 1863, Letters and Telegrams, NARA. Gilmer's letter to Grant of August 11, 1863, also appears in *OR*, 30(4):489, and Letters and Telegrams, NARA.

42. Gilmer to Wright, October 21, December 7, 1863, *OR*, 31(3):575-76.

43. Grant to Gilmer, October 30, 1863, and Grant to R. P. Rowley, November 4, 1863, Letter Book 9, L. P. Grant Papers, AHC; Wright to commander of the post of Marietta, December 7, 1863, and Wright to Brent, December 14, 1863, *OR*, 31(3):821-22; *Atlas to Accompany the Official Records*, plate LI, no. 2; Julian, "Atlanta's Defenses," 24; Fryman, "Fortifying the Landscape," 51.

44. Wright to Brent, December 14, 1863, *OR*, 31(3):821.

45. Lewis L. Carter statement, December 6, 1863, *OR*, 31(3):347-48; Logan to Bowers, February 24, 1864, and Dodge to Rawlins, February 26, 1864, in Simon, *Papers of Ulysses S. Grant*, 10:537-38, 540.

46. Wright to Brent, December 19, 1863, *OR*, 31(3):848; Marcus J. Wright to Moses H. Wright, March 12, 15, 29, 1864, Marcus J. Wright Service Record, NARA; Grant to Alfred L. Rives, March 8, 1864, and Grant to J. J. Clark, March 28, 1864, Letter Book 9, L. P. Grant Papers, AHC; A. L. Rives to L. P. Grant, March 17, 1864, Letters and Telegrams, NARA; Moses H. Wright to Marcus J. Wright, April 1, 20, 1864, and Moses H. Wright to George W. Brent, April 20, 1864, Reel 17, Confederate Inspection Reports, NARA; Special Order No. 22, Office of Chief Engineer, Army of Tennessee, December 28, 1863; Moses H. Wright to Jeremy F. Gilmer, March 14, 1863; E. Starnes to Louis T. Wigfall, March 15, 1863; and L. P. Grant to Jeremy Gilmer, March 14, 1863, James J. Davies Service Record, NARA.

47. Grant to Moses H. Wright, April 12, 1864, and Grant to Alfred L. Rives, May 17, 1864, Letter Book 9, L. P. Grant Papers, AHC; Julian, "Atlanta's Defenses," 24.

48. J. M. Glass statement, June 24, 1864, *OR*, 38(4):584.

49. Johnston, "Opposing Sherman's Advance," 274; Johnston, *Narrative of Military Operations*, 347.

50. Shoup, "Dalton Campaign," 265; Gustavus W. Smith, "Georgia Militia," 334; Connelly, *Autumn of Glory*, 368.

51. Connelly, *Autumn of Glory*, 368; field visit to Atlanta defenses, May 9, 1987.

52. Fryman, "Fortifying the Landscape," 50; Lockett, "Defense of Vicksburg," 488; Hess, *Field Armies and Fortifications*, 41-43, 99-101, 111-15, 171-73, 237-40.

53. Poe to [Delafield], October 8, 1865, *OR*, 38(1):131.

54. Sherman to Halleck, July 6, 1864, *OR*, 38(5):66; Van Buren Oldham Diary, July 8-9, 1864, UTM; Poe to [Delafield], October 8, 1865, *OR*, 38(1):129; Barnard, *Photographic Views*, no. 33.

55. Reese to Poe, September 14, 1864, *OR*, 38(3):66; diary, July 14-15, 1864, Abraham J. Seay Collection, UO; Chuck Brown, "Military Entrenchments," map; field visit to Roswell crossing, January 4, 1996.

56. Sherman to Halleck, July 6, 1864, *OR*, 38(5):66; Sherman to Ewing, July 13, 1864,

in Simpson and Berlin, *Sherman's Civil War*, 665; Stephen Davis, *Atlanta Will Fall*, 95–96; Sherman, *Memoirs*, 2:70–71.

57. Bradley to mother, July 14, 1864, Luther P. Bradley Papers, USAMHI; Gould and Kennedy, *Memoirs of a Dutch Mudsill*, 267; Sherman to commanding officer at Marietta, July 14, 1864, *OR*, 38(5):142.

58. Castel, *Decision in the West*, 348, 360; Sherman, *Memoirs*, 2:71; Thienel, *Mr. Lincoln's Bridge Builders*, 194–95.

59. Johnston to Cooper, October 20, 1864, *OR*, 38(3):618; Johnston, "Opposing Sherman's Advance," 274.

60. General Order No. 4, Army of the Mississippi, July 18, 1864, *OR*, 38(5):891; Lowrey to Benham, September 20, 1864; Stewart to Mason, January 12, 1865; French to Gale, December 6, 1864; Young to Sanders, September 17 1864; and Cockrell to Sanders, September 20, 1864, *OR*, 38(3):733, 870–71, 903, 909, 917; French, *Two Wars*, 216–17; record of events, Company B, 6th Kentucky (C.S.), *SOR*, pt. 2, 23:335; Neal to Pa, July 20, 1864, Andrew Jackson Neal Letters, EU; Hess, *Battle of Peach Tree Creek*, 34–37.

61. Johnston to Cooper, October 20, 1864, *OR*, 38(3):618; Castel, *Decision in the West*, 362; Van Buren Oldham Diary, July 18, 1864, UTM; Thomas B. Mackall journal (McMurry transcript), 31, Joseph E. Johnston Papers, CWM.

62. Tower, *Carolinian Goes to War*, 223; Hess, *Battle of Peach Tree Creek*, 56.

63. Correspondence to *Savannah Republican*, July 20, 1864, in *Charleston Mercury*, July 26, 1864; field visit to Atlanta area, June 22, 2000; Poe to [Delafield], October 8, 1865, *OR*, 38(1):131.

64. Johnston to Cooper, October 20, 1864, *OR*, 38(3):618.

65. Stephen Davis, *Atlanta Will Fall*, 127–31.

CHAPTER 10

1. Sherman memorandum, July 17, 1864, and Special Field Orders No. 39, July 19, 1864, *OR*, 38(5):167, 193.

2. Castel, *Decision in the West*, 365, 367; Hess, *Battle of Peach Tree Creek*, 30–54.

3. Hood, "Defense of Atlanta," 337; Hood, *Advance and Retreat*, 168; Castel, *Decision in the West*, 366–67; Hess, *Battle of Peach Tree Creek*, 71–73.

4. Hood, *Advance and Retreat*, 168; Crowson and Brogden, *Bloody Banners*, 84; Castel, *Decision in the West*, 368, 371–73, 375; Hess, *Battle of Peach Tree Creek*, 73–76; field visit to Peach Tree Creek battlefield, April 20, 2000.

5. Castel, *Decision in the West*, 369, 371, 373; Hess, *Battle of Peach Tree Creek*, 81; Clyde C. Walton, *Private Smith's Journal*, 169; Hynes to brother, July 29, 1864, William D. Hynes Papers, ISL; Sherman to Thomas, July 20, 1864, *OR*, 38(5):196–97.

6. Castel, *Decision in the West*, 375; Hess, *Battle of Peach Tree Creek*, 78–81.

7. Hynes to brother, July 29, 1864, William D. Hynes Papers, ISL; Howard, "Battles about Atlanta," 389; Howard, *Autobiography*, 1:613–14; J. W. M. to editor, July 21, 1864, in *Indianapolis Daily Journal*, July 26, 1864; Sherman, *Memoirs*, 2:73; Wagner to Lee, September 10, 1864, *OR*, 38(1):338; Castel, *Decision in the West*, 376; Hess, *Battle of Peach Tree Creek*, 84–95.

8. Wiley, *Four Years*, 209–210; Van Buren Oldham Diary, July 20, 1864, UTM; Hynes to brother, July 29, 1864, William D. Hynes Papers, ISL.

9. Castel, *Decision in the West*, 377; Crowson and Brogden, *Bloody Banners*, 84; Rogers to Palmer, September 7, 1864, *OR*, 38(2):50; Hess, *Battle of Peach Tree Creek*, 103–66.

10. Nichol to father, July 23, 1864, David Nichol Papers, USAMHI; Byrne, *Uncommon Soldiers*, 173; Henry Lyon to editor, July 22, 1864, in *Indianapolis Daily Journal*, August 1, 1864; Bohrnstedt, *Soldiering with Sherman*, 125.

11. Castel, *Decision in the West*, 381–82; Byrne, *Uncommon Soldiers*, 173; Merrell, "Personal Memoirs of the Civil War," LMU; Bohrnstedt, *Soldiering With Sherman*, 126; Hess, *Battle of Peach Tree Creek*, 247, 250.

12. Castel, *Decision in the West*, 377–78; DeGress to Lofland, September 1, 1864, *OR*, 38(3):265.

13. Sherman to Thomas, July 20, 1864, and Sherman to McPherson, July 20, 1864, *OR*, 38(5):198, 208.

14. McMurry, *John Bell Hood*, 129, 132.

15. Hood, *Advance and Retreat*, 173–74; Hood, "Defense of Atlanta," 338; Hood to Cooper, February 15, 1865, *OR*, 38(3):631; *Atlas to Accompany the Official Records*, plate LI, no. 2.

16. Hood, *Advance and Retreat*, 174; Hood, "Defense of Atlanta," 338, 340; Hood to Cooper, February 15, 1865, *OR*, 38(3):631; Huff, "Seeing Atlanta Shelled," 95.

17. Castel, *Decision in the West*, 383–84; [Rood], *Story of the Service*, 306; Smith to Buck, August 5, 1864, and Taylor to Sneed, July 29, 1864, *OR*, 38(3):746, 752–53; Norman D. Brown, *One of Cleburne's Command*, 109.

18. Buck, *Cleburne and His Command*, 232–33; Lowrey to Benham, September 20, 1864, and Smith to Buck, August 5, 1864, *OR*, 38(3):733–34, 746; Norman D. Brown, *One of Cleburne's Command*, 108–9; Yeary, *Reminiscences of the Boys in Gray*, 656.

19. Castel, *Decision in the West*, 386.

20. Stewart to Mason, January 12, 1865, and Walthall to Gale, January 14, 1865, *OR*, 38(3):872, 926; Ritter, "Sketch of Third Battery," 192.

21. French to Gale, December 6, 1864, and Cockrell to Sanders, September 20, 1864, *OR*, 38(3):903, 917; diary, July 21–22, 1864, Daniel Harris Reynolds Papers, UAF.

22. Castel, *Decision in the West*, 384, 387–88; Gates, *Rough Side of War*, 246; Bohrnstedt, *Soldiering with Sherman*, 126; Newton to Whipple, July 21, 1864, *OR*, 38(5):214.

23. Diary, July 21, 1864, James R. Carnahan Papers, IHS; Patrick and Willey, *Fighting for Liberty and Right*, 232.

24. Castel, *Decision in the West*, 385, 387; Tower, *Carolinian Goes to War*, 225.

25. Reese to Poe, September 14, 1864, *OR*, 38(3):66; McPherson to Blair, July 21, 1863, *OR*, 38(5):220; Munson, "Battle of Atlanta," 219; Evans, "Report of the Battle of Atlanta," 29.

26. Sherman to Halleck, July 21, 1864, *OR*, 38(5):211.

27. Castel, *Decision in the West*, 388–89; Norman D. Brown, *One of Cleburne's Command*, 110–11.

28. McPherson to Logan, July 22, 1864, *OR*, 38(5):231; Sherman, *Memoirs*, 2:74–75.

29. Reese to Poe, September 14, 1864; Griffiths to Van Dyke, July 26, 1864; and Burton to Harrow, July 25, 1864, *OR*, 38(3):66, 361, 363; Duke, *History of the Fifty-Third*, 148; Evans, "Report of the Battle of Atlanta," 29.

30. Bennett and Tillery, *Struggle for the Life*, 184; Munson, "Battle of Atlanta," 220–21.

31. Castel, *Decision in the West*, 391.

32. Bate to not stated, [July] 30, 1864, *SOR*, 101–2; field visit to July 22 battlefield,

February 26, 2001; Chamberlin, "Hood's Second Sortie," 326, 329; Adams, "Battle and Capture of Atlanta," 155; Castel, *Decision in the West*, 393–98.

33. Castel, *Decision in the West*, 398–99.

34. Giles Smith to Alexander, July 28, 1864, *OR*, 38(3):581–82; Munson, "Battle of Atlanta," 220; Cate, *Two Soldiers*, 94.

35. Castel, *Decision in the West*, 402–4.

36. Cheney to Alexander, July 25, 1864, and Giles Smith to Alexander, July 28, 1864, *OR*, 38(3):576, 581–82; Post, *Soldiers' Letters*, 401; Munson, "Battle of Atlanta," 222–23; Castel, *Decision in the West*, 402.

37. Giles Smith to Alexander, July 28, 1864, and Shane to Kinsman, July 22, 1864, *OR*, 38(3):581–82, 602; Chamberlin, "Recollections," 280; Castel, *Decision in the West*, 402.

38. Giles Smith to Alexander, July 28, 1864, and Shane to Kinsman, July 22, 1864, *OR*, 38(3):582, 602; Munson, "Battle of Atlanta," 227; Castel, *Decision in the West*, 403; cards, H. D. Lampley Service Record, NARA.

39. Giles Smith to Alexander, July 28, 1864, and Shane to Kinsman, July 22, 1864, *OR*, 38(3):583–84, 602; Post, *Soldiers' Letters*, 401–2; Munson, "Battle of Atlanta," 223–26; Tuthill, "Artilleryman's Recollections," 303–4; Frank P. Blair to J. E. Austin, February, no date, 1875, quoted in Hood, *Advance and Retreat*, 189.

40. Giles Smith to Alexander, July 28, 1864, *OR*, 38(3):583–84; Castel, *Decision in the West*, 404, 409.

41. Giles Smith to Alexander, July 28, 1864, *OR*, 38(3):584; Castel, *Decision in the West*, 409.

42. Castel, *Decision in the West*, 405.

43. Castel, *Tom Taylor's Civil War*, 146–47; Castel, *Decision in the West*, 405–6.

44. Sherman to Halleck, July 23, 1864, *OR*, 38(5):234; Tower, *Carolinian Goes to War*, 227–28.

45. Evans, "Report of the Battle of Atlanta," 29.

46. Castel, *Decision in the West*, 407.

47. Wells to not stated, July 26, 1864, *SOR*, 131; Castel, *Decision in the West*, 408.

48. Johnson to Macon, August 19, 1864, *SOR*, 127; Castel, *Decision in the West*, 408.

49. Bennett and Tillery, *Struggle for the Life*, 186–87, 232; Evans, "Report of the Battle of Atlanta," 29–30.

50. Gustavus W. Smith, "Georgia Militia," 334–35.

51. Castel, *Decision in the West*, 398.

52. Stanley to Fullerton, September, no date, 1864, *OR*, 38(1):226; Gates, *Rough Side of War*, 246–47.

53. Diary, July 22, 1864, Charles Richard Pomeroy Jr. Papers, DU; Bohrnstedt, *Soldiering with Sherman*, 128; Boughton to Pittman, September 10, 1864, and Salomon to Boughton, September 15, 1864, *OR*, 38(2):93, 100.

54. Bryant, *History of the Third Regiment*, 259–60.

55. Young to Sanders, September 17, 1864, *OR*, 38(3):910.

56. Munson, "Battle of Atlanta," 228; Dodge, *Personal Recollections*, 216–17; Logan to Sherman, July 22, 1864, *OR*, 38(5):232; Chamberlin, "Hood's Second Sortie," 331.

57. Lowrey to Benham, September 20, 1864, *OR*, 38(3):734; Chamberlin, "Recollections," 283; map enclosed in John R. McGuiness to Sherman, June 8, 1877, William T. Sherman Papers, LC.

58. Castel, *Decision in the West*, 411–12; Cryder and Miller, *View from the Ranks*, 418;

Howard, "Battles about Atlanta," 394; [Dwight], "How We Fight at Atlanta," 665; Leggett to Alexander, July 25, 1864, OR, 38(3):564.

59. [Dwight], "How We Fight at Atlanta," 666; Charles W. Wills, *Army Life*, 286.

60. Special Field Orders No. 41, Headquarters, Military Division of the Mississippi, July 22, 1864, OR, 38(5):232–33.

61. Diary, July 23, 1864, Abraham J. Seay Collection, UO; [Dwight], "How We Fight at Atlanta," 665.

62. Logan to Sherman, July 22, 1864, and General Orders No. 10, Headquarters, Seventeenth Corps, August 2, 1864, OR, 38(5):232, 338–39.

63. Sherman to Logan, July 23, 1864, OR, 38(5):237–38; Sherman, *Memoirs*, 2:87. For a full discussion of the Ezra Church phase of the Atlanta campaign, see Hess, *Battle of Ezra Church*.

64. Sherman to Logan, July 24, 1864, OR, 38(5):243; Castel, *Decision in the West*, 417.

65. Sherman to Schofield, July 27, 1864, OR, 38(5):274–75.

66. Poe to [Delafield], October 8, 1865, OR, 38(1):132; Sherman to Ellen, July 26, 1864, in Simpson and Berlin, *Sherman's Civil War*, 672; Reese to Poe, September 14, 1864, OR, 38(3):66.

67. Reese to Poe, September 14, 1864, OR, 38(3):66–67; Poe to [Delafield], October 8, 1865, OR, 38(1):132–33; diary, July 24, 1864, Orlando Metcalfe Poe Papers, LC.

68. Bell, *Tramps and Triumphs*, 20–21; Castel, *Tom Taylor's Civil War*, 151; diary, July 24, 1864, Orlando Metcalfe Poe Papers, LC. George Barnard exposed several photographs of the Union earthworks on the battlefield of July 22 in the summer of 1865. It is probable that he focused his efforts on Bald Hill. At any rate, the earthworks seen in his views represent the fortifications the Federals evacuated on the night of July 26 to move to the west of Atlanta. See Barnard, *Photographic Views*, nos. 36, 37, and William C. Davis and Wiley, *Photographic History*, 2:714.

69. Stanley to Fullerton, September, no date, 1864, OR, 38(1):226; Holzhueter, "William Wallace's Civil War Letters," 102–3; Kirkup to Creigh, September 9, 1864, OR, 38(2):175–76; Bauer, *Soldiering*, 154.

70. Holzhueter, "William Wallace's Civil War Letters," 103; Dunlap, *"Your Affectionate Husband,"* 332.

71. Venet, *Sam Richards's Civil War Diary*, 228.

72. Special Field Orders No. 42, Headquarters, Military Division of the Mississippi, July 25, 1864, OR, 38(5):255.

73. Cox to Cameron, July 23, 1864; Sherman to Logan, July 24, 1864; Fullerton to Stanley, July 26, 1864; and Special Field Orders No. 62, Headquarters, Army of the Ohio, July 26, 1864, OR, 38(5):237, 243, 263, 267–68.

74. Sherman, *Memoirs*, 2:87–88; Castel, *Decision in the West*, 424–25.

75. Cate, *Two Soldiers*, 102; Van Buren Oldham Diary, July 27, 1864, UTM; journal and letter book, November 14, 1864, M. F. Force Papers, UW.

76. Castel, *Decision in the West*, 426; Stephen Davis, *Atlanta Will Fall*, 150–51; McMurry, *John Bell Hood*, 133; Connelly, *Autumn of Glory*, 453.

77. General Field Orders No. 7, Headquarters, Army of Tennessee, July 25, 1864; [Shoup] to Hardee, July 28, 1864; [Shoup] to Lee, July 28, 1864, 2:20 P.M., 4:00 P.M.; and [Shoup] to Stewart, July 28, 1864, 3:25 P.M., OR, 38(5):909, 919–20; Hood to Cooper, February 15, 1865, OR, 38(3):632.

78. Castel, *Decision in the West*, 426, 428.

79. Hess, *Battle of Ezra Church*, 56–57.

80. Poe to [Delafield], October 8, 1865, *OR*, 38(1):133; Howard, *Autobiography*, 2:20–21; Howard, "Struggle for Atlanta," 319; Howard, "Ezra Church," 9, in O. O. Howard Papers, Bowdoin College, Special Collections and Archives, Brunswick, Maine; Sherman, *Memoirs*, 2:89.

81. Wangelin to Gordon, August 5, 1864, *OR*, 38(3):167; Bek, "Civil War Diary," 524–25; Bennett and Tillery, *Struggle for the Life*, 191; Allan to mother, July 25, 1864, David Allan Jr. Letters, MHM.

82. Lucas, *New History of the 99th Indiana*, 116; Black, "Marching with Sherman," 324; Oliver to Wilkinson, August 4, 1864, *OR*, 38(3):343.

83. Mott to assistant adjutant general, First Brigade, Second Division, Fifteenth Corps, September 9, 1864, *OR*, 38(3):218; Tapert, *Brothers' War*, 208.

84. Hess, *Battle of Ezra Church*, 58–113.

85. Hess, 114–31.

86. Hess, 172, 209, 211.

87. Reese to Poe, September 14, 1864, *OR*, 38(3):67; Cryder and Miller, *View from the Ranks*, 421.

88. Henry Pippitt Diary, July 26–28, 1864, Mohi-HS; Welton to parents, July 31, 1864, Chauncey Brunson Welton Papers, UNC; John W. Tuttle Diary, July 26–27, 30, 1864, UK; Gates, *Rough Side of War*, 248, 253; Harwell, "Campaign from Chattanooga to Atlanta," 272; Wood to Fullerton, August 14, 1864, *OR*, 38(1):388.

89. Kirwan, *Johnny Green*, 150; M. L. Wheeler Memoirs, 34, PMSHS; John Henry Marsh to Quintard, July 26, 1864, Charles Todd Quintard Papers, DU; Cate, *Two Soldiers*, 102–3.

90. Angle, *Three Years*, 247–48; Sherman to Thomas, July 28, 1864, *OR*, 38(5):280.

91. Lee to Mason, January 30, 1865, *OR*, 38(3):763; [Shoup] to Hardee, Cheatham, and Lee, July 29, 1864, 3:25 P.M., and Hood to Seddon, July 30, 1864, *OR*, 38(5):925, 930.

92. [Shoup] to Cheatham and Lee, July 29, 1864, 3:00 P.M., *OR*, 38(5):925.

93. Castel, *Decision in the West*, 434–36; Connelly, *Autumn of Glory*, 454; Lofland to Townes, September 10, 1864, and Oliver to Wilkinson, August 4, 1864, *OR*, 38(3):189, 344; Howard to Sherman, July 28, 1864, *OR*, 38(5):283; Charles W. Wills, *Army Life*, 287.

94. Diary, July 28, 1864, Daniel Harris Reynolds Papers, UAF; Bek, "Civil War Diary," 525.

95. Tower, *Carolinian Goes to War*, 236–37.

96. Worley, *War Memoirs*, 98–99; Stephen Cowley to Minor, August 6, 1864, Hubbard T. Minor Papers, USAMHI.

CHAPTER 11

1. Anderson to Ratchford, February 9, 1865, *OR*, 38(3):769.

2. Sherman, *Memoirs*, 2:92; Special Field Orders No. 82, Army of the Tennessee, July 29, 1864, *OR*, 38(5):300; Cryder and Miller, *View from the Ranks*, 423.

3. Bauer, *Soldiering*, 154–58; Shimp to wife, July 26, 1864, William Shimp Papers, USAMHI; Holzhueter, "William Wallace's Civil War Letters," 103.

4. Williams to Whipple, September 20, 1864; Ruger to Pittman, September 11, 1864;

and Boughton to Pittman, September 10, 1864, *OR*, 38(2):18, 62–63, 93–94; Marshall to mother, July 30, 1864, John Law Marshall Letters, New-York Historical Society, New York, New York; Morse, *Letters*, 182–84.

5. [Shoup] to Stevenson, July 31, 1864; [Shoup] to Cheatham, July 31, 1864; and [Shoup] to Lee, August 1, 1864, *OR*, 38(5):933, 935, 937; Lowrey to Benham, September 20, 1864, and Young to Sanders, September 17, 1864, *OR*, 38(3):734, 910.

6. [Shoup] to Beckham, July 30, 1864; [Shoup] to Stevenson, July 30, 1864; and [Shoup] to Presstman, August 1, 1864, *OR*, 38(5):931, 938; diary, August 1, 12, 15, 1864, Daniel Harris Reynolds Papers, UAF; Walthall to Gale, January 14, 1865, *OR*, 38(3):928.

7. Sherman to Thomas, July 30, 31, 1864; Sherman to Howard, July 31, 1864; and Special Field Orders No. 48, Military Division of the Mississippi, August 1, 1864, *OR*, 38(5):301, 309–10, 314, 327; Poe to [Delafield], October 8, 1865, *OR*, 38(1):133; diary, July 30, 1864, Orlando Metcalfe Poe Papers, LC.

8. Fullerton to Grose, July 30, 1864, *OR*, 38(5):301.

9. Stanley to Whipple, September 15, 1864, and Fullerton journal, *OR*, 38(1):212, 912.

10. Stanley to Whipple, September 15, 1864, and Fullerton journal, *OR*, 38(1):212, 912.

11. Castel, *Decision in the West*, 453–54; Poe to [Delafield], October 8, 1865, *OR*, 38(1):133; Schofield to Sherman, August 2, 1864, *OR*, 38(5):334; Sherman, *Memoirs*, 2:92; Black, "Marching with Sherman," 325.

12. Poe to [Delafield], October 8, 1865, *OR*, 38(1):133.

13. Black, "Marching with Sherman," 325; Henry H. Wright, *History of the Sixth Iowa*, 312–13.

14. Gibson to Bestow, August 3, 1864, *OR*, 38(1):400–401.

15. Post to Mason, September 15, 1864, *OR*, 38(1):264.

16. Sherman to Grant, August 4, 1864, *OR*, 38(5):350; field visit to Utoy Creek, May 9, 1987.

17. Special Field Orders No. 51, Headquarters, Military Division of the Mississippi, August 4, 1864, and Special Field Orders No. 71, Headquarters, Army of the Ohio, August 4, 1864, *OR*, 38(5):364–66.

18. Sherman to Schofield, August 4, 1864, *OR*, 38(5):360.

19. Special Field Orders No. 88, Headquarters, Army of the Tennessee, August 4, 1864, *OR*, 38(5):366–67.

20. Castel, *Decision in the West*, 455–56.

21. French to Gale, December 6, 1864, and Clark to West, September 18, 1864, *OR*, 38(3):904, 921–22; [Shoup] to Lee, August 4, 1864, *OR*, 38(5):943.

22. Sherman to Thomas, August 5, 1864, *OR*, 38(5):372.

23. Cox to Schofield, August 5, 1864, and Schofield to Cox, August 5, 1864, *OR*, 38(5):385.

24. B. F. Thompson, *History of the 112th Regiment of Illinois*, 231–32.

25. Angle, *Three Years*, 250; Gleason to Lowrie, August 16, 1864, *OR*, 38(1):791; Morgan, "Home Letters," 234, AHC; Castel, *Decision in the West*, 456.

26. Banning to Wilson, September 9, 1864, *OR*, 38(1):706; Castel, *Decision in the West*, 456.

27. Sherman to Thomas, August 5, 1864, *OR*, 38(5):371.

28. Lee to Mason, January 30, 1865, *OR*, 38(3):763; Castel, *Decision in the West*, 458–59; Kirwan, *Johnny Green*, 151; Ed Porter Thompson, *History of the Orphan Brigade*, 264.

29. Davis to Hood, August 5, 1864, *OR*, 38(5):946; Kendall, "Recollections of a Confederate Officer," 1193.

30. Cox to Campbell, September 10, 1864, *OR*, 38(2):689.

31. Cox to Campbell, September 10, 1864, *OR*, 38(2):689; James M. Merrill and Marshall, "Georgia through Kentucky Eyes," 331; Kirwan, *Johnny Green*, 151; Ed Porter Thompson, *History of the Orphan Brigade*, 264; Castel, *Decision in the West*, 459.

32. Ed Porter Thompson, *History of the Orphan Brigade*, 264; Kirwan, *Johnny Green*, 151; James M. Merrill and Marshall, "Georgia through Kentucky Eyes," 332; Schofield to Sherman, August 6, 1864, *OR*, 38(5):399; Castel, *Decision in the West*, 459.

33. Thomas to Sherman, August 6, 1864, *OR*, 38(5):392; French, *Two Wars*, 220.

34. General Orders No. 62, Headquarters, Lee's Corps, August 7, 1864, *OR*, 38(3):765; Kirwan, *Johnny Green*, 151.

35. Castel, *Decision in the West*, 460; Ed Porter Thompson, *History of the Orphan Brigade*, 265; Ragle to Hubbell, no date, *OR*, 38(2):629.

36. Castel, *Decision in the West*, 460–61; Ragle to Hubbell, no date, *OR*, 38(2):629; Sherman to Thomas, August 7, 1864, and Howard to Schofield, August 7, 1864, *OR*, 38(5):412, 416; Poe to [Delafield], October 8, 1865; Banning to Wilson, September 9, 1864; and Baird to McClurg, September 7, 1864, *OR*, 38(1):134, 706, 747; Ellison, *On to Atlanta*, 72; Slack to father and mother, August 7, 1864, Albert L. Slack Letters, EU.

37. Kirwan, *Johnny Green*, 151; record of events, Company B, 6th Kentucky (C.S.), *SOR*, pt. 2, 23:335; [Shoup] to Lee, August 7, 1864, and Ratchford to Bate, August 7, 1864, *OR*, 38(5):948, 949; Ratchford to Clayton, August 9, 1864, and General Orders No. 63, Headquarters, Lee's Corps, August 12, 1864, *OR*, 38(3):766.

38. M. L. Wheeler Memoirs, 34–35, PMSHS; Buck, *Cleburne and His Command*, 249; Cleburne to Roy, August 7, 1864, and Roy to Cleburne, August 7, 1864, *OR*, 38(5):949–50; Lowrey to Benham, September 20, 1864, *OR*, 38(3):734.

39. Sherman to Howard, August 1, 8, 1864, and Sherman to Halleck, August 7, 1864, *OR*, 38(5):325, 408–9, 429; Sherman to Ellen, August 2, 1864, in Simpson and Berlin, *Sherman's Civil War*, 681; Stephen Davis, *Atlanta Will Fall*, 159.

40. Sherman to Thomas, August 7, 1864, and Thomas to Sherman, August 8, 1864, *OR*, 38(5):412, 419; diary, August 10, 1864, Orlando Metcalfe Poe Papers, LC; Bauer, *Soldiering*, 163; Stephen Davis, *Atlanta Will Fall*, 159.

41. Osborn to Marshall, September 16, 1864, *OR*, 38(3):60; Harwell and Racine, *Fiery Trail*, 17–18.

42. Osborn to Marshall, September 16, 1864, and Corse to Barnes, September 8, 1864, *OR*, 38(3):60, 411; Sherman to Thomas, August 10, 1864, and Howard to Sherman, August 10, 1864, *OR*, 38(5):449, 453.

43. French to Gale, December 6, 1864, *OR*, 38(3):904.

44. Sherman to Thomas, August 8, 1864; Sherman to Halleck, August 9, 1864; Sherman to Thomas, August 10, 1864; and Sherman to Howard, August 10, 1864, *OR*, 38(5):431, 434, 448, 449, 452–53.

45. Franklin M. Garrett, "Civilian Life in Atlanta," 31–32; Venet, *Sam Richards's Civil War Diary*, 232.

46. Davis to wife, July 23–24, 1864, Leander E. Davis Letters, NYSL; Poe to wife, September 7, 1864, Orlando Metcalfe Poe Papers, LC.

47. Cate, *Two Soldiers*, 108; Hood, "Defense of Atlanta," 342–43; Castel, *Decision in the West*, 464; unidentified Southern newspaper correspondent quoted in Neal, *Illustrated History*, 261–62.

48. William E. Sloan Diary, 72, TSLA.

49. Gould and Kennedy, *Memoirs of a Dutch Mudsill*, 282; Bauer, *Soldiering*, 168; Bohrnstedt, *Soldiering with Sherman*, 147; Rieger, *Through One Man's Eyes*, 126.

50. Schofield to Sherman, August 9, 1864, *OR*, 38(5):441; Watkins to not stated, August 24, 1864, John Watkins Papers, UTK.

51. Schofield to Sherman, August 8, 1864, 8:30 P.M.; Sherman to Thomas and Howard, August 9, 1864; and Sherman to Schofield, August 9, 1864, *OR*, 38(5):423, 435, 441.

52. Sherman to Thomas and Howard, August 10, 1864; Sherman to Thomas, August 10, 1864; and Schofield to Sherman, August 10, 1864, *OR*, 38(5):448–51.

53. Sherman to Grant, August 10, 1864, 8:00 P.M.; Sherman to Schofield, August 10, 1864; Howard to Sherman, August 10, 1864; and Sherman to Howard, August 10, 1864, *OR*, 38(5):447, 451, 453.

54. Sherman to Schofield, August 10, 11, 1864; Schofield to Sherman, August 11, 1864, 3:45 P.M.; and Schofield to Hascall, August 11, 1864, *OR*, 38(5):461–64, 467.

55. Schofield to Sherman, August 11, 1864, 9:30 P.M., *OR*, 38(5):462.

56. Taggart to Blair, August 9, 1864; Dodge to Clark, August 9, 1864; Lightburn to Townes, August 9, 10, 1864; Harrow to Townes, August 9, 1864; Special Field Orders No. 94, Headquarters, Army of the Tennessee, August 10, 1864; Logan to Clark, August 10, 1864; Woods to Townes, August 10, 1864; and Blair to Clark, August 11, 1864, *OR*, 38(5):443–44, 454–55, 470; Maharay, *Lights and Shadows*, 202–3.

57. Stanley to Whipple, September 15, 1864, and Fullerton journal, *OR*, 38(1):212, 923.

58. Proposal signed by Howard, August 13, 1864, and Schofield to Sherman, August 14, 1864, *OR*, 38(5):487–88, 498–99.

59. Thomas to Sherman, August 12, 15, 1864, and Sherman to Halleck, August 13, 1864, 8:00 A.M., *OR*, 38(5):472, 482, 507.

60. Sherman to Schofield, August 15, 1864, and Schofield to Sherman, August 14, 16, 1864, *OR*, 38(5):499, 511, 534; Henry Pippitt Diary, August 16, 1864, Mohi-HS; B. F. Thompson, *History of the 112th Regiment*, 239.

61. Hardee to wife, August 12, 1864, Hardee Family Papers, ADAH.

62. Hardee to wife, August 13, 1864, Hardee Family Papers, ADAH.

63. J. Milton Glass statement, August 18, 1864; [Shoup] to Hardee, August 13, 1864; and Roy to Cleburne, August 19, 1864, *OR*, 38(5):580, 961, 976; Bennett and Tillery, *Struggle for the Life*, 206.

64. *History of Company B*, 80.

65. Sherman, *Memoirs*, 2:102–3; Sherman to Thomas, August 16, 1864, *OR*, 38(5):528.

66. Sherman to Thomas, August 16, 1864; Hood to Seddon, July 30, 1864; and Wheeler to Shoup, August 16, 1864, *OR*, 38(5):528, 930, 967; Hood, *Advance and Retreat*, 198; Wheeler to Mason, October 9, 1864, *OR*, 38(3):957; Castel, *Decision in the West*, 466; Stephen Davis, *Atlanta Will Fall*, 171.

67. Sherman to Thomas, August 15, 1864, *OR*, 38(5):506; Castel, *Decision in the West*, 469–73.

68. Sherman to Thomas, August 17, 1864, *OR*, 38(5):548.

CHAPTER 12

1. Circular, [Headquarters, Army of Tennessee], August 13, 1864, *OR*, 38(5):962; Circular, Headquarters, Army of Tennessee, August 13, 1864, George Washington Finley Harper Papers, UNC; Isaac Gaillard Foster Diary, August 14, 1864, James Foster and Family Correspondence, LSU.

2. Circular, Headquarters, Loring's Division, August 13, 1864, Samuel Thompson Papers, UNC; Circular, Headquarters, Loring's Division, August 19, 25, 1864, Featherston Order Book, Winfield Scott Featherston Collection, UM; Stewart to Mason, January 12, 1865, and Walthall to Gale, January 14, 1865, *OR*, 38(3):872, 928.

3. [Shoup] to Lee, August 11, 1864, *OR*, 38(5):956; Circular, Headquarters, Lee's Corps, August 12, 1864, General Orders and Circulars, MOC.

4. Tower, *Carolinian Goes to War*, 237–38.

5. Joseph B. Morrison to [T. G.] Morrison, August 8, 1864, and Circular, Headquarters, First Brigade, Second Division, Sixteenth Corps, August 11, 1864, G. B. Cockrell Collection, LMU; Holmes to Swift, September 7, 1864, *OR*, 38(1):730; Bennett and Tillery, *Struggle for the Life*, 194; Partridge, *History of the Ninety-Sixth*, 387n; Cryder and Miller, *View from the Ranks*, 429, 432–33; Black, "Marching with Sherman," 326–27; "Enlistment and in Camp," Raymond Harper Collection, Dunkirk, New York.

6. Holzhueter, "William Wallace's Civil War Letters," 104; Bryant, *History of the Third Regiment*, 264.

7. Anderson to Ratchford, February 9, 1865, and Young to Sanders, September 17, 1864, *OR*, 38(3):770, 910–11.

8. Henry H. Wright, *History of the Sixth Iowa*, 314.

9. Diary, July 24, 1864, Daniel Harris Reynolds Papers, UAF; Young to Sanders, September 17, 1864, *OR*, 38(3):911; Foster to not stated, August 25, 1864, *OR*, 38(5):989; Howe, *Marching with Sherman*, 55; Gates, *Rough Side of War*, 275; Jarman, "History of Company K," MDAH; Norman D. Brown, *One of Cleburne's Command*, 121; Bauer, *Soldiering*, 163; Muir, "Battle of Atlanta," 110–11.

10. Young to Sanders, September 17, 1864, *OR*, 38(3):912.

11. Byrne, *Uncommon Soldiers*, 183; Gates, *Rough Side of War*, 279; Lucas, *New History of the 99th Indiana*, 124; Partridge, *History of the Ninety-Sixth*, 387n–388n.

12. Hood to Cooper, February 15, 1865, and Anderson to Ratchford, February 9, 1865, *OR*, 38(3):632, 770–71; Tower, *Carolinian Goes to War*, 254.

13. French to Gale, December 6, 1864, and Clark to West, September 18, 1864, *OR*, 38(3):905, 921.

14. Henry H. Wright, *History of the Sixth Iowa*, 313.

15. Partridge, *History of the Ninety-Sixth*, 387; Bryant, *History of the Third Regiment*, 260.

16. Harwell and Racine, *Fiery Trail*, 5; Poe to [Delafield], October 8, 1865, *OR*, 38(1):134–35; Sherman to Ellen, August 9, 1864, in Simpson and Berlin, *Sherman's Civil War*, 685.

17. Cate, *Two Soldiers*, 105; Isaac Gaillard Foster Diary, August 11, 1864, LSU.

18. Corse to Barnes, September 8, 1864, and French to Gale, December 6, 1864, *OR*, 38(3):411, 905; Ellison, *On to Atlanta*, 73.

19. Corse to Barnes, September 8, 1864, and Blodgett to Morrison, September 5, 1864, *OR*, 38(3):410, 472–73; Boughton to Pittman, September 10, 1864, *OR*, 38(2):94.

20. Poe to [Delafield], October 8, 1865, *OR*, 38(1):135; Harwell and Racine, *Fiery*

Trail, 7; M. D. Leggett to Force, August 4, 1864, M. F. Force Papers, UW; Swett remarks accompanying abstract of inspection report, September 20, 1864, *OR*, 38(3):684; [Dwight], "How We Fight at Atlanta," 666.

21. Gary to Mickle, September 7, 1864, *OR*, 38(2):485–86; Special Field Orders No. 59, Headquarters, Left Wing, Sixteenth Corps, August 11, 1864, *OR*, 38(5):471.

22. Anderson to Ratchford, February 9, 1865, *OR*, 38(3):769–70.

23. W. L. Truman Memoirs, August 11–12, 1864, www.cedarcroft.com; Kendall, "Recollections of a Confederate Officer," 1180; Isaac Gaillard Foster Diary, August 8, 1864, LSU.

24. Tower, *Carolinian Goes to War*, 241, 253–54.

25. Neal to Ella, August 4, 1864, Andrew Jackson Neal Papers, EU.

26. Chamberlin, "Skirmish Line," 192; Lee to Mason, January 30, 1865, and Anderson to Ratchford, February 9, 1865, *OR*, 38(3):763, 770.

27. Baumgartner, *Blood & Sacrifice*, 160, 163.

28. Bauer, *Soldiering*, 160–61.

29. Ellison, *On to Atlanta*, 73; Maharay, *Lights and Shadows*, 204; Partridge, *History of the Ninety-Sixth*, 387; Walthall to Gale, January 14, 1865, *OR*, 38(3):928.

30. Tower, *Carolinian Goes to War*, 238–39.

31. Ibid., 239, 253.

32. Ibid., 239.

33. Ibid., 253; Isaac Gaillard Foster Diary, August 29, 1864, LSU.

34. Diary, July 24, 1864, Daniel Harris Reynolds Papers, UAF.

35. General Orders No. 63, Headquarters, Lee's Corps, August 12, 1864, *OR*, 38(3):766.

36. French to Gale, December 6, 1864, *OR*, 38(3):905; French, *Two Wars*, 220, 222.

37. Dustin to Grubbs, September 15, 1864, *OR*, 38(2):362.

38. Harrison to Speed, September 14, 1864, *OR*, 38(2):349.

39. Stanley to Fullerton, September, no date, 1864, *OR*, 38(1):226.

40. Kirby to Mason, August 18, 1864, *OR*, 38(5):576; Anderson to Ratchford, February 9, 1865, *OR*, 38(3):770.

41. Baird to McClurg, September 7, 1864, *OR*, 38(1):747, 754; M. D. Leggett to Force, August 10, 1864, M. F. Force Papers, UW; Willis Perry Burt Diary, August 14, 1864, Georgia Historical Society, Savannah, Georgia; list of casualties in Mercer's Brigade, July 20 to September 1, 1864, and French to Gale, December 6, 1864, *OR*, 38(3):756–58, 907.

42. Hazen, *Narrative of Military Service*, 419–20.

43. William Walton, *Civil War Courtship*, 95–96; Quaife, *From the Cannon's Mouth*, 336; Chamberlin, "Skirmish Line," 193.

44. Fullerton journal, *OR*, 38(1):919.

45. *History of Company B*, 78.

46. Hughes, *Civil War Memoir*, 185.

47. Isaac Gaillard Foster Diary, August 14, 1864, LSU; Elmore to parents, July 26, 1864, Day Elmore Letters, CHM; Dent to wife, July 9, 1864, Stouten Hubert Dent Papers, ADAH; Maxwell, *Autobiography*, 247; Bryant, *History of the Third Regiment*, 260.

48. Isaac Gaillard Foster Diary, August 8, 1864, LSU; Comey, *Legacy of Valor*, 190.

49. Griffin to wife, August 11, 1864, Daniel F. Griffin Papers, ISL.

50. Robertson, " 'Such Is War,' " 332; Bennett and Tillery, *Struggle for the Life*, 194; Philips to Campbell, September 9, 1864, *OR*, 38(3):312–13; Butler, *Letters Home*, 141.

51. William E. Sloan Diary, 118, TSLA.

52. Black, "Marching with Sherman," 327.

53. Maharay, *Lights and Shadows*, 205.

54. Isaac Gaillard Foster Diary, August 8, 1864, LSU; Maxwell, *Autobiography*, 247.

55. Lea to father, August 12, 1864, in Cull, "Civil War Letters," MDAH; Davis to Bettie, August 9, 1864, Newton N. Davis Papers, ADAH; A. T. Holliday to Lizzie, July 28, August 3, 1864, A. T. and Elizabeth Holliday Civil War Correspondence, AHC.

56. Maxwell, *Autobiography*, 247; Kerwood, *Annals of the Fifty-Seventh*, 273; Circular, Headquarters, Army of Tennessee, July 30, 1864, Featherston Order Book, Winfield Scott Featherston Collection, UM.

57. Henry H. Wright, *History of the Sixth Iowa*, 316.

58. Ibid., 315; Tower, *Carolinian Goes to War*, 240.

59. Bryant, *History of the Third Regiment*, 264; Bohrnstedt, *Soldiering with Sherman*, 135; Circular, Headquarters, Lee's Corps, August 12, 1864, General Orders and Circulars, MOC.

60. Speir to wife, August 14, 1864, J. S. Speir Collection, AHC; Walthall to Gale, January 14, 1865, *OR*, 38(3):928; diary, August 13, 1864, Abraham J. Seay Collection, UO.

61. Bek, "Civil War Diary," 526; Isaac Gaillard Foster Diary, August 14, 1864, LSU; diary, August 29, 1864, Avington Wayne Simpson Papers, UNC.

62. Isaac Gaillard Foster Diary, August 8 1864, LSU; Henry H. Wright, *History of the Sixth Iowa*, 316.

63. Charles D. Gammon Diary, August 7, 1864, EU; Henry H. Wright, *History of the Sixth Iowa*, 316.

64. W. L. Truman Memoirs, August 7, 1864, www.cedarcroft.com; Brackett, "With Sherman at Atlanta," 432.

65. Bronson, "Recollections," 61, TC; Butler, *Letters Home*, 143.

66. "Sketches of the Confederate War," 8, in Thomas T. Smith Papers, MDAH; W. L. Truman Memoirs, August 7, 1864, www.cedarcroft.com; Ragle to Hubbell, no date, *OR*, 38(2):629; Isaac Gaillard Foster Diary, August 5, 1864, LSU.

67. Henry H. Wright, *History of the Sixth Iowa*, 315; O'Leary and Jackson, "Civil War Letters," 175.

68. Ellison, *On to Atlanta*, 74.

69. Ratchford to Clayton, August 13, 1864, and General Field Orders No. 15, Headquarters, Army of Tennessee, August 15, 1864, *OR*, 38(5):962, 965; Circular, Headquarters, Lee's Corps, August 13, 1864, General Orders and Circulars, MOC.

70. Ellison, *On to Atlanta*, 76; Patrick and Willey, *Fighting for Liberty*, 241.

71. Patrick and Willey, *Fighting for Liberty*, 241.

72. Tower, *Carolinian Goes to War*, 240.

73. Smith to Dustin, September 23, 1864, *OR*, 38(2):356; Jones to Lofland, August 17, 1864, *OR*, 38(5):558.

74. Benjamin Putnam Weaver to father and mother, August 18, 1864, Benjamin Putnam Weaver Letters, EU.

75. Hopkins to Taylor, August 9, 1864; Burton to Case, August 17, 1864; Hopkins to Williams, August 22, 1864; and Edge to Logan, August 22, 1864, *OR*, 38(5):437, 552, 630–31.

76. Thomas H. Herndon to R. A. Hatcher, August 14, 1864, John B. Jordan Service Record, NARA; statement of John B. Jordan, August 14, 1864, *OR*, 38(5):494–95.

77. Statement of John B. Jordan, August 14, 1864, *OR*, 38(5):494–95.

78. John B. Jordan to D. W. Flimener, February 21, 1865; Thomas H. Herndon to Samuel Cooper, March 6, 1865; and index cards, John B. Jordan Service Record, NARA.

79. Index cards, John B. Jordan Service Record, NARA.

80. Douglas J. Cater to Fannie, August 4, 1864, Douglas J. Cater and Rufus W. Cater Papers, LC; Benjamin Putnam Weaver to father and mother, August 18, 1864, Benjamin Putnam Weaver Letters, EU.

81. Bennett and Tillery, *Struggle for the Life*, 196–97.

82. Salomon to Boughton, September 15, 1864, *OR*, 38(2):100–101.

CHAPTER 13

1. Poe to [Delafield], October 8, 1865, *OR*, 38(1):135; Reese to Poe, September 14, 1864, *OR*, 38(3):67.

2. Poe to [Delafield], October 8, 1865, *OR*, 38(1):135; Boughton to Pittman, September 10, 1864, *OR*, 38(2):94; Reese to Poe, September 14, 1864, *OR*, 38(3):67.

3. Sherman to Thomas, August 24, 1864, *OR*, 38(5):651.

4. Howard to Sherman, August 24, 1864, and Sherman to Howard, August 24, 1864, *OR*, 38(5):654.

5. Orders, Headquarters, Twentieth Corps, August 24, 1864, *OR*, 38(5):660.

6. Special Field Orders No. 108, Headquarters, Army of the Tennessee, August 24, 1864; Thomas to Howard, August 25, 1864; and Howard to Thomas, August 25, 1864, *OR*, 38(5):661, 664; *History of the Fifteenth Regiment*, 390–91.

7. Schofield, *Forty-Six Years*, 154–55.

8. Ellison, *On to Atlanta*, 79–80; Bauer, *Soldiering*, 164; Jackson, *Colonel's Diary*, 145; Cryder and Miller, *View from the Ranks*, 433–34; Sherman, *Memoirs*, 2:105; Castel, *Decision in the West*, 485–87.

9. Bauer, *Soldiering*, 165; Forbes to Perkins, August 26, 1864, and Perkins to Kelly, August 28, 1864, *OR*, 38(5):671, 692; Bauer, *Soldiering*, 165; Boughton to Pittman, September 10, 1864; Stevens to Creigh, September 8, 1864; and Craig to Creigh, September 10, 1864, *OR*, 38(2):95, 185, 202; Morse, *Letters*, 186–87; Holzhueter, "William Wallace's Civil War Letters," 107; Comey, *Legacy of Valor*, 192; Nichol to father, August 31, 1864, David Nichol Papers, USAMHI.

10. Stanley to Whipple, August 26, 1864, *OR*, 38(5):669; Ellison, *On to Atlanta*, 80–81.

11. Lee to Mason, January 30, 1865, *OR*, 38(3):763–64.

12. French, *Two Wars*, 221; George Anderson Mercer Diary, August 29, 1864, UNC; diary, August 28, 1864, Avington Wayne Simpson Papers, UNC; Baumgartner, *Blood & Sacrifice*, 163; Wilson, *Reminiscences*, not paginated.

13. French to Gale, December 6, 1864; Young to Sanders, September 17, 1864; and Walthall to Gale, January 14, 1865, *OR*, 38(3):906, 912, 929; French, *Two Wars*, 221.

14. Gates, *Rough Side of War*, 278; Clayton to wife, August 24, 28, 1864, Henry De Lamar Clayton Papers, University of Alabama, William Stanley Hoole Special Collections, Tuscaloosa, Alabama.

15. Hood to Bragg, September 4, 1864, *OR*, 52(2):729.

16. Thoburn, *My Experiences*, 115–17; Harwell and Racine, *Fiery Trail*, 12; Logan to Clark, August 27, 1864, and Hazen to Townes, August 27, 1864, *OR*, 38(5):680; Doan to [Fortner], September 9, 1864, *OR*, 38(1):800.

17. [Shoup] to Lee, August 27, 1864, *OR*, 38(5):994; Stephen Davis, *Atlanta Will Fall*, 177–78.

18. Sherman, *Memoirs*, 2:105; Poe to [Delafield], October 8, 1865, *OR*, 38(1):136; Cryder and Miller, *View from the Ranks*, 434; Harwell and Racine, *Fiery Trail*, 11; diary, August 29, 1864, Abraham J. Seay Collection, UO; Castel, *Decision in the West*, 491.

19. Castel, *Decision in the West*, 489.

20. [Shoup] to Brown, August 28, 1864, *OR*, 38(5):998; Cabaniss, *Civil War Journal and Letters*, 70; Kirwan, *Johnny Green*, 152–54; record of events, Company B, 6th Kentucky, *SOR*, pt. 2, 23:336; Castel, *Decision in the West*, 491.

21. Diary, August 28–29, 1864, Daniel Harris Reynolds Papers, UAF.

22. Castel, *Decision in the West*, 494–95; Black, "Marching with Sherman," 328; diary, August 30, 1864, Daniel Harris Reynolds Papers, UAF.

23. Cox, *Military Reminiscences*, 2:282; Henry Pippitt Diary, August 30, 1864, Mohi-HS.

24. [Shoup] to Jackson, August 30, 1864, *OR*, 38(5):1005; Stephen Davis, *Atlanta Will Fall*, 179–81; Buck, *Cleburne and His Command*, 250.

25. Stephen Davis, *Atlanta Will Fall*, 182, 184–85; Martin L. Smith Diary, August 30, 1864, Mary-HS; Dodge to Stewart, August 29, 1864, *OR*, 38(5):999.

26. Lee to Mason, January 30, 1865, and Anderson to Ratchford, February 9, 1865, *OR*, 38(3):765, 772–73; Cabaniss, *Civil War Journal and Letters*, 71; Castel, *Decision in the West*, 495–96.

27. Castel, *Decision in the West*, 497–98; Dawson, *Life and Services*, 80; Jackson, *Colonel's Diary*, 148; Cryder and Miller, *View from the Ranks*, 436; *Story of the Fifty-Fifth Regiment*, 367.

28. Hardee to Cooper, April 5, 1865, and Maney to Buck, September 28, 1864, *OR*, 38(3):700, 710–11; diary, August 31, 1864, Daniel Harris Reynolds Papers, UAF; Castel, *Decision in the West*, 498–502.

29. Maney to Buck, September 28, 1864; Lee to Mason, January 30, 1865; and Anderson to Ratchford, February 9, 1865, *OR*, 38(3):708, 764, 773; [Shoup] to Hardee, August 31, 1864, 3:00 A.M., 3:10 A.M., 3:20 A.M., 10:00 A.M., *OR*, 38(5):1006–7.

30. Maney to Buck, September 28, 1864; Weir to Milner, September 6, 1864; and Granbury to Milner, September 5, 1864, *OR*, 38(3):711, 735, 744; Kirwan, *Johnny Green*, 154–55; Castel, *Decision in the West*, 502–3.

31. Mott to assistant adjutant general, First Brigade, Second Division, Fifteenth Corps, September 9, 1864, and Anderson to Ratchford, February 9, 1865, *OR*, 38(3):218, 773–74.

32. Tower, *Carolinian Goes to War*, 246–47; Anderson to Ratchford, February 9, 1865, *OR*, 38(3):775.

33. Tower, *Carolinian Goes to War*, 247; Gibson to Macon, September 16, 1864, *OR*, 38(3):857–58.

34. Anderson to Ratchford, February 9, 1865, and Gibson to Macon, September 16, 1864, *OR*, 38(3):775, 858; Sherman to Schofield, September 1, 1864, *OR*, 38(5):755; Castel, *Decision in the West*, 503.

35. Lee to Mason, January 30, 1865, *OR*, 38(3):764.

36. Tower, *Carolinian Goes to War*, 245.

37. Jones to Macon, September 16, 1864, *OR*, 38(3):835.

38. Phillips, *Personal Reminiscences*, 54.

39. Hood, "Defense of Atlanta," 343; Hardee to Cooper, April 5, 1865, *OR*, 38(3):702.

40. Hood to Bragg, September 4, 1864, *OR*, 52(2):730.

41. Fullerton journal, *OR*, 38(1):931; Sherman to Howard, August 31, 1864, *OR*, 38(5):726; Castel, *Decision in the West*, 504; Stephen Davis, *Atlanta Will Fall*, 185, 187.

42. [Shoup] to Hardee, August 31, 1864, *OR*, 38(5):1007; Lee to Mason, January 30, 1865, *OR*, 38(3):765; Castel, *Decision in the West*, 505, 507, 509–10.

43. Castel, *Decision in the West*, 511.

44. Sherman to Schofield, September 1, 1864, *OR*, 38(5):755; Buck, *Cleburne and His Command*, 253; Lowrey to Benham, September 10, 1864, and Granbury to Milner, September 5, 1864, *OR*, 38(3):728, 745; Lowrey, "General M. P. Lowrey," 372–73; Castel, *Decision in the West*, 510–11.

45. Weir to Milner, September 6, 1864; Granbury to Milner, September 5, 1864; and Olmstead to Palmer, September 5, 1864, *OR*, 38(3):735–36, 744, 756; M. L. Wheeler Memoirs, 35, PMSHS; Hughes, *Civil War Memoir*, 234, 237.

46. Lowrey to Benham, September 10, 1864, and Green to [Buck], September 5, 1864, *OR*, 38(3):728–29, 742; Buck, *Cleburne and His Command*, 253–54; field visit to Jonesboro, May 9, 1987.

47. Buck, *Cleburne and His Command*, 253–54; Castel, *Decision in the West*, 512–13.

48. Ed Porter Thompson, *History of the Orphan Brigade*, 266–67; Grainger, *Four Years*, 20; Kirwan, *Johnny Green*, 157–58.

49. Capers to Smith, September 12, 1864, *OR*, 38(3):718–19.

50. Girardi and Hughes, *Memoirs of Brigadier General*, 135; Castel, *Decision in the West*, 515–16; Buck, *Cleburne and His Command*, 254; Green to [Buck], September 5, 1864, *OR*, 38(3):742.

51. Mizner to Morrison, September 2, 1864, *SOR*, 13–14; Green to [Buck], September 5, 1864, *OR*, 38(3):742; Castel, *Decision in the West*, 517.

52. Mizner to Morrison, September 2, 1864, *SOR*, 13–14; Green to [Buck], September 5, 1864, *OR*, 38(3):742; Mizner, "Reminiscences," 80–81.

53. Green to [Buck], September 5, 1864, *OR*, 38(3):742; Mumford H. Dixon Diary, September 1, 1864, EU; Christ, *Getting Used to Being Shot At*, 104.

54. Moore to Smith, September 3, 1864, and Given to Montague, September 5, 1864, *OR*, 38(1):600, 617; Kirwan, *Johnny Green*, 160.

55. Kirwan, *Johnny Green*, 161; Ed Porter Thompson, *History of the Orphan Brigade*, 267; record of events, Company B, 6th Kentucky, *SOR*, pt. 2, 23:336.

56. Capers to Smith, September 12, 1864, *OR*, 38(3):719; Castel, *Decision in the West*, 518, 520; Stanley to Whipple, September 1, 1864, *OR*, 38(5):747; Stanley to Whipple, September 15, 1864, *OR*, 38(1):215.

57. Capers to Smith, September 12, 1864, *OR*, 38(3):719.

58. Granbury to Milner, September 5, 1864, *OR*, 38(3):745; Buck, *Cleburne and His Command*, 254–55; Norman D. Brown, *One of Cleburne's Command*, 128.

59. Buck, *Cleburne and His Command*, 254; Green to [Buck], September 5, 1864, *OR*, 38(3):743.

60. Lowrey to Benham, September 10, 1864; Green to [Buck], September 5, 1864; and Granbury to Milner, September 5, 1864, *OR*, 38(3):729, 743, 745; Buck, *Cleburne and His Command*, 254–55.

61. Swett remarks accompanying abstract of inspection report, September 20, 1864; Lowrey to Benham, September 10, 1864; and Green to [Buck], September 5, 1864, *OR*, 38(3):685, 729, 743; Cate, *Two Soldiers*, 126–27.

62. Baird to McClurg, September 7, 1864, *OR*, 38(1):752.

63. Angle, *Three Years*, 258.

64. Buck, *Cleburne and His Command*, 255; Granbury to Milner, September 5, 1864, *OR*, 38(3):745; M. L. Wheeler Memoirs, 35–36, PMSHS; Mizner to Morrison, September 2, 1864, *SOR*, 14; Walker to Lowrie, September 8, 1864, *OR*, 38(1):766.

65. Castel, *Decision in the West*, 524, 526; Hardee to Cooper, April 5, 1865, *OR*, 38(3): 701–2; Norman D. Brown, *One of Cleburne's Command*, 131; McMurry, *Atlanta*, 174.

66. Swett remarks accompanying abstract of inspection report, September 20, 1864, *OR*, 38(3):684; Morse to Robert, August 30, 1864, Charles F. Morse Papers, Massachusetts Historical Society, Boston, Massachusetts; Castel, *Decision in the West*, 527; unidentified diary, September 1–2, 1864, UTA.

67. Quaife, *From the Cannon's Mouth*, 341.

CHAPTER 14

1. George Anderson Mercer Diary, September 2, 1864, UNC; Harwell and Racine, *Fiery Trail*, 22; Buck, *Cleburne and His Command*, 258; Weir to Milner, September 27, 1864, *OR*, 38(3):736; Philip D. Jordan, "Forty Days," 139; Norman D. Brown, *One of Cleburne's Command*, 129; M. L. Wheeler Memoirs, 36, PMSHS; Castel, *Decision in the West*, 530.

2. Whipple to Davis, September 2, 1864, and Davis to Whipple, September 2, 1864, *OR*, 38(5):766–67; Howard, *Autobiography*, 2:42–43; Castel, *Decision in the West*, 530–31.

3 Stout to Erb, September 14, 1864, and Fullerton journal, *OR*, 38(1):470, 933–34; Stanley to Whipple, September 2, 1864, 7:30 P.M., 8:40 P.M., and Whipple to Stanley, September 2, 1864, 8:30 P.M., *OR*, 38(5):765–66; Gates, *Rough Side of War*, 271; Castel, *Decision in the West*, 531–32.

4. Sherman to Howard, September 2, 1864, and Townes to Osterhaus, September 2, 1864, *OR*, 38(5):771–72; Reese to Poe, September 14, 1864, *OR*, 38(3):67; Harwell and Racine, *Fiery Trail*, 22.

5. Howard, *Autobiography*, 2:43; Harwell and Racine, *Fiery Trail*, 22; Day, *Story*, 262; Stanley to Whipple, September 2, 1864, and Stanley to Thomas, September 2, 1864, *OR*, 38(5):765.

6. Sherman to Schofield, September 2, 1864; Townes to Harrow, September 3, 1864; and Special Field Orders No. 116, Headquarters, Army of the Tennessee, September 3, 1864, *OR*, 38(5):774–75, 785, 790; Gates, *Rough Side of War*, 271.

7. Hood to Bragg, September 3, 1864, *OR*, 38(5):1017; French to Gale, December 6, 1864, *OR*, 38(3):906.

8. French to Gale, December 6, 1864, and Young to Sanders, September 17, 1864, *OR*, 38(3):906, 912; French, *Two Wars*, 222.

9. Durham, *Blues in Gray*, 234; Norman D. Brown, *One of Cleburne's Command*, 130; George Anderson Mercer Diary, September 3, 1864, UNC.

10. Thomas to Sherman, September 4, 1864, *OR*, 38(5):795; Fullerton journal, September 4, 1864, *OR*, 38(1):935; Harwell and Racine, *Fiery Trail*, 22.

11. Hazen, *Narrative of Military Service*, 382–83.

12. Sherman to Halleck, September 4, 1864, in Simpson and Berlin, *Sherman's Civil War*, 697, 699.

13. Hood to Bragg, September 4, 1864, *OR*, 38(5):1018.

14. [Shoup] to Lee, September 4, 1864, and [Shoup] to Smith, September 4, 1864, *OR*, 38(5):1018–19.

15. Bennett and Tillery, *Struggle for the Life*, 205; Cockrell to Sanders, September 20, 1864, *OR*, 38(3):918–19; Blair to Clark, September 5, 1864, *OR*, 38(5):803.

16. Special Field Orders No. 64, Headquarters, Military Division of the Mississippi, September 4, 1864, and Sherman to Stanton, September 6, 1864, *OR*, 38(5):801, 809.

17. French to Gale, December 6, 1864, and Cockrell to Sanders, September 6, 1864, *OR*, 38(3):907, 915–16; Ratchford to Clayton, September [6], 1864, and [Shoup] to Hardee, September 7, 1864, *OR*, 38(5):1024, 1028.

18. Hood to Davis, September 6, 1864, *OR*, 38(5):1023; Phillips, *Personal Reminiscences*, 55.

19. Hood to Davis, September 6, 1864, and [Shoup] to Smith, September 7, 1864, *OR*, 38(5):1023–24, 1029; Martin L. Smith Diary, September 10–21, 26, 29, October 1, 5–6, 1864, Mary-HS.

20. Neal, *Illustrated History*, 145; record of events, 1st Missouri Engineers, *SOR*, pt. 2, 36: 169; Special Field Orders No. 104, Headquarters, Army of the Ohio, September 8, 1864, *OR*, 38(2):521; Rieger, *Through One Man's Eyes*, 127; Howe, *Marching with Sherman*, 60.

21. Poe to [Delafield], October 8, 1865, *OR*, 38(1):138; Bauer, *Soldiering*, 169.

22. Poe to [Delafield], October 8, 1865, *OR*, 38(1):138; Hooker to wife, September 17, 1864, Horace B. Hooker Letters, VT; Special Field Orders No. 67, Headquarters, Military Division of the Mississippi, September 8, 1864, *OR*, 38(5):837; William Kossak Journal, September 28–29, 1864, WCL-UM.

23. Sherman to Hood, September 10, 1864, *OR*, 39(2):416.

24. Sherman to Halleck, September 13, 20, 1864, *OR*, 39(2):370, 414. While Sherman refrained from telling Hood the real reason for his evacuation of civilians from Atlanta, he apparently was free to tell a resident named King the true cause for the policy. King had gone on to Savannah by the latter part of September 1864 and divulged the reason to Confederate authorities there. See Oeffinger, *Soldier's General*, 241.

25. Buck, *Cleburne and His Command*, 259; Tower, *Carolinian Goes to War*, 254; Gillette to not stated, September 28, 1864, *OR*, 39(2):513; Castel, *Decision in the West*, 550.

26. Baumgartner, *Blood & Sacrifice*, 168–70; Cater, *As It Was*, 193; diary, September 20–23, 1864, Daniel Harris Reynolds Papers, UAF; Cate, *Two Soldiers*, 137–38; Norman D. Brown, *One of Cleburne's Command*, 132; Semmes to wife, September, no date, 1864, Benedict Joseph Semmes Papers, UNC; Douglas, *Douglas's Texas Battery*, 134–36; Gillette to not stated, September 28, 1864, *OR*, 39(2):513; cards, Asbury C. Dale Service Record, NARA.

27. Tower, *Carolinian Goes to War*, 254; Stewart to Mason, January 12, 1865, *OR*, 38(3):872; Norman D. Brown, *One of Cleburne's Command*, 132; Castel, *Decision in the West*, 551.

28. Record of Events, September 28, 1864, 1st Missouri Engineers, *SOR*, pt. 2, 36:169; Shiman, "Engineering Sherman's March," 552–53; David Russell Wright, "Civil War Field Fortifications," 162.

29. Robinson to Robinson, December 28, 1864, and Brant to Kellam, December 26, 1864, *OR*, 39(1):659–61, 689.

30. Byrne, *Uncommon Soldiers*, 196; Tappan, *Civil War Journal*, 160.

31. Neal, *Illustrated History*, 145; Poe to [Delafield], October 8, 1865, *OR*, 38(1):138; David Russell Wright, "Civil War Field Fortifications," 162; Hooker to wife, October 14, 1864, Horace B. Hooker Letters, VT.

32. Journal and letter book, November 14, 1864, 613, M. F. Force Papers, UW; Poe to [Delafield], October 8, 1865, *OR*, 38(1):138–39.

33. Robinson to Robinson, December 28, 1864, and Brant to Kellam, December 26, 1864, *OR*, 39(1):661, 690.

34. Hess, *Civil War in the West*, 249–52.

35. Journal and letter book, November 14, 1864, 613, M. F. Force Papers, UW; Watkins to John, November 2, 1864, John Watkins Papers, UTK; Poe to wife, November 6, 1864, Orlando Metcalfe Poe Papers, LC; Poe to [Delafield], October 8, 1865, *OR*, 38(1):139; Keith F. Davis, *George N. Barnard*, 78.

CONCLUSION

1. Hooker to wife, August 26, 1864, Horace B. Hooker Letters, VT.

2. Diary, July 8, 1864, James R. Carnahan Papers, IHS; [Dwight], "How We Fight at Atlanta," 664; Bauer, *Soldiering*, 118–19; Poe to [Delafield], October 8, 1865, *OR*, 38(1):136; Floyd, *History of the Seventy-Fifth Regiment*, 290.

3. Kendall, "Recollections of a Confederate Officer," 1176.

4. "'Unseen Message,'" 370.

5. Wagner, "Hasty Intrenchments," 146; Hagerman, "From Jomini," 217; Hagerman, *American Civil War*, 293.

6. Sherman, *Memoirs*, 2:396–97.

7. Cox, *Military Reminiscences*, 2:223; Fennell, "How the Orphans Learned," 210–12.

8. W. L. Truman Memoirs, May 20, 1864, www.cedarcroft.com.

9. Pearce to Wilson, September 9, 1864, *OR*, 38(1):692. Richard McMurry in *Atlanta* (93–94) also sees the pace of fortifying picking up in operations south of the Etowah River.

10. Diary, August 8, 1864, Abraham J. Seay Collection, UO; W. L. Truman Memoirs, July 3, 1864, www.cedarcroft.com; Gould and Kennedy, *Memoirs of a Dutch Mudsill*, 250.

11. Cox, *Military Reminiscences*, 2:223–24.

12. Sherman to Ellen, May 20, June 12, 30, 1864, in Simpson and Berlin, *Sherman's Civil War*, 638, 647, 660; Sherman to Stanton, May 23, 1864, *OR*, 38(4):294.

13. Sherman to Halleck, July 9, 1864, and Sherman to Howard, August 31, 1864, *OR*, 38(5):91, 726.

14. Johnston to Cooper, October 20, 1864, *OR*, 38(3):619. As Richard McMurry has pointed out, there was an alternative to passive defense and wasteful attacking, and that was for Johnston to hold his fortified positions with minimal force and mass the rest of his manpower for an attack on a vulnerable point; see McMurry, *Atlanta*, 112. To his credit, Johnston tried to do so at Cassville and along the New Hope Church, Pickett's Mill, and Dallas Line, but in both cases the planned attacks were canceled by developments beyond his control.

15. Castel (*Decision in the West*, 381, 412, 434) estimates Hood's losses from July 20 to 28 conservatively at 11,000.

16. Hood, *Advance and Retreat*, 171, 185–86; Hood, "Defense of Atlanta," 337.

17. Roy, "General Hardee," 379.

18. Hood, *Advance and Retreat*, 129–30; Hood, "Defense of Atlanta," 336; Hood to Cooper, February 15, 1865, *OR*, 38(3):629, 636.

19. Hood to Bragg, September 5, 1864, *OR*, 38(5):1021.

20. Lee to Hood, January 26, 1864, quoted in Hood, *Advance and Retreat*, 138–39.

21. Schofield, *Forty-Six Years*, 153.

22. Hood, *Advance and Retreat*, 131–32.

23. McMurry, *John Bell Hood*, 150.

24. Hardee to wife, August 4, 1864, and Hardee to Johnston, April 10, 1867, Hardee Family Papers, ADAH.

25. Tower, *Carolinian Goes to War*, 251; Haughton, *Training, Tactics and Leadership*, 152–53. Col. John G. Mitchell believed his Fourteenth Corps brigade was "under constant fire" for three-fourths of the time during the four-month-long campaign; see Mitchell to Wiseman, September 4, 1864, *OR*, 38(1):682.

26. Price, "Skirmish Line," 97; Chamberlin, "Skirmish Line," 182; Howard, *Autobiography*, 1:548–49.

27. Alpheus Baker to Johnston, July 4, 1874, Joseph E. Johnston Papers, CWM.

28. Gates, *Rough Side of War*, 215, 220, 234.

29. Morgan, "Home Letters," 212, 225, AHC.

30. Stone, "From the Oostenaula to the Chattahoochee," 413; Gates, *Rough Side of War*, 252; [Thomas M. Jack] to French, Cantey, and Featherston, June 17, 1864, Special Orders from May 9th 1864 to June 19th 1864, NARA.

31. Price, "Skirmish Line," 2; J. C. Thompson to A. P. Stewart, December 8, 1867, Joseph E. Johnston Papers, CWM.

32. Haughton, *Training, Tactics and Leadership*, 155; [Dwight], "How We Fight at Atlanta," 666.

33. Stone, "From the Oostenaula to the Chattahoochee," 413; Thaddeus S. C. Brown, Murphy, and Putney, *Behind the Guns*, 113; "At the Hospital in Dallas, Ga," folder 454, series 1, reel 3, U.S. Sanitary Commission Records, New York Public Library, Rare Books and Manuscripts, New York, New York.

34. Sherman to Schofield, July 23, 1864: Sherman to Palmer, August 5, 1864, *OR*, 38(5):237, 384; Howard, "Battles about Atlanta," 395.

35. [Dwight], "How We Fight at Atlanta," 666; J. C. Thompson to A. P. Stewart, December 8, 1867, Joseph E. Johnston Papers, CWM; Herr, *Nine Campaigns*, 231.

36. Harwell and Racine, *Fiery Trail*, 17; Sherman, *Memoirs*, 2:396.

37. Josiah C. Williams to Edistina, July 12, 1864, Worthington Williams Papers, IHS; Sherman to Halleck, September 8, 1864, *OR*, 38(5):830.

38. [Dwight], "How We Fight at Atlanta," 665; Goodloe, *Some Rebel Relics*, 180; William C. Davis, *Diary of a Confederate Soldier*, 136.

39. Ario Pardee Jr. to Pa, June 8, 1864, Pardee-Robison Family Papers, USAMHI; D. T. letter, June 8, 1864, in *Soldier of Indiana*, 714.

40. Schofield, *Forty-Six Years*, 144–45.

41. Alonzo Abernethy, "Incidents of an Iowa Soldier's Life," 419–20; Mahon, "Civil War Letters," 252; Sherman, *Memoirs*, 2:55.

42. Johnston to "Folks at Home," July 25, 1864, Andrew J. Johnson Papers, IHS;

Charles W. Wills, *Army Life*, 260; Henry H. Wright, *History of the Sixth Iowa*, 299; Angle, *Three Years*, 236; Byrne, *Uncommon Soldiers*, 162; William Harrison Githens to wife, June 15, 1864, William Harrison Githen Letters, Cornell University, Rare Book and Manuscript Collection, Ithaca, New York; Bohrnstedt, *Soldiering With Sherman*, 120; Little to Lizzie, June 7, 1864, Alexander C. Little Papers, CHM; Angle, *Three Years*, 223; Bryant, *History of the Third Regiment*, 271.

43. Charles W. Wills, *Army Life*, 261, 263; Bohrnstedt, *Soldiering with Sherman*, 120.

44. Robinson to Hunt, May 21, 1864, James Sidney Robinson Papers, Ohio Historical Society, Archives/Library, Columbus, Ohio.

45. Mary Miles Jones and Martin, *Gentle Rebel*, 43; Thomas L. Clayton to wife, July 6, 1864, Clayton Family Papers, UNC. After the campaign, John James Reeve, an officer on Carter L. Stevenson's division staff, had an opportunity to see many of the Confederate lines of fortifications Johnston had abandoned, and he was glad that the general had been relieved for giving up so many strong positions; see Reeve to "My dear friend," November 14, 1864, John James Reeve Letters, Virginia Historical Society, Richmond, Virginia.

46. Hughes, *Civil War Memoir*, 225; Mathis, *In the Land*, 109–10.

47. Hughes, *Civil War Memoir*, 185; Charles W. Wills, *Army Life*, 255; J. Litton Bostick to mother, June 13, 1864, Bostick Papers, TSLA; Ridley Wills, *Old Enough to Die*, 114–15.

APPENDIX

1. Cox, *Atlanta*, 83.

2. Tower, *Carolinian Goes to War*, 253.

3. Gates, *Rough Side of War*, 212, 271; Winther, *With Sherman to the Sea*, 109; Floyd, *History of the Seventy-Fifth Regiment*, 290–91; Hawes, "Memoirs of Charles H. Olmstead," 428.

4. Sherman, *Memoirs*, 2:55; Johnson and Hartshorn, "Development of Field Fortification," 579; Cope, *Fifteenth Ohio*, 447; Norman D. Brown, *One of Cleburne's Command*, 101; Gates, *Rough Side of War*, 232; Howard, "Battles about Atlanta," 398; Byron R. Abernethy, *Private Elisha Stockwell*, 95. Arthur Wagner claimed that he discovered evidence that the Confederates were the ones to think of placing skids under the ends of head logs to prevent them from falling into the trench and that the Federals picked up on the idea, but Wagner did not provide evidence of his find. See Wagner, "Hasty Intrenchments," 142–43.

5. Gould and Kennedy, *Memoirs of a Dutch Mudsill*, 250; Gates, *Rough Side of War*, 233; Ackley to wife, July 1, 1864, Charles Thomas Ackley Civil War Letters, University of Iowa, Special Collections, Iowa City, Iowa; Trowbridge to wife and baby, July 24, 1864, George Martin Trowbridge Papers, WCL-UM; Joslyn, *Charlotte's Boys*, 234; W. S. Morris, Hartwell, and Kuykendall, *History 31st Regiment Illinois*, 104; Cram to Erb, September 14, 1864, *OR*, 38(1):463.

6. Sherman, *Memoirs*, 2:55; Hawes, "Memoirs of Charles H. Olmstead," 428; Norman D. Brown, *One of Cleburne's Command*, 100; [Dwight], "How We Fight at Atlanta," 664.

7. Newton, "Battle of Peach Tree Creek," 160–61.

8. Norman D. Brown, *One of Cleburne's Command*, 101; Muir, "Battle of Atlanta," 111; Wynne and Taylor, *This War So Horrible*, 108–9; Bohrnstedt, *Soldiering with Sherman*, 120. Chesley Mosman provided details about Confederate chevaux-de-frise located along

the line defended by Polk's Brigade of Cleburne's Division at Kennesaw Mountain. Each section was twenty feet long, with a tree trunk from five to twelve inches wide from one end to the other. Auger holes had been bored two inches wide, with sticks six feet long stuck through them and telegraph wire to fasten the sections to the ground. The line of chevaux-de-frise was positioned forty feet in front of the main line. See Gates, *Rough Side of War*, 232.

9. Quaife, *From the Cannon's Mouth*, 334; Partridge, *History of the Ninety-Sixth*, 347; [Dwight], "How We Fight at Atlanta," 665.

10. Maxwell, *Autobiography*, 227, 247, 250–51.

11. A. T. Holliday to wife, July 14, 1864, A. T. and Elizabeth Holliday Civil War Correspondence, AHC; Bronson, "Recollections," 52, TC.

12. Orders, Headquarters, Hardee's Corps, May 14, 1864, "Records Cleburnes Div Hardees Corps A of Tenn," NARA.

13. Fullerton journal, August 16, 1864, *OR*, 38(1):919.

14. Graham to McGrath, September 18, 1864; Stout to Erb, September 14, 1864; Fearing to Curtis, August 16, 1864, *OR*, 38(1):405, 471, 787; Brant to Coburn, September 9, 1864, *OR*, 38(2):420. For other estimates of the number of lines constructed or the total length of these lines, see Simmons, *History of the 84th*, 195; Stout to Erb, September 14, 1864, and Fearing to Curtis, August 16, 1864, *OR*, 38(1):471, 787; Austin to wife, August 17, 1864, Judson L. Austin Papers, University of Michigan, Bentley Historical Library, Ann Arbor, Michigan; and Williams to father, September 10, 1864, Thomas H. Williams Papers, University of Michigan, Bentley Historical Library, Ann Arbor, Michigan.

15. W. L. Truman Memoirs, August 23, 1864, www.cedarcroft.com.

16. Johnson and Hartshorn, "Development of Field Fortification," 592; Stone, "From the Oostenaula to the Chattahoochee," 413; F. Halsey Wigfall to Papa, August 4, 1864, Louis Trezevant Wigfall Family Papers, LC; Poe to [Delafield], October 8, 1865, *OR*, 38(1):137; Sherman, *Memoirs*, 2:56.

17. Samuel Eugene Hunter to wife, June 24, 1864, Samuel Eugene Hunter Letters, LSU; Sherman to Halleck, July 5, 1864, *OR*, 38(5):50.

18. Correspondence in *Cincinnati Commercial*, July 8, 1864, reprinted in *Washington Daily National Intelligencer*, July 20, 1864.

19. Hughes, *Civil War Memoir*, 251. See also Ayers to wife, August 7, 1864, Alexander Miller Ayers Papers, EU.

20. Payne to wife, July 6, 1864, Edwin W. Payne Papers, ALPL; Cooper to assistant adjutant general, Department of the Cumberland, October 11, 1864, *OR*, 38(1):177; Reeve to "My dear friend," August 11, 1864, John James Reeve Letters, Virginia Historical Society, Richmond, Virginia; Butler, *Letters Home*, 130–31; William Anderson Stephens to wife, May 7, 1864, quoted in Haughton, *Training, Tactics and Leadership*, 152.

21. Kellenberger to Pollard, August 29, 1864, Peter B. Kellenberger Letters, LC.

22. Geary to Rodgers, July 29, 1863, *OR*, 27(1):826, 831–32.

23. Butterfield to Hooker, May 7, 1864, *OR*, 38(4):60.

24. William Clark McLean diary, July 6, 1864, McLean Family Papers, NYSL.

25. Tower, *Carolinian Goes to War*, 253; Crowson and Brogden, *Bloody Banners*, 69; Bircher, *Drummer-Boy's Diary*, 118; Gates, *Rough Side of War*, 271; McConnell to Crowell, September 10, 1864, *OR*, 38(1):438.

26. Howard to Whipple, July 21, 1864, *OR*, 38(5):213.

27. Bradley to Buel, September 19, 1864, Luther P. Bradley Papers, USAMHI.

28. Goodloe, *Some Rebel Relics*, 181–82.

29. Hurd to Lawton, September 13, 1864, *OR*, 38(1):281; Post, *Soldiers' Letters*, 391–93.

30. F. Morris to Olds, June 30, 1864, William C. Olds Papers, ISL; Quaife, *From the Cannon's Mouth*, 316; Howard, "Struggle for Atlanta," 307; Kendall, "Recollections of a Confederate Officer," 1177; Partridge, *History of the Ninety-Sixth*, 388n.

31. Cox, *Military Reminiscences*, 2:282.

32. [Dwight], "How We Fight at Atlanta," 664; Herr, *Nine Campaigns*, 230; Hagerman, *American Civil War*, 295–96.

33. Barnum to Forbes, September 11, 1864, *OR*, 38(2):272.

34. Hughes, *Civil War Memoir*, 252; W. L. Truman Memoirs, August 5, 1864, www .cedarcroft.com.

35. Hickenlooper, "Our Volunteer Engineers," 315; Maurice to not stated, September 9, 1864, *SOR*, 55.

36. McAdams, *Every-Day Soldier Life*, 86; Harrison to Speed, September 14, 1864, *OR*, 38(2):349; Special Field Orders No. 52, Headquarters, Army of the Ohio, July 13, 1864, *OR*, 38(5):136.

37. Gates, *Rough Side of War*, 220; Charles D. Gammon Diary, May 31, 1864, EU; Wynne, and Taylor, *This War So Horrible*, 102; Wagner to Lee, September 10, 1864, *OR*, 38(1):338.

38. Henry Campbell Diary, June 17, 1864, Indiana University, Lilly Library, Bloomington, Indiana; Hickenlooper, "Reminiscences," 54, USAMHI; Sherman to Grant, July 12, 1864, *OR*, 38(5):123.

39. Circular, Headquarters, Department of the Cumberland, June 25, 1864, *OR*, 38(4):594.

40. Fullerton journal, ca. May 22, 1864, *OR*, 38(1):860; Gould and Kennedy, *Memoirs of a Dutch Mudsill*, 250; Bauer, *Soldiering*, 119.

41. Malmborg to Cox, June 21, 1864, *OR*, 38(3):560; [Rood], *Story of the Service*, 306.

42. J. Condit Smith to Hartz, June 10, 1864; [indecipherable signature] to H. M. Smith, June 11, 1864; L. C. Easton to Hartz, June 14, 25, 1864; and H. Skinner to Hartz, July 8, 11, 1864, Edward L. Hartz Papers, DU.

43. Howard, "Battles about Atlanta," 396; Humphrey to wife, June 18, 1864, John Humphrey Papers, EU.

44. Miller to Crawford, July 17, 1864, *OR*, 38(2):397.

45. Gates, *Rough Side of War*, 206–207, 220, 223.

46. Diary, May 31, June 3, 1864, Thomas B. Byron Papers, WCL-UM.

47. Charles W. Wills, *Army Life*, 285.

48. Gould and Kennedy, *Memoirs of a Dutch Mudsill*, 250.

49. General Orders No. 2, Headquarters, Army of Tennessee, January 3, 1864, Orders and Circulars, NARA; Circular, Headquarters, Loring's Division, August 23, 1864, Featherston Order Book, Winfield Scott Featherston Collection, UM.

50. Circular, Headquarters, Army of the Mississippi, June 10, 1864, Special Orders from May 9th 1864 to June 19th 1864, NARA; Kendall, "Recollections of a Confederate Officer," 1177; French, *Two Wars*, 215.

51. Tower, *Carolinian Goes to War*, 164–65.

52. Ibid.

53. Lockett to wife, June 12, 1864, Samuel Henry Lockett Papers, UNC.

54. Hughes, *Civil War Memoir*, 185–86, 252.

55. Reinhart, *Two Germans*, 136; Nichol to father, July 8, 1864, David Nichol Papers, USAMHI; Morgan to father, July 12, 1864, in Morgan, "Home Letters," 222–23, AHC.

56. Hughes, *Civil War Memoir*, 251–52.

57. Bohrnstedt, *Soldiering with Sherman*, 147; Brant, *History of the Eighty-Fifth Indiana*, 69; Charles O. Brown, *Battle-Fields Revisited*, 62–63.

58. Pierson, "From Chattanooga to Atlanta," 343.

59. Lossing, *Pictorial Field Book*, 3:402.

60. Johnson and Hartshorn, "Development of Field Fortification," 591.

bibliography

ARCHIVES

Abraham Lincoln Presidential Library, Springfield, Illinois
Allen L. Fahnestock Papers
Edwin W. Payne Papers
Alabama Department of Archives and History, Montgomery, Alabama
Edward Norphlet Brown Letters
Newton N. Davis Papers
Stouten Hubert Dent Papers
Hardee Family Papers
American Antiquarian Society, Worcester, Massachusetts
Philo Beecher Buckingham Papers
Atlanta History Center, Atlanta, Georgia
Davidson Family Collection
L. P. Grant Papers
A. T. and Elizabeth Holliday Civil War Correspondence
Otho Herron Morgan, "Home Letters, 1861–1864"
J. S. Speir Collection
Harry Stanley Diary, Antebellum and Civil War Collection
Augusta State University, Special Collections, Augusta, Georgia
George S. Storrs Papers
Judy Beal Collection, Harrogate, Tennessee
John K. Ely Diary
Bowdoin College, Special Collections and Archives, Brunswick, Maine
O. O. Howard Papers

Chicago History Museum, Chicago, Illinois
  Day Elmore Letters
  Alexander C. Little Papers
The Citadel, Archives and Museum, Charleston, South Carolina
  Irving Bronson, "Recollections of the Civil War," Bruce Catton Collection
College of William and Mary, Manuscripts and Rare
  Books Department, Williamsburg, Virginia
  Joseph E. Johnston Papers
Cornell University, Rare Book and Manuscript Collection, Ithaca, New York
  William Harrison Githens Letters, Gail and Stephen
    Rudin Collection of Civil War Letters
Duke University, David M. Rubenstein Rare Book and
  Manuscript Library, Durham, North Carolina
  Alfred W. Bell Papers
  J. T. Bowden Letter, *Confederate Veteran* Papers
  B. F. Grady Letter, *Confederate Veteran* Papers
  Edward L. Hartz Papers
  Charles Richard Pomeroy Jr. Papers
  Charles Todd Quintard Papers
  James M. Willcox Papers
  J. B. Work, "Map of the 'Dead Angle,' Cheatham's Hill, Kenesaw Mountain,
    GA., June 27 to July 2–3, 1864," *Confederate Veteran* Papers
Emory University, Manuscript, Archives, and Rare Book Library, Atlanta, Georgia
  Alexander Miller Ayers Papers
  Mumford H. Dixon Diary
  Charles D. Gammon Diary, Union Miscellany Collection
  John Humphrey Papers
  John S. Lightfoot Diary
  Andrew Jackson Neal Papers
  Albert L. Slack Letters
  Benjamin Putnam Weaver Letters, Confederate Miscellany Collection
Filson Historical Society, Louisville, Kentucky
  Thomas Speed Papers
  John H. Tilford Diary
Georgia Historical Society, Savannah
  Willis Perry Burt Diary, Laura Burt Brantley Collection
Raymond Harper Collection, Dunkirk, New York
  "The Enlistment and in Camp at Jamestown and the Several Camps While
    in the Service of the United States," based on William D. Harper Diary
Earl J. Hess Collection, Knoxville, Tennessee
  Thomas J. Head Letters
Indiana Historical Society, Indianapolis, Indiana
  James R. Carnahan Papers
  Daniel Wait Howe Papers
  Andrew J. Johnson Papers
  Worthington Williams Papers

Indiana State Library, Indianapolis, Indiana
    Daniel F. Griffin Papers
    William D. Hynes Papers
    William C. Olds Papers
Indiana University, Lilly Library, Bloomington, Indiana
    Henry Campbell Diary
Kennesaw Mountain National Battlefield Park, Kennesaw, Georgia
    W. J. McDill Letter
    Edward Spear Diary
Library of Congress, Manuscripts Division, Washington, D.C.
    Douglas J. Cater and Rufus W. Cater Papers
    John S. Jackman Journal
    Peter B. Kellenberger Letters
    Orlando Metcalfe Poe Papers
    William T. Sherman Papers
    Louis Trezevant Wigfall Family Papers
Lincoln Memorial University, Abraham Lincoln Library
   and Museum, Harrogate, Tennessee
    G. B. Cockrell Collection
    William Merrell, "Personal Memoirs of the Civil War"
Louisiana State University, Louisiana and Lower Mississippi
   Valley Collections, Baton Rouge, Louisiana
    Isaac Gaillard Foster Diary, James Foster and Family Correspondence
    Samuel Eugene Hunter Letters, Hunter-Taylor Family Papers
    James G. Marston Diary, Henry Marston Family Papers
Maryland Historical Society, Baltimore, Maryland
    Martin L. Smith Diary
Massachusetts Historical Society, Boston, Massachusetts
    Charles F. Morse Papers
Mississippi Department of Archives and History, Jackson, Mississippi
    Robert J. Cull, comp., "The Civil War Letters of George S. Lea, 1861–1864"
    R. A. Jarman, "The History of Company K, 27th Mississippi
      Infantry, and Its First and Last Muster Rolls"
    Thomas T. Smith Papers
Missouri History Museum, St. Louis, Missouri
    David Allan Jr. Letters
    Osterhaus Family Papers
    John Wharton Papers
Mohican Historical Society, Loudonville, Ohio
    Henry Pippitt Diary
Museum of the Confederacy, Richmond, Virginia
    General Orders and Circulars, Hood's Corps
    John L. Inglis Letters
    Archie Livingston Letters
National Archives and Records Administration, Washington, D.C.
    Thaddeus Coleman Service Record, M258, Corps of Engineers, Compiled

Service Records of Confederate Soldiers Who Served in Organizations
Raised Directly by the Confederate Government, RG109

Confederate Inspection Reports, M935

Asbury C. Dale Service Record, 2nd and 6th Missouri, M322,
Compiled Service Records of Confederate Soldiers Who Served
in Organizations from the State of Missouri, RG109

James J. Davies Service Record, M258, Compiled Service Records
of Confederate Soldiers Who Served in Organizations Raised
Directly by the Confederate Government, RG109

Mathew E. Ezell Service Record, 3rd Confederate Engineers, M258,
Compiled Service Records of Confederate Soldiers Who Served in
Organizations Raised Directly by the Confederate Government, RG109

George H. Hazlehurst Service Record, Corps of Engineers, M258, Compiled
Service Records of Confederate Soldiers Who Served in Organizations
Raised Directly by the Confederate Government, RG109

John B. Jordan Service Record, 36th Alabama, M311, Compiled
Service Records of Confederate Soldiers Who Served in
Organizations from the State of Alabama, RG109

H. D. Lampley Service Record, 45th Alabama, M311, Compiled
Service Records of Confederate Soldiers Who Served in
Organizations from the State of Alabama, RG109

Letters and Telegrams Sent by the Engineer Bureau of the
Confederate War Department, 1861–1864, M628, RG109

Letters Sent by the Chief of Engineers, 1812–69, M1113, RG77,
Records of the Office of the Chief of Engineers

"Map Showing Approximate Position and Entrenchments of
the Army of Miss., May 25–July 9, '64," N220, RG77

Walter J. Morris Service Record, M331, Compiled Service Records of Confederate
General and Staff Officers and Non-regimental Enlisted Men, RG109

Orders and Circulars, Army of Tennessee and Subordinate
Commands, 1862–1864, chap. 2, vol. 53, RG109

James R. Percy Service Record, 53rd Ohio, Compiled Service Records of Volunteer
Union Soldiers Who Served in Organizations from the State of Ohio, RG94

"Records Cleburnes Div Hardees Corps A of Tenn," RG109, chap. 2, no. 265

Service Records of 3rd Confederate Engineers, Roll 99, M258, Compiled
Service Records of Confederate Soldiers Who Served in Organizations
Raised Directly by the Confederate Government, RG109

Francis A. Shoup Service Record, M331, Compiled Service Records of Confederate
General and Staff Officers and Non-regimental Enlisted Men, RG109

Special Orders from May 9th 1864 to June 19th 1864, Headquarters,
Army of the Mississippi, chap. 2, no. 2211/2, RG109

D. Wintter Service Record, Pickett-Flynn Company of
Sappers and Miners, M258, Roll 115, RG109

Marcus J. Wright Service Record, M331, Compiled Service Records of Confederate
General and Staff Officers and Non-regimental Enlisted Men, RG109

New-York Historical Society, New York, New York
  John Law Marshall Letters
New York Public Library, Rare Books and Manuscripts, New York, New York
  U.S. Sanitary Commission Records
New York State Library, Albany, New York
  Leander E. Davis Letters
  McLean Family Papers
Ohio Historical Society, Archives/Library, Columbus, Ohio
  James Sidney Robinson Papers
Pickett's Mill State Historic Site, Dallas, Georgia
  M. L. Wheeler Memoirs
Rice University, Woodson Research Center, Houston, Texas
  W. H. Brooker Diary
State Historical Society of Iowa, Des Moines, Iowa
  Grenville Mellen Dodge Papers
Tennessee State Library and Archives, Nashville, Tennessee
  Bostick Papers
  Joseph W. Kimmel Memoir, Civil War Collection
  William E. Sloan Diary, Civil War Collection
U.S. Army Military History Institute, Carlisle, Pennsylvania
  Luther P. Bradley Papers
  Fergus Elliott Diary, *Civil War Times Illustrated* Collection
  Gordon Hickenlooper, ed., "The Reminiscences of General Andrew
    Hickenlooper, 1861–1865," *Civil War Times Illustrated* Collection
  Hubbard T. Minor Papers
  David Nichol Papers, Harrisburg Civil War Round Table Collection
  Pardee-Robison Family Papers
  William Shimp Papers, Civil War Miscellaneous Collection
  Levi Wagner, "Recollections of an Enlistee 1861–1864,"
    Civil War Times Illustrated Collection
**University of Alabama, William Stanley Hoole Special
  Collections, Tuscaloosa, Alabama**
  Henry De Lamar Clayton Papers
University of Arkansas, Special Collections, Fayetteville, Arkansas
  Daniel Harris Reynolds Papers
University of Georgia, Hargrett Rare Book and Manuscript Library, Athens, Georgia
  Branch Family Papers
  Alexander Peter Stewart Letter
University of Iowa, Special Collections, Iowa City, Iowa
  Charles Thomas Ackley Civil War Letters
  John C. Brown Diary
University of Kentucky, Audio-Visual Archives, Lexington, Kentucky
  John W. Tuttle Diary
University of Michigan, Bentley Historical Library, Ann Arbor, Michigan
  Judson L. Austin Papers

Thomas B. Byron Papers
Thomas H. Williams Papers
University of Michigan, William L. Clements Library, Ann Arbor, Michigan
Schoff Civil War Collection
Thomas B. Byron Papers
William Kossak Journal
George Martin Trowbridge Papers
University of Mississippi, Archives and Special Collections, Oxford, Mississippi
J. A. Bigger Memoir
Winfield Scott Featherston Collection
**University of North Carolina, Southern Historical
Collection, Chapel Hill, North Carolina**
Clayton Family Papers
Joseph B. Cumming Papers
Harry St. John Dixon Papers
George Washington Finley Harper Papers
Samuel Henry Lockett Papers
George Anderson Mercer Diary
Benedict Joseph Semmes Papers
Avington Wayne Simpson Papers
Samuel Thompson Papers
Chauncey Brunson Welton Papers
University of Oklahoma, Western History Collections, Norman, Oklahoma
Abraham J. Seay Collection
University of Tennessee, Special Collections, Knoxville, Tennessee
"Autobiography of Edwin Hansford Rennolds, Sr."
Edwin H. Rennolds Diary
John Watkins Papers
University of Tennessee, Special Collections, Martin, Tennessee
Van Buren Oldham Diary
University of Texas, Center for American History, Austin, Texas
Truair Family Papers
Unidentified diary by a member of the 85th Indiana, Civil War Miscellany
University of the South, Archives and Special Collections, Sewanee, Tennessee
Leonidas Polk Papers
University of Virginia, Special Collections, Charlottesville, Virginia
Benjamin and John Green Letters
University of Washington, Special Collections, Seattle, Washington
M. F. Force Papers
Virginia Historical Society, Richmond, Virginia
John James Reeve Letters, Bagby Family Papers
**Virginia Polytechnic Institute and State University,
Special Collections, Blacksburg, Virginia**
Horace B. Hooker Letters

NEWSPAPERS

Charleston Mercury	*Nashville Daily Times and True Union*
Chicago Daily Tribune	*New York Herald*
Indianapolis Daily Journal	*St. Louis Daily Missouri Democrat*
Memphis Daily Appeal	*Washington Daily National Intelligencer*

WEBSITES

W. L. Truman Memoirs, www.cedarcroft.com

MAPS

Cartersville and White West Quadrant Map, U.S. Department of the Interior
Marietta Quadrant Map, U.S. Department of the Interior

ARTICLES, BOOKS, AND REPORTS

Abernethy, Alonzo. "Incidents of an Iowa Soldier's Life, or Four Years in Dixie." *Annals of Iowa*, 3rd ser., 12, no. 6 (October 1920): 401–28.

Abernethy, Byron R., ed. *Private Elisha Stockwell, Jr. Sees the Civil War.* Norman: University of Oklahoma Press, 1958.

Adams, Robert N. "The Battle and Capture of Atlanta." In *Glimpses of the Nation's Struggle: Fourth Series, Papers Read before the Minnesota Commandery of the Military Order of the Loyal Legion of the United States*, 144–63. Saint Paul, Minn.: H. L. Collins, 1898.

Anderson, Ephraim McD. *Memoirs: Historical and Personal.* Dayton, Ohio: Morningside Bookshop, 1972.

Angle, Paul M., ed. *Three Years in the Army of the Cumberland: The Letters and Diary of Major James A. Connolly.* Bloomington: Indiana University Press, 1959.

Aten, Henry J. *History of the Eighty-Fifth Regiment Illinois Volunteer Infantry.* Hiawatha, Kans.: printed by the author, 1901.

Atlas to Accompany the Official Records of the Union and Confederate Armies. Washington, D.C.: Government Printing Office, 1891–95.

Bailey, Ronald H. *Battles for Atlanta: Sherman Moves East.* Alexandria, Va.: Time-Life Books, 1985.

Barnard, George N. *Photographic Views of Sherman's Campaign.* New York: Dover, 1977.

Barnes, W. T. "An Incident of Kenesaw Mountain." *Confederate Veteran* 30 (1922): 48–49.

Barnhart, John D., ed. "A Hoosier Invades the Confederacy: Letters and Diaries of Leroy S. Mayfield." *Indiana Magazine of History* 39 (1943): 145–91.

"Battle of Kennesaw Mountain." In *The Annals of the Army of Tennessee and Early Western History.* Vol. 1, edited by Edwin L. Drake, 109–17. Nashville: A. D. Haynes, 1878.

Bauer, K. Jack, ed. *Soldiering: The Civil War Diary of Rice C. Bull, 123rd New York Volunteer Infantry.* San Rafael, Calif.: Presidio Press, 1977.

Baumgartner, Richard A., ed. *Blood & Sacrifice: The Civil War Journal of a Confederate Soldier.* Huntington, W.Va.: Blue Acorn Press, 1994.

Bek, William G., trans. and ed. "The Civil War Diary of John T. Buegel, Union Soldier." Part 2. *Missouri Historical Review* 40, no. 4 (July 1946): 503–40.

Bell, John T. *Tramps and Triumphs of the Second Iowa Infantry*. Omaha, Neb.: Gibson, Miller, and Richardson, 1886.

Bennett, Stewart, and Barbara Tillery, eds. *The Struggle for the Life of the Republic: A Civil War Narrative by Brevet Major Charles Dana Miller, 76th Ohio Volunteer Infantry*. Kent, Ohio: Kent State University Press, 2004.

Bierce, Ambrose. "The Crime at Pickett's Mill." In *The Collected Works of Ambrose Bierce*. Vol. 1. New York: Neale, 1909.

Biggs, Greg. "The 'Shoupade' Redoubts: Joseph E. Johnston's Chattahoochee River Line." *Civil War Regiments* 1, no. 3 (1991): 82–93.

Bircher, William. *A Drummer-Boy's Diary: Comprising Four Years of Service with the Second Regiment Minnesota Veteran Volunteers, 1861 to 1865*. St. Paul, Minn.: St. Paul Book and Stationery, 1889.

Black, Wilfred W., ed. "Marching with Sherman through Georgia and the Carolinas: Civil War Diary of Jesse L. Dozer." Part 1. *Georgia Historical Quarterly* 52, no. 3 (September 1968): 308–31.

Blair, J. L. W. "The Fight at Dead Angle." *Confederate Veteran* 12 (1904): 532–33.

Blair, William Alan, ed. *A Politician Goes to War: The Civil War Letters of John White Geary*. University Park: Pennsylvania State University Press, 1995.

Blomquist, Ann K., and Robert A. Taylor, eds. *This Cruel War: The Civil War Letters of Grant and Malinda Taylor, 1862–1865*. Macon, Ga.: Mercer University Press, 2000.

Bohrnstedt, Jennifer Cain, ed. *Soldiering with Sherman: Civil War Letters of George F. Cram*. De Kalb: Northern Illinois University Press, 2000.

Brackett, Albert G. "With Sherman at Atlanta." In *Battles and Leaders of the Civil War*. Vol. 6, edited by Peter Cozzens, 431–35. Urbana: University of Illinois Press, 2004.

Braley, Chad O. "The Battle of Gilgal Church: An Archeological and Historical Study of Mid-nineteenth Century Warfare in Georgia." Prepared for Oglethorpe Power Corporation by Southeastern Archeological Services, Athens, Ga., 1987.

Brant, Jefferson E. *History of the Eighty-Fifth Indiana Volunteer Infantry*. Bloomington, Ind.: Cravens, 1902.

Breckinridge, W. C. P. "The Opening of the Atlanta Campaign." In *Battles and Leaders of the Civil War*. Vol. 4, edited by Robert Underwood Johnson and Clarence Clough Buel, 277–81. New York: Thomas Yoseloff, 1956.

Brown, Charles O. *Battle-Fields Revisited*. Kalamazoo, Mich.: Eaton and Anderson, 1886.

Brown, Chuck. "Military Entrenchments in North Fulton County, South of Roswell at the Chattahoochee River: June–July, 1864." N.p., 1991.

Brown, Norman D., ed. *One of Cleburne's Command: The Civil War Reminiscences and Diary of Capt. Samuel T. Foster, Granbury's Texas Brigade, CSA*. Austin: University of Texas Press, 1980.

Brown, Thaddeus S. C., Samuel J. Murphy, and William G. Putney. *Behind the Guns: The History of Battery I, 2nd Regiment, Illinois Light Artillery*. Carbondale: Southern Illinois University Press, 1965.

Bryant, Edwin E. *History of the Third Regiment of Wisconsin Veteran Volunteer Infantry, 1861–1865*. Madison, Wis.: Veteran Association of the Regiment, 1891.

Buck, Irving A. *Cleburne and His Command*. Jackson, Tenn.: McCowat-Mercer, 1959.

Butler, Watson Hubbard[, ed.]. *Letters Home: Jay Caldwell Butler, Captain, 101st Ohio Volunteer Infantry.* N.p., 1930.

Byrne, Frank L., ed. *Uncommon Soldiers: Harvey Reid and the 22nd Wisconsin March with Sherman.* Knoxville: University of Tennessee Press, 2001.

Cabaniss, Jim R., ed. *Civil War Journal and Letters of Serg. Washington Ives, 4th Florida C. S. A.* N.p., 1987.

Capron, Thaddeus H. "War Diary of Thaddeus H. Capron, 1861–1865." *Journal of the Illinois State Historical Society* 12, no. 3 (October 1919): 330–406.

Castel, Albert. *Decision in the West: The Atlanta Campaign of 1864.* Lawrence: University Press of Kansas, 1992.

————. *Tom Taylor's Civil War.* Lawrence: University Press of Kansas, 2000.

Cate, Wirt Armistead, ed. *Two Soldiers: The Campaign Diaries of Thomas J. Key, C.S.A., and Robert J. Campbell, U.S.A.* Chapel Hill: University of North Carolina Press, 1938.

Cater, Douglas John. *As It Was: Reminiscences of a Soldier of the Third Texas Cavalry and the Nineteenth Louisiana Infantry.* Austin, Tex.: State House Press, 1990.

Chamberlin, W. H. "Hood's Second Sortie at Atlanta." In *Battles and Leaders of the Civil War.* Vol. 4, edited by Robert Underwood Johnston and Clarence Clough Buel, 326–31. New York: Thomas Yoseloff, 1956.

————. "Recollections of the Battle of Atlanta." In *Sketches of War History, 1861–1865: Papers Prepared for the Commandery of the State of Ohio, Military Order of the Loyal Legion of the United States,* Vol. 6: 276–86. Cincinnati: Monfort, 1908.

————. "The Skirmish Line in the Atlanta Campaign." In *Sketches of War History, 1861– 1865: Papers Prepared for the Ohio Commandery of the Military Order of the Loyal Legion of the United States.* Vol. 3: 182–96. Cincinnati: Robert Clarke, 1890.

Christ, Mark K., ed. *Getting Used To Being Shot At: The Spence Family Civil War Letters.* Fayetteville: University of Arkansas Press, 2002.

Collins, George K. *Memoirs of the 149th Regiment New York Volunteer Infantry.* Syracuse, N.Y., 1891.

Comey, Lyman Richard, ed. *A Legacy of Valor: The Memoirs and Letters of Captain Henry Newton Comey, 2nd Massachusetts Infantry.* Knoxville: University of Tennessee Press, 2004.

Connelly, Thomas Lawrence. *Autumn of Glory: The Army of Tennessee, 1862–1865.* Baton Rouge: Louisiana State University Press, 1971.

Cope, Alexis. *The Fifteenth Ohio Volunteers and Its Campaigns.* Columbus, Ohio: printed by the author, 1916.

Cox, Jacob Dolson. *Atlanta.* New York: Charles Scribner's Sons, 1882.

————. *Military Reminiscences of the Civil War.* 2 vols. New York: Charles Scribner's Sons, 1900.

Crowson, Noel, and John V. Brogden, eds. *Bloody Banners and Barefoot Boys: "A History of the 27th Regiment Alabama Infantry CSA."* Shippensburg, Pa.: Burd Street Press, 1997.

Cryder, George R., and Stanley R. Miller, comps. *A View from the Ranks: The Civil War Diaries of Charles E. Smith.* Delaware, Ohio: Delaware County Historical Society, 1999.

Cunyus, Lucy Josephine. *The History of Bartow County, Formerly Cass.* Cassville, Ga.: n.p., 1933.

Dacus, Robert H. *Reminiscences of Company "H," First Arkansas Mounted Rifles.* Dardanelle, Ark.: Post-Dispatch Print, [1897?].

Daniel, Larry J. *Soldiering in the Army of Tennessee: A Portrait of Life in a Confederate Army.* Chapel Hill: University of North Carolina Press, 1991.

Davis, Keith F. *George F. Barnard: Photographer of Sherman's Campaign.* Kansas City, Mo.: Hallmark Cards, 1990.

Davis, Stephen. *Atlanta Will Fall: Sherman, Joe Johnston, and the Yankee Heavy Battalions.* Wilmington, Del.: Scholarly Resources, 2001.

Davis, William C., ed. *Diary of a Confederate Soldier: John S. Jackman of the Orphan Brigade.* Columbia: University of South Carolina Press, 1990.

Davis, William C., and Bell I. Wiley, eds. *Photographic History of the Civil War.* 2 vols. New York: Black Dog and Leventhal, 1994.

Dawson, George Francis. *Life and Services of Gen. John A. Logan as Soldier and Statesman.* Chicago: Belford, Clarke, 1887.

Day, L. W. *Story of the One Hundred and First Ohio Infantry.* Cleveland: W. M. Bayne, 1894.

Dean, Jeffrey S. "The Forgotten 'Hell Hole': The Battle of Pickett's Mill." In *The Campaign for Atlanta and Sherman's March to the Sea.* Vol. 2, edited by Theodore P. Savas and David A. Woodbury, 343–73. Campbell, Calif.: Savas Woodbury, 1994.

Demoret, Alfred. *A Brief History of the Ninety-Third Regiment Ohio Volunteer Infantry.* Ross, Ohio: Graphic Print, 1898.

Dickey, Tom. "Johnston's River Line." *Brown's Guide to Georgia* 3, no. 2 (March–April 1975): 24–29.

Dodge, Grenville M. *Personal Recollections of President Abraham Lincoln, General Ulysses S. Grant and General William T. Sherman.* Denver: Sage Books, 1965.

———. "Reminiscences of Engineering Work on the Pacific Railways and in the Civil War." *Engineering News* 62 (October 28, 1909): 456–58.

Douglas, Lucia Rutherford, ed. *Douglas's Texas Battery, CSA.* Tyler, Tex.: Smith County Historical Society, 1966.

Duke, John K. *History of the Fifty-Third Regiment Ohio Volunteer Infantry during the War of the Rebellion, 1861 to 1865.* Portsmouth, Ohio: Blade Printing, 1900.

Dunlap, Leslie W., ed. *"Your Affectionate Husband, J. F. Culver": Letters Written during the Civil War.* Iowa City: Friends of the University of Iowa Libraries, 1978.

Durham, Roger S., ed. *The Blues in Gray: The Civil War Journal of William Daniel Dixon and the Republican Blues Daybook.* Knoxville: University of Tennessee Press, 2000.

[Dwight, Henry O.]. "How We Fight at Atlanta." *Harper's New Monthly Magazine* 29, no. 173 (October 1864): 663–66.

Eleazer, W. D. "Fight at Dead Angle, in Georgia." *Confederate Veteran* 14 (1906): 312.

Ellison, Janet Correll, ed. *On to Atlanta: The Civil War Diaries of John Hill Ferguson, Illinois Tenth Regiment of Volunteers.* Lincoln: University of Nebraska Press, 2001.

Ervin, W. J. "Genius and Heroism of Lieut. K. H. Faulkner." *Confederate Veteran* 14 (1906): 497–98.

Evans, E. Chris, ed. "Report of the Battle of Atlanta." *Blue and Gray* 11, no. 4 (April 1994): 28–30.

Fennell, Charles. "How the Orphans Learned to Dig." *Confederate Veteran* 30 (1922): 210–12.

Fenton, E. B. "From the Rapidan to Atlanta." In *War Papers: Being Papers Read before the Commandery of the State of Michigan, Military Order of the Loyal Legion of the United States.* Vol. 1: 483–504. Wilmington, N.C.: Broadfoot, 1993.

Ferrell, Robert H., ed. *Holding the Line: The Third Tennessee Infantry, 1861–1864*. Kent, Ohio: Kent State University Press, 1994.

Fleming, James R. *Band of Brothers: Company C, 9th Tennessee Infantry*. Shippensburg, Pa.: White Mane, 1996.

Floyd, David Bittle. *History of the Seventy-Fifth Regiment of Indiana Infantry Volunteers*. Philadelphia: Lutheran Publication Society, 1893.

Foster, Wilbur F. "Battle Field Maps in Georgia." *Confederate Veteran* 20 (1912): 369–70.

French, Samuel G. *Two Wars: An Autobiography*. Nashville: Confederate Veteran, 1901.

Fryman, Robert J. "Fortifying the Landscape: An Archaeological Study of Military Engineering and the Atlanta Campaign." In *Archaeological Perspectives on the American Civil War*, edited by Clarence R. Geier and Stephen R. Potter, 43–55. Gainesville: University Press of Florida, 2000.

Garrett, Franklin M. "Civilian Life in Atlanta." *Civil War Times Illustrated* 3, no. 4 (July 1964): 30–33.

Garrett, Jill K., ed. *Confederate Diary of Robert D. Smith*. Columbia, Tenn.: Capt. James Madison Sparkman Chapter, United Daughters of the Confederacy, 1975.

Gates, Arnold, ed. *The Rough Side of War: The Civil War Journal of Chesley A. Mosman, 1st Lieutenant, Company D, 59th Illinois Volunteer Infantry Regiment*. Garden City, N.Y.: Basin, 1987.

Girardi, Robert I., and Nathaniel Cheairs Hughes Jr., eds. *The Memoirs of Brigadier General William Passmore Carlin, U.S.A.* Lincoln: University of Nebraska Press, 1999.

Goodloe, Albert Theodore. *Some Rebel Relics from the Seat of War*. Nashville: Methodist Episcopal Church, South, 1893.

Gould, David, and James B. Kennedy, eds. *Memoirs of a Dutch Mudsill: The "War Memories" of John Henry Otto, Captain, Company D, 21st Regiment Wisconsin Volunteer Infantry*. Kent, Ohio: Kent State University Press, 2004.

Grainger, Gervis D. *Four Years with the Boys in Gray*. Dayton, Ohio: Morningside Bookshop, 1972.

Grimshaw, Samuel. "The Charge at Kenesaw." *National Tribune*, January 15, 1885.

Hafendorfer, Kenneth A., ed. *Civil War Journal of William L. Trask, Confederate Sailor and Soldier*. Louisville, Ky.: KH Press, 2003.

Hagerman, Edward. *The American Civil War and the Origins of Modern Warfare: Ideas, Organization, and Field Command*. Bloomington: Indiana University Press, 1988.

———. "From Jomini to Dennis Hart Mahan: The Evolution of Trench Warfare and the American Civil War." *Civil War History* 13 (1967): 197–220.

Harmon, B. H. "Dead Angle." *Confederate Veteran* 11 (1903): 219.

Harwell, Richard B., ed. "The Campaign from Chattanooga to Atlanta as Seen by a Federal Soldier." *Georgia Historical Quarterly* 25, no. 3 (September 1941): 262–78.

Harwell, Richard B., and Philip N. Racine, eds. *The Fiery Trail: A Union Officer's Account of Sherman's Last Campaign*. Knoxville: University of Tennessee Press, 1986.

Haughton, Andrew. *Training, Tactics and Leadership in the Confederate Army of Tennessee: Seeds of Failure*. Portland, Ore.: Frank Cass, 2000.

Hawes, Lilla Mills, ed. "The Memoirs of Charles H. Olmstead." Part 9. *Georgia Historical Quarterly* 44, no. 4 (December 1960): 419–34.

Hazen, William B. *A Narrative of Military Service*. Boston: Ticknor, 1885.

Herr, George W. *Nine Campaigns in Nine States*. San Francisco: Bancroft, 1890.

Hess, Earl J. *The Battle of Ezra Church and the Struggle for Atlanta*. Chapel Hill: University of North Carolina Press, 2015.

———. *The Battle of Peach Tree Creek: Hood's First Effort to Save Atlanta*. Chapel Hill: University of North Carolina Press, 2017.

———. *Civil War Infantry Tactics: Training, Combat, and Small-Unit Effectiveness*. Baton Rouge: Louisiana State University Press, 2015.

———. *The Civil War in the West: Victory and Defeat from the Appalachians to the Mississippi*. Chapel Hill: University of North Carolina Press, 2012.

———. *Field Armies and Fortifications in the Civil War: The Eastern Campaigns, 1861–1864*. Chapel Hill: University of North Carolina Press, 2005.

———. *In the Trenches at Petersburg: Field Fortifications & Confederate Defeat*. Chapel Hill: University of North Carolina Press, 2009.

———. *Kennesaw Mountain: Sherman, Johnston, and the Atlanta Campaign*. Chapel Hill: University of North Carolina Press, 2013.

———. *Trench Warfare under Grant and Lee: Field Fortifications in the Overland Campaign*. Chapel Hill: University of North Carolina Press, 2007.

Hickenlooper, Andrew. "Our Volunteer Engineers." In *Sketches of War History, 1861–1865: Papers Prepared for the Ohio Commandery of the Military Order of the Loyal Legion of the United States*. Vol. 3: 301–18. Cincinnati: Robert Clarke, 1890.

History of Company B (Originally Pickens Planters) 40th Alabama Regiment Confederate States Army, 1861 to 1865. N.p.: Colonial Press, 1963.

History of the Fifteenth Regiment, Iowa Veteran Volunteer Infantry from October, 1861, to August, 1865. Keokuk, Iowa: R. B. Ogden and Son, 1887.

Holmes, J. T. *52d O.V.I.: Then and Now*. Columbus, Ohio: Berlin Printing, 1898.

Holzhueter, John O., ed. "William Wallace's Civil War Letters: The Atlanta Campaign." *Wisconsin Magazine of History* 57, no. 2 (Winter 1973-1974): 90–116.

Hood, John B. *Advance and Retreat: Personal Experiences in the United States and Confederate States Armies*. Philadelphia: Burk and McFetridge, 1880.

———. "The Defense of Atlanta." In *Battles and Leaders of the Civil War*. Vol. 4, edited by Robert Underwood Johnson and Clarence Clough Buel, 336–44. New York: Thomas Yoseloff, 1956.

Howard, O. O. *Autobiography of Oliver Otis Howard*. 2 vols. New York: Baker and Taylor, 1907.

———. "The Battles about Atlanta." *Atlantic Monthly*, October 1876, 385–99.

———. "The Struggle for Atlanta." In *Battles and Leaders of the Civil War*. Vol. 4, edited by Robert Underwood Johnson and Clarence Clough Buel, 293–325. New York: Thomas Yoseloff, 1956.

Howe, M. A. DeWolfe, ed. *Marching with Sherman: Passages From the Letters and Campaign Diaries of Henry Hitchcock, Major and Assistant Adjutant General of Volunteers, November 1864–May 1865*. Lincoln: University of Nebraska Press, 1995.

Huff, Sarah. "Seeing Atlanta Shelled." In *Confederate Reminiscences and Letters, 1861–1865*. Vol. 7: 94-97. Atlanta: Georgia Division, United Daughters of the Confederacy, 1998.

Hughes, Nathaniel Cheairs, Jr., ed. *The Civil War Memoir of Philip Daingerfield Stephenson, D. D.* Conway: University of Central Arkansas Press, 1995.

Jackman, J. S. "From Dalton to Atlanta." Part 3. *Southern Bivouac* 1, no. 12 (August 1883): 451–59.

Jackson, Oscar L. *The Colonel's Diary*. N.p.: no publisher, [1922?].

James, F. B. "McCook's Brigade at the Assault upon Kennesaw Mountain, Georgia, June 27, 1864." In *Sketches of War History, 1861–1865: Papers Prepared for the Ohio Commandery of the Military Order of the Loyal Legion of the United States*, Vol. 4: 255–77. Cincinnati: Robert Clarke, 1896.

Johnson, W. C., and E. S. Hartshorn. "The Development of Field Fortification in the Civil War." *Professional Memoirs of the Corps of Engineers* 7 (1915): 570–602.

Johnston, Joseph E. *Narrative of Military Operations*. New York: D. Appleton, 1874.

———. "Opposing Sherman's Advance to Atlanta." In *Battles and Leaders of the Civil War*. Vol. 4, edited by Robert Underwood Johnson and Clarence Clough Buel, 260–77. New York: Thomas Yoseloff, 1956.

Jones, Jenkin Lloyd. *An Artilleryman's Diary*. Madison, Wis.: Democrat Printing, 1914.

Jones, Mary Miles, and Leslie Jones Martin, eds. *The Gentle Rebel: The Civil War Letters of 1st Lt. William Harvey Berryhill Co. D, 43rd Regiment, Mississippi Volunteers*. Yazoo City, Miss.: Sassafras Press, 1982.

Jordan, A. L. "'Dead Angle' Tunneled." *Confederate Veteran* 17 (1909): 601.

Jordan, Philip D., ed. "Forty Days with the Christian Commission: A Diary by William Salter." *Iowa Journal of History and Politics* 33, no. 2 (April 1935): 123–54.

Joslyn, Mauriel Phillips[, ed.]. *Charlotte's Boys: Civil War Letters of the Branch Family of Savannah*. Berryville, Va.: Rockbridge, 1996.

Joyce, Fred. "A Hot May-Day at Resaca." *Southern Bivouac* 2, no. 11 (July 1884): 499–501.

Julian, Allen P. "Atlanta's Defenses." *Civil War Times Illustrated* 3, no. 4 (July 1964): 23–24.

Kelly, Dennis. "Atlanta Campaign: Mountains to Pass, A River to Cross." *Blue and Gray* 6, no. 5 (1989): 8–30, 46–58.

———. *Kennesaw Mountain and the Atlanta Campaign: A Tour Guide*. Marietta, Ga.: Kennesaw Mountain Historical Association, 1990.

Kendall, John Smith[, ed.]. "Recollections of a Confederate Officer." *Louisiana Historical Quarterly* 29, no. 4 (October 1946): 1041–228.

Kerksis, Sydney C. "Action at Gilgal Church, Georgia, June 15–16, 1864." In *The Atlanta Papers*, compiled by Sydney C. Kerksis, 831–67. Dayton, Ohio: Morningside, 1980.

Kerwood, Asbury. *Annals of the Fifty-Seventh Regiment Indiana Volunteers*. Dayton, Ohio: W. J. Shuey, 1868.

Kilpatrick, Robert Lang. "The Fifth Ohio Infantry at Resaca." In *Sketches of War History, 1861–1865: Papers Prepared for the Ohio Commandery of the Military Order of the Loyal Legion of the United States, 1890–1896*. Vol. 4: 246–54. Wilmington, N.C.: Broadfoot, 1991.

Kirwan, A. D., ed. *Johnny Green of the Orphan Brigade: The Journal of a Confederate Soldier*. Lexington: University Press of Kentucky, 1956.

Kundahl, George G. *Alexandria Goes to War: Beyond Robert E. Lee*. Knoxville: University of Tennessee Press, 2004.

———. *Confederate Engineer: Training and Campaigning with John Morris Wampler*. Knoxville: University of Tennessee Press, 2000.

Little, George, and James R. Maxwell. *A History of Lumsden's Battery, C. S. A.* Tuscaloosa, Ala.: R. E. Rhodes Chapter, United Daughters of the Confederacy, [1905?].

Lockett, S. H. "The Defense of Vicksburg." In *Battles and Leaders of the Civil War*. Vol. 3, edited by Clarence Clough Buel and Robert Underwood Johnson, 482–92. New York: Thomas Yoseloff, 1956.

Longacre, Glenn V., and John E. Haas, eds. *To Battle for God and the Right: The Civil War Letterbooks of Emerson Opdycke.* Urbana: University of Illinois Press, 2003.

Lossing, Benson J. *Pictorial Field Book of the Civil War: Journeys through the Battlefields in the Wake of Conflict.* 3 vols. Baltimore: Johns Hopkins University Press, 1997.

Losson, Christopher. *Tennessee's Forgotten Warriors: Frank Cheatham and His Confederate Division.* Knoxville: University of Tennessee Press, 1989.

Lowrey, M. P. "General M. P. Lowrey: An Autobiography." *Southern Historical Society Papers* 16 (1888): 365–76.

Lucas, D. R. *New History of the 99th Indiana Infantry.* Rockford, Ill.: Horner, 1900.

M. "The Battle of Dead Angle on the Kennesaw Line, Near Marietta, Georgia." *Southern Bivouac* 3, no. 2 (October 1884): 71–74.

Mahan, D. H. *A Treatise on Field Fortification.* 3rd ed. New York: John Wiley, 1836.

Maharay, George S., ed. *Lights and Shadows of Army Life: From Bull Run to Bentonville.* Shippensburg, Pa.: Burd Street Press, 1998.

Mahon, John K., ed. "The Civil War Letters of Samuel Mahon, Seventh Iowa Infantry." *Iowa Journal of History* 51, no. 3 (July 1953): 233–66.

Maney, T. H. "Battle of Dead Angle on Kennesaw Line." *Confederate Veteran* 11 (1903): 159–60.

Marvin, Edwin E. *The Fifth Regiment Connecticut Volunteers.* Hartford, Conn.: Wiley, Waterman, and Eaton, 1889.

Mathis, Ray, ed. *In the Land of the Living: Wartime Letters by Confederates from the Chattahoochee Valley of Alabama and Georgia.* Troy, Ala.: Troy State University Press, 1981.

Maxwell, James Robert. *Autobiography of James Robert Maxwell of Tuskaloosa, Alabama.* New York: Greenberg, 1926.

McAdams, F. M. *Every-Day Soldier Life, or a History of the One Hundred and Thirteenth Ohio Volunteer Infantry.* Columbus, Ohio: Charles M. Cott, 1884.

McMurry, Richard M. "The Affair at Kolb's Farm." *Civil War Times Illustrated* 7, no. 8 (December 1968): 20–27.

———. *Atlanta, 1864: Last Chance for the Confederacy.* Lincoln: University of Nebraska Press, 2000.

———. "Atlanta Campaign: Rocky Face to the Dallas Line, the Battles of May 1864." *Blue and Gray* 11, no. 4 (1989): 10–23, 46–62.

———. "Cassville." *Civil War Times Illustrated* 10, no. 8 (December 1971): 4–9, 45–48.

———. "Confederate Morale in the Atlanta Campaign of 1864." *Georgia Historical Quarterly* 45, no. 2 (Summer 1970): 226–43.

———. *John Bell Hood and the War for Southern Independence.* Lexington: University Press of Kentucky, 1982.

———. "A Policy So Disastrous: Joseph E. Johnston's Atlanta Campaign." In *The Campaign for Atlanta and Sherman's March to the Sea.* Vol. 2, edited by Theodore P. Savas and David A. Woodbury, 223–48. Campbell, Calif.: Savas Woodbury, 1994.

McNeill, William J. "A Survey of Confederate Soldier Morale during Sherman's Campaign through Georgia and the Carolinas." *Georgia Historical Quarterly* 45, no. 1 (Spring 1971): 1–25.

Meadows, John C. *Modern Georgia.* Athens: University of Georgia Press, 1951.

Merrill, James M., and James F. Marshall, eds. "Georgia through Kentucky Eyes: Letters

Written on Sherman's March to Atlanta." *Filson Club History Quarterly* 30, no. 4 (October 1956): 324–39.

Merrill, W. E. "Block-Houses, Etc.: The Engineer Service in the Army of the Cumberland." In *History of the Army of the Cumberland.* Vol. 2, edited by Thomas B. Van Horne, 439–58. Cincinnati: Robert Clarke, 1875.

Mizner, Henry R. "Reminiscences." In *War Papers: Being Papers Read before the Commandery of the State of Michigan, Military Order of the Loyal Legion of the United States.* 2:72–82. Wilmington, N.C.: Broadfoot, 1993.

Morris, Hobart L., Jr. *One Year at War: The Diary of Private John A. Shultz, August 1, 1863 – August 1, 1864.* New York: Vantage Press, 1968.

Morris, W. S., L. D. Hartwell, and J. B. Kuykendall. *History 31st Regiment Illinois Volunteers, Organized by John A. Logan.* Carbondale: Southern Illinois Press, 1998.

Morse, Charles F. *Letters Written during the Civil War, 1861–1865.* Boston: T. R. Marvin and Sons, 1898.

Muir, Andrew Forest, ed. "The Battle of Atlanta as Described by a Confederate Soldier." *Georgia Historical Quarterly* 42, no. 1 (March 1958): 109–11.

Munson, Gilbert D. "Battle of Atlanta." In *Sketches of War History, 1861–1865: Papers Prepared for the Ohio Commandery of the Military Order of the Loyal Legion of the United States.* Vol. 3: 212–30. Cincinnati: Robert Clarke, 1890.

Neal, William A., ed. *An Illustrated History of the Missouri Engineer and the 25th Infantry Regiments.* Chicago: Donohue and Henneberry, 1889.

Nelson, H. K. "Dead Angle, or Devil's Elbow, GA." *Confederate Veteran* 11 (1903): 321–22.

Newton, George A. "Battle of Peach Tree Creek." In *G. A. R. War Papers.* Vol. 1: 148–63. Cincinnati: Fred C. Jones Post, 1891.

Nichols, James L. *Confederate Engineers.* Tuscaloosa, Ala.: Confederate Publishing, 1957.

Noe, Kenneth W., ed. *A Southern Boy in Blue: The Memoir of Marcus Woodcock, 9th Kentucky Infantry (U.S.A.).* Knoxville: University of Tennessee Press, 1996.

Norrell, William O. "Memo Book: William O. Norrell — Co. B. 63d Ga. Regt. Vols Mercer's Brigade Walker's Division Hardee's Corps Army of Tennessee." *Journal of Confederate History* 1, no. 1 (Summer 1988): 49–82.

Oeffinger, John C., ed. *A Soldier's General: The Civil War Letters of Major General Lafayette McLaws.* Chapel Hill: University of North Carolina Press, 2002.

O'Leary, Jenny, and Harvey H. Jackson, eds. "The Civil War Letters of Captain Daniel O'Leary, U.S.A." *Register of the Kentucky Historical Society* 77, no. 3 (Summer 1979): 157–85.

Padgett, James A., ed. "With Sherman through Georgia and the Carolinas: Letters of a Federal Soldier." Part 1. *Georgia Historical Society* 32 (1948): 284–322.

Partridge, Charles A., ed. *History of the Ninety-Sixth Regiment Illinois Volunteer Infantry.* Chicago: Brown, Pettibone, 1887.

Patrick, Jeffrey L., and Robert J. Willey, eds. *Fighting for Liberty and Right: The Civil War Diary of William Bluffton Miller, First Sergeant, Company K, Seventy-Fifty Indiana Volunteer Infantry.* Knoxville: University of Tennessee Press, 2005.

Payne, Edwin W. *History of the Thirty-Fourth Regiment of Illinois Volunteer Infantry.* Clinton, Iowa: Allen, 1902.

Phillips, Brenda G., ed. *Personal Reminiscences of a Confederate Soldier Boy.* Milledgeville, Ga.: Boyd, 1993.

Pierson, Stephen. "From Chattanooga to Atlanta in 1864, a Personal Reminiscence." *Proceedings of the New Jersey Historical Society* 16 (1931): 324–56.

Polk, William M. *Leonidas Polk: Bishop and General.* 2 vols. New York: Longmans, Green, 1915.

Post, Lydia Minturn, ed. *Soldiers' Letters from Camp, Battle-Field and Prison.* New York: Bunce and Huntington, 1865.

Price, Samuel W. "The Skirmish Line in the Atlanta Campaign." In *Military Order of the Loyal Legion of the United States, District of Columbia, War Papers*, no. 53. N.p., no publisher, 1904.

Quaife, Milo M., ed. *From the Cannon's Mouth: The Civil War Letters of General Alpheus S. Williams.* Detroit: Wayne State University Press, 1959.

"A Rash Deed at Dead Angle." *Confederate Veteran* 12 (1904): 394.

Reinhart, Joseph R., ed. *Two Germans in the Civil War: The Diary of John Daeuble and the Letters of Gottfried Rentschler, 6th Kentucky Volunteer Infantry.* Knoxville: University of Tennessee Press, 2004.

Reyburn, Philip J., and Terry L. Wilson, eds. *"Jottings from Dixie": The Civil War Dispatches of Sergeant Major Stephen F. Fleharty, U. S. A.* Baton Rouge: Louisiana State University Press, 1999.

Rhodes, Steven B. "Jeremy Gilmer and the Confederate Engineers." Master's thesis, Virginia Polytechnic Institute and State University, 1983.

Rieger, Paul E., ed. *Through One Man's Eyes: The Civil War Experiences of a Belmont County Volunteer.* Mount Vernon, Ohio: Printing Arts Press, 1974.

Ritter, William L. "Sketch of Third Battery of Maryland Artillery." *Southern Historical Society Papers* 11 (1883): 186–93.

Robert and Company. "Allatoona Battlefield Master Preservation Plan." Prepared for the Etowah Valley Historical Society, Cartersville, Georgia.

Robertson, James I., Jr., ed. "'Such Is War': The Letters of an Orderly in the 7th Iowa Infantry." *Iowa Journal of History* 58, no. 4 (October 1960): 321–56.

Robinson, William M., Jr. "The Confederate Engineers." Part 2. *Military Engineer* 22 (September–October, 1930): 410–19.

Rogers, Robert M. *The 125th Regiment Illinois Volunteer Infantry.* Champaign, Ill.: Gazette Steam Print, 1882.

[Rood, Hosea W.]. *Story of the Service of Company E, and of the Twelfth Wisconsin Regiment, Veteran Volunteer Infantry, in the War of the Rebellion.* Milwaukee, Wis.: Swain and Tate, 1893.

Roy, T. B. "General Hardee and the Military Operations Around Atlanta." *Southern Historical Society Papers* 8 (1880): 337–87.

Scaife, William R. "Waltz between the Rivers: An Overview of the Atlanta Campaign from the Oostanaula to the Etowah." In *The Campaign for Atlanta and Sherman's March to the Sea.* Vol. 2, edited by Theodore P. Savas and David A. Woodbury, 269–93. Campbell, Calif.: Savas Woodbury, 1994.

Scaife, William R., and William E. Erquitt. *The Chattahoochee River Line: An American Maginot.* Atlanta: printed by the authors, 1992.

Schofield, John M. *Forty-Six Years in the Army.* New York: Century, 1897.

Secrist, Philip L. *The Battle of Resaca: Atlanta Campaign, 1864.* Macon, Ga.: Mercer University Press, 1998.

Sherman, William T. *Memoirs of General William T. Sherman, by Himself*. 2 vols. Bloomington: Indiana University Press, 1957.

Shiman, Phillip L. "Army Engineers in the War for the Union." Unpublished report for the Office of History, Office of the Chief of Engineers, 1995.

———. "Engineering Sherman's March: Army Engineers and the Management of Modern War, 1862–1865." PhD diss., Duke University, 1991.

———. "Sherman's Pioneers in the Campaign to Atlanta." *The Campaign for Atlanta and Sherman's March to the Sea*. Vol. 2, edited by Theodore P. Savas and David A. Woodbury, 251–66. Campbell, Calif.: Savas Woodbury, 1994.

Shoup, Francis A. "Dalton Campaign—Works at Chattahoochee River—Interesting History." *Confederate Veteran* 3 (1895): 262–65.

Simmons, L. A. *The History of the 84th Reg't Ill. Vols*. Macomb, Ill.: Hampton Brothers, 1866.

Simon, John Y., ed. *The Papers of Ulysses S. Grant*. 31 vols. Carbondale: Southern Illinois University Press, 1967–2009.

Simpson, Brooks D., and Jean V. Berlin, eds. *Sherman's Civil War: Selected Correspondence of William T. Sherman, 1860–1865*. Chapel Hill: University of North Carolina Press, 1999.

Smith, Gustavus W. "The Georgia Militia about Atlanta." *Battles and Leaders of the Civil War*. Vol. 4, edited by Robert Underwood Johnson and Clarence Clough Buel, 331–35. New York: Thomas Yoseloff, 1956.

Smith, Philip E. "Aboriginal Stone Constructions in the Southern Piedmont." In *University of Georgia Laboratory of Archaeology Series*, Report No. 4 (1962): 1–47.

Smith, Timothy B. *Corinth, 1862: Siege, Battle, Occupation*. Lawrence: University Press of Kansas, 2012.

The Soldier of Indiana in the War for the Union. Indianapolis: Merrill, 1869.

Stewart, Nixon B. *Dan McCook's Regiment, 52nd O.V.I.: A History of the Regiment, Its Campaigns and Battles, from 1862 to 1865*. Alliance, Ohio: Review Print, 1900.

Stone, Henry. "From the Oostanaula to the Chattahoochee." In *The Mississippi Valley, Tennessee, Georgia, Alabama, 1861–1864: Papers of the Military Historical Society of Massachusetts*. Vol. 8: 397–427. Boston: Cadet Armory, 1910.

Storrs, George S. "Kennesaw Mountain." *Southern Bivouac* 1, no. 2 (December 1882): 135–40.

The Story of the Fifty-Fifth Regiment Illinois Volunteer Infantry in the Civil War, 1861–1865. Clinton, Mass.: W. J. Coulter, 1887.

Supplement to the Official Records of the Union and Confederate Armies. 100 vols. Wilmington, N.C.: Broadfoot, 1993–2000.

Switzer, Charles I., ed. *Ohio Volunteer: The Childhood & Civil War Memoirs of Captain John Calvin Hartzell, OVI*. Athens: Ohio University Press, 2005.

Tapert, Annette, ed. *The Brothers' War: Civil War Letters to Their Loved Ones from the Blue and Gray*. New York: Vintage Books, 1988.

Tappan, George, ed. *The Civil War Journal of Lt. Russell M. Tuttle, New York Volunteer Infantry*. Jefferson, N.C.: McFarland, 2006.

Taylor, Paul. *Orlando M. Poe: Civil War General and Great Lakes Engineer*. Kent, Ohio: Kent State University Press, 2009.

Thienel, Phillip M. "Engineers in the Union Army, 1861–1865." Parts 1 and 3. *Military Engineer* 47 (January–February 1955): 36–41; 110–16.

———. *Mr. Lincoln's Bridge Builders: The Right Hand of American Genius*. Shippensburg, Pa.: White Mane, 2000.

Thoburn, Lyle, ed. *My Experiences during the Civil War*. Cleveland: no publisher, 1963.

Thompson, B. F. *History of the 112th Regiment of Illinois Volunteer Infantry in the Great War of the Rebellion, 1862–1865*. Toulon, Ill.: Stark County News Office, 1885.

Thompson, Ed Porter. *History of the Orphan Brigade*. Louisville, Ky.: Lewis N. Thompson, 1898.

Thompson, Gilbert. *The Engineer Battalion in the Civil War*, no. 44. Washington, D.C.: Press of the Engineer School, 1910.

Toombs, Samuel. *Reminiscences of the War*. Orange, N.J.: Journal Office, 1878.

Tower, R. Lockwood, ed. *A Carolinian Goes to War: The Civil War Narrative of Arthur Middleton Manigault, Brigadier General, C. S. A.* Columbia: University of South Carolina Press, 1983.

Tuthill, Richard S. "An Artilleryman's Recollections of the Battle of Atlanta." In *Military Essays and Recollections: Papers Read before the Commandery of the State of Illinois, Military Order of the Loyal Legion of the United States*. Vol. 1: 299–309. Chicago: A. C. McClurg, 1891.

"An 'Unseen Message' of President Davis's." *Confederate Veteran* 14 (1906): 364–71.

Venet, Wendy Hamand, ed. *Sam Richards's Civil War Diary: A Chronicle of the Atlanta Home Front*. Athens: University of Georgia Press, 2009.

Wagner, Arthur L. "Hasty Intrenchments in the War of Secession." In *Civil War and Mexican Wars, 1861, 1846: Papers of the Military Historical Society of Massachusetts*. Vol. 13: 127–53. Boston: Military Historical Society of Massachusetts, 1913.

Walton, Clyde C., ed. *Private Smith's Journal: Recollections of the Late War*. Chicago: R. R. Donnelley and Sons, 1963.

Walton, William, ed. *A Civil War Courtship: The Letters of Edwin Weller from Antietam to Atlanta*. Garden City, N.Y.: Doubleday, 1980.

Warner, Ezra J. *Generals in Gray: Lives of the Confederate Commanders*. Baton Rouge: Louisiana State University Press, 1959.

War of the Rebellion: A Compilation of the Official Records of the Union and Confederate Armies. 70 vols. in 128. Washington, D.C.: Government Printing Office, 1880–1901.

Watkins, Sam R. *"Co. Aytch": A Side Show of the Big Show*. New York: Collier, 1962.

Wiley, Bell Irvin, ed. "The Confederate Letters of John W. Hagan." Part 2. *Georgia Historical Quarterly* 38, no. 3 (September 1954): 268–90.

———, ed. *Four Years on the Firing Line*. Jackson, Tenn.: McCowat-Mercer, 1963.

Willett, James R. *Rambling Recollections of a Military Engineer*. Chicago: J. Morris, 1888.

Wills, Charles W. *Army Life of an Illinois Soldier*. Washington, D.C.: Globe Printing, 1906.

Wills, Ridley, II, ed. *Old Enough to Die*. Franklin, Tenn.: Hillsboro Press, 1996.

Wilson, Thomas B. *Reminiscences*. N.p.: no publisher, n.d.

Winther, Oscar Osburn, ed. *With Sherman to the Sea: The Civil War Letters, Diaries, & Reminiscences of Theodore F. Upson*. Bloomington: Indiana University Press, 1958.

Worley, Ted R., ed. *The War Memoirs of Captain John W. Lavender, C. S. A.* Pine Bluff, Ark.: Perdue, 1956.

Wright, David Russell. "Civil War Field Fortifications: An Analysis of Theory and Practical Application." Master's thesis, Middle Tennessee State University, 1982.

Wright, Henry H. *A History of the Sixth Iowa Infantry*. Iowa City: State Historical Society of Iowa, 1923.

Wynne, Lewis N., and Robert A. Taylor, eds. *This War So Horrible: The Civil War Diary of Hiram Smith Williams*. Tuscaloosa: University of Alabama Press, 1993.

Yates, Bowling C. *Historical Guide for Kennesaw Mountain National Battlefield Park and Marietta, Georgia*. Marietta, Ga.: printed by the author, 1976.

Yeary, Mamie, comp. *Reminiscences of the Boys in Gray, 1861–1865*. Dallas, Tex.: Smith and Lamar, 1912.

index